W9-CLY-968

GENOCIDE, WAR, AND HUMAN SURVIVAL

GENOCIDE, WAR, AND HUMAN SURVIVAL

Edited by Charles B. Strozier and Michael Flynn

Andrew Carnegie Library
Livingstone College
701 W. Monroe St.
Salisbury, N.C. 28144

Rowman & Littlefield Publishers, Inc.

128247

ROWMAN & LITTLEFIELD PUBLISHERS, INC.

Published in the United States of America
by Rowman & LIttlefield Publishers, Inc.
4720 Boston Way, Lanham, Maryland 20706

3 Henrietta Street
London WC2E 8LU, England

Copyright © 1996 by Rowman & Littlefield Publishers, Inc.

All rights reserved. No part of this publication may
be reproduced, stored in a retrieval system, or transmitted
in any form or by any means, electronic, mechanical,
photocopying, recording, or otherwise, without the prior
permission of the publisher.

British Cataloging in Publication Information Available

Library of Congress Cataloging-in-Publication Data

Genocide, War, and Human Survival / edited by Charles B . Strozier and
Michael Flynn.
p. cm.
Includes bibliographical references and index.
1. Genocide. 2. Genocide—Sociological aspects. I. Strozier,
Charles B. II. Flynn, Michael, 1962–
HV6322.7.G43 1996 304.6′63—dc20 96–3736 CIP

ISBN 0-8476-8226-9 (cloth : alk. paper)
ISBN 0-8476-8227-7 (pbk. : alk. paper)

Printed in the United States of America

∞ ™ The paper used in this publication meets the minimum requirements of
American National Standard for Information Sciences—Permanence of
Paper for Printed Library Materials, ANSI Z39.48—1984.

For Robert Jay Lifton

Contents

III. Witnessing

Acknowledgments

We would like to thank Jon Sisk, Steven Wrinn, and Julie Kuzneski for undertaking the project, their skilled editing, and meeting our difficult publication schedule; Lucy Silva, Robert Lifton's ever-loyal assistant, for her help in putting the book together and good-humored tolerance for the chaos our book sometimes caused; and Richard Koffler for his editorial assistance as we conceptualized the book.

And to Cathy and Yollie, who gave up much for Robert Jay Lifton.

Contributors to his volume have retained copyright of their work, as follows:

"Introduction" © 1996 Charles B. Strozier
"Hiroshima and the Politics of History" © 1996 Martin J. Sherwin
"Hiroshima: The First Response" © 1996 Paul Boyer
"Hiroshima and the Silence of Poetry" © 1996 Michael Flynn
"Life after *Death in Life*" © 1996 Greg Mitchell
"On Pseudospeciation and Social Speciation" © 1996 Kai Erikson
"To Prevent or to Stop Mass Murder" © 1996 Ronnie Dugger
"Genocide and Warfare" © 1996 Eric Markusen
"Victims, Perpetrators, Bystanders, and Rescuers in the Face of Genocide and Its Aftermath" © 1996 Eva Fogelman
"In Pursuit of Sugihara: The Banality of Good" © 1996 Hillel Levine
"Genocide, Victimization, and America's Inner Cities" © 1996 Charles Green
"Meeting the Challenge of Genocide in Bosnia: Reconciling Moral Imperatives with Political Constraints" © 1996 Richard Falk
"The Prevention and Punishment of the Crime of Genocide" © 1996 Saul Mendlovitz and John Fousek
"Saving Bosnia (and Ourselves)" © 1996 Elinor Fuchs
"Manliness and the Great War" © 1996 George L. Mosse
"U.S. over Iraq: High Technology and Low Culture in the Gulf Conflict" © 1996 John M. Broughton
"Physicians and Nuclear War" © 1996 Victor W. Sidel

"Development and Violence" © 1996 Ashis Nandy

"Tolstoi's Revenge: The Violence of Indian Non-Violence" © 1996 Wendy Doniger

"Thoughts on a Theater of Witness and Excerpts from Two Plays of Witness: *Better People, The Beekeeper's Daughter*" © 1996 Karen Malpede

"Artists Witnessing 'Ethnic Cleansing' " © 1996 Stevan M. Weine

"Religion and Violence" © 1996 Harvey Cox

"Back from the Abyss: Symbolic Immortality, Faith, and Human Survival" © 1996 Roger Williamson

"Can There be a Psychoanalysis Without a Political Analysis?" © 1996 Bennett Simon

"We Must Hear Each Other's Cry: Lessons from Pol Pot Survivors" © 1996 Lane Gerber

"History, Objectivity, Commitment" © 1996 Howard Zinn

"Exposing the Killing System: Robert Jay Lifton as Witness" © 1996 John E. Mack

Introduction

Charles B. Strozier

This book works at many levels. It is, first and foremost, a remarkable collection of essays on the deeper meanings of genocide, mass violence, *and* healing images of human survival in a dark time. In its various parts, the book probes aspects of America in the nuclear age; the tragic workings of genocide from the Holocaust to Bosnia and Rwanda, as well as other issues of war and mass violence; and artistic witnessing to genocide and the activist professional self in the wake of the new violence.

These wide-ranging themes have a conceptual and ethical unity in the work of Robert Jay Lifton, who has a special relationship to this book. Any investigation of violence and human survival that moves below the surface will soon encounter Lifton. He helped awaken a whole generation to the psychological meanings of nuclear threat (*Death in Life, Indefensible Weapons*). His study of the Holocaust redefined the historical issues of that tragic eruption of twentieth-century violence and introduced into the culture new ideas about genocide in general (*The Nazi Doctors; The Genocidal Mentality*). He has long been a major theoretical voice in American psychology (*The Broken Connection*). His groundbreaking interviewing of Hiroshima survivors taught us about victimization and psychological renewal (*Death in Life*). His pioneering work on the psychological effects on veterans of the Vietnam war was the crucial empirical basis for what was later called PTSD *and* directly influenced current thinking about trauma (*Home From the War*). His "formative" theory of the self and the life-death continuum has helped explain the human cost of living with the scientific potential of ultimate endings (*The Life of the Self; The Broken Connection*). His method that adapts the psychoanalytic interview has proven vital for qualitative researchers, especially when the subject is human distress in extreme situations *(Thought Reform and the Psychology of Totalism; Death in Life)*. But for all his focus on death and mass violence Lifton has always sought to define principles of trans-formation within the context of a psychology of the self (*The Protean Self*). That yearning to keep hope alive has remained a constant *and* has brought him into an active leadership role in the peace movement opposing wars from Vietnam to the Gulf. He also takes great pride in his role as a key figure in the anti-nuclear movement and the revitaliza-tion of Physicians for Social Responsibility in the early 1980s and the creation of the IPPNW (the extension of PSR allied with Russian medi-cal colleagues that won the Nobel Peace Prize).

This book, in fact, began as a volume of honorary essays for Lifton, a *Festschrift* in weighty German terms. It seemed to me and my colleague, Michael Flynn, that Lifton's work had introduced a number of unique perspectives on violence that deserved broader investigation. And so we asked his many friends and colleagues to think about their work in rela-tion to the intellectual architecture of violence and human survival that Lifton has constructed in his various empirical and theoretical studies. To our surprise forty-nine distinguished colleagues responded to our request with original essays for the book. Some specifically discuss Lif-ton's work in relation to their own; some reference their ideas more subtly in the context of the categories of inquiry he has established; and some contend with him vigorously.

What began to emerge, in other words, during the year in which we put this book together, was much larger and more interesting than a simple *Festschrift*. Most such volumes are collections of minor essays by the disciples of great thinkers and quickly gather dust on library shelves. Our book was something very different, a kind of *unfestschrift*, as we began calling it informally. Our contributors honored Lifton's work by moving off from it in their own creative ways. There are no panegyrics to Lifton in this book, and in many cases you won't even find Lifton in the text or the notes. Some disagree with him on issues. And yet all the essays reflect an abiding respect for the questions Lifton has raised about violence and human survival. Such is the truer form of honor accorded a major thinker by his colleagues.

Because of its size and complexity, we decided to bring out the book in two separate but companion volumes. Both *Genocide, War, and Human Survival* and *Trauma and Self* honor Lifton's work in the sequence of themes that link violence and survival. My introduction, which makes clear the larger purposes of the project, is printed in each book. At the same time, the two books are quite separate and conceptually indepen-dent. Each follows its own course and we suspect will interest rather different audiences.

This book, with its emphasis on genocide and mass violence, includes several essays on the enduring significance of Hiroshima in American culture, including an initial essay that moves from a discussion of the decision to drop the bomb to the Enola Gay controversery at the Smithsonian to commemmorate the fiftieth anniversary of that decision; further reflections on the initial cultural response to Hiroshima; and the absent voice of poetry in responding to it. Lifton's latest book, written with Greg Mitchell, returned to the general topic with *Hiroshima and America: Fifty Years of Denial* (Putnam, 1995), and the section concludes with a personal statement by Mitchell on what drew him into what has become a lifelong obsession with Hiroshima. We felt it made editorial sense to group these essays together. Hiroshima and nuclear threat have been so central to Lifton's work, and are so significant in American life, that ultimate violence should be the hub of the book's turning wheel.

Section Two includes papers on many facets of genocide, which is the "epicenter" of Lifton's work (as Richard Falk puts it in his essay), and mass violence. The section begins with an important theoretical statement on "social speciation" that is followed by two reflective comments on genocide in the second half of the twentieth-century. Three papers then describe issues that haunt the contemporary mind: the Holocaust and its genocidal echoes in American racism. Lifton's own recent special concern, as those of the rest of us at the Center on Violence and Human Survival (which Lifton directs, I co-direct, and where Flynn is in charge of programs and research), has been with Bosnia. That intense involvement is reflected in three papers in this book, including one that narrates the story of the Center's involvement in the issue. Three theoretical papers on genocide then make the connection to discussion of three wars (World War I, the Gulf, and the prospect of nuclear war), and finally two papers address aspects of the violence of development.

Genocide and mass violence prompt a variety of responses from complicit bystanding to numbed withdrawal. But sometimes genocide can evoke a more humane form of witness, which is the focus of the first part of Section Three. Witnessing is developed here in three modes: artistic, religious, and professional. In the first part, excerpts from witnessing plays, as well as an appraisal of such artistic witnessing, opens up in the section to the other forms of such pained response to the violence of our era, including contributions by two theologians who have considered issues of faith and violence, and finally by psychiatrists, psychologists, and a historian who reflects here on the relationship between politics and knowledge. The message of the section (that we also affirm as editors) is that, as intellectuals and professionals, we have obligations to act responsibly in a world of violence. The model, again, is Lifton, who always describes his work as rigorous *and* committed.

If those formal categories describe the organization of the book, there are as well other plots and themes that operate in the book's disparate parts. Bosnia is the focus of a specific section but enters as well into several other essays in a somewhat different context. World War II is the subtext of Section One, while one key dimension of World War I is the focus of concern in a paper in Section Two. The meaning of psychoanalysis in contemporary life runs throughout all the sections of the book. Lifton's notion of "symbolic immortality" comes up often and is the point of four separate papers in two different sections. And these overlapping themes further connect with many topics in the companion volume, *Trauma and Self.*

There is also much respectful disagreement between many authors on key issues. Richard Falk marks the lines of his disagreement with Lifton over intervention in Bosnia, and Elinor Fuchs details the way Lifton and I parted company over lifting the arms embargo. Harvey Cox and Roger Williamson offer quite different perspectives on the significance of fundamentalism. Kai Erikson notes the contours of his dialogue with his father, Erik Erikson, over the appropriateness of the term, "pseudospeciation."

It is all a great feast of learning and passion that we hope you will enjoy.

**Part I
Hiroshima and America**

1

Hiroshima and the Politics of History

Martin J. Sherwin

No one who looks closely at the arguments surrounding the atomic bombings of Hiroshima and Nagasaki, or the controversy fifty years later that engulfed the National Air and Space Museum's planned exhibit of the Enola Gay,[1] the B-29 that flew the Hiroshima mission, will fail to recognize that there is more than a matter of historical accuracy at stake. At their core, all arguments over why Hiroshima and Nagasaki were bombed, and whether those attacks were necessary to end the war without invading Japan, touch upon the character of the United States, and the moral authority of its nuclear arsenal. As a result, as long as nuclear weapons continue to play a central role in United States defense policy, the history of Hiroshima will remain a hostage to the politics of nuclearism that flourished during the Cold War, and that remains one of that era's most prominent legacies.[2]

Defining Nuclear America

The decision to use the atomic bomb against urban civilian targets without warning was not inevitable; nor was it unanimously supported by senior members of the Truman administration. On May 28, 1945, for example, Acting Secretary of State Joseph C. Grew told President Harry S. Truman that the Japanese recognized that they were defeated and would surrender if the safety of the emperor was guaranteed.[3] A month later, on June 27th, Under Secretary of the Navy Ralph Bard wrote to Secretary of War Henry L. Stimson, urging that the Japanese receive explicit warnings about the atomic bomb several days prior to an attack. "The position of the United States as a great humanitarian nation" Bard wrote, required such a warning.[4]

The advice of Grew, Bard, and others went unheeded and, perhaps, it should be no surprise that the initial irony of Hiroshima was that the very act symbolizing our wartime victory was quickly turned against our peacetime purposes. At the 1946–48 Tokyo War Crimes Trials, which, like the Nuremberg trials, were a symbolic expression of our moral authority, Justice Rabhabinod Pal of India cited the atomic bombings of Hiroshima and Nagasaki as evidence against our claim to rule in Asia by right of superior virtue. Those bombings, he wrote in a dissenting opinion, were "the only near approach [in the Pacific War] to the directive . . . of the Nazi leaders during the Second World War."[5]

Anticipating the issues of just cause and morality that Pal raised, the earliest public explanations for the bombings sought to assure the world that our actions had been morally justified. "We have used [the atomic bomb]," President Truman announced, "in order to shorten the agony of war, in order to save the lives of thousands and thousands of young Americans."[6]

However, Truman's private explanation, written on August 11, 1945, in response to criticism of the atomic bombings from none other than John Foster Dulles, was more revealing: "Nobody is more disturbed over the use of Atomic bombs than I am but I was greatly disturbed over the unwarranted attack by the Japanese on Pearl Harbor and their murder of our prisoners of war. The only language they seem to understand is the one we have been using to bombard them. When you have to deal with a beast you have to treat him as a beast. It is most regrettable but nonetheless true."[7]

But in the aftermath of Hiroshima, as the incredible destructive force of nuclear weapons became better known, the weapons themselves began to appear increasingly beastial and, therefore, to some at least, ideal as the instruments for a new national security policy: nuclear deterrence. Yet even here, the debate over the atomic bombings of Hiroshima and Nagasaki was relevant, for it was of paramount importance to those who wished to rely on nuclear weapons for national security that they not be tarnished with a sense of guilt that could inhibit their use as instruments of diplomacy and, if necessary, war.[8] Thus, how the history of the decision to use atomic bombs was written quickly became associated with the politics of national security policy.

Constructing the Hiroshima Narrative

Henry L. Stimson, Secretary of War from 1940–1945, was the most important formulator of the history of the atomic bombings of Hiroshima and Nagasaki; in modern political parlance, he was its chief "spin doctor." Writing in 1947 to President Harry S. Truman to explain why he wrote his seminal article, "The Decision to Use the Atomic Bomb,"[9] Stimson noted that his "article has also been intended to satisfy the doubts of that rather difficult class of the community which will have charge of the education of the next generation, namely educators and historians."[10]

To satisfy those potential doubters, Stimson explained that the Truman administration faced the choice of either using atomic bombs or invading Japan. The sole motivation for the atomic attacks, he wrote, had been to save American lives by ending the war as quickly as possible.[11] Missing were references to the idea, frequently discussed in his diary, that a dramatic demonstration of the bomb during the war would help to control Stalin's ambitions afterwards. Nor did he discuss the Japanese messages intercepted by United States military intelligence indicating that the Japan had been trying to surrender "conditionally" since June 1945.[12] Assisted by the chilling effect that the cold war had on debate, and the long delay before the relevant documents became available to historians, Stimson achieved his goal.[13] Most Americans— and for a very long time perhaps most educators and historians as well— accepted his explanation of "the decision to use the atomic bomb."

Ending the war quickly was certainly *one* of the motivations for using the atomic bombs. But there were others that promoted, reinforced, and perhaps even overtook the one put forward by Stimson. These included: (1) the impact that the bomb(s) were expected to have in curbing Stalin's ambitions in Eastern Europe and the Far East; (2) the pressure that senior Manhattan Project administrators felt to validate the tremendous cost in money, materials, and talent spent to build atomic bombs; (3) the momentum to use these new weapons created by the strategy of urban bombing; (4) revenge for Pearl Harbor and the ghastly treatment of American prisoners of war that Truman's letter to John Foster Dulles reflected.[14]

Reinforcing the political motivations behind the Stimson article is another letter, this one from the man who first urged Stimson to write it. James B. Conant, President of Harvard and former chief science administrator of the Manhattan Project, had written to Stimson in the autumn of 1946—in the aftermath of the publication and radio broadcast of John Hersey's *Hiroshima*—that the growing criticism of the atomic bombings was undermining the credibility of the United States' nuclear monopoly. These criticisms had to be countered, Conant warned, and Stimson was the only person who could do that effectively.[15]

So politics was introduced from the first into the discussion of why atomic bombs were used at the end of World War II, and politics has continued to undermine and circumscribe the effort to bring to public attention the research that has been done on this subject over the past thirty-five years.

Atomic Politics and Diplomacy

Research in the President's Official File and in the diaries, correspondence and records of his closest wartime advisers reveals that while the war was an ever-present consideration, its conduct was not among Truman's primary tasks. The record of military successes, Roosevelt's deteriorating health, a growing concern with postwar problems and Truman's inexperience had shifted the management of the conflict away from the White House during 1945. The new President would officiate over victory, but he could not be credited with having led the nation to it. The problems of the postwar world loomed larger before Truman than they ever had before Roosevelt, and they occupied more of his time. His performance would be judged on what he accomplished after the war.

The Soviet Union appeared to Truman as certain to be his primary postwar problem. Joseph Stalin was breaking the Yalta Agreement, Secretary of State Edward Stettinius reported to the President at their first meeting on April 13, and soon after, Averell Harriman, ambassador to Moscow, characterized Soviet behavior as nothing less than a "barbarian invasion of Europe."[16]

Operating on the principle that toughness was the best way to deal with Stalin, Truman launched several initiatives during his early weeks in office. His first—subjecting Foreign Minister V. M. Molotov to a tongue-lashing—had disastrous results. His second—the precipitous termination of lend-lease aid to the Soviet Union the day after Germany surrendered—produced an even worse reaction.[17] Casting about for a more effective diplomatic strategy, Truman turned to Stimson, whose experiences as the overseer of the atomic bomb project inspired the policy of caution and reasonable accommodation he recommended. It seemed to Stimson "a terrible thing to gamble with such big stakes in diplomacy without having your master card [atomic bomb] in your hand."[18] He viewed the bomb as the key to the postwar world. It would be "the most terrible weapon ever known in human history," he told Truman, noting that "if the problem of the proper use of this weapon can be solved, we would have the opportunity to bring the world into a pattern in which the peace of the world and our civilization can be saved."[19]

By the late spring of 1945, the implications of this weapon which had been created to win the war had become more problematic than the war itself. As the bomb moved toward completion, a dangerous (though soon to become familiar) illusion was nurtured in the White House: the idea that the bomb was a panacea for America's diplomatic and military problems. As preparations for the Potsdam Conference got underway, assurances that the weapon would work became increasingly important to the President. On June 6, he told Stimson that he had even "postponed" the summit conference "until the 15th of July on purpose to give us more time."[20] Stimson and Truman agreed, in an early linkage of arms control and diplomacy, that after the first bomb had been successfully used against Japan, a fitting exchange for an American offer to the Soviets for the international control of atomic energy would be "the settlement of the Polish, Rumanian, Yugoslavian, and Manchurian problems."[21] And even before this discussion, Secretary of State-designate James F. Byrnes had told Truman that the bomb "might well put us in a position to dictate our own terms at the end of the war."[22]

Truman inherited the basic policy that governed the atomic bomb, just as he inherited every other policy related to the war, a point that commentators on all sides of the debate over Hiroshima often ignore. It was therefore *possible* to use the bomb only because Roosevelt had authorized preparations to do so. Truman was *inclined* to use the bomb because of those preparations. But he *decided* to use it because there seemed no good reason not to. On the contrary, the bombs were available and the Japanese fought on; the bombs were available and precedents of burned cities were numerous; the bombs were available and $2 billion had been spent to create them; the bombs were available and revenge had its claim; the bombs were available and the Soviet Union was claiming too much. "The bomb," to quote Stimson, was "a badly needed equalizer."[23] Its use held out not only the hope of shocking Tokyo into submission, but also the possible dividend of jolting Moscow into cooperation. "No man, in our position and subject to our responsibilities, holding in his hands a weapon of such possibilities," Stimson wrote in 1947, "could have failed to use it and afterwards looked his countrymen in the face."[24]

Could the Atomic Bomb Have Prolonged the War?

But a critical question remains: Were the bombings of Hiroshima and Nagasaki, as is so often claimed, the quickest way to end the war? A considerable body of evidence suggests that the decision to use the bomb, which involved a decision to reject another recommended initiative, delayed the end of the war.

American cryptographers had broken the Japanese diplomatic code before the war had begun, and senior members of the Administration were aware near the end of the war of a struggle between peace and war factions within the Japanese government. Based on this privileged information, and on his knowledge of Japanese politics gained from long experience as ambassador to Japan, Acting Secretary of State Joseph C. Grew urged Truman during the final days of May to clarify the unconditional-surrender policy. It was an insurmountable barrier for the peace faction, he explained, for no Japanese government would surrender without assurances that the Emperor would not be deposed or harmed. But Truman rejected Grew's advice. Why?

One answer is that he would not accept the political consequences that might result from a public retreat from a policy that had become a political shibboleth since Roosevelt introduced the idea in 1943. Another answer is that he preferred to use the atomic bomb. Any serious effort to understand Truman's motives must consider this possibility, for there is significant evidence in Stimson's diaries, in the Manhattan Project files and in the president's papers that support it. "The bomb as a merely probable weapon had seemed a weak reed on which to rely," Stimson wrote in his memoir, "but the bomb as a colossal reality was very different."[25] This expected difference may have made *the* difference when Truman chose between clarifying the Emporer's status after unconditional surrender and the atomic bomb.

On July 13, 1945, the "Magic" diplomatic summary made it clear to the president and his advisors that Japan not only understood that it was defeated, but that the Emperor himself had joined the effort to seek surrender terms. "His Majesty the Emperor," Prime Minister Togo had wired Ambassador Sato in Moscow, "mindful of the fact that the present war daily brings greater evil and sacrifice upon the peoples of all belligerent powers, desires from his heart that it may be quickly terminated. But so long as England and the United States insist upon unconditional surrender the Japanese Empire has no alternative but to fight on with all its strength for the honor and the existence of the Motherland. . . . It is his [Majesty's] desire for the welfare of humanity to restore *peace with all possible speed*"[26] [emphasis added]. The central point had been made earlier by Stimson's assistant, John McCloy: "We should have our heads examined if we don't consider a political solution."[27] But no political solution was attempted and, ironically, as Grew had warned Truman, the unconditional-surrender policy had served to hold together the fracturing war party in Japan.

Unconditional surrender remained an obstacle to peace even after atomic bombs destroyed Hiroshima and Nagasaki, and the Soviet Union entered the war against Japan. The Japanese did not surrender until the government of the United States offered assurances that neither the Emperor nor the imperial dynasty would be endangered. In the early morning hours of August 10, in the Emperor's bomb shelter adjoining the imperial library, Premier Kantaro Suzuki startled his divided colleagues on the Supreme Council with the announcement, "Your Imperial Majesty's decision is requested." That decision, "to accept the Allied proclamation on the basis outlined by the Foreign Minister," brought the war to its conclusion—on the condition that the United States not compromise the prerogatives of the Emperor as supreme ruler or the survival of the dynasty.

When he came to consider those final, dramatic months of the war and the momentous decisions he influenced so heavily, Stimson wrote, "*that history might find that the United States, by its delay in stating its position [on the conditions of surrender], had prolonged the war*"[28] [emphasis added].

The Enola Gay War

In writing this observation for his memoirs, Stimson was responding to a letter from Joseph Grew reminding Stimson that his *Harper's* magazine article ignored the efforts that Grew had made to have unconditional surrender clarified.[29] Thus, as early as 1948, the debate over the history of the atomic bombings of Hiroshima and Nagasaki, a debate that the Enola Gay exhibit sought to explain, began between the former Acting Secretary of State and the former Secretary of War.

I was a member of the advisory committee of historians to the ill-fated Enola Gay exhibit. When first recruited, I told the museum staff member who phoned that I opposed calling celebratory attention to the Enola Gay on the fiftieth anniversary of its historic mission. Even if one believed that it had played a critical role in ending a terrible war, I was opposed to an exhibit that might be interpreted as celebrating the deaths of 150,000 to 200,000 Japanese civilians, mostly old men, women and children.

My view was not a comment on the courage or morality of the men who manned the B-29s. It was based on my belief that killing—even in war—is something that we should publicly regret rather than celebrate.

Furthermore, this fiftieth anniversary presented a unique opportunity for Americans and Japanese to heal the wounds of war by jointly celebrating its most positive result, the birth of Japanese democracy. Mourning together for those who died on both sides of the war is a necessary step toward healing the wounds of war. (Just such a healing event was held in Dresden, Germany, on February 13, 1995, when "General John M. Shalikashvili, Chairman of the Joint Chiefs of Staff," the *New York Times* reported, "joined his German and British military counterparts and the Duke of Kent, representing Queen Elizabeth II, to lay wreaths at a vast cemetery called Heidefriedhof, where many of the dead from 50 years ago are buried."[30])

The counter-argument was that the historical exhibits that were being planned to accompany the Enola Gay would make it clear that this was not a celebration of nuclear destruction, but an educational exhibit about the origins of the nuclear age. Even the Hiroshima and Nagasaki peace museums had agreed to lend NASM several artifacts. Although skeptical that an exhibit that adequately reflected critical historical research could be mounted at NASM, I accepted a position on the advisory committee with the understanding that I came to it with deep reservations.

On February 7, 1994, the advisors, having received a draft of the exhibit script several weeks earlier, met at NASM for their first, and only, meeting. I was critical of the script. My complaints can be summarized under two headings: First, the historical section was not attractively designed. The history of the decision-making process was told through documents that were to hang passively on the museum's walls. I urged the curators to create an interactive exhibit that challenged visitors to assume the roles of Truman, Stimson, James Byrnes, or others involved in the decision-making process, and discover what had influenced their views in the spring of 1945.

Second, and more seriously, many important documents that revealed what the decision makers thought were missing from the exhibit. No one who read the selected documents would understand why so many historians have come to believe that the president and secretary of war had been less than candid in their explanations of why atomic bombs had been used. The documents I was referring to included excerpts from Stimson's diary that repeatedly referred to the important postwar advantages the United States would gain in dealing with the Soviet Union if atomic bombs were used successfully against Japan.[31]

I also wanted to include Under Secretary of the Navy Ralph Bard's memorandum to Stimson of June 27, 1945 that recommended a "political solution" before using the atomic bomb, urged that we give the Japanese at least two or three days warning, and provided the Joint Planning Staff estimates of the number of Americans likely to be killed if an invasion was necessary. The estimate, based on an analysis of other Pacific theater operations such as Iwo Jima and Okinawa, was considerably lower than the figure of 500,000 killed that both Stimson and Truman had published.[32] Finally, while the artifacts from Hiroshima and Nagasaki were powerful reminders that atomic bombs do horrible things to people, they would not help visitors understand *why* the bombs were dropped on cities. In summary, I judged the commemorative character of the exhibit dominant and ubiquitous, and the historical portion incomplete, marginalized, and unappealing.

My view was contradicted by the reactions of the other advisors, most especially the historians from the Air Force, Dr. Richard Hallion and Dr. Herman Wolk, who staunchly defended the script. "Overall this is a most impressive piece of work," Hallion wrote to one of the curators after the meeting, "[it is] comprehensive and dramatic, obviously based upon a great deal of sound research, primary and secondary."[33]

The script was based on sound research. The curators had studied the literature thoroughly. They had a sophisticated understanding of the evidence and the arguments. But under the circumstances, their approach to the exhibit had been extremely cautious, for political reasons.

It was this caution that Hallion and Wolk supported, and that led another advisor, Edwin Bearss, Chief Historian of the National Park Service, to endorse the Air Force view with a letter of his own. "As a World War II combat veteran," Bearss wrote to a curator, "I commend you and your colleagues who have dared to go that extra mile to address an emotionally charged and internationally significant event in an exhibit that, besides enlightening, will challenge its viewers."[34]

John Correll, the editor of *Air Force Magazine*, had a decidedly different opinion of the exhibit. In his view, it not only suffered from too much of the PC he disliked, but even worse, it was insufficiently endowed with the PC he exploited for his living, *Patriotic Correctness*. Correll considered the exhibit biased against the Air Force, pro-Japanese, and anti-American. His article condemning the exhibit script, "War Stories at Air and Space," which served as a clarion call to veterans groups, was a deceptive critique that took quotations out of context and used McCarthyite innuendo to impugn the patriotism of Martin Harwit, the director of NASM. "For most Americans," Correll quoted the script as stating, "this war was fundamentally different than the one waged against Germany and Italy—it was a war of vengeance. For most Japanese, it was a war to defend their unique culture against Western imperialism." What Correll failed to note, and what journalists who repeated this inflamatory quotation without reading the original script failed to discover, was that this sentence came near the end of a section that frankly and clearly summarized the brutality of Japanese militarism: "Japanese expansionism was marked by naked aggression and extreme brutality. The slaughter of tens of thousands of Chinese in Nanking in 1937 shocked the world. Atrocities by Japanese troops included brutal mistreatment of civilians, forced laborers and prisoners of war, and biological experiments on human victims," the section reads in part.[35]

Correll's article reflected his longstanding disaffection with the curators and historians at NASM who, under Harwit's administration, had been mounting exhibits that included critical discussions of the consequences of air and space technology. The Air and Space museum, he insisted, was ignoring its "basic job . . . the restoration and preservation of aircraft." Yet in the past decade, other Smithsonian museum directors had successfully sponsored challenging exhibits, and previous critical exhibits at the NASM had received some excellent reviews.[36]

But the Enola Gay exhibit was different for several reasons. First, the public criticism of the exhibit began in the planning stages and just six months before a congressional election in which conservative forces were in the ascendancy. Second, the event being commemorated was the 50th anniversary of the end of World War II, the "Good War," and the museum's administration failed to publicly respond (until it was too late) to charges that it was denigrating the memory of the men who had fought in that crusade. And, finally, the curators had created an exhibit that probed how the Japanese thought about the war, a virtue that critics distorted by interpreting any recognition of the humanity of Japan's soldiers as an anti-American bias.

Within a month of the publication of "War Stories," and a companion article, "The Decision that Launched the Enola Gay," that ignored thirty years of critical historical research on the subject, a broad spectrum of veterans groups, led by the 3.1-million-member American Legion, had enlisted congressional allies in support of their criticisms of the script.[37] Senators and congressmen eagerly rushed to condemn the exhibit.[38] Senator Nancy Kassebaum offered a resolution in the Senate, and dozens of Congressmen signed letters implying and threatening retribution against the staff and the museum if the script were not modified to the satisfaction of its critics. Behind these letters and resolutions (in addition to politics as usual) was an astonishingly self-righteous view of the atomic bombings. "There is no excuse," Congressman Sam Johnson and six of his colleagues wrote to I. Michael Heyman, secretary of the Smithsonian, "for an exhibit which addresses *one of the most morally unambiguous events of the 20th century* to need five revisions" [emphasis added].[39]

What had begun as a debate over interpreting and balancing the public presentation of an historical event of transcendent importance was quickly turned by congressional intervention into a "political cleansing" operation against both the exhibit and NASM's staff.[40] The political agendas of those who joined in this assault varied: the veterans sought to control the public presentation of the Hiroshima narrative; the Air Force Association wanted NASM's administration returned to more accommodating hands; and conservative politicians saw another issue they could use in their culture wars crusade.

The exhibit's critics called for two very different sorts of fundamental changes to the script. In the first instance, they demanded that the exhibit be expanded to include a history of Japanese aggression and atrocities that began with Japan's invasion of China in the 1930s, an arguably reasonable alternative framework for the exhibit.[41] But they also insisted upon something that was objectionable and unconscionable: the removal of all documents critical of the use of the atomic bombs. This blatant demand for censorship eliminated passages from the memoirs of Dwight D. Eisenhower and Admiral William D. Leahy, among other texts. The American Legion also insisted on the removal of the statement (generally recognized as a fact) that, "to this day, controversy has raged about whether dropping this weapon on Japan was necessary to end the war quickly."[42]

Heyman, who had inherited this unenviable situation in the fall of 1994, chose the path that Japan had resisted: unconditional surrender. Without ever saying a word against censorship, on January 30, 1995, he canceled the exhibits that were to accompany the Enola Gay. "I have concluded," he stated in his announcement of the cancellation, "that we made a basic error in attempting to couple a historical treatment of the use of atomic weapons with the 50th anniversary commemoration of the end of the war."[43] His actions and explanation have led me to revise Santayana's famous aphorism, "Those who cannot remember the past are condemned to repeat it." I am now more inclined to worry that "Those who insist only on their memories of the past condemn others to remain ignorant of it."

The Enola Gay debacle at the National Air and Space Museum is a reminder of how completely the politics of the cold war—in its reinforcement of America's collective memory of the Good War—circumscribed all discussions of the war's ambiguities. This special protection accorded the history of Hiroshima for so many decades unites the task of "unspinning" Stimson's history of Hiroshima with the more considerable challenge of disentangling U.S. politics from its cold war culture.

Epilogue: A Hiroshimaless Narrative

For fifty years the public memory of the atomic bombings of Hiroshima and Nagasaki has been sustained and distorted by a non-event: the invasion of Japan. Yet, as even Stimson finally recognized,[44] the need for an invasion was remote, and the war might very well have ended without the use of nuclear weapons. To frankly confront the legacy of Hiroshima and Nagasaki, it is necessary, therefore, to consider an alternative past, one in which atomic bombs had *not* been used against Japanese cities.

It is generally assumed that the atomic destruction of Japanese cities acted as a deterrent to the future use of nuclear weapons: in Korea, Berlin, Cuba, or Vietnam.[45] But this sort of reasoning is more rationalization than logical deduction. Consider what might have occurred if Stimson had followed the logic of his own assessment of the dangers of a nuclear arms race, and had convinced Truman that the United States should avoid using the atomic bomb.

As all senior administrators of the Manhattan Project feared, a congressional committee would have conducted an investigation into why the Truman administration had failed to use an extraordinarily expensive new bomb that had been ready before the end of the war. Stimson, a Republican who served two Democratic administrations that had led the country to victory, would have been called to defend his recommendation. In his defense, he would have said to Congress—and the American public—what he had said to Harry Truman on April 25, 1945: "The world in its present state of moral advancement compared with its technical development would be eventually at the mercy of such a weapon. In other words, modern civilization might be completely destroyed." It is our nation's responsibility, he might have gone on to argue, to avoid such destruction, and "if the proper use of this weapon can be solved, we would have the opportunity to bring the world into a pattern in which the peace of the world and our civilization can be saved."[46] In support of his decision he might have quoted the Franck Report that was sent to him in June 1945 from the atomic scientists at the University of Chicago. "We urge that the use of nuclear bombs in this war be considered as a problem of long-range national policy rather than military expediency," they had written, arguing against dropping atomic bombs on Japanese cities.[47]

Stimson might have gone on to say that our nation is too moral to set a precedent of using such a weapon. He would have insisted that the American people would not want their government to behave like the German government, which had initiated gas warfare in World War I, or like the Japanese government, which had initiated urban bombing of civilians in China. Once a precedent is set, he would have said, its repetition follows inevitably. Perhaps he would have borrowed some language from Bard's memorandum of June 27, 1945, that spoke of "the position of the United States as a great humanitarian nation."[48] He would have explained that the United States had built atomic bombs in self-defense having reason to believe that the Germans were working along the same lines. But to have initiated nuclear war when there were alternatives (other than invasion) available would have sunk America to the level of the Nazi and Japanese governments. We have our own values, our own standards, he would have said. They are the standards that must guide our behavior. These weapons not only burn and blast, but they also kill by radiation. They have the characteristics of poison gas and biological weapons. Americans would not want their government to be the first to use them, he would have concluded.

Congress and the American people would have agreed that President Truman had done the right thing in avoiding the use of nuclear weapons. The press would have written editorials affirming that we are morally superior, as we have always insisted. To save the lives of American soldiers we had reluctantly accepted the Nazi–Japanese precedent of strategic bombing, but to save civilization we had resisted the temptation to use nuclear weapons.

Such a hearing would have had exactly the opposite effect that Hiroshima and Nagasaki had on American (and Soviet) attitudes toward nuclear weapons. Rather than validating them as weapons of war, our refusal to use them would have relegated them to the category of chemical and biological weapons—weapons beyond the moral pale.

Perhaps the international control of atomic energy would have been achieved. But even if not, it is doubtful that Stalin, faced with the challenge of rebuilding a devastated nation, would have initiated a crash program to build a weapon that the United States had refused to use in war. It is also doubtful that the U.S. would have lunged toward nuclear deterrence if relations with the Soviets had deteriorated into a cold war. Such a reversal of policy would have been extraordinarily difficult after Stimson's testimony and the policies of marginalizing nuclear weapons that would have followed in its wake.

A principled stand against nuclear weapons at the outset of the nuclear age, by the nation that possessed a nuclear monopoly, might very well have changed world history. The lesson of Hiroshima is not that atomic war is too horrible to contemplate again. As we have relearned from Robert McNamara's memoir, the Joint Chiefs of Staff did not hesitate to recommend the use of nuclear weapons in Vietnam when they ran out of conventional solutions.[49] What Hiroshima appears to have taught those who plan and fight wars is that nuclear weapons are useful, if you can get away with using them.

The atomic bombings of Hiroshima and Nagasaki did not contribute to preventing the next nuclear war—it made it more likely.

Notes

1. Martin J. Sherwin, "The Assault on History," *The Nation Magazine* (May 15, 1995), pp. 692–94; Tony Capaccio and Uday Mohan, "Missing the Target," *American Journalism Review* (July/August 1995), pp. 19–26; "History and the Public: What Can We Handle? A Round Table About History after the Enola Gay Controversy," *The Journal of American History* (December 1995), 1029–1144.

2. Robert Jay Lifton, *The Broken Connection* (New York: Simon and Schuster, 1979), pp. 369–87. Lifton defines this "ultimate contempory deformation" as "the passionate embrace of nuclear weapons as a solution to death anxiety."

3. Joseph C. Grew, *Turbulent Era: A Diplomatic Record of Forty Years, 1904–1945*, vol. 2 (Boston: Houghton Mifflin, 1952), 1406–1442.

4. Ralph Bard to George Harrison, June 27, 1995, and George Harrison to Henry L. Stimson, June 28, 1945, are reprinted in Martin J. Sherwin, *A World Destroyed: Hiroshima and the Origins of the Arms Race* (New York: Vintage, 1987), pp. 307–8. For dissenting opinions of military leaders, see Gar Alperovitz, *The Decision to Use the Atomic Bomb and the Architecture of An American Myth* (New York: A. A. Knopf, 1995), 321–71.

5. Rabhabinod Pal quoted in Richard Falk, Gabriel Kolko, Robert Lifton, eds., *Crimes of War* (New York, Vintage Books, 1971), 136. Pal misses the critical distinction; the goal of the Holocaust was genocide, which was not the goal of the atomic bombings.

6. The most thorough analysis of the construction of the "Hiroshima narrative" is in Robert Jay Lifton and Greg Mitchell, *Hiroshima in America: 50 Years of Denial* (New York: G.P. Putnam's Sons, 1995), chapters 1, 2.

7. Harry S. Truman to Bishop Oxnam and John Foster Dulles, n.d., approximately 15 August 1945, quoted in Sherwin, *A World Destroyed*, xvii–xviii.

8. "I am firmly convinced that the Russians will eventually agree to the American proposals for the establishment of an atomic energy authority of world-wide scope, *provided* they are convinced that we *would* have the bomb in

quantity and would be prepared to use it without hesitation in another war. Therefore, I have been fearful lest those who have been motivated by humanitarian considerations in the arguments against the bomb[ing of Hiroshima] were as a matter of fact tending to accomplish exactly the reverse of their avowed purpose." James B. Conant to Stimson, Jan. 22, 1947. The papers of Henry L. Stimson, Sterling Library, Yale University, New Haven, CT.

9. Henry L. Stimson, "The Decision to Use the Atomic Bomb," *Harper's Magazine* (February, 1947), 97–107.

10. Stimson to Truman, January 7, 1947. Stimson papers.

11. Stimson, "Decision to Use the Atomic Bomb," 106.

12. The "Magic" intercepts were declassified early in 1995. A July 13, 1945 message states that "His Majesty . . . desires from his heart that [the war] may be quickly terminated." Foreign Minister Togo to Ambassador Sato in Moscow. Ultra intercepts, War Department, Office of A.C. of S., G-2, National Archives, Washington, D.C.

13. Henry L. Stimson's diaries, the first major source for revising Stimson's own explanation for the atomic bombings of Hiroshima and Nagasaki, first became available to researchers in 1959. They are available on microfilm at the Sterling Library, Yale University.

14. For impact on Soviets see Stimson's diary, December 31, 1944; February 15, May 10, 13, 14, 15, and June 6, 1945. For pressure on administrators see Sherwin, *A World Destroyed,* p. 199; for strategic bombing, see Michael Sherry, *The Rise of American Air Power* (New Haven: Yale University Press, 1987).

15. Conant to Stimson, January 22, 1947, quoted in Sherwin, *A World Destroyed,* p. xix. For a thorough discussion of the role that Conant played in initiating and shaping Stimson's article, see James Hershberg, *James B. Conant: From Harvard to Hiroshima and the Making of the Nuclear Age* (New York: Knopf, 1993), chap. 16.

16. Quoted in Sherwin, *A World Destroyed,* 187.

17. Ibid., 176–85. See also Gar Alperovitz, *Atomic Diplomacy: Hiroshima and Potsdam* (New York: Penguin Books, 1985), 81–88.

18. Stimson diary, May 15, 1945.

19. Ibid. April 25, 1945. Memo discussed with the President, April 25, 1945; reprinted in Sherwin, *A World Destroyed,* appendix 1, 291–92.

20. Ibid., June 6, 1945.

21. Ibid.

22. Harry S. Truman, *Memoirs,* vol. 1, *Year of Decisions* (Garden City, NY: Doubleday, 1955) p. 87.

23. Henry L. Stimson and McGeorge Bundy, *On Active Service in Peace and War* (New York, Harper & Brothers, 1948), 638.

24. Stimson, "The Decision to Use the Atomic Bomb," 106.

25. Stimson, *On Active Service,* 637.

26. Ultra, "Magic"—Diplomatic Summary, No. 1205—13 July 1945, War Department Office of A.C. of S., G-2, National Archives, Washington, D.C.

27. Kai Bird, *The Chairman: John J. McCloy and the Making of the American Establishment* (New York, Simon and Schuster, 1992), 246. See also pp. 244–50.

28. Stimson, *On Active Service*, 629.

29. Joseph C. Grew to Stimson, February 12, 1947, Stimson papers. See also Kai Bird, *The Chairman*, p. 247.

30. *New York Times*, Feb. 14, 1995, A6.

31. Stimson diaries, December 31, 1944; February 15, May 13, 14, 15, and June 6, 1945.

32. Both documents are reprinted in full in the appendices of Sherwin, *A World Destroyed* (1987 edition): Bard, 307–8; casualty estimates, 335–63.

33. NASM "News." A press release, no date, with the title: "Favorable Comments about the Exhibition" "The Last Act: The Atomic Bomb and the End of World War II." The subtitle reads: "Advisory Board Comments on the January and April Scripts." p.1. For the point of view of the director of the National Air and Space Museum during this controversy see, Martin Harwit, "Academic Freedom in The Last Act," *Journal of American History* (December 1995), 1064–82.

34. Edwin Bearrs to Tom Crouch, February 24, 1994.

35. John T. Correll, "War Stories at Air and Space," *Air Force Magazine*, April 1994, pp. 24–29. "The Crossroads: The End of World War II, the Atomic Bomb, and the Origins of the Cold War" [script no. 1, January 12, 1994], 5.

36. Correll, "War Stories," pp. 26–27, 29. In response to the controversial exhibit at the National Museum of American Art, "The West as America," a *Washington Post* editorial had praised the "move away from the traditional heroes, politicians, and objects in glass cases and toward a wide, fluid, social-history approach." Quoted in Correll, "War Stories," 27.

37. John T. Correll, "The Decision that Launched the Enola Gay," *AFM*, (April 1994), 30–34.

38. The Air Force Association has compiled for distribution a bound volume, "The Enola Gay Debate, August 1993–May 1995" [hereafter AFA, EGD]. It is a broad ranging collection that contains, among much other information, numerous letters from Congressmen to senior Smithsonian Institution administrators.

39. Senate Resolution 257, 103rd Congress, 2nd Session, submitted by Senator Nancy Kassebaum, "A resolution to express the sense of the Senate regarding the appropriate portrayal of men and women of the armed forces in the upcoming National Air and Space Museum's exhibit on the Enola Gay;" agreed to by unanimous consent, September 24, 1994. Sam Johnson et al. to Heyman, December 13, 1994, AFA, EGD.

40. On November 16, 1994, approximately fifty historians (which expanded to over 100 during the following week) signed a letter to Heyman urging him to resist censorship ("historical cleansing") of the exhibit. The secretary's failure to respond led to the formation of "The Historians' Committee for Open Debate on Hiroshima."

41. The original exhibit, as its subtitle noted, was planned as an introduction to the nuclear age: "The End of World War II, the Atomic Bomb, and the Origins of the Cold War." The alternative framework demanded by the exhibit's critics included a history of the Pacific War.

42. Ralph Bard's memorandum of June 27, 1945, urging advance notice to the Japanese and noting that the Japanese were looking for a way to surrender, had been inserted into the (April '94) second script at my suggestion, but later was eliminated during negotiations with the American Legion. The "to this day" quotation was in the first draft script, "The Crossroads: The End of World War II, The Atomic Bomb and the Origins of the Cold War," January 12, 1994, 2.

43. "Smithsonian Scuttles Exhibit," *Washington Post*, January 31, 1995, A1.

44. Stimson, *On Active Service*, 628–29.

45. See, for example, *Newsweek* (July 24, 1995), "Why We Did It." The article concludes on this point: "[The atomic bombings] also allowed the world to see how truly awful the bomb was—one reason, perhaps, that it has not been used since," p. 30. See also Karl T. Compton, "If the Atomic Bomb Had Not Been Used," *The Atlantic* (December 1946), 54–56.

46. Memo discussed with the President, April 25, 1945; Sherwin, *A World Destroyed*, 291–92.

47. Sections of the Franck Report are reproduced in Sherwin, *A World Destroyed*, 323–32.

48. Ralph Bard to George Harrison (Stimson's assistant), June 27, 1945, Harrison passed Bard's memorandum to Stimson with a cover note on June 28. Sherwin, *A World Destroyed*, 307.

49. Robert McNamara, In Retrospect: The Tragedy and Lessons of Vietnam (New York, Times Books, 1995), 160, 234, 275, 243–44.

2

Hiroshima: The First Response

Paul Boyer

To understand our nuclear history, we must go back to the beginning. Washington's initial handling of nuclear-related issues; the media's coverage of the new reality; and the troubled and contradictory responses of the American people in the immediate aftermath of Hiroshima all deserve careful attention for the light they shed on the public's subsequent responses to the nuclear threat. In this process of historical excavation of a now-distant era, we can find the roots of the psychological techniques for dealing with nuclear fear that Robert Jay Lifton has so penetratingly explored.

Very early in the postwar period—indeed, within weeks of the devastation of Hiroshima and Nagasaki—nearly every theme that would shape the nation's nuclear discourse for more than four decades had already been articulated. These included determined efforts to rationalize and defend President Truman's decision; a surge of fear ("muted terror" is not too strong a term) that a future atomic holocaust could engulf the United States itself; and sketchy but unmistakable strategies of denial and evasion—often reflecting explicit governmental policy—that Lifton would later call nuclear numbing.

Justifying the Decision

From the moment on August 6, 1945, when President Truman announced the atomic bombing of Hiroshima, government officials and a swelling chorus of media voices mounted determined efforts to persuade the public that the President and his advisors had made the only possible choice in authorizing the destruction of a Japanese city (and

21

then a second one), with a massive toll of civilian life and suffering, and without meaningful prior warning.

Indeed, Truman's announcement itself provided the elements for such a justification. The President described Hiroshima as "a military base," obscuring the magnitude of the civilian slaughter. Further, Truman insisted, establishing a link that would figure in most future discussions of the bomb decision, Japan's 1941 surprise attack fully justified this act of terrible retribution. "The Japanese began the war from the air at Pearl Harbor," the President's statement intoned; "they have been repaid manyfold."

The media at once picked up on these themes. Japan's surrender a few days after the Nagasaki bombing seemingly underscored the correctness of Truman's action. Newspaper editorials, radio commentators, and political cartoonists almost unanimously agreed in hailing the atomic bombing of Hiroshima and Nagasaki as wholly defensible measures to defeat a monstrous and treacherous foe.

This commentary often betrayed the crude racism that, as historian John Dower has shown in *War Without Mercy: Race and Power in the Pacific War*, characterized much of the propaganda of the Pacific conflict. A political cartoon in the *Atlanta Constitution* on August 8, showing bodies flying into the air from a massive explosion, bore the witty caption "Land of the Rising Sons." Another, published in the *Philadelphia Inquirer* on August 7, personified the Japanese as a brutish, ape-like creature staring up in dumb incomprehension as an atomic bomb bursts overhead.

The Pearl Harbor–Hiroshima symmetry proved especially compelling. A *Chicago Tribune* cartoon of August 8, illustrating a point being made in countless editorials, pictured a long fuse running from Pearl Harbor to Hiroshima. The annihilation of two cities, in short, hardly involved human volition at all: it was simply an automatic, cause-and-effect consequence of a chain of events extending back to Japan's initial perfidy.

A powerful additional argument soon surfaced in defense of Truman's decision: that the atomic bomb had offered the only alternative to an invasion of the Japanese main islands in which countless thousands of Americans would have died. President Truman advanced this contention in an October 1945 message to Congress on atomic-energy legislation, and again at the annual Gridiron Dinner in Washington that December, when he summed up what he claimed to have been his thought processes in making the atomic-bomb decision: "It occurred to me, that a quarter of a million of the flower of our young manhood were worth a couple of Japanese cities, and I still think they were and are."

Again, the media echoed and amplified this theme. Another political cartoon, for example, entitled "Bloodless Invasion," pictured a U.S. soldier striding peacefully ashore in Japan as part of the occupation force, looking gratefully at the phantom image of a dead G.I. sprawled face-down in the sand: a victim of the invasion that would supposedly have become inevitable had the atomic bombs not been employed.

This was a major theme of "The Decision to Drop the Atomic Bomb," a highly influential and much-reprinted 1947 *Harper's Magazine* article. Published under the name of Henry L. Stimson, recently retired as secretary of war, the piece was in fact ghost-written by Stimson's aide Mc-George Bundy with the close oversight of Harvard president James B. Conant, a key figure in the tight circle of wartime atomic advisors. Eager to influence teachers, historians, and other opinion-molders, the trio insisted that an invasion would have been nearly inevitable had the atomic bomb not intervened, pushing the war into 1947 at a cost of "over a million casualties in American forces alone."

The multi-faceted defense of America's use of the atomic bomb against Japan, initially advanced by men with an obvious vested interest in securing their historical reputations, penetrated deeply into the American consciousness. Reassured by their leaders and by an almost unanimous media, and relieved by the Japanese surrender that followed so shortly after the bombings, an overwhelming majority of Americans supported the atomic-bomb decision.

To be sure, a few raised ethical doubts, or questioned whether the story was as simple and clear-cut as the administration and the press were suggesting. Indeed, in 1946 the U.S. Strategic Bombing Survey, implicitly challenging the argument that the war would have dragged on for years without the atomic bomb, concluded that the Japanese would certainly have surrendered by the end of 1945, and probably by the end of October, even without the bomb, Russia's intervention, or the threat of an invasion. But at the time, this seemed an isolated dissent from an overwhelming consensus.

Subsequent historical scholarship, beginning with Gar Alperovitz's *Atomic Diplomacy* of 1965, would argue convincingly that the bomb decision involved a considerably more complex set of issues, and was more ethically ambiguous, than policymakers and the media insisted at the time. Scholars would point out that Japan's war government was on the point of collapse in August 1945 and that urgent peace feelers were emanating from Tokyo—a matter known to Washington by virtue of the fact that U.S. cryptographers had broken the Japanese diplomatic code. Historians would further argue that calculations involving America's postwar relations with the Soviet Union loomed large in the minds of top U.S. policymakers in July 1945 as the atomic-bomb decision was made. At the Yalta conference in early 1945, Joseph Stalin pledged to declare war on Japan within three months of Germany's surrender—in other words, as events unfolded, by August 10, 1945. The real issue confronting Truman and his key advisors in July and early August, one may plausibly conclude, was not the prospect of a massive invasion of Japan months in the future, but the precise means by which the end game of the Pacific war would be managed, given the convergence of Japan's imminent collapse, Stalin's approaching entry into the conflict—and the successful test of an atomic bomb at Alamogordo, New Mexico, on July 16.

But amid the euphoria of V-J Day and the joyous scenes of returning G.I.s embracing wives and sweethearts, few challenged the officially endorsed justifications offered for the obliteration of two enemy cities. A war-weary nation, after nearly four years of bloody conflict (and of virulent anti-Japanese propaganda), accepted the arguments advanced by the government and embraced by the media. Indeed, some grassroots voices angrily complained that the United States had not finished the job and extermined the entire Japanese population. "When one sets out to destroy vermin, does one try to leave a few alive in the nest?" one advocate of genocide asked rhetorically in a letter to the *Milwaukee Journal*, "Certainly not!"

This justificatory view of America's initial use of the atomic bomb, firmly implanted in the public mind at the moment of victory (and the moment when the atom's awesome power first became manifest) continues to determine public opinion on the subject, revisionist historians to the contrary. The conviction that "the atomic bomb prevented an invasion and saved a quarter of a million [half a million, a million] American lives," first advanced in 1945 by President Truman and others immediately involved in the decisionmaking process, and buttressed by influential media outlets, remains an article of faith for millions of Americans.

Yet Truman's fateful decision, which so profoundly influenced the subsequent course of the world's nuclear history, can still rouse passionate reactions. Despite determined efforts to silence it, the debate goes on. Indeed, the angry controversy that in 1994 swirled around the Smithsonian Institution's planned fiftieth-anniversary commemorative exhibit of the Hiroshima-Nagasaki bombings was only the latest round in a controversy that began in the earliest moments of the atomic age, and that still stirs uneasily in the public mind.

Visions of Atomic Menace Ahead

While most Americans rallied behind their government in endorsing the atomic bombing of Japan, they also immediately put two and two together and realized that the same weapon the United States had employed against Japan could one day be directed against America. The fear of an all-destroying nuclear holocaust that would shadow American life for more than four decades, periodically surging to intense levels, dates literally from the earliest moments of the atomic age.

Initially, powerful media voices reenforced these fears. "For all we know, we have created a Frankenstein!" declared radio news commentator Hans Von Kaltenborn on the evening of Truman's announcement. Commentators and editorial writers projected with chilling specificity the effect of a Hiroshima-sized bomb on U.S. cities of comparable size. As Don Goddard somberly told his listeners on CBS radio that same memorable evening:

> There is reason to believe tonight that our new atomic bomb destroyed the entire Japanese city of Hiroshima in a single blast. . . . It would be the same as Denver, Colorado, with a population of 350,000 persons being there one moment, and wiped out the next.

In November 1945, *Life* magazine, a vastly influential media voice in this pre-television era, published a scary scenario of World War III—"The 36-Hour War"—in which missiles bearing atomic bombs streak toward the United States. (With the Soviet Union still an erstwhile ally, not yet the Cold War adversary, *Life* remained vague about the source of the attack, implausibly identifying it only as somewhere deep in Africa.) But if the identity of the attacker was unclear, the effects were not: *Life*'s artists graphically portrayed missiles raining down on America's major urban centers, and a flattened New York City in which only the stone lions of the New York Public Library still stand, eyelessly surveying a vanished city as investigators wearing protective suits probe the rubble.

In June 1946, the Mutual radio network's program *Exploring the Unknown* dramatized the outbreak of an atomic war, recreating the casual, workaday activities of a typical American city in the final moments before the first bomb strikes. After an unearthly blast, the narrator, Clifton Fadiman, intoned: "Silence—complete and total silence. The infinite silence of death. In a fraction of a second—you and thousands of your neighbors . . . vaporized. . . , blown to bits. . . , to nothingness."

The Manhattan Project veterans who formed the Federation of American Scientists (FAS) in 1946 and plunged into the campaign for the international control of atomic energy deliberately played upon this wave of atomic fear, and—like many later activists—tried to channel it for their own political purposes. FAS presentations typically began with a horrifying description of the devastation of Hiroshima and Nagasaki, went on to a reminder that American cities lay naked to the same fate, and concluded with an urgent plea for support of the Acheson-Lilienthal Plan for atomic-energy control by the United Nations.

One World Or None (1946), the FAS's most compelling piece of international-control propaganda, began with a gripping account by physicist Philip Morrison of an atomic attack on New York City, full of details drawn from the effects of the bomb on Hiroshima and Nagasaki, translated to an American setting. "From the river west to Seventh Avenue and from south of Union Square to the middle Thirties," wrote Morrison; "the streets were filled with dead and dying."

While some of these dreamscapes of the nuclear future anticipated intercontinental ballistic missiles (years before ICBMs in fact became operational), others conjured up atomic menaces involving means all-too-readily available in 1945: an enemy smuggling in the components of an atomic bomb, for example; secretly assembling them in some hidden site in Manhattan; and then demanding Washington's capitulation as the price of sparing New York City's seven million inhabitants. *One World or None* invested even the most innocuous settings with hidden menace: "In any room where a file case can be stored . . . a determined effort can secret a bomb capable of killing a hundred thousand people and laying waste every ordinary structure within a mile." Such dramatizations of atomic horrors ahead deepened fears already roused by the first news of a city-destroying bomb.

The Acheson-Lilienthal Plan soon fell victim to Cold War animosities, but the fear that the international-control campaign had intensified remained. By the early 1950s, however, the officially endorsed strategy for dealing with the atomic danger had shifted 180 degrees: not international control and disarmament, but keeping ahead of the Russians in a grim spiral of nuclear-weapons competition. The Soviets' successful A-bomb test in late summer 1949 offered a propitious moment for another serious effort at international control (as McGeorge Bundy argues in *Danger and Survival: Choices About the Bomb in the First Fifty Years*), but this was not to be. Prodded by Edward Teller, and over the objections of David Lilienthal, J. Robert Oppenheimer, James Conant, and others, President Truman endorsed a crash program to build the hydrogen bomb. Once again the American people, with no advance notice or public debate, expressed overwhelming retroactive support for Truman's decision.

The basic dynamic of the nuclear arms race, in short, took shape in the earliest postwar period: pervasive nuclear fear, coupled with the official manipulation of that fear to rally support for the nuclear arms race—a competition that generated still more fear as it threatened the well-being if not the very survival of the population it was ostensibly designed to protect.

Nuclear Numbing: The First Phase

The open manifestations of raw atomic fear that gripped the nation in the immediate aftermath of Hiroshima soon diminished. Within a few years, the lurid scenarios of atomic annihilation that so pervaded early postwar American culture became more and more rare.

In part, this reflected a natural human psychological response: the mind cannot remain fixated on even the most fearsome prospect indefinitely. But the suppression of atomic terror was also abetted by the mass media. Even as newspapers, magazines, and the radio networks reflected the spasm of fear that gripped the populace in the early post-Hiroshima months, they also treated the bomb as a subject of nervous humor. Editorial writers and radio comedians spoke of Japan's "atomic ache" and compared Hiroshima to Ebbett's Field after a game between the Giants and the Dodgers. Bartenders mixed "atomic cocktails." On August 13, 1945, the *Chicago Tribune* ran an entire column of "Atomic Anecdotes." Milton Berle, of all people, was the only comedian who explicitly refused to make jokes about the atomic bomb.

And entrepreneurs quickly saw the potential for profit in the new weapon. Department stores ran "Atomic Sales"; advertisers promised "Atomic Results." By 1947 the Manhattan telephone directory listed forty-five companies that had incorporated the magic word "Atomic" into their names. For fifteen cents and a Kix Cereal boxtop, the General Mills Corporation in 1947 offered kiddies an "Atomic 'Bomb' Ring" complete with "sealed atom chamber" and "gleaming aluminum . . . warhead." (At least one boy who sent in his fifteen cents found the ring a bit of a disappointment.)

The link between nuclear cataclysm and erotic arousal, often noted by psychiatrists, surfaced early. Within weeks of Hiroshima, *Life* published a full-page photograph of "The Anatomic Bomb": a Hollywood starlet posed fetchingly at poolside in a revealing bathing suit. In "Atom Bomb

Baby," a pop song of 1947, the bomb became a metaphor for sexual orgasm. The French designer who dubbed his skimpy new swimsuit the "Bikini" in 1946, after the U.S. atomic test site in the Pacific, was only echoing a pervasive cultural linkage. Admiral W. H. P. ("Spike") Blandy, commander of the Bikini tests, smilingly posed with his wife cutting a "wedding cake" in the shape of a mushroom cloud.

The pattern of denial was encouraged by government propaganda touting the vast promise of the "peaceful atom." Even before 1945, popular magazines had offered occasional glimpses of an atomic utopia ahead, and with the awesome demonstration of the atom's power in 1945, the dreams suddenly seemed to take on tangible reality. In the months after Hiroshima the popular press endlessly featured starry-eyed predictions of the transformative impact atomic energy would have on all areas of American life: electricity too cheap to meter, miracles of medicine, massive public-works projects facilitated by atomic explosions that would change the face of the earth itself. One article envisioned using atomic bombs to melt the polar ice caps.

Much of this fantasizing initially arose from innocent journalistic hype and spontaneous fascination with the new scientific wonder. But Washington policymakers warmly encouraged such speculation as a way of muting nuclear fear and diverting a public gripped by nightmares of atomic war. While atomic energy had been developed under the spur of wartime necessity, and initially used for destructive purposes, the argument went, it would in fact have highly beneficial consequences.

With the creation of the Atomic Energy Commission in 1946, this program of politically inspired positive thinking gained a powerful institutional voice. The first AEC chairman, David E. Lilienthal, formerly head of the Tennessee Valley Authority, a New Deal agency, devoted much of his efforts to writing and speechmaking extolling the vast promise of atomic energy. In magazine articles and nationally broadcast radio addresses to high school graduating classes, farm organizations, and other assemblages of anxious Americans, Lilienthal expansively pictured the shining new era that lay ahead thanks to peacetime applications of atomic energy.

Privately, Lilienthal grew increasingly morose as the scope of the government's atomic-weapons program became clear. In bleak diary entries and conversations with aides, Lilienthal brooded that the AEC had become nothing but a conduit for supplying atomic weaponry to the military. But in public, until his resignation in 1950, Lilienthal maintained his cheerful facade—at who knows what psychic cost.

The media readily fell into line. The stories of the atom's peacetime benefits continued to flood the press, now encouraged by the AEC. Local communities, again with Washington's prodding, organized "Atomic Energy Weeks" and "Atomic Energy Fairs." In 1947, in cooperation with the AEC, CBS-Radio ran a program called "The Sunny Side of the Atom." Narrated by Agnes Moorhead, the show deplored the preoccuation with the atom's death-dealing power and insisted on its many peacetime benefits, from oil exploration to new surgical techniques to possible cures for cancer. In a photo montage accompanying a 1947 *Collier's* story on the atom's medical benefits, a smiling paraplegic emerges from a mushroom cloud, his empty wheelchair in the background.

A high point in this campaign was "Man and the Atom," a month-long exhibit in New York's Central Park in the summer of 1948 sponsored by the AEC and its two major contractors for atomic-power development, Westinghouse and General Electric. Visitors to GE's exhibit received a comic book in which Mandrake the Magician introduced Dagwood and Blondie to the exciting world of atomic energy.

The federal government also countered atomic fear by touting the theme of security through civil defense. Even if atomic war did come, the reassuring message went, it would not be so bad if citizens were prepared. Richard Gerstell's *How to Survive an Atomic Bomb* (1950), a quasi-official publication, advised men to wear hats, and women long-sleeved dresses, to prevent burns in the event of atomic attack. Gerstell urged property owners to rake up autumn leaves promptly, especially around their houses, to minimize fire damage in an atomic blast. While waiting in the basement during the attack itself, Gerstell suggested, recite nursery rhymes or repeat the multiplication tables to keep calm.

Again, the mass media compliantly echoed the official line. *Life* sent a newlywed couple into a fallout shelter for their honeymoon, publishing photographs of the smiling bride and groom as they disappeared underground for several days of connubial bliss. In 1950, as the H-bomb project swung into high gear, *U.S. News and World Report* pooh-poohed the atomic danger and attacked the negativity of those who advised relocation to rural areas:

> Forget most stories you read about atomic radioactivity, mass evacuation of cities, devastation of whole regions. If there were a "hydrogen super-bomb," for example, 100 times as powerful as the actual modern atomic bombs, it would reach only [sic] about 9 miles from the center of the explosion—not clear across a state. The new line on atomic attack is to figure on staying and living. The whole country cannot run away and hide.

Cruelly deceptive and absurdly heavy-handed as it seems in retrospect, such propaganda helped soothe a society that still trusted the government and the press. Civil defense and media placebos contributed to the process by which atomic jitters were eased and advocates of international control silenced as the military geared up for a full-scale nuclear arms race with the new global enemy.

Back to the Future

To sum up, the fundamental political and psychological contours of the nuclear age took shape with surprising suddenness after the atomic bombing of Hiroshima and Nagasaki. As it would continue to do, the government worked strenuously to calm any doubts about the fateful initial decision to drop the bomb; to mute public anxiety by proclaiming the exciting potential of the peacetime atom; and to offer reassurance that through the magic of civil defense, atomic war need be little more than a brief annoyance.

All these themes and strategies, more subtly employed and adapted to new circumstances, would continue to shape Americans' response to the bomb for the next four decades. The nuclear numbing that Robert Jay Lifton later identified in the *hibakusha* of Hiroshima, and employed so creatively as a concept to illuminate the evasions and denials of an entire era shadowed by the bomb, had its roots in popular responses, government propaganda, and media themes that emerged in the earliest moments of the atomic age.

3

Hiroshima and the Silence of Poetry

Michael Flynn

Theodor Adorno's statement—"to write poetry after Auschwitz is barbaric"[1]—emerged as a central mantra in discussions addressing the situation of art and aesthetic consciousness in the post-Holocaust age. Several years later, in his exploration on the role of metaphysics and art in the wake of the Nazis' "final solution," Adorno made what to some intellectuals seemed a retraction and to others an understandable revision in stating "it may have been wrong to say that after Auschwitz you could no longer write poems. But it is not wrong to raise the less cultural question whether after Auschwitz you can go on living—especially whether one who escaped by accident, one who by rights should have been killed, may go on living."[2]

In an even later essay Adorno was able to combine, in the same paragraph, the audacity of his original statement "I have no wish to soften the saying that to write lyric poetry after Auschwitz is barbaric" with a claim that artistic expression (presumably including poetry) was uniquely qualified to the represent the agonies inherent to twentieth-century human existence. "It is virtually in art alone that suffering can find its own voice, consolation, without immediately being betrayed by it."[3] As evidenced by these quotes, Adorno was rarely guilty of equivocation; but he was far too intimate with the lethal possibilities of any totalitarian regime to prescribe a singular purpose for poetry. Yet by so forcefully raising the question of poetry's relevance in an age of mass slaughter, Adorno insisted on the radicalization of poetry.

To say that after the Holocaust nothing has been the same seems to many a cliché. Yet no historical event, including World War I, has so radically altered the ontological foundations of the poetic endeavor. After the Holocaust, poetry's primary political and moral responsibilities became those of dissent and opposition. No longer was it acceptable for the poet to serve the ruling elite, nor craft poems intended to glorify, minimize, or excuse evil or oppressive governmental policies and action. As Helene Cixous' declaration "a state will never accept a poet, and a poet will never accept a state"[4] alludes, the post-Holocaust poet's condition became one of self-appointed inhabitor of the margins. In this space, unchained from the fictional security and uniqueness furnished by nationalistic myth and heterodoxy, the poet's duty involved the creation of images and narratives countering any state's attempts to legitimize slaughter, brutality, or oppression.

The Holocaust administered the deathblow to the cherished, but counterfeit, separation of the personal from the political in poetry. The Nazi's success in infiltrating relational dyads previously considered inviolate—mother–child, doctor–patient, Christian believer–Incarnate God —demonstrated the porousness of categories philosophers and psychologists had spent countless pages proving as mutually exclusive. Public and private, once understood as separate and unequal, percolated together in every human act. Poetry, long understood as the most personal of literary acts, became a social act. As evidenced by the poetry of Celan, Saks, Levi, Borowski, Pagis, and Bruck (and the many others influenced by these masters) the poet's mandate became one of witness to the "noises of history."[5] Whether confronting the incineration of the Jews, the ravages of the Gulag, or the soul-killing effects of American racism, poetry's provocation became one of simultaneously bearing witness to the experiences of traumatized individuals and peoples and against the atrocities perpetrated in the name of national, religious, ethnic, or ideological salvation.

Not that it became necessary for every post-Holocaust poem, nor poet, to chronicle historical or contemporary evil, confront twentieth-century despair and nothingness, or annotate the infinite forms of suffering, disease, and injustice threading existence. Consigning poetry, or any art form, to this exclusive motivation would truly engender the "death of art" that critics and nihilists have spent countless pages announcing and forecasting with a sanctimonious admixture of glee, despondency, and insight. Poetry, according to Bachelard, "speaks on the threshold of Being" and even in our genocidal age "Being" consists of much more than suicidal or homicidal chaos.[6] It simply became unacceptable for the poet to collude with forces that constituted the twentieth century as an age "where murder is legitimate and where human life is considered trifling."[7]

Decrying the state of modern poetry has become a favored avenue in the literary critics' quest for intellectual relevance. The death of poetic vision and the constriction of symbolic breadth are mourned (witness Adorno's famous "the dimensions of poetry have shrunk") along with the rise of confessional subjectivism. Comparisons with the masters of the not-so-distant past—Eliot, Stevens, and even the fascist Pound—are made to document the fall from the figurative to the literal, the transcendent to the mundane.

These criticisms possess a kernel of truth. Contemporary poetry can be diminished by an exaggerated emphasis on individual emotional experience and, as Terrence Des Pres argues, a misunderstanding of "self as a world rather than self in the world."[8] But these criticisms overlook the extent to which, because of its commited opposition to evil and advocacy for the wretched of the earth, the widening of the experiential parameters of poetry have resulted in a greater, rather than lesser, public and moral significance.

II

The impact on poetry of the war's other genocidal noise, Hiroshima, has been far less profound. Outside a handful of powerful poems by such poets as Robert Penn Warren, Carolyn Forché, Campbell McGrath, and Galway Kinnell the event of Hiroshima, and specifically its psychological and moral meanings for Americans, has gone unaddressed. Nor is poetry the only artistic reprobate; Hiroshima has been largely ignored in American literature, painting, and drama. Given Hiroshima's immensity, both as the most violent moment in human history and the actuation of existence with the threat of nuclear annihilation, its absence is deeply troubling.

Accounting for this lack requires a multi-level analysis. It can be seen as simply another manifestation of a larger cultural pattern of avoidance and denial; it would be fair to say that the issue of Hiroshima has never been prominent in American consciousness. In fact most Americans' exposure to Hiroshima is probably limited to a high school reading of John Hersey's *Hiroshima,* a truncated historical sketch detailing the factors that brought about the end of World War II courtesy of a college teaching assistant, and a ninety-second network news segment outlining the intricacies of the Smithsonian's Enola Gay controversy. Yet given the disposedness of postwar American poetry to address the underbelly of American life, the lack of treatment is perplexing and disappointing. Over the course of the past fifty years some of the most profound and memorable American poetry has, with great honesty and unyielding insight, confronted madness, sexual abuse, violence (including the atrocities committed by American soldiers during the Vietnam War), racism, and even the absurd vicissitudes of living in the nuclear age.

To be fair, Hiroshima, together with the Holocaust, presents unique challenges to the poetic imagination. Both are *sui generis* and, due to the traditionally unthinkable scale, grotesqueness, and technicized delivery of death, reside beyond the "traditional presuppositions of history, psychology, politics, and morality."[9] The Holocaust's historical imprint is that of a civilized, modern nation-state engaged in a systematic, undisguised attempt at the extermination of one race. Hiroshima, on the other hand, marks the literalization of the possibility of the complete annihilation of life itself through a deed of human agency. As Hiroshima represents an ultimate threat to organic continuity, and writing is an organic process perpetrated with the hope of human permanence, it is tempting to state that Hiroshima represents the "limit of writing."[10] This sentiment received perhaps its strongest endorsement with Faulkner's "there is only the question: When will I be blown up? Because of this, the young man or woman writing today has forgotten the problems of the human heart in conflict with itself which alone can make good writing."[11]

Faulkner's Nobel statement has a certain appeal: living under the nuclear umbrella greatly increases the possibility of psychic numbing as well as paralyzing states of despair, meaninglessness, and apathy—states counter to the creation of great literature. Yet since 1945 there has been no shortage of great American literature and poetry. Nor has American poetry shied away from nuclear concerns. In fact, of all the literary forms, poetry has most forcefully confronted the ontological predicaments of existence in the nuclear age. Over the course of the past fifty years Frost, Williams, Jarrell, Lowell, Ginsburg, Snyder, Levertov, Kumin, Levine, Clifton, Jong, Jordan, Hudgins, Rodney Jones, and Thomas McGrath have written extraordinary poems confronting issues as varied as the lunacy of nuclear testing, living in the shadow of nuclear apocalypse, and the lethal senselessness of nuclear arms stockpiling.[12] Why not Hiroshima?

Some important clues can be found in Hiroshima's moral and politcal narration. As evidenced by the very different spirit accompanying the recent wave of commemorations, Hiroshima and the European Holocaust occupy very different positions in public consciousness and memory. With the exception of a small group of discredited Holocaust deniers and minimizers, the Nazi's "Final Solution" has been universally understood as the apotheosis of human evil. Hiroshima, on the other hand, has been widely understood, even by many in the anti-nuclear movement, as a tragically regrettable, but necessary, event in a just war to defeat a fascist enemy. This viewpoint derives much of its sustenance from the official narrative—constructed by Secretary of War Henry Stimson (more than a year after the bombing) and supported in Truman's and Churchill's later autobiographical writings—maintaining that the bombing of Hiroshima was carried out to prevent an allied invasion of Japan; an invasion that would have entailed up to a million American casualties, and untold Japanese deaths. Given this historiography the bomb becomes narrated as a humane and courageous act, a technological triumph of democratic good over totalitarian evil. Such a triumphal narrative serves as wonderful fertilizer for patriotic odes but effectively smothers any chance for profound poetry. Thankfully, for both the artist and those interested in the complicacy of historical truth, recent scholarship by Robert Jay Lifton and Greg Mitchell, Barton Bernstein, Charles Strozier, Martin Sherwin, and Gar Alperovitz revisiting the motives underlying the decision (and the questions of the number of lives saved) has raised strong questions regarding the veracity of Stimson's narrative.[13]

Any discussion of Hiroshima must confront the reality of Japanese evil. Whereas the victimization of the Jews, Gypsies, and, to a lesser degree, the European citizenry is widely accepted, suggestions that the bombing constituted a war crime have been branded as traitorous. And given the brutal realities of Japanese aggression and the atrocities perpetrated against the Chinese, Koreans, Filipinos, and Allied and American POW's it is little wonder. Japanese wartime conduct can only be described as evil. This record, combined with Japan's steadfast refusal to authentically acknowledge and apologize for these atrocities, leaves little room for feelings of remorse or sympathy. Consequently, the impulse to excuse, even celebrate, any military action resulting in Japan's demise is regrettably understandable.

The continued insistence on Japanese evil has, however, another, more sinister, source; the obviation of American guilt. As long as the Japanese are dehumanized as the "evil other" the responsibility for the bombing and the generations of resultant suffering falls entirely on their military and political leadership. Maintaining such a position provides the moral and psychological benefit of allowing Americans to feel pity for the ordinary citizens of Hiroshima (especially the women and children) while simultaneously perceiving it as a military triumph worthy of national commemoration. Japanese evil results in America being a victor, not a perpetrator. It is interesting to note that Bill Clinton's recent defense of Truman's decision (eliminating, at least in this anniversary year, any possibility for an official apology or even national debate) followed this line. While extremely seductive for a campaigning politician, this victorious position renders serious, searching poetry impossible.

III

In arguing for the centrality of Hiroshima in any narration of twentieth-century history, Robert Jay Lifton has written, "like any powerful text, Hiroshima must be read, absorbed, and recreated by each generation searching for its own truths."[14] The controversy over the Enola Gay exhibition at the Smithsonian's Air and Space Museum vividly demonstrates that the truths of Hiroshima are, for this generation and the generation that lived through the war, still a matter of great discord. The emotional and moral vehemence shown by the many camps involved in the debate makes it most clear that Hiroshima is far from a dead issue, it remains a "raw nerve."[15] And far more than the moral and military "correctness" of the bombing is at stake. Such issues as the influence of private groups on the public representation of history, the dissimilitude of history and memory, the role of museums in the process of commemoration, the psychological and moral dangers of nostalgia, and the enduring the glorification of American military prowess lurk within the folds of the acrimony.

If the current controversy can be said to have a moral, it is the need for a sustained and critical reconsideration of Hiroshima. The goals of such a reconsideration should be threefold: a greater appreciation of the dynamics of Hiroshima, that is, how the unique blending of the individual motivations of the principle actors involved and the historical/political circumstances resulted in the decision to use the bomb (despite Truman's claim of being sovereign arbiter, the responsibility must be shared by a group of men); to deconstruct the untruths and semi-truths proffered over the course of the last fifty years by the supporters and apologists for the bomb; and an honest appraisal of the psychological, moral, and political legacies of Hiroshima. This reconsideration should be performed in the service of increasing public awareness and activating *informed* moral discourse rather than "laying it to rest." Forgetting or burying an atrocity does increase the risk of reoccurrence. It was Hitler who said, "Who now remembers the Armenians?" (Unfortunately, as the continuing genocide in Bosnia and Rwanda tragically attests, memory and recognition do not ensure prevention.)

Any critical intellectual act involves the laceration of established and sanctioned myths. Consequently, a reconsideration of the existing narratives, narratives which secure a comfortable national righteousness, will face great resistance and outright aggressive opposition (and not only from the Right and military groups). Accusations of revisionism and national betrayal will be leveled with obligatory vehemence. To such charges David Tracy's "our history is the way it is not because of any natural necessity but only because equally historical individuals have struggled before us" is an excellent rejoinder.[16] Hiroshima's textualization, as Lifton and Tracy make evident, is a product of human, not divine or "natural," authorship. Consequently in order to remain relevant it must be "re-read" in light of available historical scholarship and wider moral understandings. Many opposed to a reconsideration voice concerns that such an enterprise only result in a wave of self-condemnation and faultfinding that would result only in greater fragmentation and ideological polarization. Their fear has validity; if the reexamination results in a quagmire of "universal and ineffectual guilt" rather than the animation of responsibility, nothing is gained.[17]

IV

Such a reconsideration requires the involvement of poetry. It might seem odd to champion a literary form that occupies so little space in contemporary public imagination (although there is much to support Robert Pinsky's statement "any room full of Americans has more poetry in it than they may suppose, in memories").[18] Yet due to its noncompliance with the dictates of logocentricity, its freedom from the stipulations of causality, and, most importantly, its faith in the restorative and generative properties of unqualified language, poetry is unique in its capacity to effect radical change. Helene Cixous' declaration regarding poetry's potency that "in some way, power is afraid of poetry, afraid of what has no strength, only the power of words. How much the word is feared—as much as the people, more than bombs—the history of our century has everywhere shown. Poetry is power, and the proof is the extent to which poets are persecuted" may possess a particular salience in political situations where repression, torture, and political imprisonment are commonplace, but is also true for the banal moral and political climates of contemporary first-world democracies.[19]

Another source of poetry's political and moral power resides in its marginality, its refusal to obey the dictates of national "common sense."

Poetry seeks to deconstruct the false distinctions and rationales for destruction or indifference so common in contemporary political discourse while simultaneously highlighting the injustices and traumas suffered by the victims of history. In this way poetry seeks to become the "country beyond all countries."[20] Because poetry centers on the "ambiguities and contradictions" of history rather than aspiring to "either historical record or mythography," Frank Kermode is quite correct in his insistence that "good poems about historical crises speak in a different language from historical record." This "different language" can translate into different, more radical "forms of knowledge," forms that "stand apart from opinion" and "protect us from the familiar."[21]

Poetry derives much of its psychological power from its unparalleled ability to animate emotional life. Due to its ability to weave its meanings around the seemingly unpenetrable psychological defenses necessary for survival in our violence-soaked, technocratic world, poetry can "break open locked chambers of possibility, restore numbed zones to feeling, and recharge desire."[22] Freed from literature's commitment to taletelling, and photography's duty to visually capture and thus aestheticize, poetry has the capacity to serve as the most radical antidote to the age's truncated psychological life. Its power lies in its practice of championing the raw, traumatized soul and allegiance to the truth as witnessed by the dead and brutalized rather than the adaptive, efficient self so prized by social science.

Two days after Hiroshima, Camus wrote that "before the terrifying prospects now available to humanity, we see even more clearly that peace is the only goal worth struggling for. This is no longer a prayer but a demand to be made by all peoples to their governments."[23] Camus' insistence on universal involvement in the service of human continuity is certainly morally sound and laudable. Tragically, though, the movements aspiring to peaceful coexistence have been repeatedly outflanked by forces advocating policies principled on the threat of nuclear slaughter. The public representatives of these forces (witness Kissinger, McNamara, Teller, Joseph Nye) appear regularly in print and media venues demonstrating, always with the most exquisite argumentation, the necessity of Hiroshima and the glories of capitalistic peace rooted in deterrence. It is against such genocidal logic that post–Hiroshima poetry must struggle; as Denise Levertov states, "If there begins to be a poetry of peace, it is still, as it has long been, a poetry of struggle."[24]

Susan Sontag's assessment that "one great poet alone cannot change the moral weather" has real validity.[25] Even those most committed to revolutions in consciousness must acknowledge the obstinacy of value systems. Yet weather systems, both atmospheric and moral, are not immortal; they lose their potency and grow weary with time and distance. Approaching their inevitable demise, they fretfully review their triumphs and failures and worry about what will follow. They want that which succeeds them to be less chaotic, more peaceful and amenable to life. Shaking with ambivalence, they sometimes look to the poetry appearing on the horizon for a sign of hope.

Notes

1. Theodor Adorno, *Prisms* (Cambridge, Mass.: MIT Press, 1981), 28.

2. Adorno, *Negative Dialectics* (New York: Continuum, 1973), 362–63.

3. Adorno, "Commitment," in *The Essential Frankfurt School Reader*, eds. Andrew Arato and Eike Gebhardt (New York: Continuum, 1982), 313.

4. Helene Cixous, " We Who Are Free, Are We Free?" in *Freedom and Interpretation*, ed. Barbara Johnson (New York: Basic Books, 1993).

5. Ibid., 23. See also *Against Forgetting: Twentieth Century Poetry of Witness*, ed. Carolyn Forché (New York: Norton, 1993).

6. Gaston Bachelard, *On Poetic Imagination and Reverie*, tr. Colette Gaudin (Dallas: Spring, 1987), 16.

7. Albert Camus, *Between Hell and Reason*, tr. Alexandre de Gramont (Hanover: Wesleyan University Press, 1991), 119.

8. Terrence Des Pres, *Writing into the World* (New York: Viking, 1991), 178.

9. Arthur Cohen, *The Tremendum: A Theological Interpretation of the Holocaust* (New York: Crossroads, 1981), 32.

10. Maurice Blanchot, *The Writing of the Disaster*, tr. Ann Smock (Lincoln: University of Nebraska Press, 1986), 7.

11. Nobel Speech

12. *Atomic Ghost: Poets Respond to the Nuclear Age* , ed. John Bradely (Minneapolis: Coffee House Books, 1995).

13. See Robert Jay Lifton and Greg Mitchell, *Hiroshima in America: Fifty Years of Denial* (New York: Putnam, 1995); Martin J. Sherwin, *A World Destroyed: The Atomic Bomb and the Grand Alliance* (New York: Knopf, 1975); Charles B. Strozier, "Unconditional Surrender and The Rhetoric of Total War: From Truman to Lincoln," *Military History Quarterly* 2 (1990): 8–15.

14. Robert Jay Lifton, *The Future of Immortality* (New York: Basic, 1987), 38.

15. Lifton and Mitchell, *Hiroshima in America*, 6.

16. David Tracy, *Plurality and Ambiguity: Hermenuetics, Religion, Hope* (San Francisco: Harper & Row, 1987), 70.

17. Ibid., 73.

18. Robert Pinsky, "A Man Goes into a Bar, See, and Recites: 'The Quality of Mercy is Not Strained,' " *New York Times Book Review* (April 19, 1994), 32.

19. Cixous, "We Who are Free, Are We Free?," 20.

20. Ibid., 18.

21. Frank Kermode, *Poetry, Narrative, History* (Cambridge, Mass.: Blackwell, 1990), 32.

22. Adrienne Rich, *What is Found There: Notebooks on Poetry and Politics* (New York: Norton, 1993), 42.

23. Camus, *Between Hell and Reason,* 78.

24. Denise Levertov, *New and Selected Essays* (New York: New Directions, 1992), 167.

25. Susan Sontag, *On Photography* (New York: Farrar, Straus and Giroux, 1977), 81.

4

Life after *Death in Life*

Greg Mitchell

One way to judge Robert Jay Lifton's influence in the field of Hiroshima studies is to locate *Death in Life* in the bibliographies or end notes of other important books. And, of course, one finds it everywhere: from Richard Rhodes' *The Making of the Atomic Bomb* to Carolyn Forché's *The Angel of History*. The poet Mark Kaminsky based much of his volume, *The Road from Hiroshima*, on the accounts of survivors captured by Lifton. In his recent book, *Literary Aftershocks*, Albert E. Stone called *Death in Life* one of three "prose masterpieces" of the nuclear era. (The others were John Hersey's *Hiroshima* and Jonathan Schell's *The Fate of the Earth*.) And this does not account for the impact of Lifton's many articles and essays about Hiroshima, his books on various aspects of the nuclear dilemma, nor his most recent study, *Hiroshima in America*, which I had the privilege of co-authoring.[1]

Nearly thirty years after publication, *Death in Life* remains unique. Others have explored the experience of small groups of survivors, but no American has attempted the kind of wide-angled study accomplished by Lifton during the 1960s. So it is not too much to say that nearly everyone who wants to write about the social and psychological effects of the bomb—and anyone (expert, journalist or peace activist) who plans to visit Hiroshima—must turn to *Death in Life* as a primary text.

The influence of *Death in Life*, however, extends beyond Hiroshima, beyond even the world of nuclear weapons. Others have used Lifton's concept of "psychic numbing" to describe the human response to many other forms of violence and terror. And as Albert Stone observed, *Death in Life* has become "the era's seminal study of survivorship." There may be more significant scholarly achievements, but not many.[2]

Concerning Hiroshima, and nuclear weapons in general, Lifton insisted on the primacy of the survivor. This was a critical assertion. It

41

reminded Americans that the atomic bombings were not just a military feat and a historical controversy, but a human tragedy; and it proclaimed that the victims of the bomb, not scientists or defense intellectuals, were the world's leading authorities on nuclear war. Hiroshima, he wrote, should not be portrayed "as an event of the past, but as a source of necessary knowledge for the present and the future." The two atomic cities in Japan "convey to us a sense of nuclear actuality. The bombs were really used there. We can read, view, and, if we will allow ourselves, feel what happened to people in them."[3]

This sentiment hardly seems radical today. In 1985, at the fortieth anniversary of the atomic bombings, and then again at the fifty-year commemoration in 1995, the testimony of the *hibakusha*, the Japanese survivors, was included in much of the media coverage. But, as Martin Sherwin explains the controversy that erupted in 1994 and 1995 over the Enola Gay exhibit at the National Air and Space Museum in Washington, D.C., suggests that, today, Americans have as much difficulty marking what happened to the victims in Hiroshima and Nagasaki as they did when *Death in Life* appeared nearly thirty years ago.

From the first day of the nuclear age—August 6, 1945—American officials attempted to obscure the number and the nature of the casualties in Hiroshima. In his official announcement, President Truman referred to Hiroshima—a city of 300,000—as a Japanese "Army base." Three days later, Nagasaki was described simply as a "naval base" and industrial shipyard. It took months for the U.S. military to estimate civilian casualties, and then its count—a little over 100,000 in the two cities—amounted to less than half the actual total.

Beyond that, officials attempted to hide not merely how many civilians died, but how they died. Within days of the atomic attacks, reports from Japan indicated that thousands of those who had survived the initial blast were dying from radiation disease. Besides adding to the death toll, this threatened to create a moral disaster for the United States, and the timing could not have been worse. America was still celebrating the end of the war. The vast majority of Americans supported the use of the atomic bomb against Japan. The bombings had seemed to spur the Japanese surrender offer, which emerged eight days after the bombing of Hiroshima. Few commentators in the media questioned this cause-and-effect approach. Officials failed to disclose information about other approaches to ending the war that Truman had rejected: negotiating a surrender; demonstrating the power of the new weapon before using it on two cities; waiting to see if the Soviet declaration of war against Japan in August would provoke a surrender.

Most Americans knew, at least vaguely, that the atomic bombs had slaughtered many civilians, but they accepted this as a necessary evil. The victims had apparently died suddenly, like so many others in Europe and Asia, from the blast of bombs that fell from the sky. But the reports of radiation disease threatened this consensus. The Allies had treated the use of poison gas as taboo throughout the war, and polls showed that most Americans (recalling the horrors of chemical warfare in World War I) supported this prohibition. Now unofficial reports were emerging from Japan of thousands of civilians suffering a cruel, lingering death from a new and even more appalling "poison"—radiation.

Evidence would later reveal that military and scientific leaders of the Manhattan Project knew in advance that the atomic bomb would kill Japanese through radiation as well as blast and burns. Yet, in the weeks after the atomic attacks, they expressed surprise over the reports from Hiroshima and Nagasaki—and then labelled them "propaganda," as General Leslie Groves, head of the Manhattan Project, put it. When American investigators arrived in Hiroshima a month after the atomic attack, and saw hospitals crammed with victims of the new disease, the tragic phenomonon could no longer be denied completely, but it could be downplayed; a U.S. military spokesman declared that only "a few" Japanese were perishing from the disease (later reports put the number at ten to twenty thousand). General Groves asserted that, in any case, this was a "pleasant" way to die.[4]

To control the radiation story, it was vital to restrict press reports and visual images from Hiroshima and Nagasaki. Under the American occupation, few reporters were allowed to visit the two cities, they were chaperoned by military officers and their articles were subjected to censorship. The first Amercian journalists to arrive in Hiroshima visited patients in hospitals but the reporters were not allowed to describe the victims or their medical condition. The first American reporter to enter Nagasaki sent his landmark eyewitness account to MacArthur's headquarters in Tokyo—where it disappeared completely, and forever.[5]

Visual images were even more tightly manipulated. Newspapers and magazines published photographs of endless rubble, charred trees and mangled machinery, but were not permitted to carry pictures of the dead or injured, or any effects of the bomb on people. To enforce this policy, the U.S. military even seized all pictures taken by Japanese photographers. The first photos of human victims did not appear in the U.S. until 1952, when *Life* magazine published a portfolio under the title, "When the Atomic Bomb Struck—Uncensored." These and other "stark" pictures "had been suppressed by jittery U.S. military censors through seven years of the Occupation," *Life* revealed. This meant that for years "the world . . . knew only the physical facts of atomic destruction."[6]

Film footage shot in the two cities was suppressed for an even longer period. In October 1945 the military seized black-and-white footage shot in the two cities by a Japanese newsreel team. It would be suppressed until the late 1960s, when it was finally returned to Japan. The footage was edited by Erik Barnouw into a 15-minute documentary that appeared on public television in 1970—the first time most Americans confronted vivid images of the human suffering in Japan. A U.S. military film unit had shot 90,000 feet of color footage in 1946—much of it documenting the brutal radiation burns and other medical effects—but this footage was also declared top secret by the Pentagon, and not shown to the public, in either America or Japan, until the early 1980s. The director of the American film unit, Daniel McGovern, later told me that "the AEC [Atomic Energy Commission], the Pentagon and the Manhattan Project people wanted it buried. . . . They were fearful because of the horror it contained. I was told that under no circumstances would it be released. They didn't want that material shown, because it showed effects on men, women and children . . . because they were sorry for their sins—and because they were working on new nuclear weapons."[7]

It is little wonder, then, that Mary McCarthy once called Hiroshima "a hole in human history." More than three decades after the atomic bombings, Ralph Lapp, the physicist, asked: "If the memory of things is to deter, where is that memory? Hiroshima has been taken out of the American conscience, eviscerated, extirpated."[8]

The only two occasions that survivors of the atomic bombings received more than cursory attention in the U.S. was during the second half of 1946, with the publication of John Hersey's *Hiroshima*, first as a magazine article and then a book, and again in the mid-1950s, when the so-called Hiroshima Maidens came to New York for surgical attention. Otherwise, the *hibakusha* remained shadowy figures, and never studied in depth—until Robert Lifton arrived in Hiroshima in 1962.

To Lifton's surprise, he learned that seventeen years after the atomic bombing no one had probed "the impact of that event . . . no systematic examination of what had taken place in people's lives, of the psychological and social consequences of the bomb." This led him to adopt a new rule of thumb: "The more significant an event, the less likely it is to be studied." One reason for this, he added, had to do with the "fear and pain the event arouses—the unacceptable images to which one must, as an investigator, expose oneself." Fortunately, Lifton not only recognized the need for his study, but accepted the consequences, and plunged ahead. "I felt a survivor-like responsibility to make known in my own country, through writings and talks, what I found there," he explained many years later. He also disclosed that "what I learned there has affected everything I have done or felt since."[9]

Death in Life was published to much acclaim in 1967, and soon won a National Book Award. The *hibakusha* had reappeared in American life and would never completely disappear again. Lifton's act of witness would be cited or joined over the years by a wide range of scholars, journalists, poets and artists, film-makers and peace activists. A reviewer for *Newsweek* had gotten it right when he called *Death in Life* "one of those rare works destined to bear witness and change the lives of those who read it."

To reveal the significance of *Death in Life* in more specific, personal terms, it may be useful to briefly explore its impact on one individual: myself.

There are many ways to become interested in, and write about, Hiroshima. Some scholars focus on Los Alamos and the building of the first atomic bomb. Many probe Truman's decision to drop the bomb. Others examine how the use of the bomb affected U.S.-Soviet relations and the nuclear arms race. Lifton and only a few others have been primarily concerned with the victims of the bombing. I place myself in that latter group, due in no small part to Lifton.

I came to *Death in Life* only in 1982, with the resurgence of the anti-nuclear movement. A few weeks later, I learned that an American who had shot film of Hiroshima survivors in 1946 was scheduled to appear at a press conference before the screening of a new Japanese film which would unveil some of his long-suppressed images. The American, Herbert Sussan, had been a key member of the Strategic Bombing Survey film unit led by Daniel McGovern. Primed by *Death in Life*, I attended the screening. For some reason, none of the other journalists decided to investigate the story of the suppression of the footage, but I was determined to do it. Partly inspired first by Lifton, and then Sussan, I sought the position of editor of *Nuclear Times* magazine; and after accepting that job, the first story I assigned was an exposé on the suppressed film footage.

All of this, in turn, led me to visit Hiroshima and Nagasaki for several weeks in the summer of 1984 on a grant program, and interview dozens of survivors of the atomic bombing. How does one prepare for such an extraordinary and challenging experience? There was virtually only one place to turn, and that was *Death in Life*. My immersion in Hiroshima and Nagasaki was, as Lifton had testified, painful yet fruitful. I had been editor of *Nuclear Times* for almost two years, but after a single day in Hiroshima I realized I knew nothing of significance about nuclear weapons and nuclear war until that moment.

When I returned to the U.S., I felt driven to write dozens of articles about the legacy of Hiroshima and about the survivors themselves: the only photographer who took pictures in Hiroshima on August 6; a peace activist who came to the U.S. to meet with Paul Tibbets, pilot of the Enola Gay; a man who had survived both the Hiroshima and Nagasaki blasts; a severely retarded woman who was A-bomb–damaged while in her mother's womb on August 6, 1945; and many others. Coming full circle, this eventually led to co-authoring a book with Lifton which linked our two closely related Hiroshima concerns: the Japanese survivors, and the American suppression or denial of their experience over the past half century.

As Lifton has observed, all we know of Hiroshima comes from the survivors. They teach us everything about the impact of atomic warfare, both physical and psychological. They tell us the story—a special constellation of truth that informs everything we have to say about nuclear threat today. The *hibakusha* narrative is very different from the official American narrative, which holds that nuclear weapons, theoretically, can be used in a war to prevent even greater bloodshed. The *hibakusha* narrative is one of actuality, of consequences. It starts in Hiroshima and goes beyond Hiroshima. Listening to the survivors becomes more, not less, urgent as years pass, for now there are fewer of them, and soon there will be none.

We have discussed the themes and consequences of Robert Lifton's pioneering work in this field, but what is its message? For me it can be summarized in three simple words: Go to Hiroshima. A visitor, any visitor, can learn much from Hiroshima even if he or she rarely encounters a survivor. The atomic bombing still reverberates in the city. In a sense it has never left Hiroshima. If not a palpable presence, it is there in the imagination. Yet one of the most compelling images does not suggest itself immediately. In fact, one must journey to the highest point in the city.

Hijiyama Hill overlooks Hiroshima. It has a haunted feeling, for it is a place where many of the victims of the atomic bombing fled on August 6, 1945, and where many of them died. A survivor, a history professor, told Lifton more than thirty years ago about climbing Hijiyama Hill on that day and then looking back at the city. "I saw that Hiroshima had disappeared," he said. "I was shocked by the sight. . . . What I felt then and still feel now I just can't explain with words. . . . But Hiroshima didn't exist—that was mainly what I saw—Hiroshima just didn't exist."[10]

Today, one observes from Hijiyama that the new city of Hiroshima not only exists but thrives. Yet it is still very easy, from this vantage point, to imagine the old Hiroshima, for the topography has not changed. We see the bay, the six branches of the Ota River snaking through the city, and the other hills that surround the city on nearly every side. These are the hills that provided what General Groves's target committee called a "focusing effect" that would turn the force of the first atomic blast back on the city.

Looking down from Hijiyama one sees the city in the deep bowl formed by the hills. Hiroshima stretches farther and has more than twice the population it had half a century ago, but in general appearance it is much the same: a densely populated Japanese city in the bottom of a bowl. But another vision inevitably comes to the visitor. One imagines a weapon of mass destruction exploding in a bright flash over the middle of that bowl—not on a specific target on the ground, and not above the industrial section by the sea, but high in the air, directly over the center of the city. One can almost see the flash, and the rays of heat and radiation shooting out to envelop every inch of the bowl, fierce and inescapable.[11]

The image of a flash over the center of a city is hard to forget, for it conveys, better than any historical document, the intentional targeting of masses of civilians for instant, indiscriminate and certain death. Having witnessed this, one may decide to spend a lifetime attempting to discover how and why this particular event occurred, how it affected both the victims and the perpetrators, and why relatively few have protested it since. One may wish to explore what Lifton once called the "Hiroshima connection . . . a bridge of memory between what we human beings have already done, and what we might do to change our course."

Notes

1. Books mentioned: Robert Jay Lifton, *Death in Life: Survivors of Hiroshima* (Chapel Hill: University of North Carolina Press, 1991 [New York: Random House, 1967]); Richard Rhodes, *The Making of the Atomic Bomb* (New York: Simon & Schuster, 1986); Carolyn Forché, *The Angel of History* (New York: Harp-

erCollins, 1994); Albert E. Stone, *Literary Aftershocks* (New York: Twayne, 1994); Lifton and Mitchell, *Hiroshima in America: Fifty Years of Denial* (New York: G.P. Putnam's, 1995).

2. Stone, *Literary Aftershocks*, 23.

3. "as an event of the past. . . .": Lifton, *The Future of Immortality: and Other Essays for a Nuclear Age* (New York: Basic Books, 1987).

4. Material for the preceding paragraphs drawn from Lifton and Mitchell, *Hiroshima in America.*

5. The first journalist in Hiroshima was Wilfred Burchett. The first reporter in Nagasaki was George Weller. From Lifton and Mitchell, *Hiroshima*, 46–50.

6. Photographs in *Life* in September 29, 1952 issue.

7. McGovern interviewed in 1983. Story of suppression of film footage in Lifton and Mitchell, *Hiroshima*, 57–59.

8. "a hole in human history" from Mary McCarthy, letter to editor of *Politics* magazine, November 1946. Ralph Lapp, from Paul Boyer, *By the Bomb's Early Light* (New York: Pantheon, 1985) 182.

9. "the impact of that event" to "or felt since": from Lifton, *The Future of Immortality*, 32–38.

10. "I saw that Hiroshima. . .": Lifton, *Death in Life*, 29.

11. "Hiroshima connection": Lifton, *The Future of Immortality*, 39.

Part II
Genocide and Mass Violence

5

On Pseudospeciation and Social Speciation

Kai Erikson

Memorandum: September, 1982
To: Erik H. Erikson
From: Kai Erikson

The purpose of this memorandum is to put on paper what I think I said (or at least what I meant to say) at the Wellfleet meeting last month, so that other friends can listen in on what is becoming a wider conversation.

I think that the concept of "pseudospeciation," which you first introduced at the Royal Society of London in 1965, may very well be the richest concept to come out of the psychoanalytic tradition in its ability to link the terrains of psychoanalysis and sociology. You say in your upcoming *Yale Review* article:

> Originally, pseudospeciation was meant to refer to the fact that mankind, while one species, has divided itself throughout its history—territorially, culturally, politically—into various groupings that permit their members, at decisive times, to consider themselves, more or less consciously and explicitly, the only truly human species, and *all* others (and especially *some* others) as less than human. . . .

> [M]ankind from the very beginning has appeared on the world scene split into tribes and nations, castes and classes, religions and ideologies, each of which acts as if it were a separate species created or planned at the beginning by supernatural will. Thus each claims not only a more or less firm sense of distinct identity but even a kind of historical immortality. Some of these pseudospecies, indeed, have mythologized for themselves a place and a moment in the very center of the universe, where and when an especially provident diety caused it to be created superior to, or at least unique among, all others. . . .

What renders this "natural" process a potential malignancy of universal dimensions is the fact that in times of threat and upheaval the idea of being the foremost species tends to be reinforced by a fanatic fear and hate of other pseudospecies. The feeling that those others must be annihilated or kept "in their places" by warfare or conquest or the force of harsh custom can become a periodical and reciprocal obsession of man.

Now that makes very good sense to people in my field. The social scene we look at through our disciplinary lens is of a single biological species partitioned into an endless number of national, ethnic, religious, ideological, and class groupings, each one of them capable of thinking itself special and of being somehow ordained by God or nature or history.

This idea received a biological seal of approval from Julian Huxley, Konrad Lorenz, and others of the natural scientists who were present at the original Royal Society presentation, and more recently from Stephen Jay Gould, who has written a brief comment for the *Yale Review* piece. So it has wide disciplinary appeal.

The critical difference between what you have been calling "pseudospeciation" and what Huxley, Lorenz, and Gould all call "true speciation" or just plain "speciation" is that the first is a human construct and the other an irreversible fact of nature. From a biological standpoint, then, the modifying prefix "pseudo" is essential to the concept, because it indicates that the lines one people draws to differentiate itself from another come from the realm of the imagination and have no warrant in the world of nature.

To sociologists, though, the use of a modifyer like "pseudo" (or "quasi," a term you once contemplated using) has a somewhat different ring to it, since it almost seems to indicate that the things of the social order are not quite as true or as real—not as lawful—as the things of the natural order. Biological processes have substance; social and cultural processes are a kind of contrivance or imitation.

"Pseudospeciation" does not leave traces in the germ plasm, so far as anyone knows, but I think one should argue that it, too, is a biological process and a force in nature. Suppose we were to put the matter as follows. When animal populations sort themselves into distinct biological lineages, the process is a form of speciation. When human populations sort themselves into various social and cultural divisions, the process is also a form of speciation. The first could be called *phylogenetic* speciation and the second *psychosocial* speciation.

The two processes are analogous, to be sure. They are both ways of organizing life; they are both forms of differentiation. The main difference, as Huxley and Lorenz and Gould point out, is that phylogenetic speciation is irrevocable (at least over the short evolutionary haul) while psychosocial speciation is clearly not.

But otherwise the differences are not so pronounced. What is a species, anyway? A population within which breeding can take place. And what is a true tribe or caste or "people"? A breeding population around which boundaries are drawn by law or custom prohibiting marriage with outsiders (sometimes called—extraordinary word—miscegenation).

Now it is probably important to remember that psychosocial speciation belongs in the realm of the imagination, since people who fear miscegenation the most seem to think of interbreeding as not only biologically possible but as so attractive a prospect that harsh vigilance and self-control are necessary. So long as it works, however, social speciation has the same effect as genetic speciation.

So what? I'm not sure. I would only want to suggest that social speciation is a tremendously strong and stubborn force in human life for exactly the reasons you originally pointed out, and that "pseudo"—which really means counterfeit, spurious, false—does not seem to reflect it well. That is particularly the case when one reflects that the lines of speciation drawn through social space are the lines across which the slaughter of human beings by human beings are most likely to occur.

Your turn.

Memorandum: October, 1982
To: Kai Erikson
From: Erik H. Erikson

Thank you ever so much for your letter of September, 1982, in which you briefly and very clearly restate a reservation—first voiced at one of the Wellfleet meetings—concerning my concept "pseudo-species." Your clarification could not have been more timely, for it has become impossible for me to enter the arguments over the logic of nuclear armament without coming to terms with that concept. A number of people in a variety of groups (including one or two to whom I have read your memorandum and earlier drafts of this response to it) have come vaguely to the same feeling but do not know what to do with it.

You first describe my concept as originally presented to a meeting of the Royal Society and then say that it may be "the richest one to come out of the psychoanalytic tradition in its ability to link the terrains of psychoanalysis and sociology." But then you question my very term and suspect it of implying a claim that "the things of the social order are not quite as true or as real—not as lawful—as the things of the natural order." Are you not, in fact, suggesting that I am trying to pseudo-speciate social science itself? Well, I suppose not. But such a suspicion may have found support in the fact that two of the members of the Royal Society, which is so firmly committed to natural speciation—I am thinking of Julian Huxley and Konrad Lorenz—accepted my concept so unquestioningly. My speciation, you suggest, should be called *psychosocial*.

And, Kai, I think you are right. It is true: both the biological and the social forms of speciation are "real." But then it must also be understood that my psychosocial theory is a psychoanalytic one intimately related to Freud's theory of psychosexual development and to the whole dynamic theory of man's socialization and culturalization during the longest and most complex childhood and youth lived through by any species on earth. This means that psychosocial development is characterized on the one hand by the establishment of a most rigid conscience that tries to guarantee the coherence of the cultural subspecies to which a child learns to belong and, on the other hand, by the denials and fantasies, the illusions and delusions, which characterize every human individual's conscious and unconscious inner life as well as all shared ideologies. There is, then, a pseudo-speciation *within* the psychosocial one.

Such a more sophisticated overall term as *psychosocial speciation* also would speak to the variety of outright opposite meanings of the term "pseudo." In "true" science, for example, a "pseudomorph" can be a factually deceptive resemblance of two otherwise unrelated phenomena—a resemblance, however, which is not the result of anyone's wish to deceive anyone. "Pseudology," on the other hand, does connote a fully conscious dishonesty of speech. No wonder the thesaurus lists "pseudo" under two sets of opposites: Likeness–Unlikeness, and Truthfulness–Fraud.

While man's psychosocial speciation, then, is a most real and, in fact, most "honest" division of mankind into different "kinds," it is also permeated by a process of pseudospeciation—that is, a systematic and often unconscious combination of prejudices, illusions, and suspicions in regard to one's own human kind *and* to other kinds. And all of this, so it seems, must be studied and understood before the survival of one universal mankind is possible; while nuclear conditions permit no postponement of such a twofold study.

So, as always, but with redoubled urgency, I look forward to our next discussion.

Excerpt from Memorial Address for Erik H. Erikson: January, 1995

I then proposed (this was a discussion among friends, after all) that we avoid the awkwardness of "pseudo" by distinguishing between something to be called "phylogenetic speciation" and something to be called "psychosocial speciation." Those terms turned out to have far too many syllables for an ongoing conversation, so the shorthand soon became "genetic speciation" and "social speciation." The author of the concept agreed to my suggestion at least up to a point (although I feel obliged to report on this solemn occasion that he continued to use the term "pseudospecies" as if nothing at all had happened!). But there was a logic in his doing so that had also been a part of the ongoing conversation: "pseudo" is plainly the right prefix for an evolutionary biologist to use, and, for most purposes, for a psychoanalyst as well, even if a sociologist or anthropologist might need to look elsewhere. (In yet another memorandum, which drew on both of the ones I have reproduced here, he noted: "This terminological clarification . . . points to a future in which I will have to watch my terms." But for now, at least, "I must continue to put things as I did in the past.")

So I am going to talk about *social speciation* and define it as the process by which one people manages to neutralize the humanity of another to such an extent that those others come to be regarded as (a) ineligible for marriage or citizenship or the other benefits of membership, but (b) eligible for a degree of contempt that may express itself in subjugation or enslavement or outright slaughter. At its worst, then, social speciation is a process by which one people manages to neutralize the humanity of another to such an extent that the inhibitions which normally prevent creatures of the same species from killing one another wantonly are relaxed.

If it is the task of psychoanalysis to describe a tendency of which the human mind is capable—Erik Erikson often spoke of a "pseudo-species mentality"—then it is the task of sociology to describe the social and cultural scaffoldings that frame and give shape to that tendency. Seen thus, social speciation forms the outer edges of what sociologists mean by "differentiation." It is the sharpest of the boundaries people draw, and it is the most lethal by far.

What are those scaffoldings? Language, surely, is one of the most important of them, and that was also a part of the wider conversation. Glenn Gray, who wrote a wonderful account of men in combat, points out that people almost always use the definite article in speaking of wartime adversaries. It is rarely *our* enemy or *an* enemy, but *the* enemy—a usage that seems to hint darkly of something fixed and immutable, something abstract and evil. In a similar way, the words we use to refer to *the* enemy often involve a sharp denial of his humanity (the right pronoun this time). The language used by Americans in Vietnam is so widely cited an example that it has almost lost its value as an illustration. But, as Robert Jay Lifton has noted, words like "slope," "dink," "slant," "gook," "zip"—sounding like curses when said aloud—describe a landscape without real people at all.

And the making of myths is another of those forms. The legends that people tell of their own origins usually describe themselves as living at the center of the universe, blessed by whatever divinities preside over the world, and more human by a considerable margin than all the other creatures with whom they must share the surface of the earth. Joseph Campbell writes:

> For it is a basic idea of practically every war mythology that the enemy is a monster and that in killing him one is protecting the only truly valuable order of human life on earth, which is that, of course, of one's own people.

There are others one might draw attention to. But let me bring this part of my presentation to a close by adding one more point to the list—this time one that never became a part of the conversation because it only occurred to me later. I'd write another memorandum if I knew where to send it.

The way the idea is normally used, some form of speciation—dehumanization, distancing—is thought to be a precondition to slaughter. That is, one person needs to think of another as less than truly human in order to be the agent of that other's death. The evidence for that conclusion, of course, is deep and compelling.

But I now wonder, surveying the human wreckage strewn across places like Rwanda and Bosnia, how often it is that killing—whatever the motive that induced it in the first place—becomes a *cause* of some form of speciation. That is, in the same way that the borders separating nations (and, not incidentally, the lines seperating territories among competing animals) are often drawn and sealed in active combat, the boundaries between groups of people are often drawn and sealed by the act of killing. Or to put it yet another way: there are times when it makes sense to argue that social speciation provokes slaughter, but there are also times when it makes sense to argue that slaughter provokes speciation. That is a human chemistry we need to learn a good deal more about.

Nothing works better to sharpen a boundary than for someone to be killed in its name. The line becomes more distinct for the people who do the killing, since it gives them—whether before or after the fact—a justification for the blood on their hands. And it becomes more distinct for the people who feel victimized by the killing, since they now have a defining insult to avenge. It is almost as though it takes an additional measure of savagery to keep an ethnic boundary alive and meaningful when the differences dividing people are otherwise slight.

A story in *The New York Times* that appeared on the last day of 1994 describes an episode in which a Bosnian Serb, armed with an automatic weapon, knocked on the door of a Muslim neighbor and ordered her outside. " 'I said to Visovic, you know me, you know my husband. . . . How can you do this to me?' " Viscovic is said to have replied: " 'That time is over. I no longer know you.' " Whereupon he ordered her "to crawl along the street as he kicked her repeatedly."

6

To Prevent or to Stop Mass Murder

Ronnie Dugger

No one but the victims, the perpetrators, and some of the contemporary bystanders had or has personal knowledge of the Holocaust. Each of the rest of us has had to let knowledge about it happen to us in whatever ways it has and to experience and try to understand as best we can, separately, and in frightening loneliness, what we have randomly learned. These separate, terrifying learnings, locked away in ourselves, may be the most potent personal phenomena that we have in common about the Holocaust. By sharing, in friendships, families, schools, and public discourse, the circumstances of our personal learnings, we might start to construct an emotional network from which we can act together politically to prevent or stop mass murder.

One thing we would realize through such sharings, I suspect, is the mesmerizing power of mass murder to draw each one of us into the past in which mass murder has occurred, into the specific places, times, people, and scenes which have made it most real and frightening to us about others and ourselves, and finally deeper and deeper into ourselves, to brood and wonder.

We are mesmerized, too, because we are personal and the political problem of stopping genocide and the mass murder of innocents is planetary. States themselves can barely keep abreast of their own distinctive crimes, far less those of other states. The *difficulty* of stopping genocide and the mass murder of innocents has kept us from trying, other than by piety (for example, the 1948 Convention on the Prevention and Punishment of the Crime of Genocide, which, as Leo Kuper wrote, "has been almost totally ineffective in the punishment of the crime"[1]) or by lamentation.

If I did not mistake what was happening, much of the earlier postwar thinking among many Jews which I read and listened to was, in part, an undertaking to sacralize the suffering of the Jews in the Holocaust, thereby to proscribe its recurrence by holding the memory of it holy. Nothing could be done about what had happened, it would defile the dead for it to be "understood" and thus explained away, the holy duty was witness and memory, so that "Never Again."

Now the first volume of a scholarly three-volume work has appeared concerning the question, "Is the Holocaust unique?"[2] Certainly this is a subject which merits study and reflection: anti-Semitism is a terrible disease of both Christianity and Islam. But suppose we "stipulate," as lawyers say, the uniqueness of the Jewish Holocaust. Apart from a necessary intensification of our hate of anti-Semitism—and except also as the particulars of any mass murdering are part of understanding it and predicting and preventing its and similar recurrences—what follows? The imports of the particulars of such a uniqueness are set in the case which is unique. Assuredly one holy duty is memory. Without memory there can be no informed moral action. But a Holocaust enclosed in the idea that, because some of its aspects were unique, it was Unique, leads us not so much to the present or the future, as into the past.

For it is true, is it not, that falling into memory, study, and meditation about the Holocaust, or the political mass murder in Cambodia, or the slaughters of the Tutsi and the Hutu, or any genocide, or any mass murder, we sink deep into our stillest core, stare back and forth from the memory, to the knowledge of the evil in our self, back to the memory, back to the knowledge. Oh, my God, how can I deal with this? Nothing is sacred? We will do *anything* to each other? How could he do *that?* Oh, my God, am I *this?* How could they do that? Are we *this?* Jehovah, God, Allah, we need a new doctrine! It is as if within ourselves we have become ancient sacrifices, our deep passivity exacted by the solemnity and inescability of the occasion. Dusk, yes—time for dinner, have to fix dinner, time for a drink, time, oh God, for the evening news.

But the basal fact about the approximately eleven million noncombatants whom the Nazis mass murdered is that they were mass murdered. Whether the circumstances of the mass killing of the approximately 5,100,000 of them who were Jews[3] were and still are unique, every circumstance and every cause of such a mass action merits the most intense attention, and each one of the victims was equal, in value and importance as a person, to any other person. That is the common ground on which the human race can act against mass murder in the future: all victims of mass murder are equal.

II

Our most passionate post-Holocaust exclamation, "Never Again," has died in our throats. The genocides and mass murders of our immediate past and present are so numerous and so hideous that we feel that we are all failing, we are failing as a species. As earlier generations of bystanders were guilty of the Holocaust we bystanders in the 1990s are now guilty, for example, of the genocides and mass murders in Bosnia, Rwanda, and Burundi—more so, in ways, because we have the recent history they did not have and we are much better informed while mass murders are occurring than they were. If we had the collective will we could stop them. The acceptance of mass murder by the governments and peoples of even the most powerful nations signifies that the world system of states is morally inadequate.

But we have not failed until we have failed, and despair, as Camus said, is the one sin we are not permitted.

The principal question must become not the past but the future for which we now living are responsible. To act from the past in the present we have to form an idea, a vision, if you wish, an ideal, of a future in which mass murder has been halted. Each of us is allotted only so much energy and can give only a definite fraction of it, if we give any, to the prevention of mass murder. The task now is to marshal those precious available energies together toward the future, to Turn Forward. Never Forget. But Turn and Go Forward.

To gather and array our wills into action we shall certainly have to focus and use as much of our energy as we can bear to wrest back from mass murder's hypnotizing past. Perhaps we are already beginning to be able to merge the separateness and loneliness of our knowings about mass murder into an ability to bear to undertake collectively its prevention and punishment. But we will not be able to change our natures quickly enough to avoid escalating, interacting horrors. In addition to trying to turn ourselves and help turn other people, one by one, into better people, we must intensively apply what we know about our human behavior in "atrocity-producing situations"[4] to the intellectual and political work of changing those situations.

We have failed to make enough use, in discourse, social policy, and social action, of the fact that the mass murder of noncombatants is potentially the most galvanizing ethical wrong in human life. Except for some of the perpetrators and some of the implicated bystanders almost nobody will defend it; even those who will usually prefer to lie, denying history. The genocidalist, the mass murderer, is the worst of all criminals. The mass murder of innocents is the one horror which has the potential to move people who geopsychically are still tightly enclosed within tribe, religion, nation, race, or state to loosen their bonds enough to see or sense our common need for a change so great that if it occurs it will seem to be a mass natural event.

What would be this future in which mass murder no longer happens? It would be a world in which, whenever necessary in order to stop genocide or other kinds of mass murder while they are going on, offending tribes, religions, nations, and states are *forced* to submit to international governance. Whenever necessary to stop mass murder while it is happening, the rest of the world goes to war against the perpetrators—intervenes by military force, stops the slaughter, and punishes the criminals, from the order-givers to the obeyers, as mass murderers.

Deep in our neocortices we know this, I believe. After all, it is so obvious. We don't see yet how to get there, but we know, conceptually, what an end to mass murder requires. Mass murder is not going to stop because people become nicer, because the hate and murder in people just die out, evolution somehow purifying us, or because God, or Jehovah, or Allah, or Muhammed, or Jesus stops it. Murder is a part of the human situation. Murder is a part of the human nature. On the evidence before us the capacity to murder is given to each of us as part of our being, and so, I think, is the capability of doubling,[5] tripling, or quadrupling. Organized as we are into tribes, religions, nations, races, or states, either as perpetrators or as implicated bystanders who do little or nothing, or do not do everything, that we might do to stop it, from time to time we are all mass murderers.

We can take some heart that after millenia of localism, unknowingness and indifference we sense, in the idea, at least, what future we want and we have reached the question of How. How do we gather ourselves to do something effective? How do we stop these actions and punish those who are committing them? As Leo Kuper, the sociologist who became a specialist in mass murder, put the question, "How . . . are we to modify and transform these anonymous and amorphous worldwide structural forces and to create a new world order in time to respond to the many genocidal emergencies?" What can change genocidal situations—what can change what Kuper calls "annihilatory contexts"?

To such vast questions, for answers, I believe, one's mind must turn toward the very structures of human enclosures, the tribe, the religion, the nation, the race, the state. How do we criticize ourselves enough within these various enclosures—how do we liberate ourselves from them enough—to create and enforce a minimalist humanist ethic? What then about reparations, healing, and rehabilitation?

"My major preoccupations," Kuper wrote in the early 1990s, "relate to the possibilities of preventing genocide." In the mid-eighties Kuper assumed that only a small contribution could be expected from the United Nations in the immediate future and hence that "some form of organization," perhaps "an international grass-roots organization" or a collaboration of existing non-governmental organizations (NGOs), was needed to launch "a general campaign against genocide." To proscribe mass murders that are not genocide, he wrote, the states should sign a new treaty against political mass murder. He thought a World Genocide Tribunal might be established by multilateral treaty. The UN-created international criminal tribunal for Rwanda which convened in The Hague in June 1995[6] is a real-world start in that direction. So are the indictments on Bosnia.

Within the UN, Kuper meditated, nations should establish standards for governments and multinational corporations whose development projects endanger indigenous populations. States should prepare lists of mass murderers and punish their own citizens who are on them; the UN should appoint a High Commissioner for Human Rights; an early warning system concerning "potential genocidal situations" would help predict mass murders. The foreign minister of the Netherlands suggested this year that such a system should be multidisciplinary and should be located at UN Headquarters in New York City.[7]

More recently, Kuper descried in the international public education campaign of the communities of the Bahá'í religion against their persecution by the Iranian government a model for any endangered group's use of media and public forums to avert a genocidal situation. He hoped that groups victimized by mass murders would extend their public actions to oppose all mass murders. "The objective," he wrote, "is the promotion of a social movement comparable to the peace movement."[8]

The murderous guilt taken upon themselves by the two American reporters, Walter Duranty and Louis Fischer, in the early 1930s, when they lied in their journalistic dispatches from the Soviet Union to conceal Stalin's intentional famine which starved to death millions of people, suggests, by its obverse, the moral responsibility of the press to provide highest-quality international reporting about genocide and mass murder. Even a preliminary list of methods available to help prevent mass murder must lay a burden of star-quality reportorial competency on the press. The fairy tale that the press is "objective" cannot relieve television, radio, newspapers, and magazines of their large share of the work to stop mass murder. As newspaperman Walter K. Ezell says, the media should deploy top reporters, possibly in a pool, who can make it clear when mass murder is happening and who is doing what.[9]

Despite the absence of international criminal sanctions (we have no international prison yet) anti-genocidal states can, if they will, engineer appropriate sanctions of states and punishments for those convicted of crimes against humanity by international UN courts. Chapter II, Article 6 of the UN Charter provides for the expulsion, upon the recommendation of the Security Council, of member states which "persistently violate" the principles of the Charter. The UN should summarily expel any member state which commits or complicitously permits mass murder or refuses to ratify the findings and exact the sentences of the UN's courts concerning any of that state's citizens convicted of crimes against humanity.

Whether the Security Council does that or not, groups of states in concert should break off all diplomatic and most commercial relationships to brand such states as world pariahs. No trade, no tourists, no aid, no commerce except for food, medicines, medical supplies, and pamphlets, plus withering condemnation as specific and pointed as possible in aggressive electronic messages beamed in! Make the leaders and the people of mass murdering tribes, religions, nations, races, and states suffer for their and/or their group's deeds so that they learn through their suffering from the world's reaction the common human meaning of the mass murder and stop it.

During the forty-five years of the Cold War any idea of multinational military intervention to stop genocide or mass murder while it was happening was discredited before it could be considered by the commonplace imperialistic misuses of military force during that era. Since the early 1990s, however, multinational military action—that is to say, multinational war—against the committers of genocide and other mass murder while it is going on has been slowly gaining the credence which its patent moral necessity calls for. Except for purest pacifists (with whom I, for one, would be happy to debate on this issue), the very champions of peace and justice, confronted on their TVs nightly by undeniable evidence of mass slaughter in progress, feel increasingly drawn to support the use of international force to stop it. Standing by is standing for the slaughter.[10]

In January 1992 President Mitterrand of France proposed that states should keep national military units permanently available for deployment by the UN Security Council and that the UN's Military Staff Committee should be revived to make the plans for that. A doctrine of Just Intervention, grounded in the philosophy and concepts of Just War, has been vigorously and persuasively advanced by Jane M. O. Sharp, director of the Defence and Security Program of the Institute for Public Policy Research in London. "When force is needed to discipline rogue nations," she writes, "[an effective collective security system] must provide for the major powers to intervene for the common good, even when their own short-term national interests are not at risk." The western security community should have intervened with a serious military operation to halt Serbian and Croatian aggression against Bosnia, Sharp asserts, to uphold the principle that borders must not be changed by force, "to demonstrate unambiguously that genocide must not be tolerated," and "to uphold the vision of a federal pluralistic multi-ethnic Europe."

"Bosnia may mark a turning point in public perception," Sharp writes, "from seeing intervention as intrusive and negative, to be avoided where possible, to a growing realization that emancipatory military intervention could be a positive healing process in defense of human and minority rights. . . . If Europe is to be equitable, secure and pluralistic, western governments must acquire the capability and exercise the will to stop bully states early in their rampages and halt the practice of land grabbing and of ethnic cleansing."[11]

III

Human society—5,600,000,000 or so people living, being, in complicated interactive solitary, familial, religious, ethnic, neighborhood, local, regional, national, racial, state, and international configurations on the earth—is still a loose confederation of states whose interactions are rooted in and controlled by self-interested nationalism and its corollary doctrines (each state's absolute right of self-determination, its total sovereignty over its internal affairs, and so on). In the main, ordinary people still live, see, think, and value within the strictly bordered enclosures of their nations. The accident of a person's birth still determines the person's theater of thinking and destiny because, starting at birth, blinders are formed onto almost every child's mind by the local and national culture, education, and government. Everywhere it is still true that before boys can think autonomously as adults they learn they are expected to kill for where they are. All this, determined by the where of birth, the what of culture, and the weight of being as against the distance of travel and the dimness of communications from far away, is thought of as nationalism. As internationalized transportation, electronic media, and dirt-cheap personal communications enlarge the stages of our knowledge to world society, our minds are gradually recomposing nationalism into an overview of enclosures. But world history is still being determined by separate enclosured nationalisms acting with and against each other whatever the case may accidentally be. We might wish to call this nationalistic chaos, or the anarchic interactions of separate enclosures, but most simply it is Enclosurism.

The rest of our moiling current world history as tribal, ethnic/racial, and religious amity or conflict organically rises and unfolds from the other accreted, layered foundations of enclosurism which have evolved from our beginnings lost in time, limiting each person's circle of identification and ethical concern to the persons within his or her own enclosures. It is harmonizing and logical simply to fit these various kinds of our grouped identities into the model of nationalistic Enclosurism.

Seeing all this as evolutionary, we may, if we will, be optimistic. We can perceive progressively enlarging concentric circles of family, families, settlements, tribes, tribes of tribes, cities, city-states, nations, alliances of nations, empires, alliances of empires, single-issue treaty-signing communities of nations, the League of Nations, the United Nations. But if we look ahead from our present disorder a mere fifty years, a normal adult lifetime, to the exponential multiplication of every human need as world population increases to between 9 and 15 billion, we must at least conjecture that we are in true danger of terminal evolutionary maladaptation.

The United Nations is not the United Human Species, it's still the United *Nations*, its very name a misrepresentation, a hope misdescribed as a fact. Neither the nations nor the states are united. The UN is a confederation, it is not a federation; the unit of rule is still the state. Almost every attempted international remedy for famine, war, or mass murder is foiled by the ubiquitous competing national interests (which are, in each case, "the national interest"), by the law of unintended consequences, and by the far more destructive law of unforeseeable interactions. As the international ethicist and economist Hasan Özbekhan has perceived, international society is now so tumultuous that we are compelled to stop trying to solve world problems because the ferocious turbulence forces us to aim lower, at just coping. The weapons-making industries observe no national boundaries or ethical norms. As the "costs per death" of nuclear, chemical, and especially biological weapons plummet, more and more states have the power to kill any set of other states, and well-financed religious and ideological faiths and cults can kill whatever thousands or tens of thousands or millions of people they may select as representatives of whatever they wish to exterminate. In the economic sphere where the daily well-being of humankind should abide, 1.3 billion people live in what the World Bank calls "absolute poverty."[12] With no governing force in the world curbing them, multinational corporations continue to ravage the environment of the world, exploit the cheapest and least organized workers, and amass larger and larger government-threatening treasuries of irresponsible wealth and power. Nationalistic, tribal, ethnic, religious, and corporate Enclosurism, low-cost killing technology, and the ever-widening worldwide gap between the royally rich and the pitifully poor are propelling us zig-zag into hell on earth, more mass poverty and revolution, more mass murder, the murder of whole cities, whole nations seen merely as well-defined targets, whole peoples, whole continents.

We must try something that we have never tried before. I believe the only something new that might become large and strong enough swiftly enough to give us some surcease from the mass violence and some advance toward an ethical system of worldwide economic governance is a worldwide breakthrough to minimalist international values. Paradigm shifts do occur quite suddenly. Minimalist international humanism, which we might well rename personism,[13] is the only plausible foundation for our personal and common security which we can realistically imagine constructing in the time we may have left before maladaptive disaster.[14]

For example, it is the received doctrine that U.S. (or any other state's) "foreign policy" abroad should be guided by "the national interest," but in minimalist humanist ethics it should also be guided by the interests and well-being of people abroad. As the President of the United States has a Secretary and Department of State, he should also have what we might call a Secretary and Department Concerning the Interests and Wellbeing of People Abroad. Likewise, other states. If the Americans led in such a new direction many nations would follow, with consequences we might barely imagine.

The United Nations should announce that it will accept individual volunteers from any nation and train and equip them for service in a UN military force that could engage, not only in peacekeeping, but also in active military intervention to stop genocides and mass murders while they are happening.[15] Surely it would please most of us to speculate that we would have the idealism and the courage to volunteer or that we would have when we were younger. That really would be fighting for the human race.

Would *governments* tolerate the mounting by the union of nations of an international volunteer military force made up in part of those government's own potential or actual "military personnel"? What if young Americans could have chosen between fighting in Vietnam and fighting to stop a genocide? And what nation's history is so free of mass murders—ours certainly is not—that some of its prominent jingoes could not plausibly warn that such a new world military force to stop mass murder might be used against *us*?

Still, the power of the idea might grow so strong as to overwhelm such considerations. In September 1994 at the UN Hans van Mierlo, the Netherlands Minister for Foreign Affairs, re-launched the idea of a volunteer UN Rapid Deployment Brigade, on which the Netherlands' government has been working with Canadian officials. Van Mierlo, discussing an informed view that the rapid deployment of a brigade in Kigali could have prevented the slaughter of hundreds of thousands of people in Rwanda, declines to blame anyone for the fact "that under the circumstances no government was prepared to risk the lives of its citizens," but cites the situation as compelling proof of the need for an international volunteer brigade. An associated Netherlands study hypothesizes that the brigade will be full-time, professional, available at all times, and deployable in fourteen days or more quickly for three months at most, then to be superceded by multinational UN forces; estimates the annual cost of a 5,000-man brigade with armored vehicles at $300 million; and specifically contemplates the brigade's deployment by the Security Council "with or without the consent of local rulers, to prevent or stop crimes against humanity, mass murders, and genocide."[16]

How would we pay for an international volunteer armed force? The UN should let individuals from any nation become citizen-members and use our dues to pay those costs.

I am an American citizen. I also want to be a citizen of the United Nations. I want to join it as a person. This has been in my mind ever since that fellow Gary Davis made a minor stir in the world in the late forties because he wanted to be a citizen of the world. (I proposed to my wife at that time that to make our first child a real international citizen she give birth to him or her in a medical van on the UN plaza, which is not U.S., but international territory. She didn't say she wouldn't, but quite understandably she didn't.) Four decades later we still are not permitted to be citizens of the world because the UN is only an organization of states as states. If you're just people you can't join. The UN has no citizens. No, it's no democracy: governing the world is the business of governments and *only* governments, however corrupt, unrepresentative, and terrorizing many of them may be. Yet if we're contemporary and morally alive, inside our minds we're already citizens of the world as well as our own nations.

For, say, $25 a year (or dues could be keyed to each nation's average per-capita income), anyone should be able to get a UN citizenship card and a monthly UN report. At 5.6 billion, we're quite a market, as the multinational corporations might say—surely millions of us would want to help stop mass murder and take a first small step toward becoming world citizens. Joining the UN personally would help us unreel ourselves off the tightly wound spools of our nations and begin to weave together as if we were so many stitches in the human race, closing its seams.

I would also care to be a citizen of Great Britain (my mother was born in Glasgow), and I'd like to be a citizen of the Netherlands, and South Africa. Canada, too—why not? We kill each other in wars because of where we're from. Why not be citizens of more than one place?—maybe fewer of us would kill each other.

Easily enough the governments could work out differences between a person's base-nation citizenship and his or her additional citizenships. But we're expected to kill for where we're from—there's the rub. The theories and practices of nationalistic Enclosurism will not tolerate the idea of a *person's* sovereignty. Citizens may or may not have rights, but sovereignty is the state's, and reasons of state preclude large numbers of a nation's citizens from being citizens of other nations as well: the trajectory of such a development will threaten nationalism. Yet if some of the nations had enough ethical originality and audacity they could give us the chance.

As our understanding of each other increases, so does the basis in the nature of human life which tends to draw us together in empathy. In an important political sense it is a truth rooted in physical reality that one of us is all of us and all of us are one. When Robert Jay Lifton was forming his theories for *The Protean Self*,[17] I took the position with him (in a discussion on the subject which we had by premeditation, in his Wellfleet study) that each one of us, every one of us, is not one self, but thousands, millions, billions of potential selves, that we stay whole as we change through serial reconfigurations, and that also, we are all one person. Each of us is—each of us are—recursive sets of possibilities inward toward zero or outward toward infinity even as each of us channels down into what we misconceive to be our only self. Inversely, we are all one person, the cosmic string of the recursive compounds of our possibilities. Each of us is unique, we are all one kind, and through our kind as possibility I am you and you, me. One is all, all are one.[18]

Should we not begin to organize ourselves worldwide as people instead of as nations and governments? Granted, it's quite a leap. But taken collectively the NGOs, more responsive to the personal convictions of their members than to the reasons of state of the UN's member nations, already far better represent the opinions and interests of the people of the world than the UN does. Presuming that the United Nations won't be starting tomorrow to turn itself into a democratic organization of people, why shouldn't the Non-Governmental Organizations, the 1,500 NGO's of the world, convene a founding convention of a United Peoples Organization which, once it exists, will invite people anywhere to become citizens of it? If the UN continues to stand between every person and world citizenship, why, hell, why not found a democratic world organization of people to rise up beside, to rival, and in due democratic course to overshadow the United Nations. Here would be "an international grassroots organization" where we could try to invent real democracy for the first time.

The citizen-members of the United Peoples might meet in neighborhood, local, regional, in-nation, regionwide and eventually world assemblies, keeping themselves vividly democratic up and down the line by required periodic body-to-body accountability sessions between the represented and the representers. Write a Constitution. Establish an independent international judiciary. In due course, by democratic elections among the citizen-members, elect representatives from the nations and governors from the continents, although perhaps not a President of the world. In the world democratic parliament enact a new body of international criminal and civil law. Let the UN continue its peacekeeping, if it will, but form a volunteer United Peoples military force, free of Big Five vetoes, to stop genocides and mass murders in progress. Stop such outrages as the international arms trade and the mass export of cigarettes, which are killing hundreds of millions of unwary people, yet the states and their UN refuse to stop. And ultimately in league with the United Nations of governments require the international rechartering of multinational corporations whereby to turn them into social ventures that are governed by and accountable to all their stakeholders and to "We, the people" who permit them to exist and operate. As for those multinationals which refuse to submit to democratic authority and law: decharter, dismantle, decentralize, and redistribute them.

Pipedreams, quixotic, utopian—as you will. Nothing like this is going to happen? You may be right. We're not going to police the world just because far-off peoples slaughter each other, you say? Your view may prevail. What's that—the global corporations are beyond control, there's no way the international economy can be governed? I wouldn't bet, in this millenium, that you're wrong. But the next one starts in four years. If the UN will start representing people I'm ready for its second fifty years. If it won't I'm ready for a new start. Let one be billions of people, let billions of people be one.

Notes

The closing part of this essay was developed initially as a contribution to a discussion among twenty-one invited participants at Brandeis University in June 1995 concerning goals and activities of the prospective International Center on Ethics, Justice, and the Public Life at Brandeis. A few ideas among those advanced here were also broached in "Create a World Army," an op-ed piece in *The New York Times* of June 27, 1995.

The author dedicates this essay to Sam Bearak.

1. Leo Kuper, *The Prevention of Genocide* (New Haven: Yale University Press, 1985), 173–74.

2. Steven T. Katz, *The Holocaust in Historical Context,* Vol. 1, *The Holocaust and Mass Death before the Modern Age,* New York: Oxford University Press, 1994. Katz concludes his first volume with the generalization that ". . . close, detailed analysis of (the Sho'ah's) defining character over against the nature of other mass tragedies establishes its phenomenological distinctiveness and in so doing makes it possible—and only so is it possible—to comprehend its actuality" (pp. 1, 581).

3. Raul Hilberg, *The Destruction of the European Jews* (New York: Holmes & Meier, 1985), Vol. III, p. 1219. Concerning three summary tables of Europe-wide Jewish dead in the Holocaust, Hilberg notes that certain categories of victims are rounded to the nearest hundred thousand, other categories to the nearest fifty thousand.

4. Robert Jay Lifton, *Home from the War: Learning from Vietnam Veterans* (Boston: Beacon Press, 1992) as at 16.

5. Under extreme stress, Lifton wrote in his book about the Nazi doctors at Auschwitz, a person can become a *second* person by "the division of the self into two functioning wholes, so that a part-self acts as an entire self." Robert Jay Lifton, *The Nazi Doctors: Medical Killing and the Psychology of Genocide* (New York: Basic Books, 1986), 7, 488, *passim.*

6. "U.N. Panel Opens Inquiry on Rwanda," *The New York Times,* June 28, 1995.

7. "A Netherlands Non-Paper: A UN Rapid Deployment Brigade, 'A Preliminary Study,' " revised version, April 1995, 34–35.

8. Leo Kuper, *The Prevention of Genocide* (New Haven: Yale University Press, 1985), pp. 21–22, 186, 187, 199, 193, 212, 213, 215–216, 1818; Leo Kuper, "Reflections on the Prevention of Genocide" in Helen Fein, ed., *Genocide Watch,* 135, 138, 139, 142, 148, 150, 157.

9. Ed., Fein, *Genocide Watch, op. cit.*, 111, 113–32.

10. Lifton, whose gentle nature and detestation of violence have made him an occasional target for a certain kind of contemptible cynicism, is an example of this. He wrote in 1993: "Genocide, by definition, is an ethical scandal. But the added scandal of Bosnia is the whole world's viewing genocide and doing no more than pretending to combat it. The official world organization, the United Nations, has been made into an agency of compliance—even, at times, of over-seeing the killing." The UN, Lifton concluded, should "intervene to stop the killing and establish conditions for democratic behavior and sustained peace." (Lifton in his Introduction to Zlatko Dizdarevic, *Sarajevo: A War Journal*, trans. Anselm Hollo, New York: Fromm International, 1993, xv, xxvi.)

11. Jane M. O. Sharp, "Appeasement, Intervention and the Future of Europe," in Lawrence Freedman, ed., *Military Intervention in European Conflicts* (Oxford: Blackwell Publishers), 1994, 34, 41, 43, 54, 55.

12. The Commission on Global Governance, *Our Global Neighborhood*, Oxford: Oxford University Press, 1995, p. 21, cited in Sissela Bok, *Common Values* (Columbia: University of Missouri Press, forthcoming).

13. Özbekhan, after reading this essay in draft, objected that the term "humanism" connotes to him, not its meaning that I intended—devotion to human interests—but another of its meanings, devotion to studies, especially of the Greek and Roman classics, which promote human culture. Yet "humanitarianism," which he proposed in the alternative, is, in my opinion, a term (like "liberal" in current American politics) which in many American quarters automatically activates cynicism, hostility, or contempt. After reflection aroused by this discussion, I prefer a new term for an old doctrine that has not been made clear enough. When Jefferson wrote that "all men are created equal"—and when in 1985 the film director Frank Capra (quoted in *The New York Times*, May 19, 1985) referred to "the equal importance of each individual"—they meant, in my opinion, that from the point of view of a just government, solely because a person has human consciousness (is human and has consciousness), he or she is the basic locus of human value and is just as valuable and important as anyone else. By minimalist international personism I mean a doctrine, intended to be applied in social and governmental planning and action at any level, that each person has human value equal to that of every other person; that for purposes of social or governmental planning, being a human being is the basal and always equal unit of human value regardless of one's place of birth, culture, religion, race, tribe, nation, or state or one's gender, personal inheritance, talents, attainments, appearance, "IQ," or skills in the accumulation of money or power or both.

14. Bok, in the aforecited work, seeks to begin that construction by positing minimalist "common values" in every human society. I acquired my understanding of the importance of minimalism in this realm from Dr. Bok.

15. Ronnie Dugger, "Create a World Army," *The New York Times* (op-ed), 6/27/95. A "UN Legion" and volunteer reserve force was proposed by the first

UN Secretary-General, Trygve Lie, of Norway. In 1993 that idea was renewed by Sir Brian Urquhart ("For a UN Volunteer Military Force," *New York Review of Books*, June 10, 1993).

16. Letter, Adriaan Jacobovits de Szeged (Ambassador to the Netherlands) to the author, 7/12/95; Remarks of van Mierlo at an international syposium in the Netherlands in March 1995; "A Netherlands Non-paper," *op cit.*, 2, 4, 10, 11, 18, 38, 323.

17. Lifton, *The Protean Self: Human Resilience in an Age of Fragmentation* (New York: Basic Books, 1993).

18. Bernard Rapoport, an insurance executive, political activist, and progressive philanthropist in Texas, laid a curl of logic into my mind which contained the first part of this idea by saying to me: "Have you ever thought, have you realized, that every choice you make at any moment is closing off hundreds, thousands, millions—all the other things you might do or directions you might go at that moment?"

I appreciate the value of Lifton's therapeutic conviction that the work of a healthy person is adaptation, growth, and radical shifts of orientation when the truth requires them, within an ethics-moored, protean, but still single and unifying personality. But when I consider myself and the complexities at hand I need the visualization of serial repositionings and rolling equipoise that is metamorphous, continuingly rebalancing, and neomorphous.

Lifton refers to points involved in this matter in *The Protean Self* at 30, 237n.

7

Genocide and Warfare

Eric Markusen

Of all the problems confronting humanity during the remaining years of the twentieth century and into the twenty-first, none is more urgently in need of solution than the deliberate killing of masses of defenseless people. One need only read the daily newspaper or watch the evening news on television to be innundated by a mind-numbing array of human-caused atrocities and tragedies—wars, famines, and genocidal massacres—occurring in many corners of the world.

Although countless millions of men, women, and children have been slaughtered by their fellow human beings throughout history, there is persuasive evidence that the present century is the most murderous of all.[1] Political scientist Roger Smith aptly characterized the twentieth century as "an age of genocide in which 60 million men, women, and children, coming from many different races, religions, ethnic groups, nationalities, and social classes, and living in many different countries, on most of the continents of the earth, have had their lives taken because the state thought this desirable."[2] Fellow political scientist R. J. Rummel put the number of people "killed by government" during this century nearly twice as high—119,394,000, to be precise.[3]

The vast majority men and women responsible for the slaughter of their fellow human beings have not been sadistic or psychopathic. As psychologist Israel W. Charny concluded from his extensive study of genocidal killing, "the mass killers of humankind are largely everyday human beings—what we have called normal people according to currently accepted definitions by the mental health profession."[4] Robert Jay Lifton, on the basis of extensive interviews with former Nazi physicians who had in various ways contributed to the Holocaust, called attention to "the disturbing psychological truth that participation in mass murder need not require emotions as extreme or demonic as would seem appropriate for such a malignant project. Or to put the matter another way, ordinary people can commit demonic acts."[5] These are conclusions of major importance. How ostensibly normal, "good" people can be able and willing to contribute to atrocity is a question that merits serious study.

However, despite the vital contributions of scholars, human rights activists, and others from around the world, the energy and attention devoted to understanding and preventing governmental mass killing have been negligible when compared with the scale and urgency of the problem itself. Although scholarship on genocide and related forms of violence increased steadily during the past decade, it is still insufficient and rudimentary. Much of the literature is preoccupied with debates over how genocide should be defined. Many scholarly books have been written on specific genocides, like the Holocaust, but only a handful on genocide in comparative perspective.[6]

This essay addresses a controversial issue in the fledgling field of genocide studies—the relationship between genocide and modern warfare—and argues that this relationship is much closer than some scholars have been willing to admit. The essay concludes with reflections on the implications of this conclusion.

The Controversy Over the Relationship Between War and Genocide

The polarization among scholars on the question of the relationship between genocide and total war is quite striking. In the first major sociological study of genocide, Irving Louis Horowitz wrote that "it is operationally imperative to distinguish warfare from genocide" and asserted that the decision to emphasize the distinction between the two types of mass killing is "warranted by the weight of current empirical research that indicates that domestic destruction and international warring are separate dimensions of struggle."[7] More recently, sociologist Kurt Jonassohn asserted that:

> nobody has yet shown that our understanding is enriched by comparing such unlike phenomena as wartime casualties and genocides. The fact that both war and genocide produce massive casualties is a terrible commentary on man's inhumanity to man, but it does not help to understand either phenonemon. We do not believe that there is anything to be gained analytically by comparing cases that have little in common except that they produce large numbers of casualties.[8]

In strong contrast to this view, sociologist Leo Kuper, widely regarded as the world's leading scholar of genocide in comparative perspective, steadfastly maintained that there is in fact overlap between genocide and warfare. In his pathbreaking 1981 book, Kuper wrote:

> The changing nature of warfare, with a movement toward total warfare, and the technological means for the annihilation of large populations, creates a situation conducive to genocidal conflict. This potential was realized in the Second World War, when Germany employed genocide in its war for domination, but I think the term must also be applied to the atomic bombing of the Japanese cities of Hiroshima and Nagasaki by the U.S.A. and to the pattern bombing by the Allies of such cities as Hamburg and Dresden.[9]

How is it possible that experts can be in such fundamental disagreement on such a basic issue? There are at least three reasons for the persistence of this controversy, which can only be mentioned in the present context. First, there is the sheer variety of forms that both genocide and warfare have assumed. Both wars and genocides can vary widely in terms of numbers of parties and people involved, death tolls, and motives. A second factor that complicates definitions of genocide and thereby helps account for the persistent controversy over the relationship of genocide and warfare stems from the fact that labeling an event as "genocide" or "genocidal" is inevitably a politically volatile act. Third, both the variability of the phenomena of genocide and war, as well as the political implications of allegations of genocide, have created serious problems in developing widely accepted definitions that can serve as a consensual basis for analysis and comparison. The same can be said for definitions of war.[10]

Modern Warfare Has Become Increasingly Genocidal

After reviewing the scholarly literature on modern warfare and genocide, and after engaging in a comparative analysis of the Holocaust and strategic bombing, my colleague, historian David Kopf, and I reached the conclusion that they should not be regarded as mutually exclusive phenomena, but instead as forms of governmental mass killing that, in many but not all cases, are closely related and do in fact share important commonalities. Moreover, specific instances of modern war may be appropriately regarded as genocidal, if not actual cases of genocide. Put differently, we concluded that the line between genocide and warfare has often become very blurred.[11]

One connection between genocide and warfare on which there is a wide consensus in the scholarly community is the tendency for war to create social and psychological conditions conducive for the outbreak of genocide and genocidal killing. Leo Kuper noted that "international warfare, whether between 'tribal' groups or city states, or other sovereign states and nations, has been a perennial source of genocide."[12] Among his examples from the post-World War II era are the Chinese invasion of Tibet in 1950 and the invasion and occupation of East Timor by Indonesia in 1977, both of which entailed extensive genocidal killing. Likewise, referring to the Armenian genocide of 1915–17 and the Nazi Holocaust against the Jews, sociologist Vahakn Dadrian observed that "It is no accident that the two principal instances of genocide of this century coincided with the episodes of two global wars."[13] Civil wars also create the potential for genocidal killing. Indeed, Henry Huttenbach has warned that it is "probably one of the most likely settings for genocide in the future."[14]

Several dimensions of modern war expedite genocide. First, war—particularly on the losing side—produces widespread psychological and social disequilibrium. This creates the potential for pre-existing intergroup tensions in a culturally and/or racially diverse society to flare into violence directed by the majority against members of a minority group. The threat and disruption is blamed not only on the external enemy but also can be directed at members of a minority group within the society. The minority group may be accused of collaborating with the enemy and/or be used as a scapegoat for the frustrated aggression of the dominant group, especially when the war begins to go poorly.[15]

Second, governments engaged in total war, whether democratic or totalitarian, tend to become more centralized, secret, and powerful. They commonly use official censorship and propaganda to increase support for their belligerent policies. This can take a variety of forms, including vilification of the enemy and cover-ups of mistakes or atrocities conducted by one's own forces. The result can be diminished popular awareness of, and resistance to, ruthless governmental actions against both external and internal enemies.[16]

Third, the government at war can utilize the military forces—men who have been trained to kill in the service of their nation—for the perpetration of genocide. This occurred in both the Armenian genocide and the Holocaust. Other twentieth century genocides in which soldiers and paramilitary personnel played key roles as killers include, but are not limited to, the following: the 1904 slaughter of more than 65,000 Hereros in German South West Africa (now the nation of Namibia); the killing of half a million Southern Sudanese civilians by the Sudanese army between 1955 and 1972; the massacre of as many as 3,000,000 Bengalis by the army of East Pakistan in 1971; the killing of tens of thousands of Timorese by the Indonesian army in 1975; and the slaughter of millions of their fellow Cambodians by the Khmer Rouge in 1975–79.[17]

Fourth, just as conditions of war significantly increase the power of the government, they also tend to increase the vulnerability of the governmentally targeted victim groups, which tend to be, as Dadrian noted, "isolated, fragmented, and nearly totally emasculated through the control of channels of communication, wartime secrecy, the various sections of the wartime apparatus, police, and secret services, and the constant invocation of national security."[18]

Finally, a number of scholars have suggested that modern war creates a climate of moral and psychological numbing or desensitization that increases popular tolerance of cruelty, whether directed against an external or internal enemy. For example, in his analysis of the role of the military in the Turkish genocide of the Armenians in 1915, James Reid found that earlier attacks by the Turkish army against civilians helped to psychologically facilitate their later involvement in the even more ruthless killing of Armenians.[19]

The Deliberate Massacre of Noncombatants

"Massacre," according to *The Oxford Universal Dictionary*, has a number of meanings, including, in the noun form, "a general slaughter (of human beings)," and "a cruel or peculiarly atrocious murder." As a verb, its meanings include "to kill indiscriminately," and "to murder cruelly or violently."[20] A fundamental commonality between genocide and much modern warfare is that both employ massacre of large numbers of innocent, helpless noncombatants as a means of obtaining their objectives. One of the reasons for which genocide is universally reviled as a uniquely atrocious international crime is the innocence of its victims, the majority of whom are children, women, and the elderly. In their study, *The Fate of Polish Children During the Last War*, for example, Hrabar and his colleagues estimated that more than two million Polish children (both Jewish and non-Jewish) were killed by the Germans between 1939 and 1945.[21] These innocents were murdered in a variety of ways: by gunfire and bombs during the initial Nazi invasion, particularly the ruthless bombing of Warsaw; by being worked to death as slave laborers; because of starvation and disease in concentration camps; and in the gas chambers of Treblinka and other death camps—to name just a few. Referring to the child victims of the Nazi genocide, Raul Hilberg suggested "that is what makes the Holocaust a holocaust!"[22]

However, it is essential to recognize that most of the victims of modern war are also innocent in the sense of playing no direct role in the waging of the war and/or having absolutely no choice in the decision of their government to engage in war. This is particularly true of citizens in dictatorial regimes. It is worth emphasizing in this context that while civilians accounted for only 5 percent of the deaths in World War I, they accounted for more than 60 percent of the deaths in World War II; and in the wars of the 1970s and 1980s, civilians accounted for more than 80 percent of the deaths.[23]

Surprisingly, some scholars of genocide appear not to appreciate this crucial fact—or at least its staggering scale. For example, when Barbara Harff, under the heading, "Death in War and Genocide: The Means and Ends of Destruction," writes that "During war civilians get killed, sometimes by the thousands," I certainly agree with the first part of her statement.[24] The second part, however, conveys but a pale hint of the actual scale of civilian casualties in wars of the twentieth century, particularly during and since World War II, when the vast majority of the millions killed have been civilians. Moreover, in the same book chapter from which I just quoted, Harff also claimed that, "Most civilized states adhere to the rules of war, which proscribe the intentional killing of civilians during war. These principles rarely are applied fully, but the intent therefore is to avoid killing noncombatants."[25] While I agree with Harff that most "civilized states" (i.e., democratic and nonaggressive states) do tend to "adhere" to the "rules of war," I must also stress that such adherence is all too often violated. Such was certainly the case during World War II, when both the United States and Great Britain firebombed heavily populated enemy cities. Also, the sheer destructiveness of modern weapons makes it very difficult to avoid killing noncombatants.

A number of scholars differentiate genocide and war on the grounds that the victims of genocide are helpless, while the victims of warring nations are far less so. Sociologist Helen Fein, for example, wrote that war "is ideally conceived of as a symmetrical conflict between two forces. Genocide, by contrast, is usually conceived of as an asymmetrical slaughter of an unorganized group or collectivity by an organized force."[26] Later in her paper, she reiterated that her "paradigm of genocide . . . presumes a powerful perpetrator and relatively powerless victim."[27] Similarly, Frank Chalk and Kurt Jonassohn stated that "When countries are at war, neither side is defensless. Although individually the civilians may be defenseless, they are part of the group or nation that is at war." They noted also that in genocide, as opposed to war, "the victim group has no organized military machinery that might be opposed to that of the perpetrator."[28]

While I agree that the victims of genocides are far less powerful than the perpetrators, I also suggest that Fein, Chalk, and Jonassohn fail to sufficiently appreciate the fact that many wars are clearly asymmetrical, rather than symmetrical. Indeed, aggressors are often stimulated to undertake invasion precisely because they believe that they can prevail with relatively low "costs" to their own nation. This was the case with Nazi attacks against Poland, France, the Netherlands, and other nations during World War II, and it was true also of the Iraqi invasion of Kuwait in 1991. Moreover, Fein and others do not sufficiently acknowledge the powerlessness of civilians under attack by modern military forces and weapons. For example, despite their formidable military forces, the governments of Germany and Japan were able to do little to spare their civilians from the ravages of strategic bombing by Great Britain and the United States. The reality is that in total war civilians become helpless pawns of their governments and, in many cases, defenseless targets of enemy artillery shells, bombs, and missiles.

Overlap among War Crimes, Crimes against Humanity, and the Crime of Genocide

Leo Kuper has asserted that "war crimes, crimes against humanity, and genocide are by no means exclusive categories."[29] To the extent that these three offenses contain overlapping provisions, a case can be made against the "mutual exclusivity" position on the controversy over the relationship between war and genocide.

Although constraints on the practice of war, particularly the careful discrimination between combatants and noncombatants, have been a feature of international common law for several centuries, as well a crucial feature of the Christian just war tradition, and even though the concept of "crimes against humanity" was first articulated in a legal forum in May of 1915 (in response to Turkish atrocities against the Armenians), the legal status of war crimes and crimes against humanity was not firmly institutionalized until August 8, 1945. On that date, the nations of the United States, the Soviet Union, Great Britian, and France signed the London Agreement, which established the Charter of the

International Military Tribunal (IMT). They did so in order to provide a legal forum for the prosecution of Nazi leaders, both military and civilian, who had contributed to the many atrocities perpetrated by Germany during World War II.[30]

Three categories of crime were established by the IMT. Crimes against peace referred to the initiation and waging of a war of aggression. War crimes referred to "violations of the laws or customs of war," including "murder, ill-treatment or deportation to slave labor or for any other purpose of civilian population of or in occupied territory." This category also prohibited mistreatment of prisoners of war, killing hostages, plunder of private property, and related acts.[31] The third type of crime, crimes against humanity, included a number of specific acts, including:

> murder, extermination, enslavement, deportation and other inhumane acts committed against any civilian population, before or during the war, or persecutions on political, racial, or religious grounds in execution of or in connection with any crime within the jurisdiction of the Tribunal, whether or not in violation of the domestic law of the country where perpetrated."[32]

The category of crimes against humanity was designed to provide a legal basis for prosecuting the Germans for actions that had not been included in previous international law concerning warfare. One major loophole, however, was that the IMT applied only to crimes against humanity that had been committed in conjunction with other criminal actions in which Germany had engaged during the war, e.g., taking of civilian hostages or reprisals against civilians. In order to include genocide, per se, as a crime under international law, a further step beyond the precedents established by the IMT was required, namely, the formal establishment of genocide as a crime.

While the International Military Tribunal was conducting its trial of the major German war criminals, Raphael Lemkin, who originated the concept of "genocide" in 1944, was in the United States lobbying at the recently formed United Nations on behalf of a resolution that would clearly establish the offenses he had collected under the label of "genocide" as constituting an international crime. His efforts were rewarded on December 9, 1948, when the United Nations General Assembly unanimously adopted the Convention on the Prevention and Punishment of the Crime of Genocide. The Convention was explicit in listing specific actions which constitute the crime of genocide. Article 2 states:

In the present Convention, genocide means any of the following acts committed with intent to destroy, in whole or in part, a national, ethnical [sic],
racial, or religious group, as such: (a) Killing members of the group; (b)
Causing serious bodily or mental harm to members of the group; (c) Deliberately inflicting on the group conditions of life calculated to bring about
its physical destruction in whole or in part; (d) Imposing measures to prevent births within the group; (e) Forcibly transferring children of the
group to another group.[33]

Thus, the crime of genocide shares with certain kinds of war crimes and
with crimes against humanity the prohibition against killing civilians. In
this respect, we suggest that genocide, whether perpetrated during a war
or not, clearly overlaps with crimes against civilian populations that are
committed during warfare. The reasons discussed above do not exhaust
commonalities between war and genocide. In *The Holocaust and Strategic
Bombing,* David Kopf and I show that genocide and war are frequently
facilitated by similar psychological and social facilitating factors, including a tendency to regard the victims of killing as subhuman, the use of
euphemistic language to obscure the full reality of the mass killing, several features of the bureaucratic organization of both modern war and
genocide, and, finally, the use of technological means of killing to im-
pose physical and emotional distance between killers and victims.[34]

Implications

Unfortunately, there is not enough space to do more than briefly allude
to some of the implications of the conclusion that genocide and warfare
are not always distinct and discrete phenomena, that warfare can and
does degenerate into genocidal killing. If, in fact, common practices in
modern warfare, particularly the deliberate slaughter of helpless civilians, warrant being labeled as "genocidal," then thinking about genocide, both by the general public and the scholarly community, needs to
be expanded to include a wider range of cases than many have been
willing to consider. Such expanded thinking must contend with the
premise that the capacity for genocidal killing is not limited to obvious
monsters like Joseph Stalin, Adolf Hitler, Idi Amin, and Pol Pot, but is
widely shared. We must also face the fact that religious conviction, advanced education, and scientific expertise do not automatically confer
immunity from the capacity to become implicated in a genocidal project, nor does the fact that one is a loving husband and father. Psychologically normal, "good," people can and have participated in demonic

projects. Not only totalitarian regimes, but also democracies have been willing to directly engage in genocidal killing, to support client states that engage in it, and to make the preparations for it. The conclusion also warns us that under the brutalizing conditions of modern war waged with weapons of unprecedented destructiveness, even democracies can succumb to the genocidal temptation.

Finally, it demonstrates the importance and urgency of greater understanding of the phenomenon of genocidal killing, in order that future incidents can be anticipated and prevented. Further scholarly study of the problem is essential, as are ongoing efforts to strengthen international legal sanctions against the slaughter of innocents. However, in order for such sanctions to be successfully and meaningfully integrated into the international political arena, new generations of students and citizens must appreciate just how serious the epidemic of genocidal killing has become. Moreover, in addition to recognizing the scale and urgency of the problem, they must learn about how it might be reduced and eventually eliminated. For this to occur, a necessary, though not sufficient, condition is the development of college and university courses on genocide as a subject in its own right and in comparative perspective.

Such education, while certainly no panacea, would generate at least two salutary effects. First, a growing number of college and university educated men and women would have have what Lifton has called a "formed awareness" of the problem. By "formed" as opposed to partial or "fragmentary" awareness, Lifton refers to "awareness that *in*forms our sense of self and world, that affects our actions and our lives and is part of an evolving pattern of illumination and commitment"(italics in original).[35] As citizens of democracies, individuals with such an awareness of genocide are in a position to support political candidates and policies that address the problem in useful ways and can thereby contribute to concrete, political and legal steps to anticipate and prevent future outbreaks of genocidal violence—and when prevention fails, to intervene and punish the perpetrators. Second, out of such courses will come future scholars, who will make important contributions to our understanding of the problem of governmental mass killing, as well as future diplomats and jurists and human rights advocates who will become directly engaged in the struggle to transcend it.

Notes

1. Eric Markusen and David Kopf, *The Holocaust and Strategic Bombing: Genocide and Total War in the Twentieth Century* (Boulder, CO: Westview Press, 1995): 27–34.

2. Roger Smith, "Human Destructiveness and Politics: The Twentieth Century as an Age of Genocide," Isidor Wallimann and Michael Dobkowski, eds., *Genocide and the Modern Age: Etiology and Case Studies of Mass Death* (New York: Greenwood Press, 1987): 21.

3. R. J. Rummel, "Power Kills; Absolute Power Kills Absolutely," *Internet on the Holocaust and Genocide,* June (1992): 1.

4. Israel W. Charny, "Genocide and Mass Destruction: Doing Harm to Others as a Missing Dimension in Psychopathology," *Psychiatry* 49 (1986): 144.

5. Robert Jay Lifton, *The Nazi Doctors: Medical Killing and the Psychology of Genocide* (New York: Basic Books, 1986): 5.

6. Markusen and Kopf, *The Holocaust and Strategic Bombing:* 2–15.

7. Irving Louis Horowitz, *Taking Lives: Genocide and State Power,* 3rd ed. (New Brunswick: Transaction Books, 1982): 32.

8. Kurt Jonassohn, "What is Genocide?," ed. Helen Fein, *Genocide Watch* (New Haven: Yale University Press, 1992): 22.

9. Leo Kuper, *Genocide: Its Political Use in the Twentieth Century* (New Haven: Yale University Press, 1981): 46.

10. Markusen and Kopf, *The Holocaust and Strategic Bombing:* 57–62.

11. Ibid., 55–78.

12. Leo Kuper, *The Prevention of Genocide* (New Haven: Yale University Press, 1985): 157.

13. Vahakn N. Dadrian, "A Typology of Genocide," *International Review of Modern Sociology* 15 (1975): 206.

14. Henry R. Huttenbach, "Locating the Holocaust on the Genocide Spectrum: Toward a Methodology of Definition and Categorization" *Holocaust and Genocide Studies* 3 (1988): 297.

15. Dadrian, "A Typology of Genocide," 206.

16. Marjorie Farrar, "World War II as Total War" in *War: A Historical, Political, and Social Study,* ed. L. L. Farrar (San Francisco: ABC-Clio, 1978): 173.

17. Barbara Harff, "The Etiology of Genocides," in *Genocide and the Modern Age: Etiology and Case Studies of Mass Death,* ed. Isidor Wallimann and Michael Dobkowski (New York: Greenwood, 1987): 46.

18. Vahakn N. Dadrian, "The Structural-Functional Components of Genocide: A Victimological Approach to the Armenian Case," in *Victimology,* eds. Israel Drapkin and Emilio Viano (Lexington, MA: Lexington Books, 1974): 129.

19. James J. Reid, "The Concept of War and Genocidal Impulses in the Ottoman Empire, 1821–1918," *Holocaust and Genocide Studies* 4 (1988): 184.

20. C. T. Onions, ed., *The Oxford Universal Dictionary* (Oxford: Clarendon Press, 1955): 1213.

21. Roman Hrabar et al., *The Fate of Polish Children During the Last War* (Warsaw: Interpress, 1981).

22. Raul Hilberg, "Opening Remarks: The Discovery of the Holocaust," in *Lessons and Legacies: The Meaning of the Holocaust in a Changing World,* ed. Peter Hayes (Evanston, IL: Northwestern University Press, 1991): 15.

86   *Eric Markusen*

23. Markusen and Kopf, *The Holocaust and Strategic Bombing*: 1–2.

24. Barbara Harff, "Recognizing Genocides and Politicides," in *Genocide Watch*, ed. Helen Fein (New Haven: Yale University Press, 1992): 39.

25. Ibid., 25.

26. Helen Fein, "Discriminating Genocide from War Crimes: Vietnam and Afghanistan Reexamined," a paper prepared for the First Raphael Lemkin Symposium on Genocide, Yale University Law School, February 1991: 5–6.

27. Ibid., 18.

28. Frank Chalk and Kurt Jonassohn, *The History and Sociology of Genocide: Analyses and Case Studies* (New Haven: Yale University Press, 1990): 23–24.

29. Leo Kuper, "Genocide and the Technological Tiger," *Internet on the Holocaust and Genocide* 32 (1992): 1.

30. Sydney Goldenberg, "Crimes Against Humanity 1945–1970" *Western Ontario Law Review* 10 (1971): 5.

31. Quoted in ibid., 1.

32. Quoted in ibid., 3.

33. Quoted in Kuper, *Genocide*: 19.

34. Markusen and Kopf, *The Holocaust and Strategic Bombing*, 183–240.

35. Robert Jay Lifton, "Imagining the Real," in Lifton and Richard Falk, *Indefensible Weapons: The Psychological and Political Case Against Nuclearism* (New York: Basic Books, 1982): 117.

8

Victims, Perpetrators, Bystanders, and Rescuers in the Face of Genocide and Its Aftermath

Eva Fogelman

On April 1, 1933, the Nazis called for a boycott of Jewish businesses. This call was the first instance of state-sponsored anti-Semitism, an organized and official attempt to stamp Jews as "other." Guards stood outside stores and doctors' and lawyers' offices owned by Jews in order to intimidate callers. This was a key moment. Would it work? Would Germans refuse to be bullied into singling out their neighbors and friends?

A few individuals defied the boycott, but most stayed away. Significantly, "the universities were silent, the courts were silent; the President of the Reich, who had taken the oath on the Constitution, was silent," Leo Baeck, Berlin's preeminent leader of the liberal Jewish community, wrote. To Rabbi Baeck, this was "the day of the greatest cowardice. Without that cowardice, all that followed would not have happened."[1]

The Third Reich's systematic destruction of European Jewry would have been impossible if decent, law-abiding, citizens had said "no" to this early-warning sign of genocide. The few who ultimately did protest, or took up arms, or engaged in sabotage work, or protected the victims from a certain death, did not change the course of history. But, in fact, they teach us the most important lesson: even under conditions of extreme terror people have a choice.

To this day, the train conductors, the judges, the lawyers, bankers, teachers, civil servants, members of the SS, concentration camp guards, factory workers, and most notoriously the doctors who were killing for the sake of healing do not regret their choice. They feel justified in enhancing the life of the Aryan "pure" race and killing everyone else. Robert Lifton's interviews with the Nazi doctors are so revealing of this lack of guilt, it is chilling. Nazi doctors and other henchmen of the Nazi machinery still feel they did the "right thing."

It is noteworthy to mention that doctors and even SS guards who said that they could not follow the order of spending their day in a mass shooting or gassing were excused and given another job. Few requested such transfers; the others complied and numbed themselves nightly in a drunken stupor.

Without the villians there would have been no need for rescuers during the years of Nazi occupation, or for that matter during any historical period when a group of people was being killed for the mere reason that they were "different," or because they were being irrationally perceived as a threat to the survival of another group.

Those who risked life and limb, their families, and in many instances their own children have said: "This is the only way to act towards another human being," "I couldn't live with myself if I let these people die."

How do we, fifty years later, understand the perpetrators and the rescuers? After all, each thinks that she or he did the right thing? We need go no further than Lifton's own writings to understand both the perpetrators and the rescuers. Although Lifton does not directly analyze the rescuers, his theory on the "species self" is at the core of the rescuer self. I make this leap because of my research on non-Jews who risked their lives to save Jews without an external profit motive.

After my initial interviews with more than 100 rescuers of Jews during the Holocaust, I was fortunate to be able to consult with Lifton on how to do a sequential analysis of the narratives. I was further encouraged to re-interview each person no matter how many hours I had spent the first time. A second interview has been an invaluable suggestion for conducting psychohistorical interviews.

The diversity among the rescuers of Jews during the Holocaust would dissuade any social scientist from making generalizations about motivations. However, a closer systematic analysis of rescuers' family backgrounds, personalities, and situational conditions begins to suggest a way of understanding what enabled some rare people to take extraordinary risks to save the lives of others.

Through the rescuing relationship the values and beliefs of the innermost core of the rescuer were expressed. The core was nurtured in childhood, came to full expression during the Holocaust through rescue, and then continued in the post-war years. Saving Jews came from the inner core of a person, and became part of that person: a *rescuer self.* Although created during the Holocaust, the rescuer self continued to be an integral part of the rescuer's identity.

In examining the initial act of rescue there is a consensus among rescuers that such behavior was not premeditated and planned. Whether it was gradual or sudden, there was little mulling over the moral dilemmas, conflicts and life-and-death consequences involved in the decision to help. The decision to harbor Jews was often an impulsive response to an immediate life-and-death situation rather than a contemplated, thought-out decision. In fact, taking on the responsibility to save a person's life came from an integrated expression of the core self.

In most cases, transformation from bystander to rescuer was gradual, and characterized by an increasing commitment. Most people did not initiate rescues on their own. A friend, an acquaintance, or a friend of a friend came and asked for help. Rescuers thought about the person in trouble, not how their help would endanger them and their family. One thing led to another, and they experienced an "upward curve of risk," starting with smuggling food and messages into a ghetto, then transporting a Jew out of the ghetto, and gradually sheltering the Jew for several years.

Rescuers became outlaws in a Nazi no-man's land. Their ideas of right and wrong were not widely held. Being isolated was new for them, since before the war, they had been very much part of their communities. Prior to the rescue they tended not to be loners or people who felt alienated from society. But the secret of rescue effectively isolated them from everyone else. Neighbors who suspected people of harboring Jews viewed them as selfish and dangerous because they risked their lives and the lives of those around them.

A rescuer's life was intricate and terrifying. A careless word, a forgotten detail, or one wrong move could lead to death. Dutch rescuer Louisa Steenstra recalled that German soldiers arrested the 16-year-old daughter of a friend for merely saying "hello" to a resistance man who was in their custody. She was sent to a concentration camp where one hour later a guard shot her for insolence.

At home the strains were often just as great. Overnight, dynamics changed as families adjusted to the new member being sheltered. The home atmosphere could become poisonous if one spouse did not support the other's rescuing efforts. Comfortable routines were upset and new patterns had to be developed. Husbands and wives gave up their privacy. Children found themselves sleeping with strangers they had to learn to call brother, sister, aunt, uncle—whatever the situation or the occasion required. "Sibling" rivalries and jealousies developed.

A core confidence, a strong sense of self, and a supportive situation had allowed bystanders to undertake the rescue. But once the decision to help had been reached and the rescue had begun, a different self—a *rescuer self*—emerged, to do what had to be done and to keep rescuers from becoming overwhelmed by new responsibilities and pressures.

A "transformation" had taken place. It was not simply behavior that changed. Successful rescuers became, in effect, different people. Robert Lifton explains the psychological process: when people find themselves in a world that no longer makes sense, their identities—the ways they behave, even notions of right and wrong—no longer seem to fit. They become "de-centered." In an effort to reestablish psychological equilibrium, they had to find new centers, to create new selves.[2] This new self, in the case of rescuers, was built on strong moral foundations. But it allowed the rescuers to do what was necessary—including plotting, stealing, lying, taking risks, enduring hardships, putting loved ones in jeopardy, and living in fear—all in the service of setting the world (and their place within it) on solid ground. These actions may not have made sense to their former selves, but they became the new essence of rescuers.

The act of rescue often entails anxiety and great risk; rescue acts could also unleash strong feelings of guilt (at not being able to do more, at risking one's family in the service of others), rage (at the oppressors), terror and sadness (at witnessing atrocities and dehumanization), all of which ostensibly could induce inner chaos. But it is apparent from my interviews that rescuers have a strong equilibrium. They can withstand intense decentering experiences and the accompanying pain and confusion. As Lifton points out, such experiences can help to *recenter* people, allowing them to achieve a new mode of flexible psychological coping. The rescuer self kept the fear of death and the knowledge of Hitler's Final Solution at bay. French pastor and underground leader Marc Donadille summed it up:

> On some level we knew [the gassings] were true, incredible as it seemed— but we pushed it to the back of our minds and got on with the daily work of rescuing. It didn't make sense to say to the Jews we were rescuing, living side by side with, in our houses 'Hitler is going to kill you all.' What haunted us was to save the Jews that were there. We had enough to do to keep them hidden, safe and fed . . .[3]

The rescuer self had to be competent, resourceful, and practical to get through each day safely. Charges had to eat and food shopping was a major problem. To avoid arousing suspicion by buying too much food at once, rescuers wandered far afield. In large cities such as Amsterdam this was not a problem at first. Miep Gies, who was buying groceries for seven people in hiding above Otto Frank's spice business, as well as for herself and her husband, distributed her purchases among several stores. These ruses were not foolproof. One day Gies' local vegetable grocer noticed that she was buying large amounts of vegetables. Without saying anything, he began putting vegetables aside for her shopping visits. Months later, when she stopped by to shop as usual, he was not there. He had been arrested for hiding two Jews.[4]

Each combination of rescuer, victim, and situation created a peculiar alchemy. Whatever its distinctive traits, the rescuer self that emerged never strayed from the person's basic, humanitarian values, which were solid and unchanging. They were democratic and humane in nature. It was easier, of course, to harbor a person who was likable than someone who was unpleasant or demanding. However, once a rescuing relationship began, it was not easily terminated because of personality differences.

A Typology of Rescuers

I analyze rescue in terms of how an individual's socialization process, personality traits, and opportunity converge in the moment of decision to risk one's life for another. I have delineated five types, based on the rescuers' values, feelings, and relationships when they initially decide to engage in rescue.

For some rescuers, the process of transformation from bystander to rescuer was directly related to gradual but increasing commitment to an anti-Nazi or religious ideology. For others, the rescue act was triggered by a sudden awareness of an imminent death of either a loved one, an acquaintance, or a total stranger.

The most prevalent were moral rescuers, who simply said, "It was the right thing to do." Morality is derived from a number of sources and finds its expression in different ways according to attitudes, beliefs, and emotions. This category can be divided into three moral types:

1. Ideological-moral rescuers are motivated by a sense of morality-based ethical behavior and justice and by moral convictions that maintain a sense of self.
2. Religious-moral rescuers are motivated by that which stems from religious beliefs and a sense of moral duty to be "thy neighbor's keeper." Some religiously motivated fundamentalist rescuers believed in the "choseness" of the Jewish people and felt a spiritual connection with the Jews through the Bible and Jesus.

3. Emotional-moral rescuers are motivated to act humanely by feelings of pity and compassion for the victims.

Moral rescuers can be distinguished from other types by examining how their helping activity began. Moral rescuers often require a trigger event to precipitate a latent altruistic response. Most often they are led to help, or they undergo a "transforming encounter" that inspires them to actively initiate help. A transforming encounter occurs when witnessing an event so assaults one's sense of decency and humanity that one is forever disfigured. Transformation usually involves an encounter with death, which leaves a person with indelible images as vivid today as they were fifty years ago. The degree of empathy with the victim is the operative factor in the potential of a witnessed act of violence to assume transforming power.

Relational philo-Semitic rescuers (Judeo-philes) all had relationships with Jews, whether with spouses, relatives, close friends, acquaintances or colleagues. In addition, these rescuers, for a myriad of reasons, had a particular affinity toward Jews. Some suspected that they had Jewish blood; others possessed warm memories of having been a *shabbos goy*. Some had a Jewish role model in childhood; others felt a sense of religious connectedness to Jesus, a Jew, or to the "choseness" of Jews. Relational philo-Semitic rescuers began their activity with people they knew and sometimes moved to helping strangers.

Next, in terms of numbers, were ideological-network rescuers, who helped Jews as part of a political or religious resistance group with intense anti-Nazi connections. Rescuers who were involved in networks were wholeheartedly immersed in anti-Nazi activities well before they aided Jews. Rescue acts escalated to meet the demands of the gradually worsening inhumane situations. Some became "professional rescuers," smuggling documents or contraband before transporting Jews. These kinds of activities became a full-time occupation.

Fourth were children and adolescents who began rescuing in obedience to their parents' wishes and then continued of their own accord. It was often safer for children to pass messages into ghettos, to bring food to people in hiding in the woods, to stand guard, and to serve as guides to bring Jews to safe houses. Until recently, this group of rescuers was almost entirely invisible, as it had been during the war.

Finally, detached professional rescuers helped Jews as part of their professional duties. Physicians, nurses, psychologists, and social workers, among others, operated both within and outside of the Nazi sphere. They maintained a kind of doctor-patient relationship with the people whose lives they saved. They were empathic while at the same time keeping a certain professional distance.

Postwar Rescuer Self

The rescuer self that had grown from each individual's core values and basic moral integrity remained after the war. For most, having saved lives was a source of quiet pride and inner satisfaction. For Jews and their rescuers, postwar Poland, former republics of the Soviet Union, and other eastern European locales were still hostile to Jews and their saviors. The rescuer self in most of these areas had to remain alert. Secrecy, vigilance, cunning, and role-playing were still needed for self-protection. Polish bandits were known to have killed Jews and those they suspected to have helped them survive. After an intense involvement, in some cases six years, rescuers extracted promises from their charges not to reveal their rescue role.

The adjustment to peacetime tranquility after years of military occupation and fear of being discovered was not always easy. Some rescuers were caught in their rescue efforts and spent months or years in concentration camps. Some rescuers overcame their psychic war wounds by continuing their anti-Nazi activities by bearing witness at war-crime trials or by helping victims in displaced-persons camps for refugees.

Death and horrific wartime remembrances intruded into postwar life and hampered many rescuers' efforts to rebuilt new lives. Wartime memories plagued other rescuers and prompted them to move to places free of past associations. However, the nightmares would follow them wherever they landed. Rescuers were known to develop post-traumatic stress disorder. These unfamiliar symptoms were often not diagnosed in conjunction with their war experiences. Until recently doctors did not know to ask about such matters particularly if one was not in a concentration camp.

The war years were filled with losses for rescuers as well as for their charges. After the war rescuers also had to mourn the loss of their charges, family members and friends who may not have survived the war, and their rescuer self. For some the war was the most exciting, meaningful part of their lives. This is quite dramatically portrayed in the story of Oskar Schindler, who performed such heroic deeds during the years of Nazi occupation, but after the war was an utter failure in business.

Anti-Nazi rescuers who lost their cause with liberation often replaced this cause with other causes, such as anti-communism, the anti-nuclear movement, the peace movement. Moral religious rescuers found solace in continuing to do good deeds in their families and in the religious community. Detached professional rescuers continued their helping activities in their professional roles as doctors, nurses, teachers, or social workers. Some of the children identified with their rescuer self by choosing occupations in the helping professions. Others among them continue to suffer emotionally from anxieties and fears, and from a lack of basic trust in the outside world. Rescuers who were motivated because of relationships continue to maintain these ties with the Jews they saved. Some Judeo-philes transferred their love of certain Jews to love for the Jewish people, and have established new lives among Jews in Israel or elsewhere.

Communal Rescue

Communal rescues took place in such towns as Le Chambone, France; Nieuwlande, Holland; Assisi, Italy; Bulgaria and Denmark. Of these, it is the Danish rescue that has received the most public and scholarly attention.

Leo Goldberger, a Danish Jew who is a psychoanalyst and teacher, has devoted much time to understanding what moved his nation to defy the Nazis and smuggle almost all of its Jews to Sweden. In *The Rescue of Danish Jews: Moral Courage under Stress*, a collection he edited, Goldberger reports that the popular myth about King Christian—that he rode through the streets on horseback with a yellow star emblazoned on his chest—is apocryphal. But, he observes, if we "substitute the symbol of the king with the Danish people as a whole, and substitute further the wearing of a yellow star with the widespread and empathic compassion for the Jewish plight," we will gain "the kernel of truth" behind the myth. Apparently, empathy can occur on a mass as well as an individual level, provided the "in group" has been inculcated with a tolerant, caring attitude toward the "out group."

Samuel Abrahamsen, a historian and Jewish survivor of Norway, in his essay in Goldberger's book, says that Denmark

> had developed over the centuries what the Danes call *livkunst*, the art of living. It was a society where people cared about one another, where respect for individual and religious differences, self-reliance, cooperation and good humor had become hallmarks of a civilized nation. These moral, intellectual, and ethical attitudes made the Danes say: "The Jews are our

fellow citizens and fellow human beings; we shall not give them up for slaughter." And they did not. . . . The diabolic plan to exterminate innocent Jews so outraged the Danish population that it united the nation against the Nazis and established a popular basis for the Danish resistance movement.

Rescuers' Childhood

Clearly, each rescuer was unique and must be seen in that light. But there are patterns in rescuers' upbringing that can provide us useful clues about nurturing and promoting altruistic behavior. In an era that was dominated by authoritarian upbringings, particularly in Germany, rescuers' childhood experiences emphasized love and nurturance. Punishment for misdeeds were often verbally explained rather than acted out with physical force and with strict obedience to authority. Rescuers recall their parents as encouraging independence of thought, self-reliance and competence. A parental role model who was involved in helping others in daily life was lurking in the background. As children, many of the rescuers also were encouraged to participate in daily helping chores.

The most salient value rescuers learned from their parents or from the primary caretaker was that of tolerance for people who were different. This does not mean that there were not some rescuers who grew up in an anti-Semitic or racist family environment, but for the most part this was an aberration. This tolerance stemmed from religious sources and simple humanitarianism.

Having tolerance for people who are different as a core value imbedded in childhood and adhered to in behavior enabled these non-Jews to strip away Nazi propanganda and see the Jews as human beings just as themselves, different perhaps, but still members of the human race.

Holocaust rescuers' keen awareness and deep empathy for the imminent death of the Jews also had its roots in early losses and in near-death illness experiences. Often, such a personal tragedy was alleviated with a warm loving caretaker. This kind of role-model for nurturing, contends sociologist Eli Sagan, is also at the foundation of conscience, and is the first stage of the development of moral capacity.[5]

According to Sagan, in the second stage children begin to identify with their immediate family and they want to give back the affection they have received. During this stage Freud's basis for moral action—compassion and pity—develops. In the final stage, children's consciences reach full maturity and they want to give love and comfort to those outside the family. It is this capacity to act lovingly toward people one does not even know that is essential for the development of a social conscience.

Other researchers corroborate that there is a high correlation between parental nurturance and a social conscience including altruistic behavior. In 1948, in one of the earliest studies of anti-Nazi behavior, psychoanalyst David Levy found that when he compared anti-Nazi German men (not necessarily involved in aiding Jews) with passive German bystanders, the resisters' childhood environments were more accepting and less rigid. Their parents were described as comparatively more affectionate and less restrained, featuring a strong and affectionate maternal influence and no severity in paternal discipline. Psychologist Frances Grossman uncovered a similar pattern of a warm loving relationship with at least one caretaker in the nine Holocaust rescuers she interviewed.

It needs to be noted, however, that love is not enough to foster the performance altruistic deeds to those outside the immediate family. Developmental psychologist Carolyn Zahn-Waxler and her colleagues at the National Institute of Mental Health found that children who were altruistically inclined had parents who tended to explain to them the consequences of hurting others and do so with an admonition such as "I don't like to be with you with when you act like that."

Everyone who studies rescuers agrees on one thing: If we instruct our children to value all human life, empathize with suffering, and tolerate differences among people, we will create a society in which Auschwitz is unthinkable. These simple lessons and imperatives for moral education are no less striking for their lack of novelty, than for reiterating principles and processes that we have long known.

In a world in which heroes sometimes are separated from villians only by their mass-media appeal, where constant yet subtle racism periodically explodes in riots and murders, the answer to preventing future genocides is imbedded in Lifton's writings. If we had more "species selves," people who can reach beyond their own nationality and race and embrace others, they would find it immoral to kill the "other," no matter what moral imperative was suggested by a legally sanctioned authority.

Notes

1. Baker, *Days of Sorrow and Pain: Leo Baeck and the Berlin Jews* (New York: Macmillan, 1978).

2. Robert Jay Lifton, *The Life of the Self: Toward a New Psychology* (New York: Touchstone Books, 1976).

3. Phillippe Joutard, Jacques Poujol, and Patrick Cabanel, eds., *Cévennes Terre De Refuge 1940–1944* (Montpellier: Presses Du Langeudoc/Club Cevenol, 1987), 242.

4. Miep Gies, *Ann Frank Remembered* (New York: Simon & Schuster, 1987), 121 and 150.

5. Eli Sagan, *Freud, Women, and Morality: The Psychology of Good and Evil* (New York: Basic Books, 1988).

9

In Pursuit of Sugihara: The Banality of Good

Hillel Levine

My dialogue with Robert Jay Lifton begins more than two decades ago when we were both at Yale. As a young professor of sociology and religion with strong interests in psychoanalytic theory, I found the language of the social sciences inadequate to describe the painful realities of recent history. Bob, with his far-ranging interests, demonstrated how one could expand the parameters of theorizing and, ultimately, the parameters of human concern. Ever so busy, Bob was graciously generous with his time. In opening his mind, his heart, and ultimately his family and home to a fellow wanderer, he helped me escape the dreary academic confines of knowing "more and more about less and less." We have since traded a misery or two, the pain made no less real by the pleasures of camaraderie. Moments spent with Bob and BJ are among my happiest. In whatever manner friends divide the world, Japan was clearly Bob's territory. So was the understanding of gratuitous goodness. I am moved by life's circumstances and the gentle Hand that guides us to be able to dedicate to him the "first fruits" of this odyssey. Bob, of course, would say that I was heading there all along.

Back in the days when "made in Japan" was synonymous with low-tech, low-quality, and cheap imitations, Japan's best known filmmaker of the post World War II period, Akira Kurosawa, was exploring the soul or, more accurately, the ostensive soullessness of the obedient Japanese bureaucrat. In his 1952 classic, *Ikiru*, an archetypical "salaryman" discovers that he has cancer and less than a year to live. After going through denial, melancholy, and a good deal of self-pity, he decides to resign from his job, do good deeds, and enjoy whatever is left of his life: "I cannot die before I know why I have been living for all of these years." His son and daughter-in-law remain unimpressed by this eleventh-hour existential quest, more concerned, as they are, by Ikiru's strange behav-

99

ior, how his indulgences in women and wine will reflect on the family reputation, and what will remain of the anticipated inheritance.

Japan looks considerably less austere these days than it did in the early Kurosawa films. The well-known products of faceless officials and salarymen capture more and more of the global market share and their wealth buys for them more of the world. Daily four-hour commutes packed in the subway or hopelessly snarled in rush-hour traffic would seemingly give them enough time to reflect upon the meaning of life if not to enjoy it. And yet, beneath the calmness and pride that many Japanese exude, there is desperation and confrontation, no less easy today than when Ikiru tried to defy death itself. There is expression of this in the destructiveness of the Aum cult and other radical sects. As we now know after the recent subway attacks, these often attract the involvement of the most successful in Japanese society rather than the down and outs.

The Ikiru theme is unfolding in a new and more positive and prosocial version, giving us a glimpse into Ikiru's successors. This difficult confrontation with "why I have been living" is not too deep beneath the surface in the attention recently being paid to Sugihara, an obscure diplomat who until close to the end of his life was ignored, even mistreated. The Japanese have their inimitable way in which they combine cottage industry and cult. Sugihara is now becoming a household name for heroism across Japan and he may soon be ready for export.

On August 12, 1992, in Yaotsu, a small town near Nagoya, Japan's third largest city, rice farmers milled around with bankers, developers, officials, media moguls, and diplomats as they dedicated The Hill of Humanity to Yaotsu's favorite son. A bronze bust of the sacked diplomat who saved lives was unveiled by his widow, son, the mayor of the town, and his former classmates at the Japanese Russian School of Harbin, powerful and prominent even in their dotage.

Sugihara, depicted uncharacteristically with a humorless grimace, appears to be staring away from the hill with its fountain and parabola of ceramic chimes that memorialize him, gazing across the wooded valley, soon to be used as a landfill for what is excavated in renewing a local dam. The six-and-a-half-million-dollar project is paid for, in part, by a grant from the government to townships across Japan in response to the acute problem of Japan's unchecked urbanization, overcrowded cities, and depopulated countryside. Yaotsu's mayor hopes that more money will be available from this "how ya gonna keep the kids on the farm" fund to finish the road leading up to the Hill of Humanity and to add a "Forest of Learning" with a concert hall and conference facility and an "amusement zone" to include a "children's playground with amuse-

ment park rides and a jumbo slide." For now, visitors who make it up
the dirt road may deposit a 100-yen coin at the base of the late diplomat's sculpture to see a light and water show, with chime accompani-
ment of "Coming through the Rye."

It was only a short time ago that I began trying to discover Sugihara
during a visit to Lithuania. In February 1993, I was invited to inaugurate
the first university program in Judaic Studies established in the former
Soviet Union. Vilna, "the Jerusalem of Lithuania," as Jews call their beloved city, for centuries had been a world center of Jewish scholarship
in its pious and more secular varieties. The political vicissitudes of the
twentieth century have taken their toll on Jewish culture and those who
appreciated it. Now, how deeply moving it is to celebrate this renewal at
the University of Vilnius, even if there are hardly any Jews left to teach,
research, and study. In this city shadows of the past are ever present.
Sitting in the audience among the government and university officials
and students are a few of the aged partisans of the Vilna ghetto for
whom fifty years ago is like yesterday and the yesterday that others experience is of little interest. At the end of a lecture, one of them introduces
himself. He recently retired after sixty-five years as engineer of the Vilnius Water Works. His unrivaled knowledge of its sewer system had enabled the partisans of this ghetto to be particularly mobile during the
dark days of Nazi siege and murder and to provide something of a communications network for resisters in other ghettos. As we talk he
sketches on my lecture notes a map of the sewer system with the main
escape routes demarcated. I will treasure that map. The partisans busy
themselves these days arguing with the mayor's office for the right to
place markers and memorials around the restored Old Town, much of
which had been the site of the ghetto. Other citizens of Vilnius complain
about the efforts of these militant octogenarians to make a "graveyard"
out of "our" city.

Notwithstanding the joyousness of the occasion and the warm hospi-
tality of my hosts, I feel chilled to the core. The extra sweater with which
my family lovingly sent me off, the insulated ski overalls that I had worn
under my tweed jacket during other lectures in the same season and at
the same longitude do not seem to be doing their job. Yeltsin's efforts
to pressure former Soviet satellite countries by cutting back on Russian
fuel delivery could account only in part for this profound cold from
which I cannot escape, not for a moment.

My hosts generously take me sightseeing. We visit places such as Ponar
and the Ninth Fort in Kaunas, the pastoral sites where Nazis and their
zealous Lithuanian collaborators shot Jews into open ditches in the days

before they introduced the higher-tech murderousness of Auschwitz and Treblinka. As I stand there, I think of the prohibition against "standing on your neighbor's blood," the powerful image with which the Bible commands us to take responsibility for others. Standing on the killing grounds I understand why it is difficult to feel human warmth.

Suddenly I recall the story of Sugihara, filed in my consciousness more under exotica than anything else. As I tour the former capital of Kaunas and see the remains of its great Jewish civilization, I ask my hosts about the half-remembered story of the Japanese consul and whether we might try to find the actual chancery that he occupied in 1939–1940. With the help of a local Jew we find the building on a small street, a few blocks from the city center. The facade was virtually unchanged from what I remembered from the famous photograph—a wrought-iron fence leading to a curved stucco staircase with large windows on each floor.

That story is deceptively simple. Nearly eighty-seven years to the date after Commodore Matthew Perry forced Japan open to the West, Chiune Sugihara opened the curtain of the front window of the Japanese consulate in Kaunas, Lithuania. On that July 1940 morning, the diplomat from the backwaters of Japan, where young men still dreamed of being samurais, saw a large group of Jews pushing against the gate of the consulate, clamoring to get in.

It was a scene that hundreds of diplomats during those years in countries threatened or actually occupied by the Nazis would witness. Such Jewish scavenger hunts for visas were plausible behavior during at least the first eight of the twelve years of Hitler's rule. In that period the Nazis were satisfied to realize their vision of Judenrein, a world cleansed of Jews, by the departure of Jews from Europe through emigration as much as through the smokestacks of an Auschwitz. There are a very few examples of officials who became rescuers such as the justifiably well-known Swedish diplomat, Raoul Wallenberg, who was sent to Hungary specifically to rescue Jews. But Sugihara's response was unique.

Sugihara had little time to be diplomatic to anyone given the political turmoil in Lithuania, the entrance of Soviet troops followed by their dreaded security forces, and the orders that he was receiving from his government to close the consulate immediately and to move to the Nazi capital. He agonized, he analyzed, he acted. Sugihara spent the next twenty days and nights issuing visas to the growing rag-tag assemblage encamped on his door-step. He soon ran out of official forms and wrote the visas by hand. For some Jews he made his inscriptions on official travel documents, for others he scribbled on scraps of paper.

When on August 31 he was finally forced to leave town by the Soviets, who now annexed Lithuania and no longer recognized foreign diplomatic legations, he continued to issue these life-saving documents even from the window of the train waiting to depart to Berlin. He recorded 2,139 visas in Kaunas though many were to heads of household for several family members. He issued more visas in Prague, one of his subsequent posts. Perhaps as many as 10,000 people received visas from Sugihara; there is no way of knowing how many were actually able to use this document to make good an escape.

Standing in front of the former consulate, I imagine the elusive Sugihara. His indefatigable hand is scribbling his life-saving bureaucratic formulae on scraps of paper. As the image comes into focus I conjure up another hand, the hand of the infamous Mengele, Nazi doctor, murderous bureaucrat of Auschwitz, soon to be moving with the same precision and grace at the entry of the concentration camp, sorting out Jews between immediate and attenuated dying. And behind him I see the hands of the millions of Nazi desk murderers, mere cogs on that big and efficient wheel of mass destructiveness. A loose cog can bring the wheel to a grinding halt but these bureaucrats are experts at fragmenting responsibility, scheduling and allocating, signing and sealing the fate of others. I stand there transfixed in the minus-twenty-degree weather— Centigrade or Fahrenheit, at that temperature, it hardly seems to matter. "Standing on the site where a miracle occurred to our ancestors," the rabbis of the Talmud urge, "one must make a blessing." What blessing does one make, I wonder, on a Japanese bureaucrat?

Defrosting back in Boston, the image of Sugihara resists being refiled in long-term memory. Some cursory searches turn up a footnote here, a paragraph there, his rescue activities told as a tale of adventure more than of edification. But nothing provides me with insight into the man or his background and motives, the act, its context and implications. I busy myself in routine but begin to realize what effort it is taking not to think of Sugihara. A fax to friends in Kyoto asks them if they know anything about Sugihara. This yields an immediate response from a T. Shino of Tokyo who indicates that he has written a book on Sugihara and that he would welcome me to Japan and assist me in making my own inquiry. I do not know what to make of Shino's flattering presumption that I could understand anything in particular in the life of a man, so separated from me by temporal and cultural gaps. Moreover, how do I understand the aggressive friendliness of the expert on Sugihara who seems to welcome my competition?

I begin to ask questions about Sugihara that I believe will lead me to motives. I wonder about little Sugihara and his parents, the schoolboy

Sugihara on the playground, the young man Sugihara and his first romance. I dust off copies of the books of my old teacher Erik Erikson, the psychoanalyst and psychohistorian who made the "identity crisis" as common and predictable as the measles for at least my generation of Americans. Can I understand what made this guy tick in the way that Erikson understood Luther and Gandhi? Having spent the better part of the last decade analyzing structures of the Polish vodka industry two hundred years ago and structures of Boston real estate twenty years ago, I begin to wonder whether I would recognize a motive even if I saw one.

Motives, I begin to realize, must be more than Pavlovian responses prompted by a bit of thinking rather than some bells. And often that thinking is obscure, even banal, for the actor and all the more so for the observer. We have profiles of mass murderers who shoot with wild abandon into playgrounds and shopping malls. But what do we know about impulsive rescuers? Who was this trained-to-be-obedient official from the provinces where Perry's door opening to the West had so little impact? And why did Sugihara consciously and with full awareness of the most dire consequences for himself and family take the risks that he did to help some Jews for whom a person from his background would likely have had no strong feelings, one way or another? Was Sugihara's incessant scribbling and waving of the hand during the summer of 1940 a spontaneous and unique manifestation of compassion, a singular example of independent thinking, self-assertion, rule-breaking, and disobedience to authority or can we identify previews to the act and patterns over the years? What do we learn from Sugihara about "rescuers" and the "altruistic personality," two areas that a few social scientists and researchers of the Holocaust, desperately in search of the "good news," have recently begun to explore?

A few days and round-trip faxes later an express package arrives from Japan with a copy of Shino's book, bound in red and yellow with the by now familiar reproduction of Sugihara's visa. The considerate Shino has prepared a wooden translation of his book into English. Attached to it is a business card, "T. Shino, technical advisor." So, this most likable and energetic Shino is, after all, himself a salaryman writing books on the side. In fact, as the modest, forty-three-year-old civil engineer subsequently explains to me, he is an international consultant on mud. He plans the construction of tunnels, subways, and sewer systems in relation to surrounding soil conditions. I remember the Vilna ghetto fighter and his underground activities.

A particular detail in Shino's book catches my attention: the young man Sugihara studied and subsequently taught at the Japanese Russian

School in Harbin, living in that city from 1919–1935. "So, here," I thought, "here is the motive! Of course the young man from the rice fields of Yaotsu would save all of these Jews in Kaunas because he knew all of those Jews in Harbin." But in comparing Harbin in the years following World War I with other multiethnic enclaves that I have known I realize that Sugihara might have lived in Harbin for a good period of time without actually knowing any Jews. Moreover, contiguity does not necessarily lead to affection and by no means would explain why he risked his career and likely his life to save some Jews. Motives are far more complex and difficult to discover than smoking guns.

But information about his schooling, I begin to realize, might provide more important clues in regard to his personality and activities. Shino's passing reference to the Harbin education suggests another tack in pursuit of Sugihara. Alumni organizations are important in Japan, particularly to the functioning of "old buddy networks." If there is a Harbin Gakuin Association, it seems to me a good place to start in trying to collect impressions of the man at different stages of his life. A few weeks later I arrive in Tokyo and am welcomed by Shino. We greet each other like long lost friends. He combines qualities of Charlie Chan, the—by now, politically incorrect but sagacious—Asiatic Sherlock Holmes with those of Nahman of Bratzlav, the East European Hasidic master who struggled mightily against depression and poured his angst into uncanny and extraordinary tales that likely influenced Kafka.

By the distance, it should not have been more than a forty-five-minute drive from Nagoya to Sugihara's home town in the mountains to the west. But even in late morning after what the Japanese call "rush hour" in its untranslated form, it is a two-hour trek. The Mayor of Yaotsu, having heard of my interest in Sugihara and my visit, planned a reception, a tour of the town and a luncheon. Following the ceremonial exchange of business cards with the Mayor's assistants whose cards bear laminated photos of the Sugihara monument, I perceive some stirrings. In misdirected faxes over the past weeks, the Mayor's office has been trying to ascertain whether the honored guest would prefer bread or rice with his lunch. This now had to be resolved. That the menu would include steak, thought more appropriate for visitors of a certain status rather than the more usual and simpler Japanese diet of noodles, was not left to my decision. Three quarters of a century after the young man Sugihara opted for a cosmopolitan existence, "ours" and "theirs," Japanese and foreign are still laden with explosive meaning, hard to comprehend for those of us accustomed to walking out of our offices and homes on any day and finding within a sphere of five blocks a global variety of foreign eateries.

Both Sugihara's father and mother descended from local clans, his father marrying "up" when he betrothed the daughter of a land owner. His father, somewhat distant, even tyrannical, was an Imperial tax collector in town until around 1910 when he joined the Japanese colonial administration of Korea. The young Sugihara was left behind in a boarding school joining his family after he graduated high school. I latch on to every unconnected bit of information about how the father went to movies and sometimes wore western clothing, uncharacteristic behavior for a proper civil servant. Aha, I think, so that's where the rule-breaking comes from. Sugihara adored his mother who died in Korea and was in protracted conflict with his father to the point that the old man disinherited him. Again, aha, we know what that is all about. Yet as my back pain from chairless sitting on the Yaotsu floor begins to increase, I feel less certain about the results of putting Sugihara on Dr. Freud's Viennese couch. If conflict with his father and issues of autonomy shed light on why Sugihara sought a lower cost education in Harbin rather than Tokyo, other obvious questions about his early years remain even more puzzling. For example, why does the young Sugihara, whose English was fluent enough after high school to provide the basis of a career, not only study Russian but become a Russophile? Who would a Japanese Russophile in the inter-war period be, culturally and politically, a modernizer or a traditionalist, Western oriented or a pan-Asia enthusiast? The cousin back in the hometown has not thought about these questions and no one has asked him about them.

Masami Tsuji, 85 years old, spry and lucid, is one of the oldest Harbin U. alums still around. He actually studied with Sugihara in the short period in the '20s between when Sugihara was himself a student and when he became a bureaucrat. I arrive in the Tsuji home, a few miles out of Kumamoto, the capital city of Japan's southern island, on a wet June morning. We sit in a Western-style livingroom but there are hints of its Eastern double behind a sliding partition. The dwarfed tree, lily pond, rock garden in the inner courtyard is of picture postcard or perhaps Japanese wall-hanging perfection, the rewards, I assume, of the devoted civil service career of a Harbin Gakuin graduate.

Mr. Tsuji is proud of his four years of study at the Gakuin, particularly of his half-year course with Professor Sugihara. Only a few years younger than Sugihara, Tsuji recalls how Sugihara was already a legend. Not only was Sugihara absolutely fluent in Russian, a daunting accomplishment for his students who were struggling with the strange sounds and irregular forms of that language. But Sugihara seemed to be able to dispense with that unique combination of shyness and arrogance that inhibited other young Japanese men. So many years later Tsuji is still full of admiration for his ease with the many Russians around town and in fact with everyone else in that cosmopolitan city.

Linguistic competence and diplomatic skills were an integral part of the educational goals at the Gakuin where Sugihara, Tsuji, and a generation of Japanese experts on the Soviet Union were trained. But it is only in speaking with several other fellow graduates of the Gakuin that I get a fuller picture of the environment and of the influences to which Sugihara was subjected. Masami Okitsu is now the chairman of FM-Nakakyushu Broadcasting Company, among other enterprises. He is flanked by male assistants and a retinue of uniformed office woman who bow upon entering and leaving. It makes for an unsentimental scene. Yet tears come to his eyes when he recalls his Harbin days. Foremost in his memory is the founder and director of the school, Shimpei Goto, who began his eclectic career as an old style Meiji bureaucrat, studied medicine in Germany, ran a hospital for many years, and was an administrator in Formosa, Korea, Manchuria. In 1906, he became the president of the South Manchurian Railroad. Goto, during his long periods abroad, picked up many of the ideas that animated student princes in the late nineteenth century. These include the idealism and mysticism of Tolstoy, which he formulated in the language of a civil service code spiced up with Japanese nationalism. This constituted what was in essence a Japanese version of manifest destiny, an ideology for colonialism sounding like the Boy Scout Code of Honor. At the same time, Goto translated into Japanese some of the German writings on biological racism that would excite the first generation of Nazis.

What Goto could not implement as a bureaucrat he tried to foster as an educator in the Harbin Gakuin that he established after World War I. Okitsu becomes particularly maudlin when he remembers the school code: (1) Do not be a burden to others; (2) Take care of others; (3) Do not expect rewards for your goodness. Goto also at this time encouraged close contact with Russians. The extent to which Sugihara worked with and was influenced by Goto is unclear. But their lives intersected at various points. Sugihara surely knew of his former headmaster's efforts as president of the South Manchurian Railroad and this must have encouraged him to work all the harder in 1935 to bring to a successful conclusion the protracted negotiations with the Soviets for the purchase of the northern extension. And stories that Okitsu and other Harbin alums recall about Sugihara sound like Tales of the Master Goto's teachings: during a flood in which Chinese residents of Japanese-controlled Manchuria suffered particularly heavy losses, Sugihara himself pulled on his boots and went out to survey the situation in the countryside and give the flood victims some encouragement rather than, in good bureaucratic form, sitting back at his desk and writing his report, sight unseen.

Yukiko Sugihara refuses to confine herself to the role of widow of the great man. She continues to do the traditional Japanese floral arrangement and write the poetry she did as a young girl. But in recent years, more of her time is taken with making sense for herself and, increasingly for others, of her life with Chiune Sugihara; that life, likely as a result of those days in Kovno, did not involve the security that she expected of an older man nor the "gorgeous life" that she thought that she would enjoy as the wife of a diplomat. Whether, at the critical moment she was indeed "listened to" is a point on which Mrs. Sugihara is hardly as clear as the price that she paid for her husband's rescue activities.

We arrive in Sugihara's last home in Kamakura, a bedroom community of Tokyo and Yokihama. The house has the feel of a shrunken version of the Levittown tract house and is of the same vintage. It saves some space by not having a Japanese double to its Western-style living room. In the corner is Sugihara's beloved piano. Family members still talk of the spirited renditions of Tchaikovsky that Sugihara would play. Mrs. Sugihara, too, remembers his fluent Russian. "When he spoke Russian, his eyes would grow large and his face would change."

The Sugiharas appeared dashing as a couple, however Japanese. But she is a bit less clear as to how Japanese they were as a couple in other matters. She describes her husband as typically Japanese as far as husbands go—strong-minded, noncommunicative, and somewhat authoritarian. At the same time, she portrays herself as the "Great woman" to the side of the "Great man," a full participant in the perilous decision. Leaving her after two meetings and many hours of discussion, the motives of the voiceless rescuer still remain elusive.

Writing in the '60s, he speaks of being motivated by "a sense of human justice and love for mankind." Without self-deprecation and without self-aggrandizement, his words would make misty the eyes of any graduate of the Harbin Gakuin who would be reminded of the somewhat banal teachings of headmaster Goto about taking care of others and not expecting rewards for one's goodness.

It is a commonplace to note that Japan is a troubled place these days. As Kazuo Ogura, former director general of cultural affairs at the Japanese Foreign Ministry, puts it

The postwar Japanese way of life seems to have reached a dead end. . . . the esteem of the international community cannot be won by holding aloft our war-renouncing Constitution. . . . Nonetheless, in the depths of the Japanese psyche resides a national aspiration, vague though it is to gain an honorable status in the international community for Japan and its people. The question is how a nation can achieve such a status when its people lack an intense dedication to ideals and when their patriotism does not inspire self-sacrificing ardor. Unable to answer this question, the Japanese have begun to despair.

An increasing number of Sugihara's countrymen, like Ikiru before them, are becoming reflective about their own lives. They confront painful aspects of Japan's past and the inadequacies of its current situation. For them, memorializing Sugihara may have special meaning. In the land of the Kamikaze, suicidal commitment is not easily channeled into civic duty; the society that idealized suicide and other dramatic displays of fault stubbornly resists accepting moral responsibility, dickering about what Japan did in Nanjing or with the Korean "comfort women," or who started the Japanese-U.S. side of World War II. The smiling and slightly exuberant Sugihara, the wise rule-breaker, the bureaucrat-as-rescuer, this Japanese version of Zorba the Greek, will not provide a compelling teaching for which Japanese citizens should gladly give their lives nor with a coherent set of principles which they might spread around the world. Neither will this "bright light," shining in the days of Japanese militarism and aggressiveness, necessarily ensure for the Japanese the respect and love of others that they so much desire and feel they deserve after this time, playing and winning by the rules. But his simple "sense of human justice and love of mankind" is certainly not a bad place to start.

The Sugihara who I have been pursuing and who I finally discover in his long-sought-after own words is human, all too human, more likable than I might have expected. He is warmer and more vulnerable than the Sugihara sculpted in bronze on the windswept Yaotsu mountain top. He presents himself neither as hero nor as martyr, unlike the taller-than-life image projected by those busily at work writing the legend. Sugihara's ordinariness is, perhaps, what is so extraordinary about this story. In illustrating for us how a common person can perpetrate a most uncommon act, he empowers us all as he challenges us to greater responsiveness and responsibility.

10

Genocide, Victimization, and America's Inner Cities

Charles Green

Genocide, the darkest hour for all of humanity, is no stranger to these American shores. Yet even in the present atmosphere of multi-cultural education and the preoccupation with political correctness, one continues to find resistance to dealing with this human enigma. Resistance flows from historic racism and the way genocide is defined and conceptualized in American society.

Because genocide is limited to the willful attempt through violent means by one group to eliminate another racial, political, or cultural group, variants of this phenomenon tend not to be fully appreciated. One such variant of genocide that will be considered in this essay is the social and psychological oppression of a subordinate group by a dominant group that leads to the former's dysfunctional state. This is evidenced in terms of the subordinate group members' persistent social and economic inequality, feelings of frustration, hopelessness, and powerlessness.

More and more Americans now accept that the violence waged against Native Americans, including their subsequent confinement on reservations, was genocidal.[1] Earlier in this century some voices were raised denouncing the near elimination of Armenian people by the Turks, and later the Jewish Holocaust at the hands of the Nazis in Germany. More recently the scourge of ethnic cleansing in Rwanda between the Tutsis and the Hutus and in the former Yugoslavia has forced the outcry of American citizens. What the experiences of these groups represent for many Americans is tangible evidence of human invasion and violation. They were targeted, demonized, and set upon for annihilation.

But the plight of African Americans, past and present, has been excluded from the general discourse on genocide in the United States. This essay extends the genocidal discourse to include the plight of dis-

111

proportionate numbers of poor and working-class African Americans who are racially segregated in urban ghettos across the United States. I will argue that, notwithstanding the horrors of enslavement and overt forms of racism, conditions such as the drug subculture, unemployment, and urban decay constitute the newest form of genocide against a historically subjugated people on the basis of race. One important consequence of this is numbing,[2] which is politically constructed to infer deepened feelings of powerlessness and political disillusionment by these urban masses in their marginalized social and economic status.

These conditions, which have been imposed on the Black community by the American capitalist state, are tantamount to genocide. They are responsible for the homicide, infant mortality, despair, and fear that presently define ghetto life. Inspired by the optimism that permeates much of Lifton's work, this essay concludes with a few policy options that might be considered in order to stem this crisis.

Genocide Past and Present

Proponents of an African American genocide were most vociferous during the 1920s and the mid 1960s. The cultural nationalist, Marcus Mosiah Garvey and his mass-based organization, The Universal Negro Improvement Association (UNIA), perceived the tide of virulent racism and the lynching of Black people in the 1920s as clear and disentangled evidence of a people under siege and therefore, sufficient cause for their repatriation with the motherland, Africa. Garvey's movement was the largest grassroots movement of Black people in this country and had roots in the Caribbean and Europe. Alongside the building of cultural awareness and pride, the movement's other mission was to raise funds to construct ships to transport diasporic Blacks back home.

The period of Black militancy and radical nationalism of the mid-1960s gave rise to the Black Panther Party (BPP). The BPP was unflinching in its position that a "Declaration of War" had been called against Black people by the white power structure in America with the single objective to eliminate the race. Files on the Federal Bureau of Investigation's counterintelligence program, COINTELPRO, made possible through the Freedom of Information Act after the Party's demise, confirmed the Party's allegations of systemic infiltration of the organization. The operation, which was choreographed by Bureau Chief J. Edgar Hoover, was set up to disrupt and dismantle organizations believed to be subversive and a threat to national security. Although the BPP was at the top of the FBI's hit list, other Black and non-Black groups were targeted, such as The Student Non-Violent Coordinating Committee, the Republic of New Africa, Students For Democratic Society, and the Weather Underground movement. Addictive, destructive drugs like heroine and cocaine are alleged to have been introduced into the Black community as part of the COINTELPRO operation. The government-led movement to eliminate the BPP inspired other agents of law enforcement to pursue Party members with lethal force and unflinching brutality. An incident that vividly portrays the genocidal intent of this operation and supports the Panther Party's claims was the infamous Chicago raid of 1969.

> On December 4, 1969, fourteen Chicago policemen raided the BPP headquarters carrying with them a warrant authorizing a search for illegal weapons. In the ensuing "gun battle," the police fired between eighty and one hundred times, killing Mark Clark and Fred Hampton, and injuring four other persons in the apartment. The official claim was that only one bullet was fired from a weapon belonging to one of the apartment occupants. In a lawsuit years later, it was proven that the bullet holes in the door were faked, evidence that the authorities had tried to cover up the facts of the raid.[3]

During the period of enslavement, millions of Blacks died on the long voyage across the Atlantic. In bondage, they became the property of their masters and were treated accordingly. They were denied their African cultural heritage, human rights, literacy, and were subjected to fierce beatings or death for running away or if charged with sedition. Emancipation in 1863 physically freed former slaves, but it would take time before their social and psychological shackles were broken.

The period of Reconstruction that lasted approximately one decade after the close of the Civil War increased the prospects for Black upliftment and inclusion in what Benjamin Ringer[4] refers to as the People's Domain. It was a period that witnessed significant gains in Black advancement in the political and educational spheres. But this twist of fate for Black people, needless to say, precipitated a thunderous white backlash. "Nigger hunts" as they were called, were regularly undertaken in which freed slaves were sought out and put to death. Between 1889 and 1899, over 1,800 lynchings were reported, but the actual number was higher since many lynchings went unrecorded.[5] During the next seventy years the NAACP would record over 5,000 known cases of lynching[6]. This system of terrorism was carried out by right-wing groups like the Ku Klux Klan and Citizens Councils whose interest it was to keep Blacks in their place and forever subjugated.

In the 1920s lynching was very much on the minds of Blacks in the South and in the North. Blacks were struck a devastating blow in the 1930s when the politically cautious hand of the liberal-Democratic President, Franklin D. Roosevelt, could not be swayed to sign into law an anti-lynching bill.

The landmark Supreme Court decision in the Brown case in 1954 that inspired the Civil Rights Act of 1964 interrupted, temporarily, the white crusade to keep Blacks subordinated. As the War on Poverty and the Great Society of the Johnson administration demonstrated, efforts to empower poor Blacks through the policy of "maximum feasible participation" was staunchly rejected in the Deep South. What comes to mind is the Office of Economic Opportunity's Head Start Program that was set up to assist poor pre-school-age children of all races procure academic enrichment at an early age. In the Mississippi Delta region, one of the nation's poorest counties, white racists rejected the idea that federal funds were being used to uplift little Black children. Fueled by the Mississippi Democrat and racist, Sen. James O. Eastland, they also objected to the use of these funds to create an atmosphere where parents could directly engage in the day-to-day educational activities of their children and secure jobs as teacher aides at wages that competed with those of white Mississippians. Head Start school sites were disrupted by the racists and there were frequent bomb threats. However, white resistance was not restricted to the south. In New York City, for example, where whites had controlled municipal services and human service programs that directly impacted the poor, the Black community's quest for greater involvement in services that affected them, as a result of the maximum feasible participation mandate, caused many whites to become uneasy.[7]

A controversial work to emerge in 1978 that sought to put into perspective the new racial order and the implications for African Americans was William J. Wilson's, *The Declining Significance of Race*. To Wilson's chagrin, his thesis was openly supported by racists and conservatives whose impatience with those who sought to equate the African American plight to the suffering of other groups had already been established.

While Wilson did not negate the fact of racism, he argued that virulent racism and the racial conflicts that had previously defined the social and material opportunities of Blacks in the job market were rapidly receding. Therefore, racism could no longer be used as a viable explanation for the lagging social and economic condition of the Black community. He believed that the attention of community leaders and policy makers should be directed instead to the urban areas where deepening class divisions were now concentrated.

Wilson's discussion of race and class set the stage for his follow-up study in 1987, *The Truly Disadvantaged*, in which the condition of the Black underclass[8] was formally addressed. What is most important about the idea of an underclass is how it connects to the genocidal oppression of Blacks. Since the issue was not race but class, it became a convenient rationale for the outright disregard of Black suffering. No longer to be viewed as the unfortunate victims of racism, Blacks' underproductiveness could only be explained in terms of laziness or as predatory. According to Wright and Devine,[9] the indifference of the "urban underclass" to the values, sanctions, and laws that dictate the behaviors of the rest of society has come to be perceived as irretrievably out of control. Framed in this manner, repression, containment, and ultimately the extinction of the people from the "dark ghetto" through the use of force by the state but also by law-abiding citizens loom as the only apparent alternatives. From the perspective of the racists, the fact that Wilson and other celebrated scholars such as Shelby Steele, Thomas Sowell, and Glen Loury who support the class analysis are Black not only sanctions but strengthens their position in the national debate.

We should return to the question that brought us to this point. Is the present condition of inner-city Blacks the result of a conspiratorial plot by the dominant white society to eliminate the race? Or is it more the case of a people who, due to their own misgivings and personal deficiencies, 133 years postemancipation, have not been able to master the skills needed to improve their lot? Eugenics and Social Darwinism have flourished throughout this century to affirm the latter question and are quintessential to the racists' arsenal of stereotypes and exclusionary practices. Like the mythological head of Cyclops, every time these theories are struck down in time they resurface. Thus another work authored by two prominent conservative thinkers, the late Robert Herrnstein and Charles Murray, *The Bell Curve*, is satisfying the appetites of racists and even some neo-liberals with spurious arguments about the relationship between intelligence, race, and societal functioning.

In the new information age, knowledge is increasingly becoming the essential conduit to the superhighway of highly specialized and technical positions. For sure, other service-sector jobs (at low- to mid-range wages) will prevail, but the supply of these jobs will diminish. The central question to be answered in the midst of this latest social and economic transition is what will be the fate of individuals who lack the required knowledge and preparation to enter the superhighway? Furthermore, if the supply of general service-sector positions will decrease and manufacturing and industrial jobs (requiring fewer skills) will continue their pattern of relocation outside the United States where wages are cheaper, what are the alternatives for those who are left outside? It is at this critical juncture that a *Bell Curve*, eugenics, and social Darwinist theories enter. They offer the rationale for the policies of neglect and abandonment of persons who fail to measure up to present standards. Neglect is observed in the form of under-funding or no funding for job training and retraining programs, dysfunctional inner-city school districts, and the renewed assault on federal, state, and locally funded human and social support services. Neglect in this instance is tantamount to the outright rejection of a people. While it can be correctly argued that policies of neglect impact all poor and working-class people alike, it can also be argued that Blacks, particularly those segregated in the urban ghettos, are disproportionately affected.

Let us consider some of the conditions that define the present Black plight. At no time in history—with the exception of the epoch of chattel slavery when they were fully engaged in southern agriculture or as household servants—has Black labor levels paralleled that of whites. To pose it somewhat differently, unemployment, which is a function of the American capitalist system and has afflicted all groups, has been unjustly foisted on the Black community. Job loss in the inner cities has taken place in stages. These centers, which were once the hub of industry and manufacturing for the nation, have been declining since the 1950s. It was the industrial factory that provided the means for mobility for unskilled nineteenth-century European immigrants and their descendants. They filled the demand for industrial jobs that required mostly entry-level skills. There was, however, a ready supply of Black labor that lay idle in the southern region of the country but due to naked racism they were bypassed in favor of white immigrants. Their turn to occupy industrial jobs and real wages would not arrive until World War I, when the United States' industrial complex was threatened by the temporary halt of European workers.

But the globalization of capital that paved the way for the postindustrial age of service and information activities also created the conditions for the flight by industrial and manufacturing operations from their traditional centres to the southern region of the United States and the Third World where labor costs were cheaper. This was concomitant with the suburbanization movement that inspired the flight by White and Black middle-class persons out of the cities and the in-migration of poor and working-class southern Blacks and newer immigrants.

The role of the federal government in the process of suburbanization and the subsequent growth of the Black ghettos should not be misrepresented. The Federal Housing Administration (FHA), for example, subsidized mortgages that made it possible for many urban whites to make the suburban leap. The highway and roads construction firms and the automobile industry that were vital to the rise of suburbs were also supported by the federal government. But while the suburbs were flowering and construction firms and oil companies feasted on the federal largesse, the urban areas and their newest residents were forgotten.[10] These demographic changes ultimately led to a reduction of the tax base for the inner-city areas, and their social and physical infrastructures began to crumble. By the late 1970s to the early 1980s when severe international recession occurred, we were suddenly faced with an inner-city cauldron that quickly moved to center stage of the national public policy debate. Several studies appeared including Roger Starr's *The Rise and Fall of New York City* and Ken Auletta's *The Underclass* that victimized the masses for their plight while exonerating their oppressors.

What is most upsetting about these and similar studies and is precisely the point that I wish to argue in this essay is that by blaming the victims while exonerating their oppressors, the irresponsibility of capital and the process of abandonment that have created the void of economic opportunity for Blacks in the urban districts are conveniently eschewed. Blacks' resistance to their condition has encountered self-destruction, a response that the media has sensationalized and feeds to the American public on a daily basis. Because the situation is seen as originating with the community and not structural, the disruptive forces that penetrate the ghetto, like drugs and guns, and the force used by police authorities to contain the resisting urban masses, have crippled the genocidal thesis.

Alex Kotlewitz's[11] ethnographic study *There Are No Children Here* describes the living environment in a Chicago, Illinois, housing project which is over 90 percent Black. He describes a blighted neighborhood where fast-food outlets, car washes, run-down convenience stores, and vacant buildings and lots define the landscape. There are no banks (just check-cashing outlets for welfare checks), no public libraries, cinemas, or bowling alleys. The two area hospitals lie on the edge of bankruptcy and the infant mortality rate exceeds that of many Third World countries. The physical infrastructure as well as the day to day violence give it the appearance of a "war zone." This description could very well fit Mike Davis'[12] description of Compton, California, located one mile south of Watts and Central Los Angeles, or perhaps one of Newark, New Jersey's most troubled wards. In other words, Kotlewitz's description provides a snapshot of the national dilemma.

In this environment where familial structures have become weakened, parents have lost control over their children. Common is the single-headed household where the head is predictably a poor female on AFDC or a working-class woman struggling to make ends meet for herself and her children. The church, an icon in the Black community, has not, with few exceptions, been successful in reaching many of these needy souls. The pews on Sunday at many Black churches are not filled with the idle, unemployed, adult males who are visible on the street corners, the despondent youth, or gang members. Instead, they tend to be occupied by women and senior citizens who in most cases no longer reside in the immediate community.[13] However, it would be unfair to imply that the church is not vigilant in its efforts to reach out to this population. The schools have now become part of the problem and, as Jonathan Kozol instructs, are the purveyors of savage inequalities. It is no wonder, in light of these declining institutional bases, that the streets have become the only reliable outlet for so many young people.

Frustration and the sense of hopelessness borne out of these circumstances are incendiary devices that have exploded in urban rebellion. We will recall the spate of rebellions of the 1960s beginning with Watts in August, 1965 and in 1968 following the King assassination. There are observed differences, however, in outcome between these earlier protests and the rebellions that occurred in the inner-city ghettos of Miami in the 1980s and 1990s or the uprising in Central Los Angeles in the spring of 1992. In 1965, the state was able to encourage capital to support, temporarily at least, the Great Society, which funneled generous amounts of resources to the rural and urban poor through its administrative bureaucracy, the Office of Economic Opportunity. A number of poverty combative programs were introduced at that time, including the Community Action Projects (CAP), that sought to transfer greater responsibility for defining needs and solutions to problems to poor people themselves. At the present juncture, capital is more constrained and parsimonious. It is less sympathetic to the suffering from below and is yet to be convinced of its responsibility to citizens at home. Thus, the process of reconstruction in the aftermath of the 1992 Los Angeles rebellion has been a slow process. Not only was the rebellion televised via CNN, the viewing public was ostensibly less sympathetic to these newer rebels or the conditions that hold them hostage. The message from the new conservative Republican majority in both houses of Congress is antithetical to the liberal platform of the past. Their Contract With America[14] appeals to Americans' high morals, hard work, law and order, and the assumption of responsibility for one's behavior as the only hope for a stronger nation and a brighter future. Most important is the limited role it prescribes for government in the lives and day-to-day suffering of citizens.

Alongside frustration and hopelessness it is important to address the fear of violence and bodily injury that inner-city ghetto residents have been forced to endure. This is true of very young children, adolescents, parents, and senior citizens. They may have different experiences regarding fear but what joins them is their preoccupation with coping with fear. Homicide we learn is the chief cause of death for inner-city Blacks and that Black youth (males most commonly) are six times more likely to become homicide victims than their white counterparts. Too, in the United States nearly one million teens are victims of violent crimes each year and the number of teens and young children killed annually by firearms has surpassed the adult population.[15]

It is always moving to hear of the entrapment of the very young who too frequently are the victims of stray bullets intended for a third party. Ironically, James Darby, a nine-year-old boy from one of New Orleans' toughest neighborhoods had written a letter to President Clinton in April 1994 for his assistance to stop the shooting and killing in his neighborhood. His fear was apparent in that letter:

> I think that somebody might kill me.
> I'm asking you nicely to stop it.
> I know you can do it.[16]

Nine days later, walking home from a Mother's Day picnic with his mother, James Darby was shot in the head and killed. He was the victim of a stray bullet shot into a crowd that was intended for someone else.

In his study of the lifestyles of inner-city youth, sociologist Kwando Kinshasa[17] cites several sources that compare the fear that so many young people internalize to the battle fatigue and shell shock that soldiers in combat have been known to exhibit. Their fears are triggered not solely by revelation but frequently through witnessing violent episodes in the streets and elsewhere. Several medical personnel from Washington, D.C., a crime-ridden city, have observed among their young patient-victims' symptoms such as uncontrollable crying, extreme suspiciousness, fatalism, and impulsiveness.

Fear and the Numbing Effect

From his interviews with survivors of the Hiroshima bomb, Robert Jay Lifton identified their deep and incapacitating psychological trauma.

The fear of another nuclear attack was long lasting. In applying the notion of "psychic numbing" as the essential experience of victimization, he surmised that it served as a protective device that enabled the individual to shut self out from everyday life. Interviews with persons living in the nuclear age revealed this tendency as well. Many Americans avoided any discussion about nuclear weapons on their soil and their effect.[18] A central theme in numbing concerns the idea of security, or what Lifton considers the "ultimate pyschologism." In the nuclear age, everyone is vulnerable.[19] Such a threat, however, is antithetical to the idea of a safe and protected environment that many Americans have come to believe in and anticipate.[20] Thus, the only way to sustain this belief, at least for some people, was to block out from view any conflicting and contradicting forces. In the case of many inner-city youths, numbing appears to be associated with other behavioral responses, such as the blatant disregard for life and limb, stoicism, and the inability to engage in warm, caring relationships.

Another consequence of numbing concerns the retreat from electoral politics. Mobilizing inner-city Blacks has become a formidable task, as many are unable to perceive politics as a means to improving their chances for survival and a better life.[21] The prevailing ethos is one of acute self-interest. What really matters is day-to-day survival and looking out for one's "back." That is the politics of the ghetto. Numbing has rendered many residents politically disengaged.

The parallel between Lifton's findings about fear of a nuclear holocaust and the fear experienced by contemporary ghetto residents in the United States is remarkable. The response to violence in both cases is what triggers the numbing. The ultimate psychologism that Lifton addresses is unattainable for either cohort of victims, since vulnerability is universal. In a nuclear war no one survives. In the inner-city ghetto, stray bullets are nondiscriminating and anyone can become the target of gang violence and street crime. In both cases, fear replaces security and the sense of environmental structure.

Conclusion

The greatest challenge facing progressive persons seeking change will be to alter the mindset of average Americans about inner-city life and its residents. That will entail assisting them to reconstruct their thinking from the present position of blaming victims to the development of a clearer understanding about the source of the problem. In that way they may become more aware of the varied forms of victimization.

For inner-city residents, the menace is the draconian U.S. political economy that has historically functioned outside their interest. In one era it was responsible for their enslavement. In the present period, it is responsible for their chronic unemployment, blighted neighborhoods, inadequate housing, and dysfunctional schools. Guns and drugs, the tools of violence, may thrive in ghetto areas but they are neither created nor manufactured there. Probably the most serious crisis of all is that many of these victims have begun to internalize their suffering through the process we have alluded to as numbing.

As dismal as it may appear, the unnumbing of inner-city residents, the return to safe and secure communities with healthy and happy children in economically thriving families (whatever their structure) are all possible as we prepare to enter the next millennium. No, it will not be the initiative of the new Republican majority, nor will it emanate from the neo-liberals in the Democratic Party. It will result from the resolve of progressive people of all races to mobilize with residents in building a mass movement for change. It will require the same momentum that was responsible for bringing the world's superpowers to the table to discuss a nuclear freeze and the long-term goal of a nuclear nonproliferation treaty.

The movement for change must build on the theme of commonality. People outside the inner cities must come to realize that their survival is inextricably linked to the conditions of those in the trenches. As long as a significant sector of the population is left outside the system, it will remain a case of bitter sweet for the fortunate few. Working towards a fully employed society at livable wages will be an important starting point. It would be impossible to lay out a precise policy in the limited space of this essay but we must recognize that to discuss an employment policy without also entertaining the need for permanent job training and retraining programs that would ensure a sustained labor force is an exercise in futility. Full employment must be accompanied by a fairer distribution of wealth through progressive taxation and the commitment to nonracial politics that will strengthen communities, not destroy them.

In conclusion, to call for a redefinition of genocide that would include the present predicament of inner-city Blacks is to recognize two very important points. First, that the scars of victimization, whether they result from nuclear catastrophe, ethnic cleansing, or the trauma of ghetto life, are remarkably similar. Second, if a group is successful in

winning the support and sympathy of outsiders on the basis of its victimization, the group's prospects for acceptance in that society will be enhanced.

The history of racism in America has effectively operated to mitigate
the latter point in the case of Black people. Affirmative-action policy,
which from the date of implementation has sat at the edge of its death
bed, is an excellent example of white America's resistance to accept its
role in the historical Black plight and its responsibility to help correct
it. The policy is attacked not solely because the critics allege that it is
tantamount to reverse discrimination, but because it upholds Blacks'
claims about their past and present victimization.

When white Americans come to realize that the search for their own
humanity is inextricably linked to the treatment of victims oppressed on
American soil, maybe then the tide will begin to turn for one of this
nation's oldest racially oppressed groups.

Notes

1. Numerous scholarly works have analyzed the treatment of Native Ameri-
cans, however, I am inspired by Howard Zinn, *A People's History of the United States*
(New York: HarperCollins, 1990); Stephen Steinberg, *The Ethnic Myth* (Boston,
MA.: Beacon, 1989); and Benjamin B. Ringer, *We The People and Others* (New
York: Tavistock Press, 1983).

2. When Robert J. Lifton delivered the keynote address at a faculty-spon-
sored forum on nuclear issues at Hunter College in 1982, the rhetoric of the
Cold War era was not to be taken lightly. Thirteen years later I am still moved
by that talk and Lifton's insightful application of the notion of "pyschic numbing" to the haunting prospect of global genocide via nuclear warfare.

3. Rhoda L. Blumberg, *Civil Rights: The 1960s Freedom Struggle* (Boston, MA.:
Twayne, 1984).

4. Benjamin Ringer, *We The People and Others: Duality and America's Treatment
of Its Racial Minorities.* (New York: Tavistock, 1983).

5. Anthony Giddens, *Sociology* (New York: W. W. Norton, 1991).

6. Frances F. Piven and Richard Cloward, *Poor People's Movements* (New York:
Vintage, 1979).

7. Frances F. Piven and Richard Cloward, *The Politics of Turmoil* (New York:
Vintage, 1972); Jonathan Rieder, *Canarsie: The Jews and Italians of Brooklyn against
Liberalism* (Cambridge, Mass.: Harvard University Press, 1985); Charles Green
and Basil Wilson, *The Struggle for Black Empowerment in New York City: Beyond the
Politics of Pigmentation* (New York: McGraw-Hill (paperback edition, 1992).

8. It should be noted that the term "underclass" has been dismissed by leading progressive scholars as just another victim-blaming ploy by the dominant

elite. See for example: Herbert Gans, "Deconstructing the Underclass," in Paula S. Rothenberg, ed., *Race, Class, & Gender In the United States* (New York: St. Martin's Press, 1992); Stephen Steinberg "The Underclass: A Case of Colorblindness," *New Politics* 1(1987): 42–60; Michael Katz, ed., *The Underclass Debate: A View from History* (Princeton, N.J.: Princeton University Press, 1993).

9. Joel A. Devine and James D. Wright, *The Greatest of Evils: Urban Poverty and the American Underclass* (Hawthorne, N.Y.: Aldine De Gruyter, 1993).

10. Loci Wacquant, "The Ghetto, the State, and the New Capitalist Economy," *Dissent* (Fall, 1989) 508–20.

11. Alex Kotlewitz, *There Are No Children Here* (New York: Anchor Books, 1991).

12. See Mike Davis, "The Sky Falls on Compton," *The Nation* (Sept. 19, 1994): 268–71).

13. For a discussion of the role of the Black church see Green and Wilson, *The Struggle for Black Empowerment in New York City*, Chapter 3.

14. The preferred phrase by CUNY historian Calvin B. Holder that I find uniquely appropriate is, "The Contract Un-America."

15. Bill Moyers, "There Is So Much We Can Do," *Parade Magazine* (Sunday, Jan. 8, 1995).

16. Ibid., 5.

17. Kwando Kinshasa, "Youth Culture and Violence as a Response to the Urban Environment: Crisis of Inner-City Bloods," in Charles Green, *Globalization and Survival in the Black Diaspora: The New Urban Challenge* (Albany: SUNY Press, 1996).

18. Robert Jay Lifton, "Beyond Psychic Numbing: A Call to Awareness," *American Journal of Orthopsychiatry* 52(1982) 619–29.

19. As long as there is one nuclear weapon on the face of the earth we should continue to talk about the nuclear age in the *present tense.*

20. Lifton, "Psychic Numbing," 623.

21. In this respect at least the urban poor are not unique. Poor voter turnout by the broader American electorate in recent years is an outward expression of the growing cynicism and disillusionment with electoral politics.

11

Meeting the Challenge of Genocide in Bosnia: Reconciling Moral Imperatives with Political Constraints

Richard Falk

Depicting the Challenge

Unquestionably, the epicenter of Robert Jay Lifton's influential and highly significant scholarly *oeuvre* is a preoccupation with genocide, and particularly with what he identifies as "the genocidal mentality." Whether it be the Holocaust itself or Hiroshima or nuclearism or the Vietnam War or even the Armenian ordeal in Turkey, Lifton's psycho-historical inquiries have exposed the main dimensions of the genocidal phenomenon, explaining how both its architects and perpetrators go about their bloody business and how a complicit population removes itself from real knowledge, and hence from any realization of its own interventionary responsibility. Lifton's most provocative and threatening, yet also most valuable, finding is the dual reality that those who commit genocide are not far removed from the rest of us and that all of us, by situation or drawing down a numbing curtain over feelings, are actual or potential culprits. In essence, Lifton's work imparts the disquieting news that there is a fearsome normalcy about genocide that makes efforts to portray its occurrence as abnormal deviance profoundly misleading, but worse, more easily evaded as a challenge to complacency.

Lifton's position is, of course, that a scholarly inquiry into the roots of genocide in human personality and social structure is indispensable for purposes of explanation, prevention, and opposition, and that a moralistic denunciation on its own is an empty gesture that obscures the pervasive and continuing threat of genocide to erupt almost anywhere on the societal landscape of humanity. For Lifton, quite obviously, his

125

studies of genocide are not at all intended to reconcile us to its occurrence, but quite the opposite. Lifton's abiding concern is to explicate evil in its most extreme forms, with the intention of identifying the menace and protecting as well as is possible against the shared human susceptibility to engage in genocidal behavior under certain conditions. Lifton believes strongly in human responsibility to avoid direct or indirect participation in genocide, and seeks to clarify the human responsibility to act against genocide whenever it presents itself in our world. To grasp Lifton's overall political message, then, is to acknowledge the pervasiveness of a genocidal threat, but simultaneously to insist on the ethical imperative of active resistance by all nonviolent means. It is important to realize that our engagement with genocide can often involve the unwillingness to confront its reality in our midst through the psychodynamics of denial, which Lifton associates with "numbing," a condition of passivity that is both deliberately induced to manage the citizenry and easily embraced by citizens to avoid the discomfort of deciding what to do about a genocidal challenge.

Given this background, then, it is hardly surprising that Lifton should have been so profoundly challenged during the past several years by the collapse of the Yugoslav state, and the ensuing ordeal of Bosnia. In the eloquent words he uses to introduce Zlatko Dizdarevic's *The Siege of Sarajevo*: "Genocide, by definition, is an ethical scandal. But the added scandal of Bosnia is the whole world's viewing genocide and doing no more than pretending to combat it." And later, "[w]e have betrayed both the Bosnians and our own more decent and responsible selves. More than that, in tolerating—and periodically facilitating—visible genocide, we have to a degree entered into a genocidal mentality" (p. 4) Indeed, Lifton contends that unlike Germany of the 1930s when the Nazis went to great lengths to hide their genocidal designs and behavior, with respect to Bosnia there has been "full knowledge of the genocide" as "nothing was hidden from us," thereby putting all of us in "a new category in our relation to genocide, that of informed bystanders." Although Lifton's preoccupation with the genocidal aspect of the Bosnian conflict is articulated in universalistic language, there is implicitly, at least, an intensifying rationale for response, given the civilizational locus in Europe, reminding us all of the pledge "never again!" made in various forms by representative civic voices in the liberal democracies, possibly as a partial atonement for the abject passivity of the West during the rise of Hitler and Naziism. Without this European locale of Bosnia, it is difficult to account for, or justify, the relative absence of concern about the more unambiguous recourse to genocide in Rwanda, and its possible imminence in Burundi, as well as such earlier genocidal episodes in Cambodia and East Timor.[1]

In avoidance of this unequivocally depraved complicity, Lifton observes that "[h]ere and there, Americans have been able to transmute their psychological confusion into a constructive stand for multilateral intervention in Bosnia." And somewhat more explicitly, even if now somewhat overtaken by the developments of the last two years, Lifton feels that it is "never too late to change course," which he explains to mean "remobilizing our world organization, and ourselves in serving it, and empowering it to make use of its own charter to intervene to stop the killing and establish conditions for democratic behavior and sustained peace" (p. 9). Lifton's call is essentially for intervention under the auspices of the United Nations of sufficient magnitude to stop the genocide. The political imperative occasioned by genocide, then, is to draw a bright line between official policies that merely "pretend" to respond but are not meant as a credible challenge to the genocidal project underway and, by contrast, what is called "constructive intervention," a coercive course of action that is intended to have a reasonable prospect of ending the genocide.

It seems appropriate to relate more personally at this point to Lifton's approach on these matters. I have over the years been deeply and variously instructed by Robert Lifton's theoretical and empirical work on genocide, including his strong appeal for responsive action based on conscience, historical memory, and species solidarity. But while fully subscribing to the framework of analysis I have had difficulty sharing the specific application of the approach to the actualities of choice in relation to Bosnia as this tragedy has unfolded. It is now my intention to explore here some of my reasons for taking a different path, not to reargue the case against "intervention," but to depict what must be done if genocide of the Bosnian sort is, indeed, to be effectively opposed.

This divergence from a close and trusted friend is anguishing, especially given a long previous experience of convergence. During the latter stages of the Vietnam War Robert Lifton and I were comrades in the civic struggle to end America's involvement in the quickest possible manner, with the least additional violence, death, and destruction. We were particularly appalled by the war's cumulative tendency to generate atrocities against Vietnamese civilians, and regarded that tendency as a direct consequence of ideas and doctrines that underpinned the American military effort in Vietnam.[2] In that setting we were united in our opposition to the American intervention in Vietnam, and called for its end, implementing that call by acts of civil resistance and expressions of solidarity with those who would not participate in the killing. In this regard, anti-interventionism united progressive opinion and activism throughout the Cold War era. And what has been striking, indeed ever since the Gulf War, is the extent to which interventionism in the period since the fall of the Berlin Wall has divided the moderate left. In passing, the Soviet collapse combined with the spread of a market-oriented ethos of political and economic development has caused widespread confusion and disarray in progressive ranks, and this condition indirectly informs and may help explain why the intervention debate within progressive circles has been so acrimonious and disappointingly inconclusive.

Is the core of this divergence factual (different readings of what is taking place on the ground, and who is responsible), hermeneutic (different readings of the overall situation), moral (different ethical assessments of the behavior), political (different views as to useful action), or some complex combination? I believe the essential disagreement relates mainly to the different ways that moral imperatives and prescribed political action are combined in practice by complementary yet distinct styles of thought in search of a proposed course of action. I believe the difference is between what I will label morally conditioned political advocacy and politically conditioned moral advocacy. In the former instance the mandate to act is derived directly from the severity of the suffering being inflicted, while in the latter the mandate to act is shaped by primary reliance on an interpretation of the mindset and probable orientation towards interventionary initiatives on the part of the main political actors upon whom one is forced to rely for implementation. Particularly crucial, here, has been how to evaluate the outlook and behavior of the U.S. Government, the United Nations, the main governments of Europe, and the various European regional actors (NATO, CSCE, WEU): in short, were these actors ever reasonably capable of mounting a morally conditioned constructive intervention against genocide in Bosnia?

It is the case that these governmental and inter-governmental actors are abstractions, not persons, and that the officials who shape the policy-forming climate are diverse and to varying degrees receptive to citizen pressures based on moral appeals, and further that in a democratic society, citizens should normally exhaust available channels of persuasion before writing off "the government" as unalterably opposed to the policy initiatives being urged, in this instance intervention to stop genocide. Let me further agree that civic encouragement for initiatives in mitigation of genocide, such as the securing of safe havens in Bosnia, was an entirely justifiable, politically plausible, humane, timely and constructive line of policy advocacy. But I am arguing that urging such a course of action was not equivalent to the sort of effort that would have been needed if genocide was to be challenged and stopped in Bosnia. In my view such an interventionary option was never seriously proposed in relation to the struggle going on in Bosnia. Regardless of subsequent events, it remains important for many reasons to understand why this was so. Such an understanding is indispensable if we are to commit ourselves to work for the ideological and institutional reforms that might yet make the twenty-first century unsafe for future practitioners of genocide.

Why Intervention to Prevent Genocide Was Never a Genuine Option for Bosnia

There is, inevitably, always an element of uncertainty in asserting what would have happened if this or that had been done in the past: What would the Bosnian Serbs have done if the gun emplacements surrounding Sarajevo had been bombed by NATO in 1993? or if the safe haven at Gorazde had been protected in March 1994? or if the arms embargo had been lifted or never imposed? It is my judgment that "shallow" intervention of this character would not have significantly altered Serb goals or behavior, nor would Serb resistance have probably led the UN, NATO, or major states to commit themselves to a deeper intervention of sufficient scale, but more likely, the reverse dynamic of withdrawal of any external presence would have ensued, and quite possibly in the context of an expanded war/genocide zone.[3]

The other kind of validation of my pessimism about a Bosnian intervention arises from the approach taken by the United Nations and other centers of international authority to humanitarian intervention in the same historical period: Somalia and Rwanda, in particular, but the wider and invariable pattern of shallow geopolitical response to severe challenges of a humanitarian character. This pattern discloses some willingness to act in a mitigating role, but not to take on the far more formidable task of political reconstruction in the face of likely entrenched, indigenous resistance. It is possible to contend that the 1994 US/UN intervention in Haiti undercuts this line of assured interpretation and, especially, raises from another angle the question as to whether Serb passivity would have followed upon a tougher UN/US/Europe stand on Bosnia early on in the conflict. My assumption here is that the Haiti intervention for various reasons did not provoke resistance, and therefore the shallowness of the commitment was never tested; given the general portrayal of the ultra-nationalist passions unleashed in Bosnia, as well as its enmeshment in intense historical recollections and in regional power rivalries, the prospect of Serb passivity of a comparable sort was virtually nonexistent.[4]

The image of sufficiency in relation to intervention in Bosnia needs to be derived from past occasions in which the persistence of genocide was successfully challenged: World War II liberating those surviving the death camps; Vietnam invading and occupying Cambodia, driving the Khmer Rouge from governmental control, back in 1979; and India, invading East Pakistan in 1971 and fostering the formation of the secessionist state of Bangladesh. In each instance the effort was massive, engaging the maximum energies of the intervening side, and in each case, emancipating the victim population was definitely *incidental* to the main interventionary goals having to do with the pursuit of strategic security interests. In other words, sufficient intervention, given the structure of world order and the mindset of political leaders is *always* interest-based, never values-driven. The tragedy of Bosnia, so conceived, was that its survival as a humanistic, multi-ethnic political entity was perceived as principally a matter of values, and only peripherally engaging interests, and then only diversely and ambiguously.[5]

There are several conclusions that emerge from this analysis of the challenge of genocide in Bosnia:

(1) External actors (both governmental and intergovernmental) did not perceive their interests to be seriously engaged in former Yugoslavia, and thus were never prepared to do more than engage in one or another variant of shallow intervention;

(2) The main realist rationale for even shallow intervention in Bosnia, aside from public relations requiring that "something" be done, was the early termination and, above all, the containment of the conflict, including the outflow of refugees, and not the prevention of genocide, or even the prevention of aggression;

(3) The humanitarian element in the unfolding diplomacy of shallow intervention was mainly a response to "the CNN factor," intended to minimize civilian suffering on route to a negotiated settlement that accepted as "fact" the results of "ethnic cleansing," and did not embody the view that genocidal policies must not be allowed to succeed or that the survival of secularism in former Yugoslavia was a strategic interest for Europe and the United States;

(4) Shallow intervention never appeared to have had any serious, credible prospect of altering Serbian goals or conduct in Bosnia, although Serb adjustments in timetable and tactics might have resulted from additional initiatives designed to challenge their project;

(5) Deeper intervention to prevent genocide and aggression would have required a major commitment of resources and occupying forces for a period of uncertain duration, which never became a possibility because of the absence of perceived strategic interests in relation to *these* goals;

(6) Challenging genocide by interventionary diplomacy is unlikely to occur, unless its occurrence is entwined in larger strategic interests, until political leaders and their main advisors are ideologically reoriented to regard moral, legal, and humanitarian concerns as integral to the pursuit of "national interests" in a globalized world order given the current conjuncture of forces in the world.

I would not seek to defend any further this assessment, which given uncertainties of facts and the unresolvable character "of what would have happened if" is necessarily contingent and conjectural. I would, however, refer to David Rieff's judgment that an appropriate intervention, given the nature of the conflict, "would have been neither cheap nor easy," and that to claim otherwise was to engage in "loose talk" inconsistent with the past history of interventionary diplomacy.[6]

Meeting the Challenge of Genocide in Bosnia and Elsewhere

If a sufficient intervention is not available, what is it that can be done to reduce the ambit of harm and to work toward the effective elimination of genocide from human experience? There are, then, two closely linked perspective: first, what can be done within current political space to go beyond the politics of gesture that has been fashioned so far by the main external political actors; secondly, what can reasonably be done ideologically and structurally to protect humanity against genocide in the future. In line with my orientation associated with politically conditioned moral advocacy I give emphasis to overcoming political obstacles that block the implementation of widely shared moral imperatives.[7] Also, each specific genocidal context presents its own problems and opportunities relevant for the formation of policy, making broad generalizations inappropriate. This section is written, then, in reaction to the circumstances presented by the Bosnian ordeal, although its implications are broader.

Democratic Empowerment

The politics of gesture in relation to Bosnia emphasized a mixture of humanitarian assistance for the civilian victims in Bosnia with a heavy diplomatic effort led by Western countries that was prepared to ratify most of the results of ethnic cleansing and to treat Serbian political and military leaders as the legitimate representatives of their people despite their role in committing severe violations of the laws of war and of the Genocide Convention. Such an approach is morally incoherent, yet it is reflective of the geopolitical priorities at stake, which are to produce a settlement that will end the violence, thereby avoiding any spillover into other parts of the Balkans, as well as to reduce pressures associated with large numbers of refugees. But it is not responsive to the essential challenge of genocide, either by way of prevention or accountability.

In this regard, transnational links with democratic anti-genocidal tendencies throughout former Yugoslavia, including among Serbs, could be of great importance in reshaping the dynamics of self-determination. Since intervention from without is unavailable, and even if available might be problematic, "intervention" from within and from below could shatter the reductive effect of treating rulers as legitimate leaders despite their criminality. Helsinki Citizens Assembly and the Campaign for Peace and Democracy have creatively been experimenting with this type of transnational civic diplomacy, drawing on the experience of the 1980s when West European and North American peace forces joined with dissidents in East Europe and the Soviet Union in support of indigenous movements for human rights and democracy that weakened governing elites, eroding their legitimacy, and even undermining their will to rule. The struggle against genocide needs to become part of the agenda of what is being called "cosmopolitan democracy," supplementing the role of states with the transnational association of citizens joined by normative commitments rather than by inter-governmental alliances seeking to promote collective state interests measured by reference to power, wealth, and influence.[8]

Criminal Accountability

It is also crucial to mobilize public opinion behind efforts to implement existing norms and procedures prohibiting genocide. The Security Council in Resolution 808 (Feb. 22, 1993), responding to pressures to act, authorized the establishment of a war crimes tribunal to address crimes associated with the wars in former Yugoslavia, later expanded to encompass the killing fields of Rwanda. It can be argued that such an initiative is ill-conceived, given the absence of other elements of an interventionary diplomacy, and tends to interfere with efforts to moderate the conflict through a negotiated settlement with the political forces in being.[9] Yet from the perspective of limiting the authority of the state and political movements to engage in genocidal violence the pedagogical and punitive potential of the war crimes approach is considerable, having already reinforced long dormant moves to establish a permanent international criminal court under UN auspices. Such an institutional innovation will not occur in a useful form unless it is promoted vigorously by transnational democratic forces as an essential ingredient of an emergent global civil society. In effect, although such a tribunal was established in an atmosphere of overall ambivalence, it can at this stage be used to document the horrors of genocide, providing that measure of solace to the peoples of Bosnia (and Rwanda), but also for strengthening an international consensus to take steps to create for the future an independent enforcement capability in relation to genocide that is autonomous, and not subject to the calculus of geopolitics.

Globalizing Citizenship

The relationship of individuals to governance remains primarily bounded by the limits of territorial sovereignty that pertain to their state. Yet the economic, political, and cultural matrix of human experience is essentially planetary in scope. At present, identity patterns are being reshaped in contradictory ways, moving toward the realities of globalization and affirming the particularities of religious and ethnic specificity, both tendencies withdrawing authority from the state as focus for identity, community, allegiance. With the intermingling of peoples on the planet it is especially important to oppose those exclusivist images of identity that underly genocidal impulses. It is not necessary from this perspective to support secularism, but it is necessary to conceive of citizenship and responsibilities as extending to the protection of all peoples from any concerted effort at their abuse, as measured by reference to legal standards that are widely accepted.

Such an ethos if extended to elites in governance structures would overcome the constricting impact of "realist" horizons that conceive of interests territorially and materially, and draw a sharp distinction between interests and values. Instead the mindset being proposed for the future would conceive of mutual tolerance among peoples as a primary global interest for the future and would help to close the gap between interests and values.

Conclusion

Whether even at this stage in mid-1995 the genocidal features of the Bosnian conflict can be challenged remains in some doubt. What is evident is that there is much to be learned by the failure of Europe, the United Nations, and the United States to do more to stop genocide. If international political life is to be better protected against genocide, transnational social forces will have to make a greater effort. Governments of liberal democracies and inter-governmental institutions can only be helpful in this effort if pushed hard from below; to rely on governmental actors to carry out an anti-genocide campaign, whether in Bosnia or in general, is to misunderstand the pattern of international relations over the course of the last 200 years.

Notes

1. Cf. Helen Fein, ed., "The Prevention of Genocide: Rwanda and Yugoslavia Reconsidered," a working paper of the Institute for the Study of Genocide, 1994.

2. In this regard, we collaborated on a collection of materials prompted by the disclosures of the massacre at Mylai. Richard Falk, Gabriel Kolko, and Robert Jay Lifton, eds., *Crimes of War* (New York: Random House, 1971); see also *In the Name of America* (New York: Clergy and Layman Concerned About Vietnam, 1968) and James William Gibson, *The Perfect War* (Boston: Atlantic Monthly Press, 1986).

3. Of these shallow measures, lifting the arms embargo is the most likely to have reshaped the conflict, and besides, it would appear that its imposition without a more substantial UN/Europe commitment to protect Bosnia against Serb aggressive moves was an instance of what might well be described as "perverse" intervention, that is, helpful to the side most responsible for the humanitarian crisis, and that its lifting would at least return the situation to zero. Again assessment is problematic as lifting the embargo, supposedly imposed to contain the magnitude and scope of conflict, was so uncertain in its likely effects.

4. See a masterful account of the conflict in Bosnia from its outset, stressing the causal contributions of a shifting geopolitical scene brought about by the

end of the Cold War, in Susan L. Woodward, *Balkan Tragedy: Chaos and Dissolution After the Cold War* (Washington, D.C.: Brookings, 1995); Woodward's conclusion that Western intervention in its shallow form aggravated, rather than moderated, behavior of the adversaries is particularly confirmatory of my critique of a reliance on shallow intervention as a tool of an anti-genocide diplomacy, at 198; see also Jasminka Udovicki and James Ridgeway, eds., *Yugoslavia's Ethnic Nightmare* (Chicago: Lawrence Hill, 1995).

5. European affinities were divided among the parties based on ethnic, religious, and historical considerations; support for the Bosnian Muslim leadership was never "easy" for Europe to swallow, given the tensions between Islam and the West that remained an influential subtext throughout.

6. Reiff, *Slaughterhouse* (New York: Simon & Schuster, 1995), 12–13.

7. Compare Saul Mendlovitz's valuable contribution to this volume that proceeds from the other orientation, namely, that of morally conditioned political advocacy.

8. For explication of cosmopolitan democracy see Daniele Archibugi and David Held, eds., *Cosmopolitan Democracy: An Agenda for a New World Order* (Cambridge, U.K.: Polity, 1995).

9. These considerations are intelligently discussed in Woodward, 322n4; for the wider rationale see Theodor Meron, "The Case for War Crimes Trials in Yugoslavia," *Foreign Affairs* 72(1993): 122–35.

12

The Prevention and Punishment of the Crime of Genocide

Saul Mendlovitz and John Fousek

"Who still talks nowadays of the extermination of
the Armenians?"

—Adolf Hitler

"As a responsible Government, you don't just go
around hollering 'genocide.' You say that acts of
genocide may have occurred and they need to be
investigated."

—David Rawson, U.S. Ambassador to Rwanda

This essay argues for the creation of a standing police force to deal exclusively with the crime of genocide. It is written at a time when the
unwillingness—*not* the impotence—of the international community to
deal with genocidal slaughters, most recently in Bosnia and Rwanda, is
glaringly apparent. Yet no one denies that genocide is a crime of the
most egregious nature. As the *New York Times* editorial page put it in July
1994, "Nearly 50 years after the defeat of Nazi Germany, the world, to
all our shame, has not yet found a morally and militarily adequate response to this recurring crime against humanity."[1] The establishment of
a United Nations Police Force for the Prevention and Punishment of
Genocide, designed specifically to enforce the 1948 Genocide Convention, would constitute just such a response.

The U.N. Genocide Police Force, as we will call it, would be a new
kind of force. It would possess assertive police powers dedicated to preventing and halting episodes of genocide, and the mandate to apprehend the alleged perpetrators and bring them to justice. Unlike U.N.
peacekeeping forces, which are formed on an ad hoc basis from *national*

military contingents provided voluntarily by member states, the Genocide Police Force would be a permanent, *transnational* institution. Its members would be recruited as individuals—as citizens of the world— and employed directly by the U.N., rather than by their national military authorities. Nation-states and ad hoc peacekeeping forces have been wholly ineffectual in enforcing the law against genocide. Institutional innovation is clearly needed if the world community is to climb out of this moral quagmire.

The notion of a transnational police force dates back at least to the period before World War I, when it was advanced by the Fabian socialists in Great Britain. The idea was also aired in the disarmament discussions of the interwar period. The horrors of World War II prompted numerous proposals for a United Nations Police Force as a means of enforcing international law and preventing future wars. Today, the recent history of mass slaughters (in Indonesia, Cambodia and the Kurdish regions of Iraq, for example, as well as Rwanda and Bosnia) and the increasingly frequent deployments of U.N. peacekeeping forces have given the idea a new currency.[2] But the force proposed here would be separate from any U.N. forces used to deal with invasions of one state by another (such as Iraq against Kuwait or Iran against Iraq) or to intervene in civil wars where genocide is not a major component of the conflict (as in Afghanistan or Nicaragua). Moreover, it would not assume responsibility for dealing with other international crimes. Our thesis is that the time has come to develop effective means of enforcing the 1948 Genocide Convention, and that a U.N. Genocide Police Force would provide those means.

Genocide as an International Crime

One hundred and twenty states have ratified the 1948 Convention on the Prevention and Punishment of the Crime of Genocide. Ordinarily, treaty obligations bind only those states that sign the treaty. But when a principle or rule of law has been articulated for the international community, and there is an acquiescence in the obligatory category of that rule for what is known in international law as *opinio juris*, the obligation becomes binding even upon states that have not signed the treaty. Not a single state has put itself on record as opposing the recognition of genocide as an international crime. Even the United States, after failing to sign and ratify the 1948 Genocide Convention for four decades, joined that convention in early 1989. Many scholars have argued further that genocide as a crime should be considered *jus cogens*, meaning a peremptory norm or axiological principle of law, binding on all states and individuals throughout the world. In this view, it cannot be derogated in any fashion.

While the term "genocide" was coined in response to the Nazi Holocaust, the practice dates back at least 5,000 years.[3] Simply establishing genocide as a crime marks a remarkable change from the past, comparable to the moment in the late nineteenth century when the world's nations moved toward outlawing slavery.[4] It is also comparable to the moment in 1973 when apartheid was declared an international crime, contributing to its demise less than two decades later.[5]

After World War II, the defendants at the Nuremberg trials were charged with having "conducted deliberate and systematic genocide" against Jews, Poles, Gypsies and others. Yet the individual Nazis convicted at Nuremberg were found guilty of crimes against humanity, not of genocide as such. Instead, the articulation of genocide as an international crime fell to the General Assembly of the newly created United Nations Organization. In a unanimous resolution of December 11, 1946, the General Assembly declared that "genocide is a crime under international law which the civilized world condemns, and for the commission of which principals and accomplices—whether private individuals, public officials or statesmen, and whether the crime is committed on religious, racial, political or any other grounds—are punishable."[6] On December 9, 1948, the General Assembly adopted the Convention on the Prevention and Punishment of the Crime of Genocide.

Although the definition of genocide remains a subject of continuing discussion, this essay employs the definition set forth in the 1948 Convention, because our aim is to propose a mechanism for enforcing the Convention.[7] Moreover, that definition provides a relatively high degree of legal precision. According to the Convention:

> Genocide means any of the following acts committed with intent to destroy, in whole or in part, a national, ethnical, racial or religious group, as such:
> (a) Killing members of the group;
> (b) Causing serious bodily or mental harm to members of the group;
> (c) Deliberately inflicting on the group conditions of life calculated to bring about its physical destruction in whole or in part;
> (d) Imposing measures intended to prevent births within the group;
> (e) Forcibly transferring children of the group to another group.[8]

The Convention has been analyzed extensively.[9] We wish to highlight four points.

First, the convention declares that genocide is a crime whether it is "committed in time of peace or in time of war." It employed this phrasing because the Nuremberg Judgment had tied the "crimes against humanity" rubric to the existence of an ongoing aggressive war. The identification of genocide as a crime independent of other considerations is, then, a historic development in itself. Second, there needs to be specific intent to destroy "in whole or in part" a group defined by its ethnic, national, racial or religious identity. In legal terms, specific intent constitutes a particularly stringent test of whether a crime has been committed. In this case, the test is not simply specific intent to kill or injure individuals but to do so because of their group identity and in order to destroy the group, "in whole or in part." Third, the Convention's definition does not include political groups, which had been included in the General Assembly's original resolution in 1946. This omission occurred because the Soviet Union opposed any definition of genocide that included political groups. It subsequently became a major reason why the U.S. refused to join the Convention for forty years. Genocide became a pawn in the Cold War. From our perspective, this omission constitutes one of the Convention's greatest weaknesses.[10] Fourth and finally, several of the acts included in the Convention's definition, such as the causing of mental harm and the forcible transfer of children, show that genocide is not just a matter of death counts.

The Convention's definition provides a reasonably clear basis for enforcement so long as operational tests can be developed to guide decisions concerning the use of the Genocide Police Force. Intent to annihilate some particular group, "in whole or in part," provides one such litmus test. The specific acts enumerated in the Convention provide a second. Perhaps the sheer numbers killed provide a third, though the questions remain as to how a threshold would be determined and what it should be: 100 or 10,000? Indeed, quantification may not be an appropriate test. The issue of numbers killed is nowhere mentioned in the 1948 Convention, so it would provide at best a secondary test, after the matters of specific intent and acts.

Perhaps this special U.N. force should be required to intervene in cases where a ruler is engaged in "cruel and barbaric treatment" of his or her own people, even when the atrocities do not fit the criteria of genocide. Egregious crimes against humanity might be appropriately placed within the force's mandate. But that would run head-on into the thickets of sovereignty, since no existing convention of international law deals with crimes against humanity. So again, this proposal focuses on the crime of genocide as articulated in the 1948 Convention.

Some Issues of Jurisdiction

Who is subject to the law against genocide—individuals, groups, or states? And who may invoke the convention? The 1948 Convention is directed against individuals rather than groups, institutions or governments. This formulation leaves some ambiguity in that genocide was seen initially as being carried out by an organized state apparatus, yet it was defined as a crime perpetrated by individuals. Before the Nuremberg Judgment, individuals charged with war crimes successfully defended themselves by arguing that they had acted solely on behalf of their government. The Nuremberg Tribunal ruled that individuals charged with war crimes and crimes of aggression, the two main crimes under its jurisdiction, could no longer use that defense. Following the Nuremberg precedent, the Genocide Convention also declared that individuals bore responsibility for their actions, and would be subject to punishment accordingly.

The spirit of the Convention leaves it to the member states to provide the enforcement machinery. But the treaty empowers any signatory state to "call upon the competent organs of the United Nations to take such actions under the Charter of the United Nations as they consider appropriate for the prevention and suppression of acts of genocide." Given the failure of the international community to develop any other effective enforcement mechanisms, this provision may serve as the basis for creating the U.N. Genocide Police Force proposed here. This force could be established under the U.N. Charter by either the Security Council (under Article 47) or the General Assembly (under Articles 10 and 11)—or preferably by both.[11]

Some scholars have argued that the crime of genocide, like piracy, is subject to universal jurisdiction, and can therefore be tried before any competent tribunal, domestic or international. But the current Convention says nothing about universal jurisdiction. Instead it specifically grants jurisdiction to courts of the state where the acts occurred or to "such international penal tribunal as may have jurisdiction with respect to those Contracting Parties which shall have accepted its jurisdiction." It did not establish any such tribunal. In fact, the International Criminal Tribunal for Yugoslavia, created by the U.N. Security Council in 1993 and subsequently expanded to cover Rwanda as well, is the first such tribunal since Nuremberg. International jurisdiction is clearly more effective than state jurisdiction, since genocide is commonly state-sanctioned. For this reason, primary or even exclusive jurisdiction should be given to the United Nations, preferably through the creation of a permanent International Criminal Court.[12]

Deciding When to Intervene

The force proposed here would perhaps play a role in preventing genocides and a significant role in halting them when they do occur.[13] At this stage of global political development, it might prove difficult to initiate preventive police intervention, although U.N. monitoring, sanctioning and judicial intervention might well be possible. But swift action is crucial to enforcing the Genocide Convention and saving lives. Some sort of early warning system is needed to provide guidelines for when the police force would be brought onto the scene. "Genocide," according to Secretary-General Boutros-Ghali, "does not happen spontaneously." Certainly the Secretary-General is correct in asserting that "In most cases there are abundant danger signs long before the killing begins."[14]

We recommend that a Genocide Watch Advisory Board be established under the Secretary-General of the United Nations. This Board would be charged with developing a detailed early warning system to identify advance signs of any incipient genocide, monitoring conflict situations in which even a latent threat of genocide seems present, and overseeing the Force's activities to protect against potential abuse of police powers. The Board should work in conjunction with transnational citizens' groups, such as Human Rights Watch and Amnesty International, already engaged in similar pursuits.

The Genocide Watch Advisory Board could be established and selected by the Security Council, and would be composed of respected, senior members of the world diplomatic community. Its membership should be constitutionally structured to ensure adequate representation of the world's cultural, socio-economic, linguistic and religious diversity, and to prevent it from serving simply as a policy instrument of permanent members of the Security Council. Unlike the Security Council, this board would not be subject to vetoes by the permanent members, and it would have an advisory role only. After studying a given situation, it could vote either to approve or disapprove the Secretary-General's decision. Alternately, it could vote to recommend action where the Secretary-General has failed to take heed. But it would have no binding authority. A "war powers" clause would give the Security Council the authority to withdraw the police force 30 to 45 days after its initial deployment. Use of the force could also be authorized under established procedures for humanitarian intervention in instances of grave and egregious deprivations of human rights, where there is reasonable evidence of intent to commit genocide.[15]

Bosnia and Rwanda provide cases where early warning signs existed but went unheeded. As soon as the international community recognized Bosnia-Herzegovina as an independent state in April 1992, it was clear that the Serbs and Croats alike aimed to destroy it. The subsequent Serb policy of "ethnic cleansing" clearly signaled genocidal intent. Western Europe, the United States, or the U.N. could have stopped the genocide at that point but lacked the political will to do so.[16] The U.N. also lacked the proper instrument. An independent, standing U.N. Genocide Police Force deployed to Bosnia in the spring of 1992, before the fighting escalated, might have saved tens if not hundreds of thousands of lives.

In Rwanda, where as many as 800,000 were massacred between April and June 1994 in a carefully planned genocide against the Tutsi minority, there was abundant evidence beforehand.[17] Human Rights Watch reported government-sponsored massacres of members of the Tutsi minority more than a year before the wholesale genocide began. In August 1993, a Rwandan television station with close ties to the government began to broadcast open incitements first to hatred then to killing. Local human rights groups warned that genocide seemed imminent. A militia was being recruited, organized and trained to kill. Guns were distributed wholesale to members of the Hutu majority. All Rwandans were required to carry ethnic identity cards, which were later used to identify those to be killed. Such a mass of evidence would have set off any early warning system designed to prevent genocide.

Functions of the Genocide Police Force

Once deployed in the field, the proposed Genocide Police Force would assume at least the following functions:

1. *Stop the genocidal behavior.* In instances of inter-group tensions within nation-states—such as those between Moslems and Hindus in India, Jews and Arabs in Israel or West Bank, and blacks and whites in the U.S.—police and para-military forces are often called in when some outbreak of violence seems imminent—not simply after it happens. Once deployed, the Force would aim to prevent or halt further acts of genocide.
2. *Implement assertive safe havens.* After suppressing the alleged geno-

cidal behavior, the U.N. Genocide Police Force will have to occupy the territory where the behavior occurred, often for quite some time. The force's occupation policy should be guided by the doctrine of assertive safe havens.[18] It would have an "assertive" mandate and power of enforcement, authorizing it to:

a. demilitarize the area surrounding each safe haven, placing heavy weapons under effective supervision;

b. disarm the populations in the areas designated as safe havens;

c. seek out and lead to safety those individuals outside the protected area who are targets of the genocidal behavior and who desire entry into a safe haven; and

d. use appropriate force to defend itself and its charges, and to carry out its mandate.

3. *Arrange for the presence of humanitarian relief agencies.* Both United Nations and voluntary citizens groups (such as the Red Cross, church and medical groups) will need to be brought in to provide basic needs and initiate civil society processes of health and housing. The police presence would make this possible.

4. *Initiate processes of humane governance.* As a corollary to halting genocide, U.N. representatives will have to assume a central role in initiating just and humane governance processes amongst the local population. These efforts should utilize a wide variety of individuals and techniques. Again, the police presence would make this possible.

5. *Apprehend alleged criminals complying with appropriate legal procedures and assist in gathering evidence for prosecution.* As soon as it is in the field, the force would be empowered to arrest and incarcerate suspected perpetrators in order to bring them to justice. It would also assist prosecutors in gathering evidence and identifying and protecting witnesses.

Structure of the Genocide Police Force

The structure of the proposed Genocide Police Force is crucial to making it both workable and feasible. By structure, we mean in particular the rules and procedures guiding the force's size and location, command and control, financing and operations.[19]

Size and Location

A standing Genocide Police Force of 10,000 to 15,000 would be housed in three or more base camps, strategically situated around the world. The force housed at each base camp would be best prepared for action in the socio-cultural, linguistic, and climatic conditions of its particular region. Yet each base-unit would also be available as necessary for deployment beyond its primary region. Bases should be located in relatively isolated areas, where they would be least subject to interference from any host nation, and where they themselves would be least likely to interfere in the life of the local community. The force could also be made available for disaster relief missions.

Control

Primary decision-making control concerning the deployment of the U.N. Genocide Police Force should be vested in the Secretary-General of the United Nations. But the Secretary-General would be authorized to deploy this force only after consulting with a standing Genocide Watch Advisory Board, which would be duly constituted for that purpose, as discussed above. This board would have the authority to declare whether any given situation constitutes genocide or incipient genocide. Decision-making powers, and day-to-day command and control of the police, would rest with the Secretary-General. The Security Council would have the authority to withdraw the force after 30–45 days.

Financing

This proposal could be financed through regular U.N. allotments, but alternative formulas seem more promising. Throughout the Cold War, payments pegged to military spending were widely cited as a potential means of underwriting U.N. peacekeeping operations. In the increasingly globalized economy of the post-Cold War era, a miniscule tax on international travel, communications or currency exchanges could easily finance expanded U.N. operations, including the Genocide Police Force. In 1992, for example, international currency exchanges totaled $280 trillion, so a tax of 0.01 percent would have yielded $28 billion.[20] The force proposed here would cost $5–10 billion annually.

Operations

Members of the force should be specifically trained to identify, apprehend and incarcerate individuals engaged in acts punishable under the Genocide Convention, and to restore order and establish Assertive Safe Havens as outlined above. To fulfill its mandate, the police force will likely need light tanks and state-of-the-art infantry equipment, as well as advanced aircraft for transportation and logistical support. Operations should be guided by the principle of using the least lethal means possible to enforce the law. Wherever possible, the Force should rely on relatively humane, nonlethal weaponry, such as rubber bullets, tranquilizers, stun-guns and tear gas. Where necessary, the Genocide Police Force could be augmented by more extensive forces authorized under existing procedures.

Political Obstacles

Today, several major political obstacles stand in the way of establishing a genocide police force. These include: the imperatives of state sovereignty; "body-bags"—domestic objections to deaths incurred through participation in any force not deemed to be in service of "the national interest"; and financing. We believe that the structure and functions of the proposed force presented in this essay go a long way toward overcoming these obstacles.

The rather gruesome and tragic image of the body-bag conveys perhaps the greatest obstacle to effective U.N. actions to halt the recent killings in both the former Yugoslavia and Rwanda. The major states of the world—the United States, Britain, France, and perhaps Russia—had the capacity to intervene in these situations in ways that would have saved countless lives. But these powerful states failed to act because their political leaders feared an irate domestic backlash if members of their military forces were killed while carrying out any humanitarian intervention. The deaths of eighteen U.S. Army Rangers in Somalia, for example, provoked a major public uproar which led President Clinton to accelerate the withdrawal of U.S. forces from that country. When France intervened in Rwanda, French leaders similarly feared casualties that the electorate at home would not tolerate. For Western society at least, policing the world has become a highly suspect endeavor in the post-Soviet era, except where an overwhelming national interest is seen to be at stake, as with Middle Eastern oil. While some small and medium-sized states may not face this obstacle, these states are inhibited from volunteering troops for U.N. actions by their own lack of financial resources.

Beyond deaths and dollars lies the issue of sovereignty. States fear that a transnational police force would erode their sovereignty in two distinct ways. First, states fear that any U.N. force, if used against the interests of a member state, would erode the general principle of state sovereignty.

Second, states fear that the U.N. might intervene into their own territory, undermining their sovereignty quite specifically.

We believe these problems can be solved. Suppose that the U.N. has a Genocide Police Force some 10,000 to 15,000 strong. Suppose further that the members of this force are individually recruited, highly-trained for intervention, well-educated, with decent salaries and benefits, including post-police career opportunities and retirement funds. These individuals would be international civil servants. Rather than being appointed by their governments, they would apply for these positions directly, just as individuals apply to join the local police force in Toledo, Harare, or Kyoto. No more than 3 to 5 percent of the personnel would come from any one member state. There would be no nationally organized units within the force, and citizens from each member state should be dispersed as widely as possible throughout the force.

Casualties suffered by such a force would not raise issues of national interest or injury to the state of any kind. Nor would they provoke the kind of nationalist backlash that swept through U.S. public opinion when U.S. soldiers were killed in Somalia. Because these individuals would serve as U.N. police, no country's honor or dignity would be at stake. No local community would feel that its national government had needlessly sacrificed its sons. A U.N. Genocide Police Force structured as a transnational entity would bypass the politically volatile issues of national identity.

According to discussions we have had with military people, a rapid deployment force of approximately 12,000, equipped with means of transport and military hardware up to and including small tanks and state-of-the-art infantry, would cost $5 to 10 billion a year. An arrangement in the middle or even the high end of this range would ultimately prove cost-effective for the international community and for leading U.N. member states. Suppose that such a force had been available early on in Rwanda or in the former Yugoslavia. The costs to the U.N. of intervening in these areas with a Genocide Police Force might well have been less than the total costs the various states have subsequently incurred for both humanitarian relief and long-delayed, largely unsuccessful military deployments.

Conclusion

Fifty years after the liberation of the Nazi death camps, the crime of genocide is very much still with us—to the shame of all the nations and the people of the world. But today genocide is universally recognized as a high crime under international law. The challenge the world community now faces is how to enforce the law expressed in the 1948 Genocide Convention.

With the tragic events of recent years in Somalia, the former Yugoslavia, and, most recently, Rwanda and Burundi, the world today is forced to confront its failure to prevent genocidal episodes all too reminiscent of Nazi horrors. For a host of reasons, intervention by individual powers or by ad hoc coalitions of nation-states, whether formed regionally or under U.N. auspices, has not provided a workable solution. Diplomacy and sanctions, of course, must always be employed fully before force is deployed. But in too many instances since 1948, they too have failed to provide effective enforcement for the Genocide Convention adopted that year.

In the case of genocide, as in heinous crimes committed within nation-states, effective law enforcement requires effective police operations. We believe the time has come for the world community to confront this fact, and deal with the crime of genocide by establishing a special transnational police force, under the United Nations, dedicated to preventing, halting and punishing this singularly grave and egregious offense.

Notes

1. David C. Unger, "U.N. Troops Cannot Stop Genocide," Editorial Notebook, *New York Times* (July 31, 1994).

2. For a variety of proposals, with editorial commentary, see Richard A. Falk and Saul H. Mendlovitz, eds., *The Strategy of World Order*, vol. 3 (New York: World Law Fund, 1966), 591–692. Perhaps the most thorough proposal of the postwar era was that put forward by Grenville Clark and Louis B. Sohn in *World Peace through World Law* (Cambridge, MA: Harvard University Press, 1958). For a prominent recent call for a permanent, voluntary U.N. force, see Brian Urquart, "For a UN Volunteer Military Force," *New York Review of Books* (June 10, 1993).

3. Raphael Lemkin, who coined the word, defined genocide as "a coordinated plan of different actions aiming at the destruction of essential foundations of the life of national groups, with the aim of annihilating the groups themselves." Lemkin also led the campaign to establish an international convention treating genocide as a distinct—and distinctly heinous—category of crime against humanity. See Lori Lyman Bruun, "Beyond the 1948 Genocide Convention—Emerging Principles of Genocide in Customary International Law," *Maryland Journal of International Law and Trade* 2 (Fall 1993): 196–97.

4. See Ved P. Nanda and M. C. Bassiouni, "Slavery and Slave Trade: Steps Toward Eradication," *Santa Clara Lawyer* 12(1972): 419–31.

5. International Convention on the Suppression and Punishment of the Crime of "Apartheid," in Burns H. Weston, Richard A. Falk, and Anthony D'Amato, eds., *Basic Documents in International Law and World Order*, 2d ed. (St. Paul: West Publishing Co., 1990).

6. Quoted in Matthew Lippman, "The 1948 Convention on the Prevention and Punishment of the Crime of Genocide: Forty-Five Years Later," *Temple International and Comparative Law Journal* (Spring 1994): 229–37.

7. Two recent contributions to this discussion neatly illustrate some of the conceptual difficulties involved in defining genocide. In a 1994 letter to *The Economist* (July 23, 1994), concerning Rwanda, Alain Destexhe, Secretary-General of Doctors Without Borders, argued that the term genocide can "probably be correctly applied only three times this century: the massacres of Armenians under the Ottoman Turks in 1915–16; the Nazi Holocaust during the Second World War; and the attempt by Hutu extremists to exterminate the Tutsi in Rwanda." The brevity of this list highlights the gravity of the situation in Rwanda, of course, but it nonetheless implies a serious yet overly strict interpretation of the term as defined in the 1948 Convention.

While Destexhe does not provide a full argument for his position, it seems fair to understand him as being extremely stringent with regard to two matters. First, that there must be specific intent to destroy a particular group. Second, that the group must be defined in terms of ethnic, national, racial or religious identity, following the categories enunciated in the Genocide Convention. Indeed, Destexhe argues that the "killing fields of Cambodia" did not represent genocide because the objective of the Khmer Rouge was to eliminate possible political opponents—"not the Khmer people as such." One might make the same point concerning the Idi Amin's Uganda, Haiti, and other instances of state-sponsored mass murder where the victims do not fit into the categories identified in the 1948 Convention. In other instances, however, such as the Serbs's euphemistic "ethnic cleansing" in Bosnia or Pol Pot's brutal treatment of the Vietnamese population within Cambodia's borders, there is clear evidence of intent to destroy an ethnic or national group at least "in part." Yet Destexhe seems to neglect the use of this phrase in the Genocide Convention.

At the opposite pole, the sociologists Barbara Harff and Ted Robert Gurr advocate a more expansive conception of genocide following the Convention's definition but adding political groups to the list of protected categories. Harff and Gurr estimate that between seven and sixteen million people have been killed in some 44 episodes of genocide and "politicide" since the end of World War II. Following Destexhe's interpretation, by contrast, total genocide fatalities since 1945 would drop from the seven to sixteen million range to between 500,000 and 800,000—the approximate number of Tutsis massacred in Rwanda in the spring of 1994. See Harff and Gurr, "Toward Empirical Theory of Genocides and Politicides: Identification and Measurement of Cases since 1945," *In-*

ternational Studies Quarterly 32(1988): 359–71. Our interpretation would yield numbers somewhere in between.

8. The text of the Convention is readily available in Weston et al., *Basic Documents*, 297.

9. For just two recent examples from law journals, see Bruun, "Beyond the 1948 Genocide Convention" and Lippman, "The 1948 Convention." See also Harff and Gurr, "Toward Empirical Theory."

10. With the demise of the Soviet Union, however, we believe that the Convention could probably be amended to correct this shortcoming, which has become especially glaring in light of the history of politically directed mass slaughter since World War II. For the time being, however, the priority should be to enforce the law against genocide as it currently stands.

11. The procedures we propose for creating and controlling the Genocide Police Force are rooted in but move beyond United Nations experience with *ad hoc* forces throughout the postwar era. Under Chapter VII of the U.N. Charter, the Security Council can legally require member states to take coercive measures against any threat to or breach of international peace. The Security Council can also ask member states to volunteer their national forces for U.N. missions. Under the Uniting for Peace Resolution, the General Assembly can recommend sending peacekeeping forces into action in cases where disagreement among permanent members of the Security Council prevent the Council from discharging its responsibility for peacekeeping. These mechanisms of enforcement would not be altered by the present proposal. See also the discussion below under the heading "Deciding When to Intervene."

12. See Tina Rosenberg, "War Crimes Then and Now: From Nuremberg To Bosnia," *Nation* (May 15, 1995). Human Rights Watch is currently campaigning for the creation of a U.N.-sponsored International Criminal Court, to be charged with investigating and prosecuting the most egregious of human rights abuses.

13. In speaking of prevention, we are looking not at underlying causes, but at what a U.N. Genocide Police Force could do to prevent future episodes of genocide. Many observers have examined the question of root causes of such behavior. For a particularly penetrating analysis, see Robert Jay Lifton and Eric Markusen, *The Genocidal Mentality: Nazi Holocaust and Nuclear Threat* (New York: Basic Books, 1990). We wish to record our profound appreciation for Lifton in sustaining the concern with genocide during a period in which too many have grown numb to it, and to other human horrors.

14. From Boutros-Ghali's opinion page piece in the *International Herald Tribune*, week of April 1, 1995. As quoted in Barbara Crosette, "U.N.: Reason, in Small Doses, May Stop Genocide," *New York Times* (April 9, 1995), Section 4, p. 16.

15. This has the advantage of following procedures which have been established in customary international law and do not need to be legitimated by a new treaty. We want to follow agreed-upon rules of humanitarian intervention,

so long as the intervening is carried out by a U.N. force, and so long as that force has built-in safeguards to prevent big powers from using it as an instrument of their own policies, whatever the authorizing agency.

16. See Misha Glenny, "Yugoslovia: The Great Fall," *New York Review of Books* (March 23, 1995); and his "Letter from Bosnia: The Age of the Parastate," *The New Yorker* (May 8, 1995); and see David Rieff, *Slaughterhouse: Bosnia and the Failure of the West* (New York: Simon and Schuster, 1995): 22.

17. This review of events in Rwanda is drawn largely from Helen Fein, "An Interview with Alison L. Des Forges: Genocide in Rwanda Was Foreseen and Could Have Been Deterred," in Fein, ed., *The Prevention of Genocide: Rwanda and Yugoslavia Reconsidered* (A Working Paper of the Institute for the Study of Genocide, 1994). See also Milton Leitenberg, "US and UN Actions Escalate Genocide and Increase Costs in Rwanda," in the same volume; and Leitenberg, "Rwanda, 1994: International Incompetence Produces Genocide," *Peacekeeping and International Relations* (November/December 1994): 216–28.

18. This discussion of assertive safe havens is largely drawn from "Safe Havens in Bosnia," a statement published in the *New York Review of Books* (May 13, 1993), by the Citizens' Committee on Bosnia-Herzegovina. The senior author is a member of that committee and helped to formulate the proposal presented in that statement.

19. The following discussion draws on material presented in Robert C. Johansen and Saul H. Mendlovitz, "The Role of Enforcement of Law in the Establishment of a New International Order: A Proposal for a Transnational Police Force," *Alternatives* 6(1980): 320–24.

20. See Robert C. Johansen, "Reforming the United Nations to Eliminate War," *Transnational Law & Contemporary Problems* 4(Fall 1994): 474–76; and Martin Walker, "Global Taxation: Paying for Peace," *World Policy Journal* 10(Spring 1993): 7–12.

13

Saving Bosnia (and Ourselves)

Elinor Fuchs

I begin this writing in the spring of 1995 at Harvard University, where I am teaching for the term. Here I receive a flyer from a student at the Law School titled, "*The War in Bosnia: What Can We Do?*" Listed are seven days of talks, films and positive actions (Write Your Congressman), innocently cast in the teeth of Europe's greatest mockery to humanistic pretension since World War II.

A few weeks later I meet an eminent member of the Harvard faculty, a Serb born in Sarajevo. "How do you respond to the war?" I ask. "I laugh," he replies. "Why laugh?" "Because," he grins, "it proves that human beings are the lowest form of life. Then come animals. Then come plants and trees. And the highest form of all, inorganic matter. Most of the universe is inorganic matter you know."

A helpless innocence, a corrosive cynicism, or worse, a numbed indifference: the gestures able to be imagined by witnesses to the post-Cold War trauma playing out on our television screens have shrunk mainly to these. In 1993–94 I took part in a group effort to displace such responses to geo-political horror with informed action. To the participants in this effort, which found a leader in Robert Jay Lifton, stopping the genocide in Bosnia–Herzegovina was taken on as a personal, and passionate, responsibility. The following is a brief personal account of this failed crusade.

Among its activities, the Center on Violence and Human Survival, directed by Lifton with Charles Strozier at John Jay College of Criminal Justice in New York, has occasionally served as an organizing magnet on issues of concern to the "peace and justice" community. In January, 1993, a group of concerned New Yorkers, attracted to a presentation on the Balkan war at the Center, spontaneously began to work together in an attempt to influence the just-emerging public debate on Bosnia.

My own route into this involvement was not untypical of others in the group. I had often asked myself what I would have done had I been in my parents' situation, an adult and able to act, when the Nazi terror against the Jews was mounting in the 1930s. With ethnic cleansing sweeping out tens of thousands of Muslims and Sarajevo under siege in the summer of 1992 it seemed to me that that moment had now come for my generation: the Bosnian Muslims were our Jews.

In the fall, as reports of concentration camps and mass rapes of Muslim women began to emerge, I had an urgent telephone conversation with Robert Lifton. I was relieved to learn that the World Order Models Project (WOMP), with the Center's help, would soon sponsor a seminar on the desirability of stepped-up international intervention in the former Yugoslavia. At this meeting, held in a seminar room on the lower level of the United Nations, a telling confrontation took place between Richard Falk, professor of international law at Princeton, and his collaborator of more than three decades in international peace efforts, Saul Mendlovitz. Falk was against intervention. He argued that the West with its premature recognitions of Croatia and Bosnia-Herzegovina, its futile negotiations and symbolic peacekeepers was if anything helping to spur and sustain the violence, and that further involvement was likely to do more harm than good. Mendlovitz, an international law professor at Rutgers Law School and founder of WOMP, heatedly arguing that intervention was needed to prevent wholesale genocide, urged judicious bombing and more United Nations troops, including some American troops. Falk argued that big countries don't take risks for humanitarian objectives: "There's no oil there." Mendlovitz was especially disturbed to hear such a "realist" analysis from an idealist like Falk. Variations on this intervention/nonintervention debate, haunted by the ghost of Vietnam, persisted until the final meeting, nineteen months later, of our soon-to-be-formed group.

The Center was waiting until Dr. Jack Geiger's return from the former Yugoslavia to hold a meeting on Bosnia in its own premises at John Jay College. Geiger, a co-founder of the Center, and a founder (as well as the then president) of Physicians for Human Rights, led a forensic team to the former Yugoslavia in late 1992 as part of a mission from the United Nations Center on Human Rights. The team's purpose was to gather evidence of human rights violations, particularly to investigate the reports of massacres and torture.

Word of Geiger's January report spread quickly. It was attended by many people who did not normally attend Center events, but were fervently interested in the developing fate of Bosnia-Herzegovina. Geiger described what he discovered in the Croatian city of Vukovar, which had been captured and totally destroyed by the Serbs after a seventy-day siege. One mass grave held two hundred Croatian defenders of the town, executed after they were marched from the hospital where their wounds were being treated. They also discovered that a mass cremation had occurred in a plant normally used for rendering animal fat. This was different from the Holocaust with its efficient schedules and records, Geiger stressed. This was "low-tech slaughter" whose victims died by beatings, machine gun fire and decapitation with chainsaws. In one particularly grisly finding, Geiger said his group had taken testimony of eye-gouging, and of victims being forced to swallow their own eyeballs.

In the question period, as discussion turned to assaults on the Muslim population of Bosnia, Lifton's response was particularly stunned. "This . . . is . . . genocide," he said, with incredulous silences between the words. Geiger agreed, but warned that searching for the exact criteria of genocide could serve to defer reaction and response. Worse: governments were already beginning to manipulate the definition of genocide in order to avoid taking action. "And this continues as we speak?" Geiger nodded. Lifton continued, "In all my years of studying genocide, this is the first time I have been witness to genocide *in-progress*. What can be done? What can people like us do?"

We threw the question open to the floor. Within several minutes, the three directions of the next year and a half of work presented themselves with remarkable clarity: some of us were interested in the crafting and publication of statements that would help to create a constituency for action on Bosnia; others in drawing up an actual plan for concerted interdiction of ethnic cleansing by the international community; and Marlene Nadle, a journalist, immediately envisioned an effort to raise moral and material support for the opposition news media in Zagreb and Belgrade (since this modest effort, the most concretely successful of the three, subsequently proceeded outside the supervision of the Center, it will not appear again in my account). The group wanted to reassemble in two weeks, with smaller groups meeting in the interim. At the end of the meeting, Lifton and Strozier looked a little dazed. The Center had other plans for the spring and both men had books to complete. That night I received a panicked telephone call from Strozier. Did I have the names and telephone numbers of all these new people? Would I handle notification for these meetings? His plate was full.

From the beginning, it seemed to be understood that our emerging venture would not be "top down." Whoever wanted to initiate or join a project did so. In the free-form constellation that constituted the committee of the whole, formal votes were not taken, but the sense of the group was worked out in searching discussions. Smaller, interim groups began to meet. At the first such meeting, Joanne Landy of the Campaign for Peace and Democracy, a strong critic of U.S. and for the most part U.N. intervention in international disputes, urged, over the moral objections to armaments of some in the group, that we publish a statement calling for the lifting of the U.N.-imposed arms embargo. Intended to be neutral, its effect was to freeze the overwhelming Serb military superiority in place and leave the Bosnian government defenseless.

I too wanted the statement. I thought showing policy-makers a constituency for action, any action, on Bosnia was urgent. Landy, the Balkan historian Manuela Dobos, and I decided to draft the statement and present it at the larger meeting the following week. No one, after all, was obliged to sign it. A larger question, we agreed, was whether the Center, essentially set up for study, would "sign on" to an effort that could project it into the political arena.

We brought the statement to the meeting with Landy's announcement that the *The New York Review of Books* would shoehorn it into the next issue, appearing in the third week of February. Through her efforts it already had the backing of a number of people in the U.S. and Europe who had long urged great powers to stay out of regional disputes. Thus it was intended to signal something of a political sea change on the left. In our own group it triggered a dramatic internal debate.

Chuck Strozier strongly expressed his dislike of the statement. He hadn't committed himself to nonviolent resolution to conflict for his entire professional and morally conscious life only to throw it over now. It was unconscionable to pour additional arms into the most inflamed area of the world. The reality of genocide persuaded him to support humanitarian intervention, but not to directly supply arms during a war. That was unthinkable for a pacifist, and could even make the advancing genocide worse. Lifton rejoined that genocide presented a special case. Uncomfortable with lifting the embargo, but even more troubled by its result, he finally replied: "I am not a pacifist. It is not ethical to deny an entire people who are being tortured, raped, forced to flee for their lives, or incarcerated in their cities and murdered in their streets the right to defend themselves." Saying he would sign the statement, Lifton commented that he had known Strozier for almost twenty years, and that this was the first time they had disagreed on an issue of substance. There was a third branch of opinion on lifting the arms embargo. This came from Bogdan Denitch, CUNY Graduate Center Professor of Sociology, who was active in organizing the democratic socialist opposition to Tudjman in Croatia. Denitch argued that weapons, especially heavy weapons to counter those of the Serbs, would have a difficult time finding their way into beseiged and landlocked Bosnia. Lifting the embargo might follow some kind of intervention, especially by air, but was hardly a "magic bullet" to avert it. He suggested that lifting the embargo appealed to some quarters in the U.S. because it relieved its advocates of further responsibility. Denitch himself would not sign the statement. It is significant that this tactical appraisal of lifting the arms embargo was offered by a European who did not see himself as part of the American peace movement.

It would not be wrong to say that Americans sensitive to the Bosnian trauma—precious few at the beginning of 1993 when this discussion took place—were divided between those for whom the war against fascism was the defining moral and political event of the century, and those in whose experience Vietnam and its arrogance represented the crucial watershed. The two types had worked together since the '60s in the coalitions generalized as the "peace movement" without apparent tension. Bosnia was opening a fissure of which we were just becoming aware. Strozier was of the Vietnam-scarred generation, convinced that war was morally reprehensible, and that big powers could only make regional conflicts worse. Lifton's career had been devoted to studying Hiroshima and the Holocaust. He was of the faith that in some few situations war was a moral necessity, and that the large democratic powers bore a special responsibility to enforce standards of human justice.

At the end of this meeting it was apparent that Lifton and Strozier were willing to commit the Center on Violence and Human Survival to providing a home, resources and leadership for the efforts of our intense, diverse group. Academics and students, lawyers and doctors, historians, psychotherapists, social workers, artists, writers, mostly Americans working with some former Yugoslavs, we had surprisingly found our way to common enterprise. It was also clear that our primary focus, and on this Lifton and Strozier were in full agreement, was not on lifting the arms embargo, but on promoting humanitarian, United Nations-led intervention to stop the Serbian genocide campaign against the Bosnian Muslim population, its culture and history. For the next meeting, Saul Mendlovitz and Peter Weiss of the Lawyers' Committee on Nuclear Policy offered to draft a proposal for a U.N. mandate "with teeth."

It was now mid-February 1993. Other groups had begun to form. Led by the Center for Women's Global Leadership at Rutgers, a women's group was drafting legal language to make organized rape in wartime a war crime. Also just forming were Sheila Geist's Coalition for Intervention Against Genocide, and a group associated with several Jewish congregations in New York, the Jewish Ad Hoc Committee on Bosnia (JACOB). Every few weeks, one group or another called a march to the United Nations or a demonstration in front of the Serbian consulate. Apart from the indefatigable Geist, who seemed to attend every demonstration and meeting of every group, these groups made little progress in coordinating efforts until the end of 1993, eighteen months into the siege of Sarajevo.

By early March, our group began to reach a consensus on the Mendlovitz plan to establish "assertive" safe havens. Written first in the form of a draft U.N. resolution, which we later re-drafted into an Open Letter from the "Citizens' Committee on Bosnia-Herzegovina," it called for a new United Nations force under an enhanced mandate to "assertively" demilitarize, and subsequently defend, the areas around designated population centers. The statement also drew a distinction between massive military intervention and the narrower task of creating and defending safe havens, which we estimated could be accomplished with 50,000 or fewer troops, no more than one-quarter of them American. The statement stressed that while the envisioned force would serve as a temporary authority establishing civil order, it was not intended to be used as a basis for shaping the future map of the former Yugoslavia. However, we insisted that the plan would improve the chances for a lasting peace, because with secure population centers, all sides would have diminished motive to resist a settlement.

With the help of Bogdan Denitch, Manuela Dobos, and a minutely well-informed Croatian psychiatrist, Dinko Podrug, we identified and named the most defensible areas where there were concentrations of population. We were careful to propose protective areas that were not only Muslim but also some that were predominantly Serb and Croat. We believed, with Sarajevo under daily shelling and fighting expected to increase elsewhere as spring approached, that our plan was necessary, rational, and moderate. The Sisyphean nature of our cause was meanwhile daily revealed as one or another of our proposed "safe havens" fell under Serb control. We scaled back the list.

Our Open Letter on safe havens appeared in the *New York Review of Books* in April, along with a shorter version published in a letter to the *New York Times*. Soon versions of it began to turn up in the press. The *Philadelphia Inquirer* and the *Boston Globe* supported it. *The Nation* named but didn't like it. Then Lifton and the Center were contacted by two peace groups in Washington to whom we had faxed the statement. If we were willing to lobby our proposal in Washington, they would set up the appointments and act as our escort.

At a meeting in April it was decided that a representative group for the Washington trip should include Lifton, Mendlovitz, Bogdan Denitch, Michael Flynn—now the central coordinator of our effort—and myself. A few days before our trip the five of us met at Lifton's apartment in New York to plan our presentation. Mendlovitz, we decided, would describe the details of the plan, while Denitch would urge its practicality from intimate, on-the-ground knowledge. Denitch would especially argue that the West was not confronting "age-old hatreds" or an invincible Serb war machine, but hatreds demagogically incited by fascistic leaders and an irregular army of bullies that would back off at a credible threat of force. I, next, would stress Clinton's responsibility to educate the American public on ethical action in a world no longer guided by the Iron Curtain compass. Lifton, finally, would speak of the profound moral consequence of televised genocide. The impact, he would say, is devastating not only on the victims, but on the witnesses who, seeing no response, grow numbly permissive to extreme cruelty.

Early on the morning of May 6, our group met at LaGuardia and flew to Washington. Our appointments included meetings with a youthful assistant to Vice President Gore, who listened politely and said nothing, with Senator Dennis DeConcini, who was elegantly critical of Administration policies, and Representative Frank McCloskey, who roared with fury at Clinton's ineptitude and the U.N.'s weak response. It seemed the farther we went from the White House the less cautious the views. McCloskey was ready to bomb not only the gun emplacements around Sarajevo, but Belgrade, "the source of this thing." The closest we came to an actual source of administration policy was an hour-long discussion with a specialist in European Affairs at the National Security Council, an officer described to us as the N.S.C.'s "brains behind U.S. strategy in Bosnia."

The N.S.C. is located in the same nineteenth-century neo-Renaissance building, now the Old Executive Office Building, that houses the light-filled ceremonial office of the Vice President. There were no light-filled rooms at the N.S.C. Entering by coded lock, we were shown to a small conference room in which every window was covered by tightly closed blinds and blocked with furniture. In front of the central window was a locked floor-to-ceiling cabinet. Still and menacing as Bluebeard's closet, I supposed that it contained recording equipment, or better a scrambling device to prevent conversations from being monitored. It was almost noon, but the room was harsh with overhead, industrial lighting.

The Bosnia expert was Jane Holl, a major in the U.S. Army and Ph.D. from Stanford in the field, previously unknown to me, of "war termination." Holl immediately described herself as a former academic. (No doubt she stressed her military training when speaking to other groups.) She was not in uniform, but wore a severely unadorned green khaki dress. Once more we went through what Mendlovitz called our four-part travelling "dog and pony show." One presentation especially attracted Holl's attention, Bogdan Denitch's argument concerning the exaggeration of Serb military strength. Holl asked questions: how many Serbs in arms? with what arms? what training? After this her interest waned. She had little patience with the moral and psychological "soft" issues that loomed large to us.

During Lifton's presentation I noticed that Holl had two small cards, the size of personal calling cards, in her hands. Shifting these abstractedly, she responded to us. "The fight in Bosnia is in part East Los Angeles: it's a turf fight." In other words, she went on, the issue for the United States was not so much that of the fight on its merits, but of the tension between it and surrounding issues. We had to consider the European NATO allies, the Russians, the neighboring states, the threat to regional security. These played out in different ways. However, from most points of view, ending the fighting, not necessarily resolving the issues being fought over, received a high priority. (We wondered how that analysis would go over in East Los Angeles.) As for our long-range concerns—that U.S. policies were fostering a damaging moral indifference among our own citizenry and signaling aggressors world-wide that it was all right to commit genocide in pursuit of their aims—"Look, we have only so many questions we can focus on. I've learned that you lose your effectiveness when you push the line of questioning out more than a point or two past the current focus."

Like a poker player with a good hand, Holl punched down one of the two cards on the table. "Here is the problem," she said, "You come from New York, let's say, you have a European point of view, maybe your relatives died in the Holocaust. You identify with the victims. And I'm personally sympathetic with that," she went on. "My mother was Jewish." She slapped down card two. "But here's the other side. You come from the midwest. Europe is far away. But your son died in Vietnam, his kids are without a father. You want to think long and hard before your country gets involved in other people's wars. And I understand that point of view very well too. I'm U.S. Army, I'm up to here in that thinking, it's very real." She looked at us. "Both sides can make humanitarian claims, can't they?"

We had differing responses to our long day. My own was quite somber. I saw how marginal our cause was, and how far outside Washington thinking our arguments to support it were. The most disturbing thought of the day came from Jane Holl: we can't push our line of questioning out more than one point, two at most, from the current center of discussion. Nor could they push it back it seemed, to Munich for instance; no farther back than Vietnam. The depressing corollary followed that this Administration could or would not use its persuasive power to move more than a point beyond the public ignorance of any issue. Our group was too many points beyond where the conversation was stalled to influence it in any significant way. These encounters demonstrated to me as nothing else could have done the gulf of moral imagination between New York and Washington.

As a coda to this illuminating experience, we replayed our "act" one week later before the deputy to Madeline Albright at the American mission to the United Nations. After our thirty-minute presentation his puzzled face cleared: "You mean your motive for this is simply humanitarian?"

In the fall of 1993, with the cold settling over Sarajevo for its second winter under siege, the pessimism of early activists was deepening even as the protest coalitions began to spread. In December, a national coalition, the American Committee to Save Bosnia, was formed in Washington under the leadership of Stephen Walker, one of five Balkan experts who quit the State Department over U.S. policy in the former Yugoslavia. The Center continued to sponsor discussions, but further action seemed stymied. Perhaps the darkest of these discussions was with David Rieff, author of *Slaughterhouse: Bosnia and the Failure of the West.* Rieff had been to the war zone a dozen times in eighteen months, and was now completely without hope for Bosnia, where he saw UNPROFOR as shamelessly complicit with the Serbs. It was at this meeting that Michael Lerner, editor of *Tikkun*, outlined a scheme for a one-minute silent work stoppage by a million or more Americans in solidarity with Bosnia. Did a million Americans know where Bosnia was? Reiff gazed at him with silent incredulity. I rejoined, ironically, that it was much more practical to think of thirty people in this room committing civil disobedience and going to jail than of a million having a moment of silence, and the press coverage would no doubt be the same.

Civil disobedience was in fact becoming a topic of discussion within the loose Bosnian protest community, often in connection with the increasingly problematical, if increasingly widespread, demand to lift the arms embargo. Most in our group did not want to take the civil disobedience route. Strozier strongly objected to using a Ghandian technique to, in effect, promote war. Others questioned the ethics of disobeying local laws which bore no relation to the issues under protest. Still, in the spring of 1994, about twenty-five individuals affiliated with a number of different groups, including a few active in our Center committee, I among them, were arrested for obstructing traffic in front of the U.S. Mission to the United Nations. In this brief choreography, cameras rolled while we were handcuffed and transported to a local police precinct. The next day the *New York Times* ran our picture without mentioning the point of the action, the demand to lift the arms embargo.

With the U.N.'s resolve on Sarajevo and the other so-called "safe havens" crumbling, and the Clinton administration fixed on health care and the approaching election, the Citizens' Committee ebbed away. Robert Lifton continued honorably to speak out for a stronger U.N. mandate and the assertive safe haven plan. In May, a year to the day from our Washington lobbying effort, the Center attempted to hold one last general meeting for the purpose of issuing a strong and unified statement. However, strong and unified statements were no longer possible. The major groups from the Bosnia-interested community thronged the room, but the philosophical differences present from the beginning had become intractable. At this meeting, the core group's continued commitment to strong multilateral action through the United Nations was confronted by a drive to lift the arms embargo and contempt for the U.N. The "peace movement" was at war with itself. The meeting ended in disarray and anger, with no action taken. On this note, our efforts to "save Bosnia" came to a close.

"How all occasions do inform against me," cried Hamlet, and so might the Bosnians. On a cultural fault line, as they have been drily told by academic political theorists, marking the boundary of Hapsburg and Ottoman Empires, and fated, according to this theory, to be a site of perpetual conflict, they have had the ill-luck or ill-timing to galvanize an extraordinary number of other real and potential divisions world-wide. They have provided a target of convenience on the margin between communism and a virulent resurgent nationalism. Their possible defense was trapped between American presidencies, from which direction the only effective leadership on their behalf might have issued. Their plight spelled discord between the American government and its former enemy, Russia, friend of the Serbs, a discord quickly smothered at their expense. Even their dedicated moral allies, as our brief experience shows, could not agree on which principle to defend them with. Finally, and most dismally, Bosnia increasingly stands at the center of a struggle between liberal internationalists who would reenforce the United Nations, and those, on the left as well as on the right, who would abandon it to the dust of failed idealist experiments.

As I complete this account, "safe havens" fall to the hellish ideal of ethnic purity, terrified refugees seek safety from rape and murder, thousands of men are taken away to suspected terrible fates, and the West undergoes its most dramatic spasm yet of embarrassed meetings and uncertain resolves. "Never again," the single great moral victory to emerge from the defeat of European fascism, and in this sense the ethical core of twentieth-century humanist reconstruction, is finished now. It has been "historicized," even if the West gathers itself to end the marriage.

Simone Weil wrote, in her matchless essay "On Human Personality," that the cruellest, most soul-destroying words one human being can visit on another are "You do not interest me." The opposite attitude is described at the end of *The Protean Self,* where Robert Jay Lifton makes an eloquent plea for individual transcendence of class and ethnic identifications towards an opening to the wider horizon of "species identification." Our struggle to engage our fellow citizens and our government in the destiny of the Bosnians was of course a failure by standards of practical achievement. But by quite another standard, we all understood how necessary our effort was. In a world where instantaneous knowledge of evil plants in each of us the seed of moral illness, we were trying to save not only the Bosnians but ourselves.

Note

I wish to thank Nannette P. Sachs, a member of the Citizens' Committee on Bosnia-Herzegovina, for her helpful comments on this article, as well as Claire Oakes Finkelstein and Dr. John D. Ryan for their thoughtful readings.

14

Manliness and the Great War

George L. Mosse

Returning in 1815 from the battle of Leipzig where the Prussians and their allies had defeated the troops of Napoleon, the poet and writer Ernst Moritz Arndt exclaimed, "I return from a bloody battle fought among men" ("Ich komm aus blutigem Männerstreit").[1] This seems to state the obvious. And yet here manliness was no mere slogan but stood for a definite moral posture, for virtues which modern society thought it required and needed. Manliness, according to the neo-classical tradition, symbolized both order and progress, through its "quiet greatness" (to use J. J. Winckelmann's phrase of 1755);[2] the harmonious proportions of the body and the virile play of muscles. Much later, directly after the First World War, Ernst Jünger will write about the lithe and taut bodies of soldiers bathing at the front during the First World War, "whose muscles move like fluid marble."[3] Modern manliness, then, incorporated both the principle of order as well as virility, the dynamic, which would propel society into the future. Power of Will and manly courage as well as self-control were expressions of this balance of order and progress, of a male stereotype whose modern foundations were laid nearly two centuries before the outbreak of the First World War.

The Great War itself made no fundamental change in the perception of normative masculinity; instead it brought to the fore some of the implications hidden in this manly ideal; features latent in respectable, peacetime manhood now came to the surface and received full play. Manliness in the Great War was isolated, cut off from its traditional social base: the family, women and the many functions it had fulfilled in civilian life. Nevertheless, the association of militarism and masculinity had a long history behind it, and the military—once universal conscription had been introduced during the Age of the French Revolution and Napoleon—had been quick to co-opt the masculine ideal. After all, in its quiet strength and self-control, this ideal was ready-made for the kind of discipline the military needed. Moreover, the education in manliness, which had been a goal of many schools since the beginning of the nineteenth century, was designed to make boys hard, training their bodies and giving them the proper moral posture. These manly qualities did not need an actual war in order to become effective. The "clean-cut Englishman," for example, went out to rule the Empire, but rarely enlisted in the peacetime army, and while the "true German" did become an officer of the reserves, even in peacetime, he lived a civilian, quite un-warlike daily existence.

Yet, even so, a more aggressive warlike posture was encouraged by that part of the manly ideal which, once again, since the age of the Revolution and the Napoleonic wars, had made the urge to serve in a cause which transcended the individual—to put manliness in the service of an ideal—an integral component of true masculinity. The new national consciousness which swept Europe in the wake of the French Revolution and the Napoleonic wars provided an outlet for enthusiasm and the will to sacrifice. Here, true manhood became the instrument for both personal and national salvation. The search for a national identity at the very beginning of modern nationhood took the creation of a virile and yet disciplined masculinity, ready to defend and to serve the nation, as one of its goals.

The First World War tied nationalism and masculinity together more closely than ever before, and as it did so, it brought to a climax all those aspects of masculinity which had merely been latent, and which now got their due. Trench warfare, as men went over the top in order to take the enemy's trench, supposedly freed aggression from that restraint which had been one of the signs of true masculinity. A famous passage from Ernst Jünger's war diary, *Thunder of Steel* (*Stahlgewitter*, 1920), was typical of this fighting spirit: trench warfare, he writes, is the bloodiest, wildest, and most brutal of all warfare, ". . . yet it too has its advocates, men whom the call of the hour has raised up, anonymous foolhardy fighters."[4] These soldiers were the "princes of the trenches" who never retreated and knew no mercy.[5] Jünger's glorification of this type of warfare was extreme, especially as a "live and let live" attitude permeated the trenches the longer the war lasted. Nevertheless, once the war was over, one can find similar statements in other nations as well; however none became so popular after the war.

The First World War, as Jünger saw it, was a struggle for existence which released man's animal instincts, but at the same time tested "manly courage" and power of will. Here masculinity was on trial at a time, when, as Joanna Bourke has written, military service not only forced men to discharge the responsibility to their nationality, but also required them to acknowledge their manhood,[6] to become more self-conscious of what it meant to be a man. Battles released stunning energy, according to Jünger, while war stripped man down to his primordial instincts as the best of men discovered their true nature as warriors. The general drift of Ernst Jünger's much acclaimed wartime writings gave a heightened meaning to what it meant to be a man, a new-found joy in struggle without mercy as part of the maturation of the individual. To be sure, the reaction to the war by the vast majority of soldiers was that they were simply doing their duty—"their bit"—and yet even among many of them what was regarded as true manliness gained a new dimension of brutality—not so much during the actual fighting, where soldiers had no time for introspection, but in retrospect, after the war. Manliness, steeled by war, seemed to legitimize the brutalization of post-war politics. For example, revelling in his manhood, Pierre Brasillach, the young French fascist, looking back at the inter-war period, wrote that only from force used in the name of a pure race and nation springs joy.[7]

The release of such feelings of aggression was related not only to the reality of combat, but also to a search for individual freedom from social imperatives, a search which had long been associated with modern warfare. For example, Friedrich Schiller's much cited poem, the *Reiterlied* (*Song of the Cavalry*, 1797), held that only the soldier is free because he has left daily cares behind him and can look death in the face, as over against cowardly and false mankind among whom all freedom has vanished and which knows only masters and slaves. The contrast here is telling, not unlike Jünger's praise for true men, foolhardy fighters, as over against the cowards behind the front. Such men were free because in Jünger's eyes they were on their own and had recaptured their individuality. Even those front-line soldiers who became widely known as opponents of the war, savored not only their manhood but also the freedom which war apparently brought them. When, for example, England's leading anti-war poet, Siegfried Sassoon, wrote his first war poem in 1915 and rhymed that "War is our scourge; yet war has made us wise," and "fighting for our freedom, we are free," he was still in training and had not yet seen combat. The horror and the anger at the foe will pass, he goes on, but the happy legion of comrades and brothers remain.[8] When he took part in battle his reaction was quite different from that of Jünger, and he bitterly condemned the war: "The rank stench of those bodies haunts me still."[9] Nevertheless, both Sassoon and England's other famous anti-war poet, Wilfred Owen, continued to see in war an instrument of their personal freedom, not only because of the shared male camaraderie in the trenches, but also through making them feel that poets were no weaklings as their stereotype had it, but could "take it like a man."

Not only the much-cited English anti-war poets, but also, for example, Ludwig Renn in Germany, shared the consciousness of their manhood with those who had kept their wartime enthusiasm intact. They were apt to criticize the reason for fighting but not the fighting itself.[10] And even the most famous of all the pacifist novels, Erich Maria Remarque's *All Quiet on the Western Front* (1929) gave Paul Bäumer, one of its central figures, the manly qualities of endurance and calmness in battle, so that one reviewer could praise him as Germany's true unknown soldier.[11] Here the ideal of masculinity was so closely linked to the fighting that it could even inform the attitudes of those who hated the military conflict. Modern manliness helped to make war acceptable even to some of its sworn enemies. The ideals of courage, sacrifice and camaraderie—indeed the warrior ideal itself—was hardly touched by their criticism of this particular war. The sense of having achieved the freedom "to be a man" through the instrumentality of war was widely shared. It did not have to lead to Ernst Jünger's brutalization, but could serve to solve other dilemmas inherent in masculinity, such as being both a poet and yet a true man.

Concepts of heroism in war glorified the male camaraderie of the trenches, and such comradeship did indeed serve to mitigate that brutality which rejoiced in killing. The front-line soldiers, Richard Aldington wrote—looking back at the war—had every excuse for turning into brutes, but they did not do so because instead of hating they developed comradeship among themselves.[12] Indeed, most war literature, and war diaries as well, put the squad into the center of their narrative, the "little band of comrades," who fought and died together. As men actually fought in squads consisting of a corporal and some dozen men in the relative isolation of the trenches, they were literally dependent upon one another for survival.

The ideal of men among themselves was not new—it was deeply in-grained in modern society. Middle and upper class life in central Europe and England took place within a network of male-only associations, from Choir Societies to professional organizations and sport as well as political clubs. Just as the war sharpened the image of modern manliness, so it gave a new dimension to the ideal of male camaraderie. Male bonding on this level was regarded as respectable, even though homoeroticism played its part and at times found expression in wartime poetry glorifying masculine beauty,[13] or even in a highly popular German work like Walter Flexe's *The Wanderer between Two Worlds* (*Der Wanderer Zwischen Beiden Welten*, 1915) with its portrait of the nude sun-drenched Lieutenant Wurche. Whatever tensions or frustrations may have existed among the squad during the war, after the war the precedent of the male camaraderie of the trenches was constantly invoked by right-wing politicians as the base upon which the politics of the nation should be reconstructed. While the Soviet of Soldiers and Workers deputies has usually been considered the one entirely new form of government to come out of the war, the ideal of a state based upon a continuation of wartime male camaraderie embraced by National Socialism and to some extent, by all fascist movements, was also unprecedented.[14]

Camaraderie directed some of the member's energies toward maintaining their community, rather than furthering an aggressive spirit. Still, one German officer later killed in the war, wrote that he felt best when bullets surround him and cannons thunder; he experienced "voluptuousness even in pain."[15] Such enthusiasm was close to Jünger's, but also to the quest for purification through suffering which intensified the association of masculinity with the ability to bear pain stoically. During and after the war such sacrifice and purification was often likened to Christ's martyrdom. The resurrection of the dead, for example, was symbolized by the crosses or chapels of resurrection in military cemeteries, while the graves in their serried ranks were reminders of wartime camaraderie: "death had lost its meaning and the will to live was now in the custody of our nation."[16] It was not so much pain or suffering itself as the will to sacrifice which counted towards an education in manliness.

Many who had stayed at home regarded the war as a welcome instrument in the fight against physical and moral degeneration. Some physicians, for example, believed that the war promised victory in this fight. Paul Weindling has written about the so-called "medical optimism" in Germany during mobilization. Not only was military service glorified as healthier than urban life, but the consumption of alcohol and tobacco (long regarded as causes of degeneration) was placed under strict control as threatening military efficiency.[17] The war was conceived as a therapeutic even though the best and most fit would be killed in great numbers. However, the gap they created could easily be filled, if the survivors, strengthened and purified through combat and the spirit of sacrifice, could produce more children; meanwhile, the victorious nation would have acquired additional territory in order to provide homes and work.[18]

German racial hygienists dreamt such dreams, but they can be found in other nations as well. Henry de Montherlant in France believed that war and sport with their male camaraderie were the antidote to degeneration.[19] Drieu La Rochelle, writer, war veteran, and subsequently a fascist, held that to put an end to all forms of warfare would weaken man's élan vital and condemn him to decadence.[20] The European Right continued the fight against so-called decadence after the war, and here war continued to be regarded as a test of true manliness. And though this view was strongest on the political right, to be codified eventually by European fascism, it was to a greater or lesser degree widely shared. And indeed, as we have seen so far, the war, even if it did not redefine masculinity, strengthened many factors which had gone into its making in the first place.

The spirit of adventure which was alive among some soldiers during and after the First World War, is difficult to capture. It had been present from the eighteenth century onward in the construction of modern masculinity, and had taken many forms: exploration of new lands, the creation and maintenance of Empire, as well as enlistment in the armed forces. The literature of adventure, of daring, had always been uncompromisingly masculine, and so it will remain, in spite of the accomplishments of women explorers. Before and after the First World War, many boys were raised on nineteenth-century adventure stories which, however, like those of G. A. Henty in England or Karl May in Germany were not necessarily war-like. The ideal of chivalry was more often than not an important component of such tales of adventure.[21] The spirit of adventure and manliness were considered all but identical.

Here was a quality which all true men must share, but which was rarely listed among the so-called masculine virtues; it was simply assumed under the rubric of will power and courage. Heinz Zöberlein in a book typically enough called *Faith in Germany* (1938) wrote, looking back at the war, that "greatness derives from danger; ordinary life means strangulation."[22] Adolf Hitler wrote a foreword to this book praising it as indispensable to those who wanted to re-capture the spirit of the front. The English popular writer Saki (Hector Hugh Monroe), to give an example from another country, often used words like "excitement" and "romance" when he wrote about the war.[23] He enlisted with enthusiasm, and though he had lost some of that spirit by the time he was killed, his stories found a greater audience after his death than when he had been alive.

Here, as in the writings of those who rushed to the colors in 1914, excitement blends with a spirit of adventure. Even Erich Maria Remarque's *All Quiet on the Western Front*, in spite of its realistic descriptions of the horrors of war, contains the ingredients of a good adventure story, which may have helped to determine its popularity. The two young soldiers, the central characters of the novel, on the one hand, are numbed by the horror which surrounds them, but on the other, play pranks and engage in what might be called schoolboy adventures even during the fighting. The absorbing way in which these adventures were told, despite the surrounding realism, made even a left-wing journal describe the book as pacifist war propaganda.[24]

Yet, when all is said and done, many of the so-called war stories are primarily tales of courage and iron devotion to duty in which a spirit of adventure is also present. The spirit of adventure was easily co-opted once the war started, used by recruiting posters, war propaganda and expressed in some of the diaries written by front line soldiers.

There was, it must not be forgotten, a certain realism to the warrior aspects of masculinity: front line soldiers had to be tough, had to have will power and a certain aggressiveness in order to survive in the trenches. Nevertheless, qualities which might have been useful in battle remained operative in peacetime as well, giving a cutting edge to the already present masculine stereotype.

War as an educator in manliness, for example, was harsher than sport, which had long been used to instill manly virtues. Those who believed that the war had made men out of boys were not necessarily mistaken. Thus Siegfried Krakauer, German sociologist and left-wing liberal, in his memoirs made fun of the reckless enthusiasm of the soldiers he met when volunteering for war, "I find so much health strenuous,"[25] and yet he believed that boys matured into men more quickly at the front. But it was an altogether different matter when Adolf Hitler reminisced in *Mein Kampf* that seventeen-year-olds returning from battle no longer seemed to be boys but looked like real men. Indeed, for Hitler himself, as he saw it, fighting the battle of Langenmarck (1914) had steeled his nerves and power of will.[26] But unlike Siegfried Krakauer, Adolf Hitler immediately transformed this experience into a principle of politics: such manliness was a battle cry against all adversaries, a belief in the politics of confrontation.

Whatever the reality behind the wartime myth of masculinity and the links between pre- and postwar man, a general feeling prevailed that a new type of man had emerged from the trenches. Ernst Jünger led the way, writing about the new race of men the war had produced, loaded with energy, men of steel with chiselled faces, ready for combat.[27] Perhaps the most striking example of all the qualities which such new types of men were said to possess was not to be found on the ground but in the sky: the fighter pilot practiced a new profession, unknown before the First World War. He became the object of romantic longing, of the spirit of adventure, and at the same time conjured up memories of knightly combat, of a more civilized kind of warfare, absent in the trenches. The "knights of the sky" became among all warring nations one of the most powerful symbols of manliness. Fighter planes, until fairly late in the war, flew in single combat, and once an enemy plane had been shot down, actual gestures of chivalry were not unknown: captured pilots were entertained at officers' mess, and at times a wreath was dropped behind enemy lines in order to honor the fallen. The "knights of the sky" were both a new race of men in their flying machines and at the same time were thought to embody the traditions of male honor and chivalry.[28]

The very fact that fighter pilots fought in the sky, "within timelessness," gave them a special aura. They were always pictured as representatives of true manhood, its looks and its virtues. Thus Oswald Boelcke, Germany's most famous flying ace during the First World War, was said to have possessed a "harmonious beauty," simple and modest, even while keeping his own strength under control—an interesting echo of the "quiet grandeur" Winckelmann's Greek youths were said to possess.[29] Such a representative of exemplary manhood had to be chivalrous as well: "Oswald Boelcke does not shoot the defenseless."[30] That pilots controlled the most up-to-date machinery no doubt re-enforced the masculine ideal, though this image was immediately spiritualized: the airplane was not just a product of technology but had to be part of the soul of the flyer, just as a rider is yoked to his horse. This new heroic ideal as it emerged from the First World War heightened the manly qualities attributed to the soldierly man, but in addition, through the concept of chivalry and the setting in timelessness, it mediated between the individual and the perils of modernity.

Many of the examples cited have been German, and indeed it is in Germany as well as in Italy that this supposed new type of soldierly man had its strongest political impact as it was co-opted after the war by the political right. However, even in England and France so-called "soldierly men" became much used symbols among postwar nationalist groups, not only for veterans or the radical right but among most conservatives as well. For the most part, however, such men were not considered new types, but were made to represent a normative manly ideal. Thus Tait McKenzie who sculpted the figures of young men on several English war monuments tried to convey their "power, beauty and virility," their physical as a symbol of their moral perfection, in tune with the accepted masculine ideal.[31] The youth upon which, so he thought, England's future depended had an alert, happy and slightly quizzical expression, as on the Cambridge War Monument.[32] The German "soldierly man" as the true inheritor of the war experience, by contrast, was supposedly close to Ernst Jünger's description, deadly in earnest, dedicated and disciplined, whose thin lips were rarely said to open for a smile.[33]

The German soldierly man marching into the peace projected a certain ruthlessness, a reminder that it was only with the lost war, the harsh peace, and the revolution which followed that German politics became brutalized, aiding National Socialism's access to power. Manliness, as refined by the war certainly played an important role in that process, and the idealized, always disciplined, and sometimes aggressive male body became through the sculptures of Arno Breker a much used symbol of National Socialism.[34] But in Italy fascism also placed its hopes in a rejuvenation of masculinity, a process which was said to have begun in the war. The new type which was said to have emerged from the war built upon normative masculinity's emphasis upon courage, will power, self control, idealism and the performance of duty. There were no surprises here, only an extension of manly virtues which were generally accepted.[35]

The association of militarism and masculinity had always been present. Yet masculinity and militarism did not have to be so closely associated. The education of boys to manliness did not require war but could, for example, make use of physical exercise in order to become effective. However, the association of manliness and nationalism as expressed through war encouraged the assertion of virility, a dynamic which could serve to defeat those manly qualities which were meant to project harmony and restraint. The result of such a defeat, the consequence of the war and its aftermath, contributed to that brutalization of politics which has blighted our century.

Notes

1. Ernst Moritz Arndt, "Die Leipziger Schlacht," *Sämtliche Werke*, vol. 4 (Leipzig, n.d.), 83.

2. Johann Joachim Winckelmann, *Gedanken über die nachahmung der Griechischen Werke in der Malerei und Bildhauerkunsst* (Insel Ausgabe, n.d.), 38.

3. Ernst Jünger, *Der Kampf als inneres Erlebnis* (Berlin, 1938), 67.

4. Ernst Jünger, *The Storm of Steel* (New York, 1975), 235.

5. Ibid., 235.

6. Joanna Bourke, *Working Class Culture in Britain, 1890–1960* (London and New York, 1994), 183.

7. Robert Brasillach, *Notre Avant Guerre* (Paris, 1941), 282; see also, George L. Mosse, *Fallen Soldiers* (New York, 1990), Chapter 8.

8. Adrian Caesar, *Taking It Like a Man. Suffering, Sexuality and The War Poets: Brooke, Sassoon, Owen, Graves* (Manchester, 1993), 56.

9. Siegfried Sassoon, "A Working Party," (1916), *The Penguin Book of First World War Poetry*, ed. Jon Solkin (Harmondsworth, 1979), 124.

10. Adrian Caesar, *op. cit.*, 155.

11. Axel Eggebrecht, "Paul Bäumer als der unbekannte Soldat, *Die Weltbühne*, xxv, erstes halbjahr 1929, 212ff.

12. Cited in *The Lost Voices of World War I*, ed. Tim Cross (London, 1988), 381.

13. I.e. Martin Taylor, *Lads. Love Poetry of the Trenches* (London, 1989).

14. See George L. Mosse, *The Measure of Man: the Construction of Modern Masculinity* (New York: Oxford University Press, 1996), Chapter 8.

15. *Lieutenant Sender. Blätter der Erinnerung für seine Freunde*, ed. M. Spanier (Hamburg, 1915), 22.

16. Ernst Jünger, *op. cit.*, 254.

17. Paul Weindling, *Health, Race and German Politics between National Unification and Nazism, 1870–1945* (Cambridge, 1989), 283.

18. Heinz-Peter Schmiedebach, "Sozialdarwinismus, Biologismus, Pazifismus—Ärztestimmen zum Ersten Weltkrieg," *Medizin und Krieg*, ed. Johannes Bleker und Heinz-Peter Schmiedebach (Frankfurt a. Main, 1987), 102.

19. I.e. Henri de Montherlant, "Les Chevaleries," *Nouvelle Révue Francaise*, vol. 54 (January, 1941), 163.ff.

20. Robert Soucy, *Fascist Intellectual: Drieu La Rochelle* (Berkeley, 1979), 265.

21. I. e. Martin Green, *The Adventurous Male, Chapters in the History of the White Male Mind* (University Park, PA, 1993).

22. Michael Golbach, *Die Wiederkehr des Wektrieges in der Literatur* (Kronberg i/T 1978), 227.

23. A. J. Langguth, *Saki. A Life of Hector Hugh Munro* (New York, 1981), 157.

24. Karl Hugo Sclutius, "Pazifistische Kriegspropaganda," *Die Weltbühne*, vol. XXV, erstes Halbjahr, 1929, 517.

25. Siegfried Kracauer, *Ginster, von ihm selbst geschrieben* (Berlin, 1928), 23.

26. Adolf Hitler, *Mein Kampf* (München, 1934), 181.

27. Ernst Jünger, *Der Kampf als inneres Erlebnis* (Berlin, 1922), 32.

28. I have analyzed this war experience in George L. Mosse, *Fallen Soldiers*, 148ff; and in "The Knights of the Sky and the Myth of the War Experience," in *War a Cruel Necessity?* ed. Robert A. Hinde and Helen E. Watson (London/New York, 1995), 132–209.

29. Johannes Werner, *Boelcke: der Mensch, der Führer der deutschen Jagdfliegerei* (Leipzigt, 1932), 10, 209.

30. Werner von Langsdorf, *Flieger am Feind* (Gütersloh, 1934), 40/41.

31. Christopher Hussy, *Tait McKenzie, A Sculptor of Youth* (London, 1929), 35–36.

32. *Ibid.*, 67; K. S. Inglis, "The Homecoming: The War Memorial Movement in Cambridge," *Journal of Contemporary History* 27(1992): 600.

33. Kurt Eggers, *Die Kriegerische Revolution* (Berlin, 1941), 21.

34. George L. Mosse, "National Socialism, Nudity and the Male Body," *Culturefront* 3(1994): 89–92.

35. Heinz-Peter Schmiedebach, "Sozialdarwinismus, Biologismus, Pazifismus—Ärztestimmen zum Ersten Weltkrieg," *Medizin und Krieg, op. cit.* (Frankfurt a. Main, 1987), 102.

15

U.S. over Iraq: High Technology and Low Culture in the Gulf Conflict

John M. Broughton

Sometimes I have wanted to go to war . . .
Who would not want to be the angel, high
Over the enemy's cities with wings
Broad as the foreshadow of death? What boy
Cannot recall from his pitiless dreams
That carnage laid about him in his bed.
                              —Robley Wilson, "War"

Despite certain continuities, warfare entered a new phase in its historical development in Vietnam, one that has been referred to aptly as "technowar"[1] and the consequence of which is more or less indiscriminate "techno-bloodshed."[2] The nature and implications of this transformation became clear only in the Persian Gulf War.[3] Many commentators have remarked on the specific role of high technology in this transition, with the emphasis on the noun, "technology." However, the adjective should not be ignored: a key feature of the transition to technowar is its altered spatiality, the *vertical* dimension of warfare becoming particularly salient.

During the Gulf War, not only the technology but also the moral rhetoric was "high."[4] The following account aims to recall the profound contradictions between the elevated, triumphalist discourse of the U.S./ U.N. alliance and the atrocities conducted by its forces in the name of peace and democracy. Such contradictions can be linked to the transition into high-technology warfare, and in particular to the escalation of violence that it both entails and requires. As we shall see, the contradictions may not reflect logical inconsistencies or failures of reason as much as the paradoxes of figurative meaning in the new battle scenario.

177

Vertically Polarized Experience and Elevated Political Morality

"High/low" (including "top/bottom," "up/down," "above/below," "north/south," "raise/lower," "ascend/descend," etc.) is a fundamental dimension organizing all human experience.[5] The vertical polarization is a primary, systematic ordering device for not just the epistemological, but the moral, political, and other domains as well. The vertical iconography captured in the opposition between "superior" and "inferior" positions slides over easily into the contrast between "noble" and "servile."[6] It pervades not only social order and cultural activities,[7] but also geographical space, psychic forms, and even the physical body.[8]

Ontological ordering in space also comprises a dimension of morality and power in the relations between people.[9] Even an activity as ordinary and everyday as *looking* has an intrinsic social and political dimension in the vertical plane. There is no literal, neutral way of talking about "looking down" on something or someone. The phrase is inherently derogatory. It implies not only a vantage but an advantage. The gaze from above elevates the seer and degrades the seen.[10] The downward gaze is an act of power—of willful self-enhancement and attempted disenfranchisement of the other.

No polar dimension remains "unmarked"; all separation achieves and maintains a system of inequality.[11] "High" implies superior class, and elevated status carries with it presumptions of entitlement.[12] The entitled carry the burdensome privilege of responsibility for formulating, applying, and enforcing the moral order, with its requisite segregation of good from bad. George Bush spoke of gaining "the moral high ground,"[13] a phrase borrowing from the terminology of the military, for whom "holding the high ground" means taking a "commanding position [from which] the enemy can be more easily observed, and if need be, targeted."[14]

The very act of taking a vertical perspective tends to involve aggression as well as empowerment: "Verticality and great height have ever been the spatial expression of potentially violent power."[15] The other is subordinated not only by objectification but also by a discourse of force. For example, in geometry or architecture, when we unpack the structure of a three-dimensional object in terms of a two-dimensional sketch, laid out as if viewed from above, this is customarily referred to as an "exploded" diagram.

Aggression, of course, maintains polarity. The legitimation of polar opposition by status and its naturalization by scientific law constitute an order of latent aggressiveness, initiated from the privileged pole. This order sustains the separation of the two echelons; it ensures a broken connection by deploying devices of "splitting"[16] that make opposites out of complementaries. Within such a systematic organization of socially sanctioned experience, any contact or overlap between "high" and "low" is strictly taboo.[17] This principle of authoritarian ordering is difficult to preserve during war, since the latter requires direct and repeated contact. In consequence, the legitimacy of military activity is constantly open to being compromised.

Military Subordination

The high/low dimension was used to powerful effect during the Persian Gulf War. The media management of the war, and even the military strategy employed during the conflict, can be seen as means to a polarized segregation of the U.S. as very high and Iraq as very low. This semiotic positioning tended to be taken by media and public alike as virtually *a priori*: by definition, enmity requires accentuated vertical dominance, which is its only legitimate expression.

> We Americans, with our complete mastery of the air, wage war in three dimensions against a foe trapped, like the creatures in certain geometrical games, in two dimensions. The result is that the killing and the dying have come apart. In this war so far and for the most part, we kill and they die, as if a race of gods were making war against a race of human beings."[18]

This strict structure of subordination, however, ran afoul of the need to make the military event resemble a battle between two comparable opponents—a real "engagement" rather than a massacre.[19] Not surprisingly, both military and government insisted that there was a certain parity of force, so that the war would not be construed as a mismatched contest, or the punishment disproportionate to the crime. There was a substantial risk that the allied forces might come to be seen as merely repeating exactly the same kind of crime that Hussein had originally committed in his invasion of Kuwait, a smaller bully being displaced by a bigger bully. After all, the last two military involvements on the part of the U.S. forces—Grenada and Panama—had both been invasions of small and relatively defenceless neighbors. The impression had to be sustained that the act of subordination was a well-deserved achievement, the fruit of arduous and skillful labor, rather than the illegitimate supremacy of a stacked deck. Otherwise, victory could have become confused with massacre, and sympathy for the underdog (the "Rocky" syndrome) could have prevailed.

As the war moved along, U.S. technology appeared not only to counter but to out-class Iraqi technology, to the point that the mismatch of combatants eventually became quite transparent.[20] Hi-tech seemed pitched against a distinctly lo-tech. One observer described the U.S. as a "wounded eagle: a large bird of prey which, injured and in decline, moves to a diet of baby rabbits."[21] One imagines that the mismatch must have added to the disenchantment of sports fans at home who were looking for a closer contest. As the news about April Glaspie's and Bob Dole's sly maneuvers leaked out,[22] the fight looked more and more like a rigged bout (cf. "Saddam on the Ropes," *Newsweek*, Feb. 25th, 1991).

Despite the need to simulate parity of forces, the media insisted on repeated allusions to the economic gap between the civilized, technological power of the U.S. and the relatively underdeveloped state of Iraq. The discrepancy in technical advancement was given an ideological gloss: "Democracy" was lauded as the pinnacle of human evolution, while the "dictatorship" of Iraq was denigrated as virtually a bestial state. Commonly heard phrases like "bomb them back into the Stone Age" were not merely crude expressions of unbridled aggression, but affirmations of the vertical distance between the despicable-murderer culture and the noble-executioner culture. It was the privilege of the latter to serve as punitive agent safeguarding the cosmic pecking order, reinforcing the hierarchy and preventing any pretensions of the lower to rise above its allotted station.

High Technology and High Society

The engagement in the Gulf was touted as the first war to exploit the true potential of the new, "high" technology. The fascination evoked by the display of this weaponry,[23] its iconic centrality in media coverage,[24] and the ease with which it provided an apparently indisputable, morally neutral criterion of superiority[25] were marks of an emergent era in warfare—a different international situation characterized by a deadly hypertrophy in the linkage between national economic advancement and military status.[26]

Of course, this transition does not represent an absolute discontinuity in military history; the emphasis on hardware is not new to war. But the graphically demonstrable transfer of cognitive function to weaponry

Figure 1. Cartoon parodying the much-cited military description of the effect of saturation bombing on the Iraqi infrastructure.

dramatizes a significant qualitative shift in the relationship of human beings to machines occurring at the end of this century.[27] The supposed perfection of missile and antimissile,[28] testifying to the preferability of electronic warfare,[29] presents itself as an indelible mark of the information revolution. Computers, lasers, and video combine to reassure us that the vast apparatus of information processing is not just a luxury, but actually guarantees our safety, protecting our boundaries and making possible the continued survival of our democratic, "high" way of life.

The corresponding, inverse inference (less frequently drawn) is that the information revolution is an elaboration of the traditional apparatus of instrumental violence. Virilio and Lotringer have described this "revolution" as the basis of a general technocultural "war for preparation for war," an acceleration of activity that weaves aggression into the fabric of all collective practices.[30] The merging of political authority with a society ordered in terms of information processing and mediated by hierarchies of systems expertise has permitted a fresh synthesis of actual military violence and symbolic cultural violence.[31]

However, if the current regime is to be maintained, the apotheosis of that which is technical—not to mention the formal, instrumental cognition that is its psychological foundation—must be accompanied by a systematic strategy for keeping "high" and "low" states distinct and separate. There must be a prevention of technological advance in alien lands, especially those of "the enemy," to match the encouragement of such advance in allied nations. What is lauded as the beneficent transfer of scientific progress between democracies must be distinguished sharply from the malignant "proliferation" of know-how among irresponsible nations and their immoral dictators.[32]

The exaggerated differences "necessitated" by technological advance are accompanied by an escalated ideology of entitlement. The nations of the world, who are purportedly in the process of becoming "united,"[33] are polarized ever more extremely into "high societies," privy to the new techniques of mastery, and "low societies," who are to be deprived of them.[34] Of course, from time to time, the latter may become the object upon which these techniques are exercised, thereby demonstrating the effectiveness of the techniques and increasing their desirability to precisely those who do not have them (at least, those who are still alive). In this sense, the Gulf War was a fitting festival for celebrating the new heights achieved in the spiral of technology.

The preferred administrative term, "R&D" (Research and Development), naturalizes the process of military self-aggrandizement, equating it with national development and human development—the two great imperatives of the modern era. The cult of esoteric weapons research and the catapulting inflation of the currency of "excellence" create the illusion of an inexorable upward thrust that is easily confused with, and insidiously becomes the criterion of, rapid progress.

Trapped in the accelerated vertical climb of production, the public is encouraged to mistake vertigo for euphoria, asphyxiation for a peak experience. The predominant sense of life becomes one of a "trajectory" in which the self is a projectile.[35] The chief form of intelligence becomes that of "artillery logic,"[36] a calculus of propulsion under the guidance of remote control. The primary image of the future becomes that of something falling precipitously from a great height, with the potential of having a big impact.

Pinpoint Bombing

As if to concretize this unconscious cultural imagery, high technology made its most salient Gulf War appearance in the form of the "smart bomb." Nowhere was the downward vector more graphically marked out than in the video clips from the nosecams of televisually guided missiles descending to their dramatic rendezvous with supposed enemy installations.[37]

High/low was here converted into a dynamic trajectory, with source defined as superior and target as clearly inferior—downright evil. Knowledge, agency, size, and power adhered to the attacker, the tiny, helpless enemies "never knowing what hit them."[38] The viewer was put in the position of eyewitness and also in the line of sight, and so implicated directly in the process of aerial attack. The video clips also cemented the two Gulf War technologies together: the weapons and the media.[39]

This type of footage became a key rhetorical device in the efforts of the U.S. military and government to persuade U.S. citizens and the rest of the world that only military targets were being bombed, and that "collateral damage" was being strictly minimized. Matters of "high" principle were at stake: clearly (and visibly), the U.S. would not sink to the level of needlessly imperiling the lives of innocent citizens. To the contrary, as President Bush announced at the start of the war, armed confrontation was being pursued in order to liberate those hapless victims from the tyrannical dictator controlling their country by force. In the public eye, holding to this moral high ground came to be attached to the presentation in evidence of the video imagery from smart bombs, which provided direct evidence of such care and control. Accuracy was transformed into a moral value.[40]

Targeting Women and Children

During the war the U.S. public was systematically shielded from information about the victims of the bombardment. Most of the people who suffered as a result of the Gulf conflict were women and children.[41] An estimated 60% of civilian casualties were children.[42] Meanwhile, the allies claimed that, in the words of Francois Mitterand, the bombing of Iraq was "a question of protecting people who are martyred, persecuted or massacred by the government of Saddam Hussein."[43]

The goal of a structural disintegration of Iraqi society was at odds with the sensed moral obligation to deliver a measured, pointed punishment via "surgical strikes" minimizing "collateral damage." The possible contradiction here was dealt with by military, government, and media largely through deliberate misrepresentation—as we now know not only from the analyses by critics[44] but also from the Pentagon's own postwar admissions.[45] However, the twisting of the facts was not entirely successful in concealing contradictory evidence. Even the smart bombs fell under critical scrutiny as a result of the massacre of 500 women and children (not to mention the aged) in the notorious case of the accurate yet "erroneous" strike on the Al-Ameriyah shelter.[46] The U.S. public's general euphoria about the action in the Gulf[47] was tempered by a growing awareness that the air war was based not on surgical strikes but on carpet bombing.

Why was the targeting of the civilian population not assiduously avoided, and why was the military not disabled by accusations of attacking "innocent women and children"? Those working in the area of gender studies have noted that vertical-vs.-horizontal tends to coincide with the dimension of gender, maleness being aligned with psychic altitude.[48] The vertical ordering is not simply superimposed upon gender in an extraneous or artificial manner. It has been repeatedly engendered through socialization processes in such a way that it has become constitutive of masculinity and its spatial orientation to femininity.[49]

Certainly, by now, we are used to the notion that aspects of space and time may be sex-typed.[50] However, the vertical dimension is not only "symbolic" of the traditionally ruling gender. It also determines, to a great extent, what is salient masculine experience. In addition, masculinity takes "up/down" as the axis along which mastery is exercised.[51] It binds boys and men to certain polar preoccupations that, in addition to determining certain preferred types of work, become a source of self and gender identification: elevation, inflation, hierarchy, erectness, rigidity, and permanence (putting up and keeping up), on the one hand, and systematic reduction, deposition, puncture, and destruction (toppling or taking down), on the other. Central to the structure is the idea that the agent of construction can also be the agent of ruination.

The effect is not purely a psychological one, not just a "bias" or "set" in masculine experience. Rather, gender itself is formed ontologically as a quasi-spatial phenomenon. Neither is the effect purely subjective; it is a universal feature of objective physical and social reality that is marked off as a domain of masculine order. "High/low," therefore, is an axis constitutive of masculinity itself, and by default, femininity also.[52] A specific positioning in the vertical results.[53]

Bombing is arguably the most crassly violent and indiscriminately hostile act in warfare. It articulates the complex, deeply buried, fused mass of infantile aggressive fantasies.[54] As we know from clinical studies of the common borderline personality, the lack of differentiation in this unconscious mass means that anxieties, impulses, and tendencies to act out around sexuality are richly infused with primitive hostility.[55] Moreover, gender dichotomizing and stereotyping are especially exaggerated at this level.[56]

Object relations theory has made us aware of the significance of the object, not just the aim, of our impulses. Given the intertwining of war with sexism,[57] the fact that the objectives of bombardment shift away from the men at the front toward the women at home is perhaps not surprising. But why are children to be selectively bombed as well?

In civilian society, organized as it is by family structure, "high/low" is a dimension readily superimposed upon the generations as well as upon gender, yielding a vertical hierarchy between adult and child.[58] Women and children therefore cluster at the low end of the scale, with the consequence that images of adult men eliminating women and children can serve to reinforce the primary order.

Ramsey Clark's[59] investigation within Iraq during the U.S. bombing has raised poignantly the question of why the military targeted a baby-milk production plant for destruction.[60] What did not occur to him, apparently, in the full flood of his moral outrage is the iconic power of images that confirm the rendering of the enemy as weak and helpless: they tend to reinforce the vertical structure and aggressive separation that sustain the moral legitimacy of war and preclude any sense of its grotesqueness.

Thus, when Gruber[61] asks, "Can a baby be an enemy?," the wartime answer is, paradoxically, the same as in peacetime: "No." In war, babies are not slaughtered *en masse* because according to some deranged perception they pose a threat to our forces, or even because they might one day grow up to revenge themselves on us for the murder of their parents. Rather, it is in the nature of the symbolic power of victimization to target the most helpless (and the least "masculine") as the most graphic demonstration of the enemy's vulnerability and the allies' dominance. Denial of one's own vulnerability is a further useful outcome. The fantasied absolute supremacy is signalled by the appearance of absolute resolve and total lack of misgiving; ruthlessness is employed as signifier of conviction about the magnitude of evil to be combatted. The stark verticality of power is thereby dramatized most sharply.

A related logic helps to account for the U.S. choice of the fuel-air explosive bomb,[62] the cluster bomb,[63] napalm,[64] and liquid phosphorus.[65] These weapons are notorious for their savagely mutilating effects on human flesh.[66] Prior to the war, the U.S. had consistently supported U.N. agreements on the banning of such weapons as inhumane.[67] Despite this history, the above weapons were used routinely in attacks on even heavily populated civilian areas (and not just to clear mines, as claimed).

Figure 2.

The malevolence of weapon choice and the targeting of civilians was not confined to bombs and missiles. See, for example, the new generation of U.S. antipersonnel mines, designed to mutilate but not kill.[68] Tested in action for the first time during the Gulf War, these mines were remotely laid from artillery, multiple rocket-launchers, and aircraft-delivered free fall containers. Scattered indiscriminately, and lacking programmable fuses, they left "a massive residue of potential death for civilians" after the war. Children at play are particularly likely to be victims, and due to the design of the detonation process, will be maimed for life, left "without hands or faces,"[69] and in a context where allied bombing strategy has ruined their chances of proper medical care.[70]

Caldicott and others are outraged at such hypocrisy, and brand it as an act of barbarity or insanity. Yet such critics may underestimate the logic behind the anomaly. Paradoxically, extreme disregard for the humanity of the enemy population, even unintended victims of attacks, serves to strengthen the impression back home that the enemy are truly depraved—barely human. The most rational answer to the question, "How could the U.S. systematically employ a weapon whose use it has itself rendered unconscionable?" appeared to be "The objects of aggression must have placed themselves beyond the pale of any ethical consideration." Ricoeur has documented how regularly in human history the damage sustained by a particular people has been turned around and used as evidence of their initial culpability.[71] After all, how could such heinous defilement possibly befall the innocent?

Such an interpretation—that defiling the enemy is a prime rhetorical objective of battle—helps to understand how the Gulf War carries over into the domestic abuse of our own children.[72] This unexpected linkage was luridly dramatized during the war in the exquisitely sadistic exploitation of a young, innocently blond boy, recruited as paramilitary personnel to represent the patriotic urge during the half-time entertainments at the Super Bowl.[73] In Lloyd deMause's terms, it was "time to sacrifice our children," not just those of the enemy.[74]

Conclusion

The savagery of a concrete attack on the enemy of the moment can distract us from a deeper and more primitive theme: an ambitious and preemptive fantasy of destabilizing or eradicating reality. Not only can we erase history like so many computer files, but to top it off we possess techniques for remaking space in the image of our own *Lebensraum*. Emerging technologies have a powerful figurative dimension, facilitating fresh and more disturbing fantasies that penetrate into the primal matrix of space itself. Lifton and Falk alerted us to the ontological deformation wreaked by the nuclear bomb in the domain of "thingness"; the bomb's-eye view of the "smart" missile introduces an equivalent mutation in the spatiality of things.[75]

The upgrading of not only the weaponry but also the values of warfare to the level of "high" technology marks a particularly pernicious attempt to escalate policies of domination. "Smart" war is not just an advance in instrumental efficiency or ideological deviousness. It is an effort to translate verticality from the physical plunge of deadly mechanisms into the symbolic elevation of exterminating angels—immortal and inscrutable beings who need no moral compunction and are immune to all criticism. This descent into the realm of sadistic fantasy is so primitive that fantasies of transforming spatiality itself in the image of violence are able to pose as scientific reason, the corresponding morality being one of harsh polarity enforced by massively punitive brutalizations.[76]

Our awareness of the psychodynamic nature of twentieth-century history is suggested by the fact that we often narrate it in terms of the progress in atrocities. Innovations in the barbaric, however, are not just psychic catharses; they deserve something more than righteous condemnation or psychodiagnosis. They reflect the point at which perverse, phobic, and paranoid subjectivities intersect with the complex crises of nations facing the instability of their false hierarchies, their inability to mourn past failures, the consequences of their contradictory precepts, and their failure to understand their own trajectories. To date, such problems have not been found susceptible to a technical solution. Rather, experience would suggest that reliance on the development of new technologies followed by exhibitions of their enhanced destructive potential tend to make such dilemmas even harder to resolve.

Notes

These ideas were first presented at a panel on Technology and the Social Imaginary at the Collegia Universitario de Cayey, Puerto Rico, in February 1991.

Heartfelt thanks to those who read and talked over some of these ideas with me: Raymond Barglow, Iain Boal, George Cavalletto, Susan Christopherson, Angela Lastella, Robert Ryan, Neil Smith, Lynne Stone, and Stephen Weart. Members of the Center on Violence and Human Survival at John Jay College provided helpful feedback on early formulations of this argument.

I would also like to thank Jennifer Christian, Barbara Esgalhado, Ricardo Hornos, Ken Smith, Michael Watts, and Starr Zimmerman for help in obtaining research materials; Sally Lee, Daniel Ness, and Rocky Schwarz for assistance in preparing the manuscript; and Ingrid Gerstmann and Michael Harrison for moral support.

1. James Gibson, *The Perfect War: Technowar in Vietnam* (Boston: Atlantic Monthly Press, 1986).

2. Robert Lifton, "Techno-bloodshed," in *Peace Pieces from the Gulf War*, ed. Ad Hoc Committee for Peace (New York: Center on Violence and Human Survival, 1991), 52–53.

3. Chris Gray, *Postmodern War: Computers as Weapons and Metaphors* (London: Free Association Books, 1995).

4. John Broughton, ed., *Friendly Fire: Psychosocial Commentary on the Gulf War* (New York: Teachers College, Columbia University, 1991).

5. Peter Stallybrass and Allon White, *The Politics and Poetics of Transgression* (Ithaca: Cornell University Press, 1986). The phenomenon of "polarization" is discussed in detail in Janet Allen and John Broughton, "Polarization in the Discourse of Peace Psychology," presented at the Pacific Sociological Association, Eugene, OR, April 20, 1987.

6. See Georges Bataille, "The Language of Flowers," in *Visions of Excess* (Minneapolis: University of Minnesota Press, 1985 [1929]), 14.

7. Henri Lefebvre, *The Production of Space* (London: Blackwell, 1991 [1974]). Louis Dumont, *Homo Hierarchus: The Caste System and Its Implications* (Chicago: University of Chicago Press, 1970).

8. Mary Douglas, *Natural Symbols* (New York: Vintage, 1973). Mikhail Bakhtin, *Rabelais and His World* (Bloomington: Indiana University Press, 1984).

9. Ward Churchill, "On Gaining 'Moral High Ground': An Ode to George Bush and the 'New World Order,'" in *Collateral Damage: The 'New World Order' at Home and Abroad*, ed. Cynthia Peters (Boston: South End Press, 1992).

10. Friedrich Nietzsche, *Genealogy of Morals* (New York: Vintage, 1967 [1887]), 65.

11. Jacques Derrida, *Of Grammatology* (Baltimore: Johns Hopkins University Press, 1976). David Lodge, *After Bakhtin: Essays in Fiction and Criticism* (New York: Routledge, 1992).

12. Robert Coles, *Privileged Ones: The Well-Off and the Rich in America* (Boston: Little, Brown, 1977).

13. Churchill, "On Gaining Moral High Ground."

14. Steven M. Shaker and Alan R. Wise, *War Without Men: Robots on the Future Battlefield* (Oxford: Pergamon, 1988), 145

15. Lefebvre, *Production of Space*, 98.

16. See Robert Jay Lifton, *The Protean Self : Human Resilience in an Age of Fragmentation* (New York: Basic Books, 1993).

17. Mary Douglas, *Purity and Danger* (Washington: Praeger, 1966). Cf. Theodor W. Adorno, Else Frenkel-Brunswik, Daniel Levinson, and Nevitt Sanford, *The Authoritarian Personality* (New York: Norton, 1950).

18. Jonathan Schell, "Modern Might, Ancient Arrogance," *Newsday*, February 12, 1991, 86.

19. Noam Chomsky "The Gulf War in Retrospect," in *War After War*, ed. Nancy J. Peters (San Francisco: City Lights Books, 1992).

20. Noam Chomsky, "'What We Say Goes': The Middle East in the New World Order," *Z Magazine* 4,5(1991): 49–64. Barbara Ehrenreich, "The Warrior Culture," in *Beyond the Storm: A Gulf Crisis Reader*, eds. Phyllis Bennis and Michel Moushabeck (New York: Olive Branch Press, 1991). Leonard Thomas, *On the Mass Bombing of Iraq and Kuwait, Commonly Known as "the Gulf War"* (Stirling, Scotland: AK Press, 1991). John Broughton, "The Pleasures of the Gulf War," in *Recent Trends in Theoretical Psychology, Vol. 3*, eds. Henderikus Stam, Leondert Mos, Warren Thorngate, and Bernard Kaplan (New York: Springer, 1993).

21. Edward S. Herman, "War's Bright Future," *Z Magazine* 4,5(1991): 11.

22. Alexander Cockburn and Andrew Cohen, "The Unnecessary War," in *The Gulf Between Us: The Gulf War and Beyond*, ed. Victoria Brittain (London: Virago, 1991). Ramsey Clark, "The April Glaspie Connection," in *War Crimes: A Report on U.S. War Crimes Against Iraq*, ed. Ramsey Clark (Washington: Maisonneuve, 1992). John K. Cooley, *Payback: America's Long War in the Middle East* (New York: Brassey, 1991). Theodore Draper, "The True History of the Gulf War," *New York Review of Books* (1992): 38–45. Sami Yousif, "The Iraqi-U.S. War: A Conspiracy Theory," in *The Gulf War and the New World Order*, ed. Nira Yuval-Davis, (Atlantic Highlands: Zed Books, 1991).

23. Carla Bluhm, "A Lasting Conversation," in *Friendly Fire: Psychosocial Commentary on the Gulf War*, ed. John Broughton (New York: Teachers College, Columbia University, 1991).

24. Fred Ritchin, "The March of Images," *New York Times,* June 10, 1991, A17.

25. Eugene J. Carroll, and Gene R. La Roque, "Victory in the Desert: Superior Technology or Brute Force?" in *The Gulf Between Us: The Gulf War and Beyond,* ed. Victoria Brittain (London: Virago, 1991).

26. Sheila Ryan, "Countdown for a Decade: The U.S. Build-Up for War in the Gulf," in *Beyond the Storm: A Gulf Crisis Reader,* eds. Phyllis Bennis and Michel Moushabeck (New York: Olive Branch Press, 1991). On the virtue attached to advanced military technology, see Raymond Barglow, *The Crisis of the Self in the Age of Information* (New York: Routledge, 1994).

27. Manuel De Landa, *War in the Age of Intelligent Machines* (Cambridge: Zone Books, 1992). Simon Penny, "Smart Bombs, Foolish Strategies," *After Image* 19,9(1992): 14–15.

28. Samuel Elliott, "The Missiles that Worked," *Flight International* 140(1991): 37–38.

29. Mario de Arcangelis, *Electronic Warfare* (Poole: Blandford, 1985).

30. Paul Virilio and Sylvere Lotringer, *Pure War* (New York: Semiotext(e), 1983), 139.

31. John Broughton, "The Bomb's Eye View: Smart Weapons and Military Television," in *Technoscience and Cyberculture,* eds. Stanley Aronowitz, Barbara Martinsons, and Michael Menser (New York: Routledge, 1995).

32. Stephen R. Shalom, "Bullets, Gas, and the Bomb: The Spread of Conventional and Unconventional Weapons," *Z Magazine* 4,5 (1991): 12–23. On the notion of "high states," compare Robert Lifton, *The Nazi Doctors* (New York: Basic Books, 1986), 475.

33. Virilio and Lotringer, *Pure War.*

34. Robert Lifton, "America triumphant," in *Peace Pieces from the Gulf War,* 77–78.

35. John Broughton, "Bomb's Eye View."

36. Peter Slojterdijk, *Critique of Cynical Reason* (Minneapolis: University of Minnesota Press, 1987 [1983]).

37. On the psychological politics of the "smart" bomb, see my "Bomb's Eye View," and "The Bomb in the Bathroom," in *Recent Trends in Theoretical Psychology, Vol. 4,* eds. Ian Lubek, Gail Pheterson, and Charles Tolman (New York: Springer, 1995).

38. Tom Clark, "Forty Days," in *War After War,* ed. Nancy J. Peters (San Francisco: City Lights Books, 1992), 70. On the disproportion between attacker and attacked, see Broughton, "Pleasures of the Gulf War."

39. W. J. Thomas Mitchell, *Picture Theory* (Chicago: University of Chicago Press, 1994); Patricia Mellencamp, *High Anxiety* (Bloomington: Indiana University Press, 1992).

40. Les Levidow, "Castrating the Other: The Gulf Massacre as Paranoid Rationality," *Psychoculture* 1,1(1995): 9–16. Avital Ronell, "Support our Tropes," in *War After War,* ed. Nancy J. Peters (San Francisco: City Lights, 1992).

41. Nawal El Saadawi, "The Impact of the Gulf War on Women and Chil-

dren," in *War Crimes*; Human Rights Watch, *Needless Deaths in the Gulf War: Civilian Casualties During the Air Campaign and Violations of the Laws of War* (New York: Human Rights Watch, 1991).

42. Helen Caldicott, *Towards a Compassionate Society* (Westfield: Open Magazine, 1991); Fadia Faqir, "Tales of War: Arab Women in the Eye of the Storm," in *The Gulf Between Us*.

43. John Brewda, "U.S. Readies Pretext to Bomb Iraq Again," *Executive Intelligence Review* (1991): 40–41. Cf. Josette Alia, *La Guerre de Mitterand: La Derniere Grande Illusion* (Paris: Orban, 1991).

44. Barton Gellman, "Allies Sought Wide Damage in Air War," *Guardian Weekly*, June 1991, 18; Murray Kempton, "The Wake of the Storm," *New York Review of Books* 18 (1991), 45; John R. MacArthur, *Second Front: Censorship and Propaganda in the Gulf War* (New York: Hill & Wang, 1992); Holly Sklar, "Brave New World Order," *Z Magazine* 4,5(1991): 29–34; Peter Walker, "The Myth of Surgical Bombing in the Gulf War," in *War Crimes: A Report on U.S. War Crimes Against Iraq*, ed. Ramsey Clark (Washington: Maisonneuve, 1992).

45. John H. Cushman, "Pentagon Report on Persian Gulf War: A Few Surprises and Some Silences," *New York Times*, April 11th, 1992, A4.

46. See 'Eyewitness Report' section of Ramsey Clark, "A letter to Javier Perez de Cuellar," in *War Crimes*.

47. Martin de C. Hinds, "Not Euphoric But Perplexed, Nation Deals with Peace," *New York Times* (Oct. 20th, 1991): 2:1,32.

48. Robert Bly, *Iron John: A Book About Men* (New York: Vintage, 1990), x. Cf. Norman O. Brown, *Love's Body* (New York: Norton, 1968).

49. We know this from the work of Lifton's mentor, Erik Erikson, in *Childhood and Society* (New York: Norton, 1950), 42–43.

50. Evelyn Fox Keller, *Gender and Science* (New Haven: Yale University Press, 1985).

51. John Broughton, "The Masculine Authority of the Cognitive," in *Piaget Today*, eds. Bärbel Inhelder and Denis de Caprona (Hillsdale: Lawrence Erlbaum, 1987).

52. Jean Comaroff, *Body of Power, Spirit of Resistance* (Chicago: University of Chicago Press, 1985).

53. Roberto Zapperi, "Above and Below," in *The Pregnant Man* (New York: Harwood, 1991). Georges Bataille, "The Pineal Eye," in *Visions of Excess* (Minneapolis: University of Minnesota Press, 1985 [1929]).

54. Joseph Redfearn, *The Exploding Self* (Wilmette: Chiron, 1992).

55. Otto Kernberg, *Borderline Conditions and Pathological Narcissism* (New York: Jason Aronson, 1975).

56. Glen A. Mazis, *Trickster, Magician, and Grieving Man* (Santa Fe: Bear & Co, 1993).

57. Dorothy Dinnerstein, "Toward the Mobilization of Eros," in *Face to Face*, ed. Meg Murray (New York: Greenwood, 1983). Betty A. Reardon, *Sexism and the War System* (New York: Teachers College Press, 1985). Susan Griffin, *A Chorus of Stones* (New York: Anchor, 1992).

58. John Broughton, "Infantile Annihilation Fantasy and the Gulf War," presented at the National Psychological Association for Psychoanalysis, New York, April 14th, 1991. Cf. John Broughton, "Babes in Arms: Object Relations and Fantasies of Annihilation," in *The Psychology of War and Peace: The Image of the Enemy*, ed. Robert W. Rieber (New York: Plenum, 1991).

59. Clark, *War Crimes*.

60. Broughton, "Infantile Annihilation Fantasy."

61. Howard Gruber, "Can a Baby Be an Enemy?" in *The Psychology of War and Peace: The Image of the Enemy*, ed. Robert W. Rieber (New York: Plenum, 1991).

62. Alexander Cockburn, "Beat the Devil," *The Nation* (July 1991): 42–43; Martin Kinsley, "Dead Iraqis," *New Republic* 6 (1991): 12–13; Leonard, *Mass Bombing*. John Schneidman, "Discount-a-Bomb," *Newsweek*, February 25, 1991, 27.

63. Michael T. Klare, "High-Death Weapons of the Gulf War," *The Nation*, June 3rd, 1991, 3–5 [reprinted in *Collateral Damage: The 'New World Order' at Home and Abroad*, ed. Cynthia Peters (Boston: South End Press, 1991)]. Mark Sacharoff, "War crimes in the Persian Gulf," in *Peace Pieces from the Gulf War*, 99–106. Howard Zinn, *Power, History and Warfare* (Westfield: Open Magazine, 1991).

64. Charles Strozier, "Learning to Cry," *Peace Pieces from the Gulf War*, 107–109; Ramsey Clark, "The Legal and Moral Basis for an International War Crimes Tribunal," in *War Crimes*.

65. Helen Caldicott, "Compassionate Society." David Levi-Strauss, "(Re)-thinking Resistance," in *War After War*, ed. Nancy J. Peters (San Francisco: City Lights, 1992).

66. Tom Gervasi, *America's War Machine: The Pursuit of Global Dominance* (New York: Grove Press, 1984).

67. Carl Ratner, "International Law and War Crimes," in *War Crimes*. Ramsey Clark, "Legal and Moral Basis."

68. Robert L. O'Connell, "The Worst Weapon," *Quarterly Journal of Military History* 4,2(1992): 56.

69. O'Connell, "Worst Weapon," 57.

70. Michael Weissbach, "Relief Mission Arrives in Baghdad," *Executive Intelligence Review*, July 1991, 42–43.

71. Paul Ricoeur, *The Symbolism of Evil* (Boston: Beacon Press, 1967).

72. Broughton, "Infantile Annihilation Fantasy." On the familial origins of aggression in the parent-child relationship, see my "Dialog of Imaginary and Symbolic," in *Lacan and War*, eds. Maria Taruzzi-Goldman, Samuel Wortzel and C. Edward Robins (New York: Nomos, in press).

73. Eric Larsen, "Gulf War TV," *Jump Cut* 36(1991): 3–10.

74. Lloyd de Mause, "It's Time to Sacrifice . . . Our Children," *Journal of Psychohistory* 18,2(1991): 135–44.

75. Robert Jay Lifton and Richard Falk, *Indefensible Weapons: The Political and Psychological Case Against Nuclearism* (New York: Basic Books, 1982).

76. For a detailed analysis of the fantasy components of massive destruction, see Broughton, "Babes in Arms."

16

Physicians and Nuclear War

Victor W. Sidel

The Hippocratic Oath is widely viewed in the United States—as in other
societies with cultural traditions that have roots in ancient Greece—as a
paradigmatic summary of the physician's role. Many of the physician's
duties set forth in the oath seem timeless and universal. These include
requiring the physician to refuse to reveal secrets confided to her or
him by the patient, to refuse to give a deadly drug even if it is requested
by the patient and to refrain from sexual relations with the patient. Indeed these duties and a number of others found in the oath appear in
similar historic documents in societies such as India and China that do
not look to Greek civilization as part of their cultural heritage.[1]

But despite the apparent universality of its provisions, using the Hippocratic Oath to epitomize our expectations of our society's doctors fails
to recognize how limited and controversial the oath, two millennia after
its compilation, has become. The duties enumerated in the oath are
limited to those that physicians owe to other physicians (as befits its
origins as an oath binding doctors to fealty to their teachers and to other
members of their guild) and that physicians owe to their individual patients; nothing in the oath explicitly defines the physician's obligations
to the broader society. Furthermore, many of the duties prescribed for
physicians by the followers of Hippocrates are today viewed as anachro-
nistic or at least subject to significant exceptions. For example, physicians today are legally required to reveal to legal authorities or public
health authorities facts about their patients, such as the presence of certain infectious diseases or of a gunshot wound, even if the patient asks
that these facts be kept secret;[2] physicians are not infrequently asked for,
and many physicians give, deadly drugs to dying patients;[3] and a few
physicians, although the practice is widely questioned, prescribe or even
practice "sexual therapy."

As a result of the narrowness of the oath and its changing interpretation, many U.S. medical schools at the time of graduation of their students ceremonially use a revised version, the "Declaration of Geneva," first adopted by the World Medical Association in 1948.[4] This "modernization" of the Hippocratic Oath includes more general and more flexible formulations of the original duties. For example, the guild obligations are reduced to two injunctions: "I will give to my teachers the respect and gratitude which is their due" and "My colleagues will be my brothers and sisters." Parenthetically, it is of interest that the first of these injunctions, by failing to insert a comma before the word "which," makes the final clause adjectival rather than appositional and limits the obligation of respect and gratitude only to those teachers, like Robert Lifton, to whom respect and gratitude are due. And it was not until 1994 that the second injunction was amended to recognize explicitly that women can be members of the guild.

The Declaration of Geneva also adds several new duties to those prescribed in the Hippocratic Oath, duties that broaden the social responsibility of the physician. Some of these are designed to prevent acts such as those perpetrated by Nazi physicians, acts so effectively analyzed by Dr. Lifton.[5] The new duties imposed by the Declaration of Geneva include: "I will not permit considerations of age, disease or disability, creed, ethnic origin, gender, nationality, political affiliation, race, sexual orientation, or social standing to intervene between my duty and my patient" and "I will not use my medical knowledge contrary to the laws of humanity."

But even these societally oriented aspects of the Declaration of Geneva, important and broadening as they are, fail to state an obligation by the physician to engage in social actions or advocacy that will contribute to the health of patients or of the community. It is of interest that both the Code of Ethics of the American Medical Association and the oath that had been taken by all medical graduates in the former Soviet Union include broader statements of social responsibility, statements that include a responsibility for social action.[6]

The range of social actions that physicians have taken over the centuries to promote the health of their patients is extremely broad. These actions go beyond simply treating a patient's current condition or urging the patient to reduce his or her individual risk. A number of physicians have attempted to change the social conditions that led to their patient's illness and that might lead to illness among other members of the community. A particularly dramatic example of the difference between preventive advice to an individual patient and actions attempting to protect everyone lies in the difference between those physicians in New York City in the early part of this century who attempted to prevent tuberculosis by advising their patients who lived in tenements to "sleep with their heads out the window" while other physicians urged social change that would reduce the risk to all tenement dwellers by replacing the tenements with better living conditions.[7]

An example of advocacy and action outside the United States may be found in the life of Rudolf Virchow, who worked during the nineteenth century in Berlin, in what was then Prussia. A renowned pathologist, he was a pioneer in using cell theory to explain the effects of disease in organs and tissues. He coined the words "thrombus" and "embolus" as well as many other still-used terms and concepts, and is remembered throughout the world for his brilliant contributions to the science of pathologic anatomy.

Virchow is remembered even more for other contributions. In 1847, at the request of the Prussian government, he traveled extensively in rural areas to investigate a severe typhus epidemic. He reported that the underlying causes of the spread of typhus were government neglect and oppression, poverty, illiteracy and religious exploitation. Based on his findings, he proposed education in the Polish language; self-government; separation of church and state; shifting of taxes from the poor to the rich; improvement of agriculture; development of cooperatives; and the building of roads. Illness, he argued, has its origins in social problems; medicine, to be successful, must be predominantly a social science. Virchow's advocacy was consistently on behalf of the poor and powerless. The physician, Virchow argued, is the "natural advocate for the poor."[8]

Virchow also combined his medical work with direct political action. In 1848 he joined the first major workers' revolution in Berlin. He was later elected to the Berlin City Council and to the Prussian Diet, where he was a founder of the Progressive Party and an outspoken opponent of Chancellor Otto von Bismarck. In that role Virchow supported legislation to regulate the processing of pork products to prevent trichinosis. A widely related story, probably apocryphal, has it that Bismarck, who opposed the legislation, challenged Virchow to a duel. Virchow, as the challengee, had the choice of weapons. He is reported to have proposed that two sausages be prepared, one full of trichinae ova, with Bismarck as the challenger to have the selection between the two weapons, that is, which sausage to eat first. Bismarck withdrew from the duel, and the legislation passed.

Social action on behalf of health, in its broadest sense, has sometimes led physicians to activities deeply controversial in their times and in the society in which they lived. Documents link, for example, the actions of physicians who advocated the abolition of slavery and those, acting more directly, who attempted to protect fugitive slaves from recapture by their owners. Indeed, some physicians have raised their voices and participated in social activism at personal peril. Dr. Salvador Allende Gossens, a physician and public health specialist who was elected president of Chile in 1970, was assassinated in a military coup in 1973. In the U.S., Dr. Edward Barsky organized medical care for the Abraham Lincoln Brigade, a contingent of U.S. volunteers who fought to defend the Spanish Republic against destruction by fascist forces in the 1930s; he was rewarded for his efforts, following his refusal to testify before the Un-American Activities Committee of the U.S. House of Representatives, by imprisonment and suspension of his medical license. Dr. Howard Levy was convicted at court-martial during the Vietnam War hysteria of the late 1960s and served three years in military prison for his refusal to participate in training Green Beret troops to use medicine as a weapon in the Vietnam War.[9] Dr. Yolanda Huet-Vaughn was convicted at court-martial during the Desert Storm hysteria of the early 1990s for "desertion to escape hazardous duty" because of her refusal to serve in the Persian Gulf area as a medical officer in the U.S. armed forces, whose actions she believed violated international law; her conviction was later overturned by the U.S. Court of Military Appeals, after she had served a long sentence at the Fort Leavenworth military prison and had been threatened with loss of her license to practice medicine.[10]

The problems inherent in social activism by physicians as part of the direct medical care of their patients are even more complex. Waitzkin and others have noted that all communications between patients and physicians have social and political components.[11] Although the very name "doctor" has its origin in the Latin "to teach," physicians, insofar as they act as teachers at all, usually teach their patients simply to "comply" with medical advice. Physicians, explicitly or implicitly, usually advise their patients to conform to the expectations of family, community and society. Only a few physicians choose explicitly to encourage their patients or members of their communities to fight back against sexism, ageism, racism, homophobia or poverty, although these are risk factors for many illnesses and interfere with effective medical care. Few U.S. physicians have ever heard of Paulo Freire, a Brazilian educator who counseled that education can only be effective when it is empowering and helps to break the bonds of oppression by involving people in groups to identify their problems and the social roots of them. Without this insight, however, most attempts at patient education or indeed any education at all may be useless or counter-productive.[12]

This analysis has a logical extension: physicians would be more effective in promoting health among their patients, the members of their communities and the people of the world if medical students were selected on the basis of interest in social activism, were educated in its techniques, and practiced them after graduation. Unfortunately such a recommendation is not likely to be accepted by those who control medical education or practice in the U.S. or by most current medical students or physicians, with whose social class interests such a recommendation would appear to conflict.

In recent times a number of social activist physicians have worked in accordance with the statement by the World Health Assembly that "the role of physicians and other health workers in the preservation and promotion of peace is the most significant factor for the attainment of health for all"[13] by participating in national organizations such as Physicians for Social Responsibility (PSR) in the United States and by working internationally through the International Physicians for the Prevention of Nuclear War (IPPNW), which was awarded the 1985 Nobel Prize for Peace.[14] Description of the work of PSR and IPPNW is particularly important in a book honoring Dr. Robert Lifton, who has played an important role in both organizations, including membership on the PSR Board of Directors, and who has alerted the world to the long-term impact on the survivors of the nuclear bombings of Japan[15] and to the "psychic numbing" caused by the nuclear threat.

In 1961 a group of Boston physicians, led by the renowned cardiologist Dr. Bernard Lown, analyzed in detail the potential medical consequences of thermonuclear war. While the physicians in the group had for years been individually concerned about the consequences of the nuclear bombing of Hiroshima and Nagasaki and the implications for the future, this concern was intensified by the development during the 1950s of much more powerful nuclear weapons based on nuclear fusion rather than nuclear fission. These new weapons, called hydrogen bombs or thermonuclear bombs, could produce an explosive force over one-thousand-fold greater than the bombs used in 1945. When the energy distribution of these new weapons was published in the open literature, the group in Boston, of which I was privileged to be a member, analyzed the potential consequences if these weapons were to be detonated over the United States. This analysis, published in the *New England Journal of Medicine* in 1962,[16] concluded that the use of thermonuclear weapons would be so destructive to human health, to the environment, and to medical personnel and facilities that attempts at response by health professionals after the bombs had fallen would be almost entirely futile.

The report argued that physicians, because of their special knowledge of the medical effects of these weapons and because of their special responsibility to protect the health of their patients and their communities, had a special responsibility to help prevent the use of nuclear weapons. The report gained worldwide attention and contributed to the rapid growth of PSR, which has worked for over one-third of a century for the prevention of the use of nuclear weapons.

The report documented both the short-term and the long-term health effects caused by the enormous blast energy, heat flux and ionizing radiation produced by nuclear weapons; trauma caused by building collapse, flying debris and the throwing about of humans caused by the blast wave; the severe burns and lung damage directly caused by the immediate radiation of heat and by the conflagrations and fires ignited; and the damage to tissues and organs caused by the neutron and gamma ray flux from the initial detonation and by alpha, beta and gamma radiation from short-range and long-range fallout of the radionuclides produced by the detonation; and the psychological damage to the survivors. We pointed out that the use of nuclear weapons is likely to cause greatest injury to those most vulnerable—infants, the elderly and the infirm—a direct violation of one of the fundamental principles of international law. We have further pointed out that the radioactive fallout, carried by the prevailing winds, would inevitably cross national boundaries and cause radiation injury among the population of neutral nations, another direct violation of a fundamental principle of international law. Furthermore, as Robert Lifton has so effectively argued, there are world-wide psychological consequences of the use of weapons and even of threat of use of these weapons.

The analysis used as its focus the consequences of a nuclear bombing of the U.S. totaling 6559 megatons, a potential scenario envisioned by U.S. civil defense planners, that would kill 86 million people in the first few hours. In the ensuing weeks and months, the fatality total would rise to 133 million; of 93 million survivors, some 32 million will have been injured. Approximately 80 percent of US medical resources—hospital beds and personnel, blood, drugs and medical supplies—would be destroyed. There would be only one hospital bed available for every 64 trauma and burn victims requiring hospitalization, only one surviving physician for every 633 injured patients, only 14,000 available units of blood when 64 million units would be needed.

During the post-attack period, tens of thousands of people would be packed together in radiation shelters usually lacking adequate water and food supplies and systems for heating, cooling, ventilation or waster disposal. Since full-time shelter occupancy would be necessary in many areas for 5 to 30 days, and part-time occupancy for as long as 9 months, the risks of dehydration, malnutrition and epidemic viral and bacterial disease will be extreme. In the post-shelter survival period the epidemic potential would continue, made more intense by malnutrition and lack of protection against cholera, typhoid, tetanus, poliomyelitis, measles and diphtheria. Communicable disease death rates as high as 25 percent were predicted.

In 1980 Dr. Lown, together with Dr. Yevgueni Chazov, a Soviet cardiologist, founded IPPNW, which now consists of affiliated physician organizations in 80 nations with some 200,000 supporters; PSR is the U.S. affiliate of IPPNW. The work of IPPNW and its affiliates was recognized by the Nobel Peace Prize in 1985. The Nobel citation in part read:

> (IPPNW) has performed a considerable service to mankind [sic] by spreading authoritative information and by creating an awareness of the catastrophic consequences of atomic warfare. . . . This in turn contributes to an increase in the pressure of public opposition to the proliferation of nuclear weapons and to a redefining of priorities, with greater attention being paid to health and other humanitarian issues. Such an awakening of public opinion . . . can give the present arms limitation negotiations new perspectives and a new seriousness.[17]

With the rapid stockpiling of nuclear weapons in recent years, the stockpiles now contain bombs with an explosive force equivalent to 11 billion tons of TNT, two tons of TNT for every human being on the planet. Detonation of even a small fraction would cause catastrophic environmental damage, including the short-term damage that massive fires and short-lived radionuclides produced by the nuclear detonation would cause to the ecosystem and the long-term damage caused by long-lived radionuclides, such as plutonium with a radioactive half-life of 24,000 years. There is a potential for a so-called "nuclear winter," a precipitous drop in surface temperatures on a hemispheric or global scale as a result of millions of metric tons of soot injected by mass fires into the upper atmosphere, blocking sunlight and absorbing heat. Even the modest temperature drop predicted by more recent calculations (which some have called "nuclear autumn") would be sufficient to cause serious disruptions of agriculture, posing a threat of malnutrition or famine among the survivors.

There is also potential damage from widespread ionizing radiation to human immune systems leading to epidemics of uncontrollable infectious disease and the potential damage to the human gene pool and its consequences for generations yet unborn. In addition to this damage to human beings and to human gene pools, the incremental international efforts of the past two decades to protect biodiversity and nonhuman gene pools could be dashed in just a few days. These worldwide environmental and ecological consequences, harming people and the environment in nonbelligerent as well as belligerent nations, we have noted, would be violations of a fundamental principle of international law.

Even if use of nuclear weapons is limited to military targets, such as command bunkers and missile silos, weapons of large yield are likely to be detonated at ground level. Such use would produce even greater radioactive fallout than would be the result of airbursts over cities; the fallout would cause damage to humans hundreds and even thousands of miles from the site of the attack. Such consequences, even if "collateral" to attacks on military targets, would affect the people of neutral nations and therefore are contrary to international law.

The damage that the use of nuclear weapons would cause to medical personnel and medical facilities is a violation of the Geneva Convention of 1949 and therefore a clear violation of international law. The 1987 WHO report, "Effects of Nuclear War on Health and Health Services," stated that the use of even a single nuclear weapon would overwhelm any health service, inflict indiscriminate and inhumane suffering on innocent civilians, and cause widespread and long-term environmental destruction that will affect many future generations. The 1987 WHO report went on to state that, since no health service in the world could adequately cope with the casualties resulting from the use of even a single nuclear weapon, "the only possible solution is primary prevention; that is, the prevention of nuclear war." Since the WHO Constitution states that "the attainment of the highest possible level of health is a fundamental human right" and that the indiscriminate destruction of medical personnel and facilities and the massive increase in injury, disease, disability and death caused by the use of nuclear weapons would therefore represent a clear violations of rights specified by the WHO Constitution.

In sum, IPPNW has argued that the use of nuclear weapons would constitute a public health and environmental disaster. Representatives of IPPNW and of other groups—including the International Association of Lawyers Against Nuclear Arms and the International Peace Bureau—therefore worked with delegates to the World Health Assembly, the governing body of WHO, to support the introduction by the delegates of a resolution that would have instructed the Director-General of WHO, as a specialized agency of the United Nations, to request the following advisory opinion from the International Court of Justice (the "World Court") in the Hague: "In view of the health and environmental effects, would the use of nuclear weapons by a State in war or other armed conflict be a breach of its obligations under international law including the WHO constitution?"

On May 14, 1993, the 46th World Health Assembly adopted this wording for their historic resolution (WHA46.40, "Health and Environmental Effects of Nuclear Weapons"). WHO officially submitted the question to the World Court on August 27, 1993 and on September 13 the World Court requested written statements on the issue from WHO member nations. With the exception of those from the nuclear powers and their allies, the statements urged the Court to respond positively to the request. More recently, the nations affiliated with the Non-Aligned Movement initiated a resolution, adopted by the United Nations General Assembly, asking the court to declare illegal both the use and *the threat of use* of nuclear weapons. Over 100 million people around the world, including 43 million people in Japan alone, signed declarations of conscience on this question; I personally had the privilege, as Co-President of IPPNW, of participating in the presentation of the signatures to the World Court at the Peace Palace in the Hague.

Work on the World Court Project is only one of the ways in which IPPNW is working for the abolition of nuclear weapons. Abolition has been the ultimate goal of IPPNW since its founding. At the IPPNW International Council meeting in October 1993 a decision was made to initiate immediate activities directed at abolition of nuclear weapons, with a goal of negotiation of a convention banning the development, production, testing, stockpiling, transfer or use of nuclear weapons by the year 2000.

In attempting to achieve this goal, IPPNW has a number of intermediate objectives. These objectives are important themselves and in addition further the effort to achieve abolition. They include:

- Prompt negotiation of a Comprehensive Test Ban Treaty (CTBT) that would be: (1) universal (all nuclear weapons states included); (2) nondiscriminatory (no exceptions to international inspections of fissile material and a cut-off in the supply of fissile materials); and (3) applicable to all tests (including "peaceful nuclear explosions").
- Limited extension of the Nuclear Non-Proliferation Treaty (NPT)

with strong conditions imposed for its further extension, including progress by the nuclear weapons nations toward abolition of all nuclear weapons.

- Cessation of fissile material production, including plutonium and highly enriched uranium, international control of all stockpiles, and prompt disposal of these materials has highly radioactive waste.
- Strengthened international safeguards against export of fissile materials and nuclear weapons, built into both international and national law.
- Completion of the destruction of nuclear weapons called for under START I and II, with inclusion of UK, France and China in START III.
- Negotiation of a convention on the illegality of nuclear weapons, similar to the 1993 Chemical Weapons Convention, banning development, production, testing, possession, transfer and use of nuclear weapons.

In sum, IPPNW urges the nations of the world that possess nuclear weapons to destroy their stockpiles as rapidly as possible and to pledge that these weapons will never again be used under any circumstances. IPPNW also urges the nations of the world that do not possess nuclear weapons to refrain from acquiring them and to insist that all nations declare by solemn agreement that nuclear weapons will be abolished by a defined deadline in the near future. Abolition of nuclear weapons—like the abolition of human slavery over a century ago—is within our grasp. In July a top U.S. military officer—Air Force General Charles A. Horner, who as head of the U.S. North American Aerospace Defense Command is responsible for defending the United States and Canada against nuclear weapons—publicly called for the abolition of nuclear weapons. He said, "The nuclear weapon is obsolete; I want to get rid of them all." "Think of the high moral ground we secure by having none," he continued. "It's kind of hard for us to say to North Korea 'You are terrible people, you're developing a nuclear weapon' when the United States has thousands of them." This is the first time to our knowledge that a high-ranking U.S. military officer on active duty has made such an explicit statement calling for abolition.

In addition to attempts to prevent nuclear war and to abolish nuclear weapons, IPPNW is concerned with prevention of the use of other weapons of mass destruction and with prevention of war itself. IPPNW helped in the development of the Chemical Weapons Convention, which, upon its ratification by a sufficient number of countries, will prohibit the development, production, testing, stockpiling, transfer or use of chemical weapons. IPPNW also had a role in attempts to strengthen the Biological Weapons Convention. It supports the work of the Commission on Disarmament Education, sponsored by the International Association of University Presidents and the United Nations Center for Disarmament Affairs, which attempts to introduce material on disarmament and prevention of war into the curricula of universities throughout the world. The curriculum for medical schools, entitled "Medicine and Peace," is in part based on curricula developed by PSR and IPPNW.

IPPNW also addresses the root causes of growing insecurity in the world through additional advocacy programs and partnerships. Specifically, IPPNW works closely with its affiliates in the Southern Hemisphere as active partners in the campaign for abolition by locating the campaign within the broader paradigm of common security. UNICEF has called the 1980s "The Decade of Despair." For the world's poorest people, average incomes have dropped by 10% to 25%. Today more than one billion—one in every five—live in absolute poverty. In the 37 poorest countries, spending on health has been reduced by 50% and in education by 25%. In over 50 nations, primary school enrollment has been falling.

IPPNW has long recognized that "destruction before detonation," the diversion of enormous human and financial resources to the arms race, is one of the major causes of delayed economic development and of poverty. For this reason many of us in IPPNW believe it must add to its goals sustainable development, cancellation of the debts claimed by the nations of the "North" against the nations of the "South," and elimination of world poverty. We must call upon the nations of the world, particularly the rich nations that profit from the poverty of the poor nations, to recognize that the health, well-being and security of the people of the North depends increasingly upon the health, well-being and security of the people of the South and to change their economic, military and political policies so as to close the gap between the haves and the have-nots, between the powerful and the powerless. IPPNW has added a third co-president from the South to its co-presidents from East and West and increasing parts of its efforts will be devoted to these issues.

In its Nobel Prize-honored work IPPNW follows in a great tradition. The physician and humanist, and Nobel Peace laureate, Albert Schweitzer wrote that "nuclear weapons are against international law and they have to be abolished," but he also warned that "all negotiations regarding the abolition of atomic weapons remain without success because no international public opinion exists which demands this abolition." His friend Albert Einstein, a Nobel laureate in physics, whose name honors the medical school at which I work, warned us that "the explosive force of nuclear fission has changed everything except our modes of thinking and thus we drift toward unparalleled catastrophe. We shall require an entirely new pattern of thinking," he said, "if mankind is to survive." To this warning Dr. Bernard Lown, IPPNW Founding Co-President, who together with Dr. Evgueni Chazov accepted the Nobel Prize on behalf of IPPNW, has added, "The new way of thinking must be an awakening—to our common origins, to our shared problems, as well as to our common fate. If we are to prevail, we must never delegate in the presence of challenge and never whisper in the presence of wrong."[18]

The work of Robert Lifton, who has never whispered in the presence of wrong, reminds us that many U.S. physicians, in their work with individual patients or in their work in the broader community, indeed recognize the importance of social action and through it make important contributions to their society and to its health. Unless this tradition is continued, reinforced and expanded in new directions, an irreplaceable source of social change for health and well-being will be lost. We ignore this important lesson at our peril.

Notes

Portions of this paper were adapted from the author's introduction to Eugene Perry Link, *The Social Ideas of American Physicians* (Selingrove, Penn: Susquehanna University Press, 1992); from the author's article, "Progress towards the Abolition of Nuclear Weapons," *Medicine and War* July 1995; and from speeches by the author on behalf of IPPNW in Geneva (June, 1994), Kuala Lumpur (October, 1994), Hiroshima (November, 1994), Bangkok (January, 1995) and the United Nations in New York (January, 1995)

1. Ludwig Edelstein, "The Hippocratic Oath: Text, Translation and Interpretation," *Bulletin of the History of Medicine*, Supplement 1 (Baltimore: Johns Hopkins University Press, 1943).

2. Victor W. Sidel, "Confidential Information and the Physician," *New England Journal of Medicine* 264 (1961): 1133–37.

3. Thomas E. Quill, "Death and Dignity," *New England Journal of Medicine* 324 (1991): 691–93.

4. *The World Medical Association Handbook of Declarations* (Geneva: World Medical Association, 1994).

5. Robert Jay Lifton, *The Nazi Doctors: Medical Killing and the Psychology of Genocide* (New York: Basic Books, 1986).

6. Christine K. Cassel, Andrew L. Jameton, Victor W. Sidel and Patrick B. Storey, "The Physician's Oath and the Prevention of Nuclear War," *Journal of the American Medical Association,* 254 (1983): 652–54.

7. Eugene Perry Link, *The Social Ideas of American Physicians* (Selingrove, PA: Susquehanna University Press, 1992).

8. George A. Silver, "Virchow, The Heroic Model in Medicine: Health Policy by Accolade," *American Journal of Public Health* 77 (1987): 82–88.

9. Robert Liberman, Warren Gold and Victor W. Sidel, "Medical Ethics and the Military," *The New Physician* 17 (1968): 299–309.

10. Victor W. Sidel, "Quid Est Amor Patriae"? *PSR Quarterly* 1 (1991): 96–104.

11. Howard Waitzkin, *The Politics of Medical Encounters* (New Haven: Yale University Press, 1991).

12. Paulo Freire, *Pedagogy of the Oppressed* (New York: Seabury Press, 1970; Continuum Publishing Company, 1990). See also Paulo Freire, *Education for Critical Consciousness* (New York: Seabury Press, 1973; Continuum Publishing Company, 1983), and Nina Wallerstein and Edward Bernstein, "Empowerment Education: Freire's Ideas Adapted to Health Education," *Health Education Quarterly* 15 (1988): 379–394.

13. World Health Assembly Resolution WHA 34.38, 1987, cited in Victor W. Sidel, "Weapons of Mass Destruction: The Greatest Threat to Public Health," *Journal of the American Medical Association* 262 (1989): 680–82.

14. Bernard Lown, "Nobel Peace Prize Lecture: A Prescription for Hope," *New England Journal of Medicine* 314 (1986): 985–87.

15. Robert Jay Lifton, *Death in Life: Survivors of Hiroshima* (New York: Simon and Schuster, 1967).

16. Special Study Section, Physicians for Social Responsibility, "The Medical Consequences of Thermonuclear War" *New England Journal of Medicine* 266 (1962):1126–55.

17. *Nobel Peace Prize* (Cambridge, Mass: International Physicians for the Prevention of Nuclear War, 1986).

18. Bernard Lown, *Never Whisper in the Presence of Wrong: Selections from Speeches on Nuclear War and Global Survival* (Cambridge, Mass: International Physicians for the Prevention of Nuclear War, 1993).

17

Development and Violence

Ashis Nandy

The problem with the idea of development is not its failure. The idea has succeeded beyond the dreams of its early partisans, who never imagined that they had hit upon something whose day had come. Developmentalism has succeeded where Western colonialism and evangelical Christianity failed. It has established itself as one of the few genuine universals of our time. It has become an intimate part of every surviving civilization and changed the self-definitions of some of the least accessible societies. Development has converted even the seemingly non-proselytizable.

These changes in self-definition have gone in two directions. First, there has been a rearrangement of the components of the self in the affected cultures. A new hierarchy of preferred traits has emerged in them. In many Asian, African and South American societies, the traditional cultural preferences are now devalued and are a source of embarrassment for the more self-conscious members of these societies. Such preferences are feared as atavistic or retrogressive, even obscurantist. The ruling élites in these societies are now engaged in various forms of cultural engineering to get rid of these qualities while they themselves get integrated into the global cultural order. They are willing to go to any extent to drive their subjects like cattle towards the better world development promises.[1] A less polite way of describing such self-engineering is to call it a mixture of self-hatred and mimicry leading to a new form of political authoritarianism.[2] The mix has become popular even in cultures being glorified the world over as great success stories in the history of development.

The often-violent retooling of the self has gone hand in hand with the loss of large parts of remembered past.[3] In society after society, uncomfortable and allegedly irrelevant aspects of the past are being shed as constructions fit only for the dustbin of history, again with the help of the coercive apparatus of the state and with much of the world looking the other way. Today, only that past is being celebrated which is seen as conducive to modernization and development; only that past is being rued which is seen as resistant to modernity and development. Together the two "relevant" pasts constitute history and become, after a time, the only memory accessible to the citizenry. The rest become ahistorical, "revivalist" myths. So do aspects of the self intertwined with the lost past. Violent suppression of that past, and the self associated with it, now enjoys enormous legitimacy as an attack against "fundamentalism" and new forms of "Oriental despotism."[4]

Yet, human nature being what it is, all hegemonic visions throw up their own distinctive strains of dissent in the form of counter-visions. During the last two decades, voices have emerged all over the world against the totalizing thrust of development. These voices seem to carry the awareness that, just when the ideology of development is winning its most impossible victories in global politics, it has exhausted its intellectual possibilities. Many of the most sensitive minds of our times now find the charms of development so much tinsel glitter. The details of development now engage mainly the specialists concerned with its pragmatics or management. This loss of intellectual shine has, however, also led to a certain carelessness towards the nitty-gritty of development in the world dominated by the global media and international development experts. The dirty work of development can go on in the backwaters of the world, with many vaguely concerned with the fate of the victims but only a few engaged intellectually and on a day-to-day basis with their fate.

Why this loss of credibility in the world of knowledge when developmentalism is so clearly triumphant in global politics?

The reasons are many, but the main ones all center around the gradual decline in the moral stature of development as an ideology. Many major criticisms of development do have a normative component—such as criticism of the development community's total faith in the global market, impersonal contractual relationships and professional expertise, its commoditification of nature, and its naïve trust in mega-organizations and mega-technology. In addition, development comes to all societies as part of a package, organized around the idea of the nation-state as the prime mover of all social change, a full-blown theory of progress through historical stages, and large-scale massification through urbanization and industrialization. All these are components of a concept of modernity that has a clear moral dimension. If development is, as

Arturo Escober suggests, "a chapter in an anthropology of modernity," it cannot avoid the moral evaluation that is being increasingly applied to the modern vision itself. This evaluation has begun to go against development.

One other factor that may be responsible for the spreading intellectual mutiny against the gospel according to the development planners also partly explains the loss of the seductive charms of developmentalism. In the name of individualism, the ideology of development has gradually denuded the idea of the individual of much of its substantive content. With the invention of development, most things that were once a matter of personal initiative and choice have been systematically handed over to agencies making impersonal, contractual, professionalized choices on behalf of the person. The only initiative the person is left with relates to choices from among available consumables offered by the global market. From health care to child rearing it is the same story. As the area of individual choice has shrunk, a false sense of freedom is created because the contextualizing role of the community has been removed from the choice situation. Indeed, atomized in the name of freedom, the person now stands alone against the forces of the global market and mega-technology.

Simultaneously, violence associated with impersonal bureaucratic structures, of the kind Hannah Arendt talked about, has now acquired freer play. As wars, direct use of violence against unarmed populations, torture and blatant violation of human rights become less and less easy to sell, there is an increase in indirect violence, surveillance and destruction of the life-support systems of communities unable to defend themselves by using modern institutional and legal remedies.[5]

These changes have been brought about not through old-style domination—through naked force and open exploitation. The changes have come through the cooptation of crucial segments of the recipient non-Western cultures into the developmental community—a new community of scholars, policy-makers, development journalists, readers of development news, development managers and activists who together sustain development as a sphere of professional, organizational and entrepreneurial activity. The global system backing the ideology of development has introduced in the recipient cultures new cognitive orders that apparently do not challenge traditions except for their "irrational", "easily disposable" aspects. Entering these cultures through well-meaning missionaries of development, preaching to all and sundry an accessible secular heaven on earth, these orders aim at nothing less than establishing an equation between the sustainability of the global development regime and the survival of cultures. So, what can be read as a major threat to the viability of non-Western cultures is identified as an emancipatory principle updating these cultures for our times and ensuring their survival.[6] Whatever may well-intentioned activists and scholars say, that is the ultimate political meaning of the slogan of sustainable development.

Why is the link between development and violence stronger in the Southern world? One reason can be that in the South, among those not fully uprooted or decultured, developmentalism is still suspect. Not because it is seen as a global conspiracy, but because it has been stripped of all geo-ethnic and temporal qualifications in many Southern societies by the local modernist élites. In societies where communities have not collapsed and the citizens are not entirely massified, there persists a suspicion of a fully universal, space-and-time-transcending sociology of utopianism. For in such societies the privilege of venturing such sociology is given only to religions or theories of transcendence.

Thus, at the very moment the ideology of development seems to have touched something universal in human nature—when from Beijing to Berlin and from Moscow to New Delhi more and more people are taking to the clichéd markers of mass culture as the indices of having made it—some Third World communities and activist-scholars have persisted in exercising a form of suspicion that is very uncomfortable to those dreaming of a homogenized global mass culture hitched to a global developmental regime. In doing so they might be speaking also on behalf of other defeated civilizations, including threatened communities in the superseded West, declared obsolete by the fully modern, reportedly the best-of-all-possible Wests. These activists assume that the struggle against developmentalism is a struggle to reclaim the dignity of cultures that have been turned into a set of experimental subjects, waiting to be sacrificed at the end of a defined set of operations—either to end in a museum or in a department of anthropology or history for a proper *post mortem.* Crucial realities of such cultures have already been excised to ensure—Arturo Escobar says citing Raúl Prebish—the "doctrinal asepsis" of a fully scientitized economics located outside time and space. For development economists, the Third World and its poverty are enabling concepts, which allow them to ply their trade as the resident doctors of our times, specializing in what is allegedly a culturally inherited but curable pathology. They would hate to admit that poverty is not an ancient disease that development cures, but an iatrogenic by-product of the healing touch of modernity itself.[7]

Apart from everything else, there is the "normal" life-span of an idea. Even the best ideas get dated and, human ingenuity being what it is, even the most emancipatory discourses get transformed after a time into new justifications for violence and exploitation. Even if development had not been a particularly oppressive idea at the beginning, it was bound to become one after being thoughtfully adopted by a series of despotic regimes as the final justification of authoritarian politics. As a product of this political process, the culture of development has to kill off all alternative visions of desirable societies. For the same reason, however, imagining a post-development era has come to represent something more than resistance to a hidden structure of dominance; it now means giving back the savage world the right to envision its own future. Such envisioning, whatever else it does or does not do, promises to de-homogenize non-Western subjectivities and to repluralize the idea of social intervention and dissent.

This is not an indirect defence of Afro-Asian nationalism or a plea for a return to the idea of the noble savage. It is an attempt to acknowledge that human beings, given long enough time, can convert any theory of emancipation into new a justification for violence and expropriation. Development has now begun to take over from old-style religious conflicts, colonial wars and racism; it has created new opportunities for a play of those traits that once found expression through standardized channels and justifications of human violence.

One specific issue remains. A painful feature of our times is, I have already hinted, that success in development has usually led to the emergence of authoritarian politics in Third World societies. One by one the societies that have succeeded in development—or shown signs of doing so—have fallen prey to the very success they have tried so hard to attain, in total defiance of existing theories of democracy and development. This correlation between development and authoritarianism has grown even in open societies like India and Sri Lanka after they have opted for more conventional forms of development in the last decade.

We were told in the past that authoritarianism was due to underdevelopment. Development, we were told, guaranteed democratic freedom, at least in the end. Both those who believed in socioeconomic prerequisites of political democracy—from Talcott Parsons to David Easton and from Edward Shils to Karl Deutsch[8]—and those who believed in state-controlled economic growth as the sure road to their utopia—from Lenin to Jawaharlal Nehru—saw Oriental despotism as the primary model of authoritarianism. Both expected economic growth to lead the Asian and African societies towards freedom, not away from it. In the 1960s some scholars like Everett Hagen and K. W. Kapp even went as far as to posit a perfectly inverse relationship between the antidemocratic

personality and the entrepreneurial man.[9] Even David C. McClelland
and company, breathlessly trying to induce economic growth through
higher achievement motive, incidentally produced the insight that the
rise in achievement motive in a society before economic take-off usually
led to lower levels of power and affiliation motives, and thus to lesser
chances of imperialism and authoritarianism.[10]

The experiences of police states such as South Korea, Singapore, Taiwan, China and Brazil have played havoc with this way of thinking in
recent times. It is not accidental that in the Third World, grassroots
movements in general and civil rights movements in particular have increasingly become hostile to the very idea of development. Some of
them do not even care whether one means by "development" conventional development or the new alternative forms of development.[11]

To a second group of scholars, authoritarianism can be a means of
development. These scholars do not formulate their thesis in exactly
these words but they cite the examples of Nazi Germany, Fascist Italy,
Stalinist Russia, Pre-war Japan, the military dictatorships of Latin
America, and Maoist China in support of their thesis. In these societies,
high-pitched mobilizational politics within a closed polity have been
used (1) to enforce consumption-restraints and collective sacrifices, and
(2) to justify enhanced spending, in the name of development, on the
military, the police and the other coercive instruments of the state.
James Gregor has analysed one subset of the genre neatly.[12] Cynical and
blatantly conservative though his thesis may look, it tallies with the experience of peoples who have been the victims of development and seen
their rulers and their First World sponsors choose development over
freedom whenever the chips are down.

There is also the inarticulate thesis—inarticulate because it is implicit
in the activism of many grassroots organizations working all over the
world in areas such as ecology, cultural survival and civil rights—that
development itself releases authoritarian tendencies after it crosses a
certain threshold. This even in societies seriously trying to combine development and democratic participation. The thesis admits that development has always included authoritarian elements, even in the democratic West. The elements were held in check in the Western societies
by colonialism (to the colonies were exported millions of people marginalized by industrial growth in the West and from these colonies were
imported into the West cheap raw materials for development), by restricted franchise (which partly filtered off from the public realm in
Europe voices of the victims of development), by the suppression of
ethnic groups that were made to pay the price of development in ecolog-

ical devastation, uprooting and extinction (as with North and South American Indians), or by the export of authoritarianism to crypto-colonies (as the United States has done in South America for many decades). Once these advantages are lost, authoritarianism reveals itself as the other side of development even in the developed societies.

Such a point of view recognizes three aspects of development that nurture authoritarianism. First, as democratic participation increases and new channels of social mobility open up in a developing society, it brings towards the center of the polity groups previously marginalized. These groups threaten the power of those who control the society and monopolize the benefits of development. Particularly so because development has come to mean in practice the takeover—by the state, the organized sector and the market—of the commons to which traditionally the weakest of the society used to have some access. These commons are then used to produce marketable goods that can never reach the original beneficiaries of the commons. So once some empowerment of the now displaced beneficiaries of the commons take place, they begin to pose a threat to the beneficiaries of development.

For instance, a tribe living in a forest may have "free access" to fuelwood but once the forest is cut down to put up a dam and a hydroelectric plant, the tribe may have no access to the new energy but could, in the process, suffer from uprooting, loss of livelihood, and deculturation. Yet, the very experience of displacement and dispossession may politicize the tribe and make them a threat to the state. Authoritarianism becomes an easy means of containing these new participants in politics and controlling their demands. The containment—A. F. K. Organski calls it the repression of the newly mobilized sectors and identifies it as the very heart of fascism—is legitimized by the manifest normlessness and crudity of the politics of the new entrants.[13] The middle classes are always appalled by the unseemly style of the lower classes in politics. Authoritarianism often takes advantage of this culture shock to contain political participation.[14] And the slogan of development in such societies legitimizes this containment.[15]

Second, development means sacrificing something of the present for the sake of the future. As development becomes a reason of the state, those who control the state feel justified in imposing these sacrifices selectively, under the guidance of experts. Authoritarianism becomes their technique of extracting sacrifices either from target groups identified by the state (in which case the sacrificial sectors on closer examination turn out to be the political dissenters or their support bases) or from those less able to resist making such sacrifices (in which case generally the ideology of "trickle-down effect" or that of "market forces" is invoked).[16]

Third, though development in its present sense is being used for only forty-five years—President Harry Truman was the first to use the term in its present sense—the concept is now retrospectively applied to the 300-year-long process through which the developed societies have passed to reach their present state. Development in non-Western societies is supposed to be a shorter route to that state. Thus, the idea of development has as its underside the memories of the violence and exploitation that went with the early phases of development in the West, and the idea includes the message that the underdeveloped world should make similar blood sacrifices to develop.

The images of the nonunionized workers coming back from work after sixteen hours to rape their own daughters, children below the age of ten working full day in the mills or in high-risk occupations like chimney sweeping, the enclosure movement in England, the women labourers and prostitutes populating the gin alleys—they survive in the Western unconscious as an abyss into which the West may again slip if it gives up the ambition of scaling newer and newer heights of prosperity or loses the will to protect its interests aggressively. These anxieties are then projected into the global politics of development. That is why the developed democratic societies are often the first to endorse a military despot elsewhere, particularly if the latter is smart enough to mouth the idiom of development. That is why the Shah of Iran seemed an overly strict schoolmaster to his Western admirers, whereas Idi Amin looked like a stone-age monster. The former was seen as a practising developmentalist, even if a misguided one, the latter as an unalloyed Oriental despot.

Finally, development tends to sharpen religious, interregional and ethnic tensions by "pitting" traditional communities against each other. This does not mean that such tensions were nonexistent in the past or that the planners provoke them. It means that by giving absolute priority to interests over passions, instrumental rationality over visions and worldviews, development converts the rich, multi-layered relationships among the communities into a unidimensional, interest-based, competitive relationship. And it usually does so in a context where it has already introduced massive environmental changes and disrupted the traditional life-support systems of the communities involved.[17] Once such a conversion has taken place, the conflicts between communities are brought into and negotiated within the modern political and economic spheres. What was a complex encounter of cultures becomes, thus, a hard-eyed battle for the "concrete," development-related gains. The result is the creation of new opportunities for the state sector to step in as the final arbiter among the communities, in the name of facilitating or monitoring development or holding in check violence and primitivism. In the Third World, this arbitration has often been the main excuse or justification for short-circuiting the political process and introducing authoritarian rule.

Notes

This paper was written during my brief tenure as UNESCO Professor at the Centre for European Studies at the University of Trier, during 1994. It draws upon sections of an earlier paper, "Development and Authoritarianism: An Epitaph on Social Engineering," *Lokayan Bulletin*, 1987, 5(1), pp. 39–50.

1. See Shiv Visvanathan, "From the Annals of the Laboratory State," Ashis Nandy (ed.), *Science, Hegemony and Violence: A Requiem for Modernity* (Tokyo: The United Nations University and New Delhi: Oxford University Press, 1988); Claude Alvares, *Science, Development and Violence* (New Delhi: Oxford University Press, 1992); Wolfgang Sachs (ed.), *The Development Dictionary: A Guide to Knowledge as Power* (London: Zed, 1992); and Ashis Nandy, "Culture, Voice and Development: A Primer for the Unsuspecting," in Japanese in Yoshikazu Sakamoto (ed.), *The Structure of World Politics* (Tokyo: Iwanami Shoten, 1993); in English in *Theses Eleven*, 1994, (39), pp. 1–18.

2. Herb Feith's name for such regimes is "repressive developmentalist regimes" and his definition would cover a galaxy of "sucess stories" in development—from Nazi Germany, Stalinist Russia and imperial Japan to South Korea, Singapore, Taiwan, Brazil, Shah's Iran, Ayub Khan's Pakistan and now Deng's China. See his "Repressive-Developmentalist Regimes in Asia: Old Strengths, New Vulnerabilities", paper presented at the conference of the World Order Models Project, New York, June, 1979, and published in International Affairs, Christian Conference of Asia, *Escape From Domination: A Consultation Report on Patterns of Domination and People's Movements in Asia*, Tokyo, Japan, April, 1980.

3. See, for instance, the papers in Frédérique Apffel Marglin and Stephen Marglin (eds.), *Dominating Knowledge: Development, Culture and Resistance* (Oxford: Clarendon Press, 1990).

4. Japan is a neat example; it enjoys unmatched power and autonomy within the world of development but is unable to use them to ensure its own cultural survival. The dominant global consciousness has reconstructed the Japanese tradition as a set of two cultural strands. One consists of a cultural package that has led to Japan's present developmental profile; the other consists of a few cultural accessories and esoterica thrown in for the amusement of Japan's admirers and critics. The former is reportedly the substance; the latter the form that the outsiders must master for the sake of predictability or profitability when dealing with Japan. Even many Japanese have begun to see themselves through these

imported glasses. For them Japanese history is becoming the history of modernization and the establishment of the development regime in Japan. The rest is becoming either folklore meant for the children and the elderly or "culture" meant for the Western thriller writers and tourists. If the present trend continues, it is doubtful if in the next century Japan's past unrelated to her developmental concerns will remain accessible to a majority of her own citizens.

5. According to one estimate, 21.6 million people—roughly the population of all the Scandinavian countries put together—have been displaced by only the construction of dams in India. Gayatri Singh, "Displacement and Limits to Legislation", in Raajen Singh (ed.), *Dams and Other Major Projects: Impact on and Response of Indigenous People* (Goa: CCA-URM, 1988), 91–7; see p. 91.

Another study estimates that of the 60 million aboriginal tribals in India belonging to some 212 tribes, 15 percent have been displaced by development projects, so that they could themselves be developed and turned into "skilled human resources." Smithu Kothari, "Theorizing Culture, Nature and Democracy in India" (Delhi; Lokayan, 1993), mimeo. Half of all the invisible refugees created by Indian development are by now tribals.

6. In a new book Arturo Escobar tells that part of the story. See his *Encountering Development: The Making and the Un-Making of the Third World, 1945–1992* (Madison: University of Wisconsin, in press).

7. "Massive poverty in the modern sense only appeared," Escobar claims, "when the spread of the market economy broke down community ties and deprived millions of people from access to land, water, and other resources."

8. See a brief critical assessment of the political development literature and the "pre-requisites" approach in Satish Arora, "Preempted Future? Notes on Theories of Political Development", in Rajni Kothari (ed.), *State and Nation Building* (New Delhi: Allied, 1976).

9. Everett Hagen, *On the Theory of Social Change* (Homewood, Ill.: Dorsey, 1962); K. W. Kapp, *Hindu Culture, Economic Development and Economic Planning* (New York: Asia, 1963).

10. D. C. McClelland, *The Achieving Society* (New York: Van Nostrand, 1961).

11. For instance, Special Issue on Survival, *Lokayan Bulletin*, October 1985, 3(4–5); Alvares, *Science, Development and Violence*; and "Deadly Development," *Development Forum*, 9(7), October 1983; Madhya-Pradesh Lokayan and Lokhit Samiti, *Vikas ki Kimat* (Ahmedabad: Setu, 1985); Kothari, "Theorizing Culture, Nature and Democracy in India"; Suresh Sharma "Development and Diminishing Livelihood" (New Delhi: CSDS, 1985), pamphlet.

12. A. James Gregor, *The Fascist Persuasion in Radical Politics* (Princeton, N. J.: Princeton University Press, 1974); also *The Ideology of Fascism* (New York: Free Press, 1969).

13. A. F. K. Organski, *The Stages of Political Development* (New York: Alfred A Knopf, 1965).

14. See Ashis Nandy, "Adorno in India: Revisiting the Psychology of Fascism," in *At the Edge of Psychology* (New Delhi: Oxford University Press, 1980), 99–111.

15. The Emergency in India (1975–77) fitted the analysis in a copybook fashion. The state violence and suspension of civil rights the the Emergency produced came packaged in the rhetoric of development and though occasionally the rhetoric of "putting democracy back on the rails" was also used, it was the emphasis on development that sought to justify the police-state methods used in areas such as family planning, control of media, and slum clearance. Similarly packaged arguments have come at different times from the Marcos regime in Philippines, from the military regimes in Pakistan and Thailand, and from Singapore and South Korea.

16. See for example Ashis Nandy, "Introduction: Science as a Reason of State", in Nandy, *Science, Hegemony and Violence.* The idea of trickle-down effect has had a particularly long tenure in the South. In Third World societies that have taken the capitalist path to development, the idea often serves the same function as the suspension of democratic rights does in the surviving socialist regimes. In both cases the aim is to extract economic or political surplus from the population through the science of development or scientific history, both of which are used to justify inequality and violence in the short run in the name of future freedom.

17. For instance, Vandana Shiva, *The Violence of Green Revolution* (Penang: Consumers Association of Penang, 1990); also see Helena Norberg-Hodge, *Ancient Futures: Learning from Ladakh* (San Francisco: Sierra Club Books, 1991), 122–30; and Joke Schrijvers, *The Violence of "Development": A Choice for Intellectuals*, tr. Lin Pugh (New Delhi: Kali for Women, 1993, and Utrecht: International Books, 1993).

18

Tolstoi's Revenge: The Violence of Indian Non-Violence

Wendy Doniger

Introduction

When Hindus and Muslims turned on one another in violence after Partition in 1948, Western intellectuals were astonished that the non-violent Hindus could do such a thing. When, in 1991, Hindus stormed the Babri mosque in Ayodhya, built by the Muslim emperor Babur over the place where the Hindu god Rama is believed to have been born, and over a thousand people died in subsequent riots, we were no longer so astonished. We had become used to the blood shed daily in India in the name of religion, to the killing of Hindus by Sikhs, Sikhs by Hindus, Hindus by Muslims, Muslims by Hindus, Tamil Hindus by Buddhists, Buddhists by Tamil Hindus, Untouchables by Brahmins, Brahmins by Untouchables, and on and on.

What was the source of our earlier Western belief in Hindu non-violence? Is there any basis for it in the intellectual history of India? It is, I think, the intellectual rather than political history of India that has given rise to the Western idea of Hindu non-violence. That is, it is what Hindus have said, and what Western intellectuals have thought that Hindus believe, rather than what Hindus have done, more precisely what Western intellectuals have thought that Hindus have done, that has given rise to the Western idea of Hindu tolerance.

Non-Violence and Vegetarianism

The emphasis on non-violence, *ahimsa*, that Gandhi made so famous in the West, is far from typical of Hindu thinking, let alone Hindu action.

219

Of course, Gandhi did not invent *ahimsa*; Hindus have sworn allegiance to the concept of non-violence at least from the time of *The Laws of Manu*. "Hindu non-violence" is certainly not an idea imposed upon Hindus by Orientalist, imperialist pressure. But it may well be that Hindus doth protest too violently about their non-violence. *Ahimsa*, usually translated as "non-violence" or "non-injury," is not merely the absence of violence; it is derived from the Sanskrit verb *han*, which means "to injure or kill," and is formed as a desiderative noun, meaning "the absence of the desire to injure or kill." It is thus a state of mind, not a policy for behavior; and, as Krsna pointed out in the *Bhagavad Gita*, it is quite possible to adhere to the mental principles of non-violence while killing your cousins in battle. Violence, like all things Indian, begins in the *Rg Veda*, the earliest and most revered text of the Hindu canon, composed sometime around 1,000 B.C.E. This is a text that reveres war, a text whose chief god is the warrior Indra; and a text that revolves around the sacrifice of animals, often depicted in gruesome terms. Thus the sacrificial horse is directly addressed: "Whatever of the horse's flesh the fly has eaten, or whatever stays stuck to the stake or the axe, or to the hands or nails of the slaughterer—let all of that stay with you even among the gods."[1]

The war and the sacrifice were continued and combined in the great Hindu martial epic, the *Mahabharata* (composed from 300 B.C.E. to 300 C.E.), which been called a "ritual of battle." A king in this text insists: "I see no being which lives in the world without violence. Creatures exist at one another's expense; the stronger consume the weaker. The mongoose eats mice, just as the cat eats the mongoose; the dog devours the cat, O king, and wild beasts eat the dog."[2] This same sentiment lies behind the text of a later caste Purana in which the Brahmins tell the king:

> It is said in the Vedas that non-violence is the supreme duty. But violence is not always to be abhorred, and when performed in a sacrifice it leads to heaven. No one can be completely non-violent. Violence is everywhere and therefore, whatever the Jain renouncers say is blind arrogance. Can anyone keep alive without eating and how is food to be got without violence? Is there anyone on earth who does not have a tendency towards violence? O King! people live by violence alone. . . . If a person thinks of his good qualities and thinks badly of others—then also he commits violence. . . .[3]

Nowhere in the *Rg Veda* is it said that "non-violence is the supreme duty." This is, as we shall soon see, a later development. But it is a common habit to attribute to "the Vedas" any sentiment that one wishes to endorse. It is therefore ironic that this text first canonizes non-violence and then challenges its canonic status. It is even more ironic that in this very text, the "violence" of thinking badly of others is committed against Jain renouncers, who are accused of "blind arrogance."

The Jains who are attacked in the brunt of this passage are part of a movement that began to advocate, against the Vedic tradition, the ideal of non-violence. For, by about 500 B.C.E., the violent Vedic world view had been challenged by the renunciant movements that included what became Buddhism, Jainism, and Vedantic Hinduism. As Frances Zimmermann points out:

> In the animal kingdom and then the human one, the dialectic of the eaten eater introduces further divisions between the strong and the weak, the predator and his prey, the carnivore and the vegetarian. Vegetarianism—a brahminic ideal and a social fact in India—precisely calls into question that fateful dialectic in which every class of being feeds on another. The prohibition of flesh, which became increasingly strict in brahminic society, was one way to break the chain of all this alimentary violence and affirm that it is not really necessary to kill in order to eat.[4]

Now, vegetarianism and non-violence are not the same thing at all. A moment's consideration will remind us that it is usual to eat without killing (most Western non-vegetarians, few of whom hunt or butcher, do it every day) and equally normal to kill without eating (what percentage of hit-men or soldiers devour their fallen enemies?).

Indeed, Jan Heesterman has suggested that vegetarianism and non-violence were originally mutually exclusive: that in the earliest period of Indian civilization, non-violent, meat-eating householders would, in time of war, consecrate themselves as (violent) warriors by giving up the eating of meat.[5] They either ate meat *or* killed. In later Hinduism, the strictures against eating and killing continued to work at odds, so that it was better to kill an Untouchable than to kill a Brahmin, but better to eat a Brahmin (presuming that one came across a dead one) than to eat an Untouchable (ditto). Nevertheless, the logical assumption that any animal that one ate had to have been killed by *someone* led to a natural association between the ideal of vegetarianism and the ideal of non-violence toward living creatures. And this ideal came to prevail in India, living cheek to jowl with the continuing ideal of animal sacrifice.

The violent Vedic worldview was both sustained and challenged by *The Laws of Manu*, a basic text of the dominant form of Hinduism.[6] Probably composed sometime around the beginning of the Common Era or slightly earlier, within a few centuries *Manu* had become, and remained, the standard source of authority in the orthodox tradition for that centerpiece of Hinduism, *varnasrama-dharma* (social and religious duties tied to class and stage of life). Over the course of the centuries, the text attracted nine complete commentaries, attesting to its crucial significance within the tradition. *Manu's* terror of anarchy, which is called the "law of the fishes," whereby bigger fish eat smaller ones in an uncontrolled universe, is a direct continuation of Vedic assumptions about natural violence, and *Manu still* upholds the centrality of the violent animal sacrifice that is the pivot of the *Rg Veda.* Thus, *Manu* states that "You can never get meat without violence to creatures with the breath of life, and the killing of creatures with the breath of life does not get you to heaven; therefore you should not eat meat."[7] But it is also said that "Killing in a sacrifice is not killing. . . . The violence to those that move and those that do not move which is sanctioned by the Veda—that is known as non-violence."[8] By defining the sacrifice as non-violent, Manu made it non-violent. In this way, he was able to list the Veda and non-violence together in his summary of the most important elements of the moral life: "The recitation of the Veda, inner heat, knowledge, the repression of the sensory powers, non-violence, and serving the guru bring about the supreme good."[9] Later Hindus attempted to enact this uneasy resolution by using ricecakes in place of the animal victim—and "strangling" the ricecakes at the appropriate moment in the ritual.

Non-violent Hinduism, which defines itself primarily by reference to the Upanishads (which are called "Vedanta," literally, "the end of the Veda") continued to thrive. Though this Vedantic Hinduism has its seeds in the Upanishads, it is fully developed only in the great commentaries on the Upanishads, particularly those of the Vedantic philosophers Sankara and Ramanuja, at the end of the first millennium of the common era. Vedantic Hinduism endorses the concept of *sanatana dharma*, which involves general moral precepts such as honesty, generosity, and non-violence.[10] This was an overarching, unitary, non-hierarchical category of the religion for everyone, a universal goal later compared with that other universal and anti-sacrificial goal, Freedom (*moksa, nirvana*).

The ideal of Freedom might have challenged the Vedic India of fabled elephants encrusted with jewels and temples covered with copulating couples, the world of sensuality from which the omphalosceptic yogis fled. Instead, it was reabsorbed into Vedic Hinduism and inverted into the desire to be reborn, but reborn better in worldly terms (richer, fatter,[11] with more sons, and so forth). And the idea of non-violence, that might have challenged the Vedic demand for violent sacrifice, came instead to supplement that demand. Alongside universal, Vedantic *sanatana dharma,* Hinduism continued to validate the *varnasrama dharma* of polytheistic Vedic sacrifice and the caste system. This resolution of the two strands was formalized in the medieval period, when Vedic Hinduism developed into Puranic Hinduism in the voluminous, encyclopedic texts called the Puranas, texts that remain the basis of both private and public worship to this day. These two basic approaches to human life, the violent (sacrificial) and worldly, and the non-violent (vegetarian) and renunciatory, continue to interact throughout Indian religious thinking. The Vedantic reverence for non-violence flowered in Gandhi; the Vedic reverence for violence flowered in the slaughters that followed Partition.

The Unreal Ideal of Non-Violence

But non-violence became a cultural ideal for Hindus precisely because it holds out the last hope of a cure, all the more desirable since unattainable, for a civilization that has, like our own, always suffered from chronic and terminal violence. Non-violence was an ideal propped up against the cultural reality of violence. Classical Hindu India was violent in its politics (war being the raison d'etre of every king), in its religious practices (animal sacrifice, ascetic self-torture, fire-walking, swinging from hooks in the flesh of the back, and so forth), in its criminal law (impaling on stakes and the amputation of limbs being proscribed punishments for relatively minor offenses), in its hells (cunningly and sadistically contrived to make the punishment fit the crime), and, perhaps at the very heart of it all, in its climate, with its unendurable heat and unpredictable monsoons. This last cause was well argued in 1965 by Nirad C. Chaudhuri in *The Continent of Circe: An Essay on the Peoples of India* (though I am in general less inclined than Nirad Chaudhuri to blame the extremes of Indian religion on the extremes of the Indian climate). Hindu sages dreamt of non-violence as people who live all their lives in the desert dream of oases.

It is against this background that we must view the doctrine of non-violence. Violence is as Hindu as curry (but much older than Indian curry, hot spices being a relatively late culinary innovation in India). In their ambivalent attitude to violence, the Hindus are no different from the rest of us. It was the neo-Vedantin idealists who gladly embraced the Gandhian hope that the Hindus might set an example for the human race in passive resistance. The naive self-image of the neo-Vedantins was encouraged by the liberal American transcendentalists (Thoreau was a great one for non-violence and the *Gita*) and by their own desire to prove to the disdainful British that the Hindus were not the lascivious, blood-thirsty savages depicted in the colonial caricature. We can therefore see a kind of pizza effect (a rather complex, Chicago deep-dish pizza effect) in the contemporary Hindu investment in non-violence: an ancient Hindu idea was appropriated and given new power by Hindus (such as Gandhi) who had been influenced by Western thinkers (such as Tolstoi) who were acquainted with the neo-Vedantins as well as with German idealists who had been reading the Upanishads, making these ideas more attractive both to Westerners and to Hindus still living under the shadow of Western domination. But Gandhi was whistling in the dark.

Hindus respond violently to any slur cast against their non-violence. Recently a member of the Fundamentalist and anti-Muslim Hindu association, the RSS, remarked that, since Hindus are, as is well-known, the least violent people in the world, they deserve to have the land of India to themselves, and therefore the (violent) Muslims should be disenfranchised:

> The spirit of broad catholicism, generosity, toleration, truth, sacrifice and love for all life, which characterizes the average Hindu mind not wholly vitiated by Western influence, bears eloquent testimony to the greatness of Hindu culture. . . . The non-Hindu peoples in Hindustan . . . must not only give up their attitude of intolerance and ungratefulness towards this land . . . but must . . . stay in the country wholly subordinated to the Hindu Nation, claiming nothing, deserving no privileges, far less any preferential treatment—not even citizen's rights.[12]

Here it is perhaps appropriate to recall that it was an RSS man who killed Gandhi. And we may also recall with particular irony, having witnessed the carnage in Bosnia, that when Gandhi was asked how India was going to be able to forge a nation out of two different religious and cultural traditions, he replied, "It can be done. Look at Yugoslavia."

The sort of non-violence that has prevailed in Hinduism was often more of a thinly veiled hegemonic appropriation than the mellow universalism that it has often claimed to be. Thus, for example, Hindus and non-Hindu Indologists often cite as an example of Hindu tolerance the story of the incarnation of the Hindu god Visnu as the Buddha. But a closer look at this myth reveals its hidden agenda: Visnu became the Buddha in order to teach the wrong-headed doctrine of Buddhism to a group of dangerously pious demons in order to lead them from the

Vedas, disarm them of their sacrificial merit, and kill them.[13] Thus the Hindus demonized the Buddhists just as the Christians demonized the Jews.

The appropriation of the Buddha by Hinduism became a staple of Orientalism ("All Indians/Indian religions look alike"). Hollywood films about Hindus in India frequently placed a statue of the Buddha in the central shrine of a Hindu temple. In 1990, a garbled version of the myth of the Buddha avatar was used in Pakistani textbooks to support anti-Hindu arguments, explaining the decline of Buddhism as in fact the Hindus do explain it in the myth of the Buddha avatar: "The Hindus acknowledged Buddha as an avatar and began to worship his image. They distorted his teachings and absorbed Buddhism into Hinduism." A Hindu critic comments on this passage: "The message is oblique, yet effective—that Hinduism is the greatest curse in the subcontinent's history and threatens to absorb every other faith."[14] Certainly this particular brand of appropriation has not led to non-violence, nor was it able to diffuse the political and economic factors that, in India as everywhere else in the world, erupt in communal violence—in India, the blood-bath of Partition. These same political and economic factors, enflamed and perhaps manipulated by the rhetoric of religious intolerance, resurfaced to demolish Babur's mosque in Ayodya.

What Can India Teach Us?

Is there something in Hinduism that could help us to develop our own brands of non-violence? Were there people in Hinduism who developed them? I think there were, and there are. I began by deconstructing the Western misconception that Hindus are naturally non-violent. But this does not necessarily eliminate the reality of Hindu non-violence. The concept of non-violence was forged in ancient India in the minds of people already shackled by the realities of social oppression and mutual hatreds. But perhaps we can learn from Hinduism's long and complex history some of the pitfalls to avoid, some of the mistakes that we need not repeat. And, on the other hand, perhaps we can emulate some of India's successes, some of the ways in which individuals like Gandhi transcended the cultural agendas that had bred as much violence as non-violence. We can also take heart from movements within Hinduism that rejected both hierarchy and violence, of which the most obviously significant is the devotional *bhakti* movement that included women and Untouchables within its ranks, rejected violent sacrifice, and advocated a theology of love. We must, however, curb our optimism by noting that *bhakti* did not overthrow the caste system but merely created a gentler, kinder strain within it. More tragically, we must also note that it was in the name of *bhakti* to Ram that the militant Hindus tore down the Babri mosque.

Yet Hindus and Buddhists in the early period shared ideas so freely that it is impossible to say whether some of the central tenets of each faith came from one or the other (just as Picasso and Braque worked so closely together that they sometimes signed one another's paintings). So, too, the great poet and saint Kabir, who self-consciously rejected both Hinduism and Islam nevertheless built his own religious world out of what he would have regarded as the ruins of Hinduism and Islam, as did many of the great Sufi saints. And the same Hindu texts that told of Visnu's avatar as the Buddha also told of his avatar as Krsna, who does not destroy the cobra Kaliya, even when Kaliya is killing Krsna's friends, but subdues him and removes him to another place; evil is tolerable as long as you can domesticate it or protect yourself from it.[15] Similarly, Hindus believe that violent goddesses are needed to deal with evil, and that they, too, must be simultaneously courted and kept at a distance. Thus Sitala, the goddess of smallpox, is both feared and sought; if she visits you and leaves you alive, the sign of her grace is the mark of the pox upon your skin.

The degree of non-violence in India has varied dramatically in different social and economic circumstances, and we must look to historical factors to explain these changes. Thus the end of the line of this essay on the intellectual tradition of non-violence in India is an anti-anti-historical argument: you cannot explain non-violence by an idea. Non-violence does not result merely from a set of intellectual ideas; violence prevails not merely when people have bad ideas about other people but, especially, when they don't have enough to eat. As Brecht put it, "Erst kommt das Fressen, dann kommt die Morale."[16] The connection between vegetarianism and non-violence may not be historical or logical, but it is certainly metaphorical: Brecht continues: "What keeps a man alive? He feeds on others." He might have been quoting the *Mahabharata*.

Notes

1. *Rg Veda* 1.162.9. Translated on p. 90 of *The Rig Veda: An Anthology Translated from the Sanskrit,* by Wendy Doniger O'Flaherty (Harmondsworth: Penguin Books, 1981).

2. *Mahabharata* (Southern Recension) 12.15.10ff., translated by David Shulman, *The King and the Clown in South Asian Myth and Poetry* (Princeton: Princeton University Press, 1985), 29.

3. Veena Das, *Structure and Cognition: Aspects of Hindu Caste and Ritual* (Delhi: Oxford University Press, 1977), 29.

4. Frances Zimmermann, *The Jungle and the Aroma of Meats* (Berkeley: University of California Press, 1987), 1–2.

5. Jan Heesterman, *The Inner Conflict of Tradition* (Chicago: University of Chicago Press, 1985).

6. For a discussion of the synthesis of sacrificial and anti-sacrificial traditions in India, and the parallel developments in Judaism and Christianity, see Wendy Doniger O'Flaherty, *Other Peoples' Myths: The Cave of Echoes* (New York: Macmillan, 1988; Chicago: University of Chicago Press, 1995), Chapter 4.

7. *The Laws of Manu* 5.48. Translated by Wendy Doniger, with Brian K. Smith (Harmondsworth: Penguin Books, 1991), 103.

8. *The Laws of Manu* 5.39, 44.

9. Ibid., 12. 83–93.

10. For the tension between *svadharma*, particular *dharma*, and *sanatana dharma*, general *dharma*, see the stories of the two demons, Harikesha and Sukeshin, 94–97 and 128–131 of Wendy Doniger O'Flaherty, *The Origins of Evil in Hindu Mythology* (Berkeley: University of California Press, 1976).

11. For worldly Hindus wisely believe that, *pace* the contemporary vogue, you can't be too rich or too fat.

12. M. S. Golwalkar, *We or Our Nationhood Defined* (Nagpur, India: Bharat Prakashan, 1947), 48–49 and 55–56.

13. See O'Flaherty, *The Origins of Evil in Hindu Mythology*, Chapter 4.

14. Lopsided Lessons, by Shekhar Gupta, *India Today*, July 31, 1990.

15. For the Kaliya myth, see O'Flaherty, *The Origins of Evil in Hindu Mythology*, 56.

16. As Marc Blitzstein translated it, "First feed the face, and then talk right and wrong."

Part III
Witnessing

19

Thoughts on a Theater of Witness and Excerpts from Two Plays of Witness:
Better People, The Beekeeper's Daughter

Karen Malpede

The theater is a place of witness; theatron: seeing place. When the first actor stepped out from the chorus to begin to tell the story of the forging of the inner life, the chorus became witness to that story which was also, because they watched it, theirs. Then the audience sat down on a hillside to begin to watch the chorus seeing. An idea of the self distinct from family, tribe, history or fate yet comprehensible only in relationship to these external realities is the magnificent creation Greek tragedy gave to us. This idea was possible because the chorus contemplated the actions of the actors while the audience witnessed the chorus in their act of contemplation. Without such seeing and being seen, the inner life could not be found.

In the twentieth century, the psychiatric consulting room has replaced the theater as the place where one goes to discover the mutilated multi-aspects of the self. The psychiatrist contemplates the fragmented story as once the chorus looked upon the linear tale. The current literature of psycho-history attempts to act as audience, publicizing and socializing the hidden drama. Greek theaters were often located in comprehensive healing centers. You went to Epidaurus, for example, to take the baths, to do dream and body work with priests and healers, and to watch the great tragedies unfold. And if I now point out that the theater has become a mainly idle superfluous spectacle in our society, it is only to suggest that this is precisely because theater has severed its connection to the real collaboration between knowing the self and being in the world which live drama before a living audience is meant to satisfactorily complete.

If the theater once gave rise to the rudiments of psychiatric under-

standing, now, perhaps, contemporary psychiatric thought might revital-
ize the theater to which it is joined in essence at the core. There is a
need in us to sit together and look upon our actions; to be in community
and watch our ideas of ourselves unfold; to become, again, a public
which undergoes the psychic transformation wrought by submission to
the shared experience of what it is we think we might be or become as
individuals responsible to a group.

The Greeks used the heroic act to invent the individual. The heroic
act requires a severing of self from family, tribe, society and an obscure,
untroubled fate. The hero kills in order to cut himself off from the common herd; he literally slices his way out in order to be free. Tragic irony
happens at the moment he discovers that he is not free and yet he has
become himself.

We arrive at a new millenium with the knowledge that selfhood depends upon our abilities to reconnect ourselves to ourselves and others.
Our new idea selfhood is also being forged from the knowledge that we
are not free from what has already happened, the violence already done,
and still to come, but our relationship to violence must be reexamined
utterly. For the Greeks, the hero could only be the man who cut, yet, at
the end, this longed-for man, the adult, was himself cut down. The legacy of Greek drama ends with the image of a dismembered Pentheus.
The warrior-son beheaded by his own mad mother, swallowed back into
the terrible self-defying womb. He is mourned by grandfather who lovingly picked up his pieces and by a tormented mother who is suddenly
returned to sense. The boy's fragmented body lies at their feet. Agave
and Cadmus weep for the failure of the self-knowing self and are sent
into exile by Dionysus, the god of transgression whom Pentheus denied.

The 2,500-hundred-year exile of Cadmus and Agave results in the theater of witness. What was dismembered needs to be remembered. The
homeless wanderers who killed what they most loved, who themselves
were destroyed by a violence out of their control, bear the tale to tell.

Through psychotherapy and psycho-history, we learn the private stories of abuses within the family along with the histories of twentieth-
century genocides. As we recover the impact of this violence another
idea of selfhood begins to emerge. Robert Lifton calls it the idea of the
protean self. The protean self longs to embrace what has been other,
alien, cast out, cut off; it requires the gathering together of forgotten
and denied fragments from dreams, memories, history. It asks to bear
witness to the shattered narratives of survivors.

The wholeness with which Dionysus taunted civilization depends
upon a loss of certainty, a giving up of boundaries, an opening out in

an embrace, a willingness to be swallowed up. This wholeness, denied by Pentheus, suggests that the true self is fluid, changeable, inclusive, in large part unknowable, moreover, that it might be broken and then be re-membered, emerging stronger and more varied than before. In the twentieth century, the act of bearing witness brings us to this place. Through bearing witness, the invidividual is reimagined, no longer as the one who cuts, but as the one who puts the pieces back together.

The Greek theater hid its violent acts behind closed palace doors. What is theater of witness? It is theater which veers away from violence because it recognizes trauma. It seeks to reverse trauma's debilitating effects on self and society by giving shape to the complex and cyclical stages of remembrance and recovery. By so doing, the theater of witness becomes again a seeing place in which the audience is able to imagine its collective self anew.

Better People:

Better People alternates between the waking lives and dream lives of four genetic and reproductive scientists. Haila Gudenschmartzer, the world's oldest living geneticist, in her youth was conscripted into service as a Nazi doctor. In an act of private atonement, she impregnated herself with the sperm of a Jewish "imbecile" she had been forced to sterilize, then she rebelled openly and was thrown into a camp. She escaped and gave birth to a son, Edward Chreode, another character in the play. In the excerpt from scene three, Philbert Wallace, four-time Nobel prize winner, chair of the biology department at this great unversity, and CEO of Gene-Recombo, Inc., seeks control of Haila's pure research and she dreams of the crucial turning in her early life.

Better People, Excerpt from Scene 3:
Haila Gudenschmartzer: In a month, I'll know exactly where and how memory is stored within the brain. I'm on the verge of understanding everything.

Philbert Wallace: That's the stuff, Haila. Get me a full report today. I'll put you on full retainer at Gene-Recombo, Inc.

Haila: Don't patronize me, young man. Give me the money I need because of my brilliant mind.

[Triumphantly, Haila hands him the proof, her research results. He takes the papers, reads. He's off into his own world of products and profits.]

Philbert: The control of human memory. That's marketable. We win the public's sympathy by offering it up as a cure for Alzheimer's disease (which I forgot, by the way, to mention in my speech). An ethics committee will be convened by the boys in Congress. Who is worthy of having a memory, that sort of thing. Meanwhile, who can resist? It's science. It's progress. It's truth. Haila, I knew you'd come through for me in the end.

[Philbert offers his hand for her to shake. She refuses, swings her wheel chair away.]

Haila: Not so fast, Philbert Wallace, I want the Nobel Prize for this. My life's work. I want to die with the Prize in my hand. I want my eggs frozen alongside all that sperm in the Nobel sperm bank. I want equality at last.

Philbert: Haila, I'm offering you millions.

Haila: I want the Prize, Philbert.

[Pause. He looks at the results again. Decides.]

Philbert: O.k., o.k. I'll see what I can do.

Haila: So you think I'm hot, at last, Philbert.

Philbert: Haila, there's no one in science whose integrity and accomplishments I admire more. You've stuck to the good, hard, theoretical work; you've never profiteered off of science. You're a well known supporter of liberal causes; you're an old line feminist, a refugee from Hitler and a single mother to boot. You've got principles, Haila. You deserve the Nobel Prize. I'm glad to have you on our team.

[He offers his hand, again. This time she takes it. They shake.]

Haila: And you, Philbert, are a slippery, self-important phallus who was badly toilet trained. But, I'm glad to be included on your team.

Philbert: With the Prize under your belt, you will finally be taken seriously.

[He puts her research paper into his left lab coat pocket then takes a contract from his inside jacket pocket.]

Philbert: This is Gene-Recombo's standard option agreement. It gives the company complete rights to market any and all memory control products we invent based upon your pure research. It also gives you quite a handsome advance. Sign it. And, Haila, no more displays like the one I witnessed at my speech. You may humiliate me in private only. You know, Haila, I was disappointed in my speech, myself. It lacked nerve. The truth is I got scared. I cut out the most radical part. I had intended to offer a concrete gene maximization plan. I was going to suggest that we simply remove the genetic material from each individual immediately after birth and then promptly sterilize that individual. The idea's been around for a long time, of course. During each individual's lifetime record would be kept of accomplishments and characteristics. After the individual's death, a committee decides if those genes are worthy of procreation into other individuals. If so, genetic material would be removed from the depository, mated suitably, and implanted into a surrogate. If not, the genetic material is destroyed. How simple, elegant, direct. But at 3 a.m., I cut the paragraph out. I shouldn't have done that, should I?

[But Haila has fallen asleep in her chair.]

Philbert: Haila, are you listening? That old trick again. What a pig-headed, impossible woman. [He whispers to her sleeping face.] You had better not make a fool out of me, Haila. You had better come through; I've invested in you.

[Philbert exits]

DREAM MUSIC & LIGHTS.

[Haila rises out of her wheel chair and exits through the large double doors. Eduard Schneider, played by the actor who plays Edward Chreode, sits weeping in a wheel chair. He is talking, as if he is a split personality, to himself.]

Eduard: Don't cry, Eduard.

Eduard: Why shouldn't I cry? I wanted to be like other people. I'm not like them at all.

Eduard: It's wrong to cry about that. You can't help the way you are.

Eduard: Other people have inner lives. They have places they can get to. Places they can hide. Other people have private thoughts.

Eduard: Shut up, Eduard, don't go soft on me. That sort of talk is better unheard. You're not like other people, Eduard. You do what you're told. You give what you're asked. You sacrifice.

Eduard: No. Stop. I had an idea. I had a thought. A thought came into my head. This time, this time, I am going to try. I am going to try to show who I am.

[Eduard Schneider reads his letter as he writes it.]

Dear Herr Doktor Wirths:

"I must refute this charge of imbecility with schizophrenic tendencies, since I am capable of writing and of doing arithmetic without error and without outside help. For this reason, I would like to request another physical examination."

[Dr. Eduard Wirths, played by the actor who plays Philbert Wallace, enters with Haila, playing herself as a young woman.]

Wirths: Good morning Herr Schneider.

[He takes the letter, pockets it, speaks out of two sides of his mouth.]

Wirths: I have received your most impressive letter. Fraulein Doktor will perform another examination on you. / Sterilize him, Fraulein. Inject this caustic substance through the urethra. It will block the testes. Check him in a week. If gangrene has set in, amputate. / Don't be afraid, Herr Schneider. You see, I've brought you a beautiful young woman doctor. What could possibly go wrong. She'll be won completely over by your charm. / Sterilize him, now, Fraulein.

[Wirths exits]

Eduard: You are a nice lady. I can see that.

Haila: Don't count your chickens before they hatch.

Eduard: That's just it. I can't help doing that. Everyone must. It's human. I feel that it is. I don't want to be sterilized.

Haila: Whoever put that idea into your head. I've come to speak with you a bit, take your blood and do a sperm count. Here, masturbate into this jar.

Eduard: I'm not as young as I was. Well, maybe I will never marry. I wanted to marry this year. Maybe the woman I love will not want to marry me. I wouldn't marry except for love. I know how to love, I do.

Haila: I've had thirty-nine lovers, I've given myself five abortions. I've cured myself three times of pelvic inflammatory disease and of countless yeast infections. I'm the last woman in Berlin who remembers the erotic life.

Eduard: It's because they found out I have a Jewish grandmother. That's why they are doing this. I'm not stupid, you know. I'm no dumber than lots of them in uniform.

Haila: I had a Jewish lover, once. But he asked for too much.

Eduard: Maybe you have been hurt in love. Too many times. I'm a dairy herdsman. I work with cows. But I've got my dreams.

Haila: Yes, yes, you can dream.

Eduard: You know, I thought, if we two could talk. If we could share, well, you won't be able to do what they want done.

Haila: I'm here on orders. Routine examination only.

Eduard: I could love a woman. I know I could.

Haila: You're not done. Quickly, finish up before he comes back. It's a simple mechanical thing. I just need a sperm count. We are doing a comparison rating. Do Jewish men produce more sperm? It's pure science. Pure research.

Eduard: I believe the amount of sperm produced must have to do with the amount of love felt. I believe it's the passion at the moment of conception which determines the joy in the soul of the unborn.

Haila: Now, then, I just must give you this injection.

[She injects his penis with the caustic substance. Sound of machine gun fire. His body reacts in a spasm to the pain.]

Eduard: No, no, why did you have to do that? I begged you. I pleaded with you. I looked into your eyes. I shared my dreams. I believed in tenderness. I believed in love.

Haila: Buck up, Eduard Schneider. Buck up. These are hard times. None of us does what we want. We are struggling to stay alive. Go home. Forget about this.

Eduard: You expect me to forget?

Haila: Look, I've saved your sperm. They wanted to destroy it. I'm going to have a child with this. I'm going to inject myself. I will sex select. I will make a son. A noble, gentle, brilliant man. A boy-child with your soul, my brains. I've had counts, classicists, artists, actors, professors of chemistry, biology, physics, poetry, history, politicians and judges, psychiatrists. You are the only man I've desired a child with.

The Beekeeper's Daughter:

The Beekeeper's Daughter takes place on an island in the Adriatic, in the summer of 1993. Sybil Blaze is the beekeeper; Rachel, her niece, is a human rights worker; Admira Ismic is a Bosnian refugee victim of genocidal rape. In this excerpt, all three are in the midst of a crisis of witnessing.

The Forest (excerpt) [Another part of the forest. Sybil is painting. Admira is sitting.]

Admira: What are you painting, Sybil?

Sybil: I'm painting your inner demons.

Admira: Those are your inner demons, Sybil. My demons are not so inner. They are all on the flesh.

Sybil: You will have a full life.

Admira: How can you say that?

Sybil: What is a full life but a life lived down to the bone. You should paint.

Admira: I can't paint anymore. My hands don't know how.

Sybil: I didn't paint before.

Admira: Before your life broke?

Sybil: Yes, before that.

Admira: I heard it in you. The branch snaps.

Sybil: The beasts that enter one's dreams, you can paint those.

Admira: I have no dreams.

Sybil: You don't know what you dream.

Admira: I don't want to know any more. I want to be left alone.

Sybil: But they are everywhere. I see them everywhere I go. Cold eyes looking down. There is nothing in those eyes. I am painting them. I am painting them so they will leave us alone.

Admira: Don't say such things.

Sybil: You brought them here. They are all around us in the air.

Admira: You have all tried so hard. But they will kill you, too.

Sybil: I'm painting to tie them down. To give them a place to go. I have hundreds of paintings like this. I paint all the time. I never show them to anyone. But your demons are not mine.

Admira: I was happy when I died. I looked down from the sky. I saw a woman chained to a bed. I heard the laughter of men. I don't want to live again.

Sybil: I don't know what colors to use.

Admira: I want to kill the child, too.

Sybil: Of course you do.

Admira: I want the child dead. It would be better for him. Then I could rest. I begged him not to join the fight. I pleaded with him. He had to he said. He had to try to save something of what we had. I told him I was pregnant. I made it up. Then we were together one more time; he left me in the middle of the night. I felt my life stop. He was also a writer. Like Robert. I hope he has died. We used to be happy. We drank wine. We talked. We held hands. Walked.

[Rachel enters with the child]

Rachel: Take the baby, Admira.

Admira: No.

Rachel: Hold your son.

Admira: Don't. He's not mine.

Rachel: Yes he is; I want you to take him.

Admira: Go away. Can't you see anything. They are everywhere. All around.

Rachel: No one is here, Admira. But you and Sybil, me and the baby.

Sybil: Stop, Rachel.

Rachel: No. It's time. She has to touch him. She has to connect. She's done enough damage to herself.

Sybil: Enough. Enough.

[Sybil approaches Rachel, takes the child]

Rachel: I want you to speak. I want you to tell me what you remember.

Admira: You don't want to know.

Rachel: I do. Everything. What it felt like. What happened. I can't stand the silence anymore.

Admira: I can't tell you.

Rachel: You must.

Admira: I can't speak before you. You are like a nun. You are too good. You have suffered so much.

Rachel: I'm not going to let you destroy yourself. Do you understand? I want you to tell me everything.

Admira: I'm dead. The dead don't speak.

Rachel: [she shakes Admira by the shoulders] You're alive, damn it. You're alive. You're alive and you're going to talk.

Sybil: Rachel!

[Rachel pushes Admira away. Admira falls to the ground, where she cowers. Rachel walks away from her, says softly under her breath]

Rachel: Oh, my god, oh, my god, oh, my god. I could kill her.

Sybil: You see how they get inside of us.

Rachel: I could wring her neck. Help me. Somebody help me.

Sybil: I must paint them.

[Rachel exits]

Admira: I want to kill my child.

Sybil: [sits on her stool, rocking back and forth with the child on her lap] I know, child. I know that.

Admira: No one should live. Not anymore. Beasts. Only monsters should walk the earth. He is too weak. I won't let him. I won't allow it. They took babies by their heels, hit their heads against rock. I saw what came out.

Sybil: I did. I did it. No one believed me. It was an accident. The wall came out of nowhere. I turned right into it. I had my foot on the gas. The air smelled like spring. I had the pedal to the ground. I could smell her sweet flesh.

Admira: They did it all in front of everyone. They took four of us. In front of everyone. On the ground. They did it. Everyone saw it. No one moved.

Sybil: It was a long time ago. Before even Rachel was born. Then no one could believe such things. I didn't believe it myself. Even with my black eyes, I couldn't see. Now people try to believe. They read in the newspapers. They see on the television.

Admira: I itched so. The smell. I couldn't stand the smell. They made me smell like that. I can't say these things to anyone. I want to shout. All the time I want to shout. I am so dirty inside. I must be dead. No one lives with so much dirt.

Sybil: She used to talk in poetry. She said to me when she was three and a half, "Mama, where do the stars go in day? Do they go down under the earth to dance with the dead bones." When she was just two, she asked: "Mama, why doesn't light always come colored like in rainbows?" I wrote the things she said down in my head. They were going to take her away from me. They were going to take her away. Because I watched him one night from the door, when he hurt her. I watched. My tongue turned to ash in my mouth.

Admira: I wanted to kill them all. I want to go back and I want to kill. I want to kill everyone who looked at me. Everyone who watched. Everyone who knows anything. Rachel knows too much. Some nights I want to take a knife. I want to cut out her heart. So she'll know. So she'll know what it felt like.

Sybil: Robert was already a poet, when her words stopped. I thought that a big fist was behind us pushing us. Now, she would only whine. She would sit on my lap and cling. She would hold onto my knees all the time. She had been free. Now I saw that someone had stopped her. Someone had put a big fist in her mouth. No one would believe. I didn't believe myself. It wasn't my life.

Admira: I knew them. I knew them because I had taught one year in their village. They were village boys. They used to do the things village boys do. It was so strange that I knew them. Ordinary boys. I knew one or two of their names. They looked in my eyes. No. I am dead. No one survives.

Sybil: My husband said I was crazy. He said I made everything up. For a long time I didn't know the truth. He said they were going to take her away from me because I was making her crazy. I knew something else. But I didn't know how to say it out loud. I was afraid he would kill us both. Afraid he would hit me again on the head, afraid he would use his gun.

Admira: I didn't mind for me. I was dead already. But I saw what they did to the others. To young girls and old woman. And their eyes were so cold. They had no life in their eyes. A mother held her child to protect him. To protect him, she held him tight. So they couldn't take him away, she wrapped her arms around his chest. She held him tight to protect him. While she held him; they cut his head off.

Sybil: It was not an accident. No. I planned it all. I planned it when I saw the wall. I put my foot on the gas. I thought I would run the wall through both of us. I never saw her again. They wouldn't let me go to her funeral. They sent me away to live with Robert. My teeth were scattered across the cement. I saw her bright blue headband alone in the middle of the street.

Admira: If it was for myself, I could stand anything. But for the others, for them, I couldn't help. I was too dirty to live. I knew this man. He was a high school teacher of mine. He was dripping with blood. He held a knife in his hand. He looked at me in the eyes. "Now you see how strong I am." I was dead already I had died so all I could do was hang from the top of the ceiling and look down.

Sybil: That's how I learned to keep bees. Dora bought me a hive. Dora was always very good to me. I found out that bees live the same way in captivity or in the wild. No one has ever been able to change the essence of bees. All we have ever been able to do is steal their honey, but the bees go on being bees just the same as always. They live as if they were free. They talk to each other with their wings. They made up dances. In times long ago, people used to understand the language of bees but now we've forgotten how to understand them.

Notes

Better People premiered in 1991 at Theater for the New City, New York City, in a production directed by the author. It was subsequently staged in concert versions at Life on the Water in San Francisco, at Harvard University and had two student productions at the University of Michigan. The play was featured on the Channel 13 "Eleventh Hour" program "Genetic Property."

The Beekeeper's Daughter premiered in 1994 at the Dionysia World Festival of Contemporary Drama in Veroli, Italy, directed by the author. A workshop production of the play was presented at the Florence Mission Project, New York City, February 1995.

20

Artists Witnessing "Ethnic Cleansing"

Stevan M. Weine

This is a text about artists witnessing "ethnic cleansing." I am a psychiatrist doing clinical, testimony, and research work with its survivors. As the genocide against Bosnia-Herzegovina and the non-Serbs who have been living there continued essentially unopposed by the West, our exploration of artists witnessing "ethnic cleansing" has necessarily changed. There was a time when we could experience these artists as primarily trying to rouse us and our governments towards action to stop the evolving genocide, but that time has passed. Given that the Serbian nationalists were just recently still at work on their "ethnic cleansing" of Bosnia, however, we have not yet crossed the historical juncture that would render these artworks of belated remembrance—serving the struggle to not forget—as we may now experience some Holocaust art. How then do we experience these works and how do we understand their significance in terms of our relationship with the "ethnic cleansing" in Bosnia?

This intellectual inquiry into a few artists "successfully" bearing witness to genocide in their artworks will be conducted from a position of awareness of the perversions and failures of witnessing that surround this genocide, including the West's failure to stop "ethnic cleansing"—a breakdown in our collective witnessing of genocide. "Ethnic cleansing" has presented us with examples of each of these realities and our understanding of witnessing genocide would be seriously incomplete if we were to ignore any of them.

In order to examine the role of artists witnessing the third European genocide of the century, we must understand some basic points concerning the unique nature of the Serbian nationalists' genocide against non-Serbs in Bosnia-Herzegovina, euphemistically called "ethnic cleansing."

This genocide has been a mass murder against Bosnian Muslims and

Croats in Bosnia-Herzegovina. And yet the uniqueness of "ethnic cleansing" as a genocide derives not from its being mass murder, which it certainly is, but from other factors, including how the committing of atrocities acts upon survivors and witnesses.[1] In "ethnic cleansing," traumas and atrocities have been systematically committed with the overwhelming intent of extending the circle of terror as far as possible. What is relentless here is not the effort at killing people, but the deliberate effort to annihilate a civilization and a person's sense of sharing in a multi-ethnic communality. This genocide strives to create witnesses who believe that Serbs are ruthless mass murderers, that Bosnian Muslims and Orthodox cannot live together, and that there is no possibility for a multi-ethnic nation. The deliberate assault on the values, norms, and ethics of a society seeks to create survivors and witnesses who will abandon their belief in multi-ethnic tolerance and communality and accept instead the image of ancient ethnic hatreds. The objective of "ethnic cleansing" is to create survivors and witnesses who will fear for their lives, flee their homes, and never wish to return.

Lifton has demonstrated how a genocidal project requires a genocidal ideology and delineated the Nazi biomedical vision in *Nazi Doctors*.[2] "Ethnic cleansing" demonstrates a new strain of genocidal ideology that might be called an ideology of conflict and division in which mental health workers have played a key role as terrorist professionals. This theory perversely emphasizes the centrality of unconscious intra-psychic conflict in explaining human behavior. Such a worldview envisions tensions and clashes between different ethnic or national groups as roughly akin to unconscious intra-psychic conflict. It depicts ethnic or national conflicts as naturally exploding into extraordinary violence, because at the essence of ethnic conflicts are unmitigated aggressive impulses stemming from unresolvable unconscious conflicts. For example, Radovan Karadzic, the psychiatrist leader of the Bosnian Serbs provided this diagnosis of the situation in Bosnia: "A big eruption of the subconscious. . . . We knew it was going to be chaos if they recognized Bosnia-Herzegovina. . . . You can't control it. In a civil war everyone is armed, everyone hates the other, everyone is frightened."[3]

In response, the terrorist professionals position themselves as healers to this unconscious conflict writ large, and seek a remedy through the division of opposed groups by expulsion or extermination. Another prominent mental health terrorist professional, the psychiatrist Serb leader Jovan Raskovic, author of *The Insane Country*,[4] was responsible for using his professional skills, knowledge, and authority to evoke memories of prior traumatization, provoke the fears of differences, and provide an intellectual justification for nationalistic ethnic hatreds. Raskovic did this in the guise of being a witness to the genocide against Serbs—bearing witness is used to promote the genocidal ideology of Serbian nationalism.

Mass destruction of a community which historically took pride in being a good example of co-existence and tolerance of ethnic and religious differences—a multi-ethnic community—leaves the survivor bereft of a sense of identity and belonging.[5] "I feel that I am not normal. I cannot go back to normal," said one; "I was born when I came out of the camp. The first birth was an accident," said another. Being subject to atrocities, witnessing atrocities, or being forced to perpetrate atrocities against another leaves the survivor feeling humiliated, helpless, no longer human—even a "true beast" oneself. Survivors of genocide, due to the nature of massive psychic trauma, often have tremendous difficulties in perceiving, registering, and assimilating their traumatic experiences. Survivors may even come to accept the ideology of conflict and division as true, inasmuch as it appears to contain their current feelings of ethnic hatreds which stem from their experience of ethnic atrocities. When the survivor embraces ethnic hatreds, it further erodes the multi-ethnic platform of Bosnian society, and it lends further support to the Serbian nationalists' ideological rationale for "ethnic cleansing."

The drive towards polarization carried by the ideology of conflict and division may marginalize or entirely divide the witnesses from their position in relation to the traumatic experiences. The rationale given is that conflict is inevitable and there is nothing the witness can do to stop it. Even worse, were the witness to intervene, the result would only be greater traumatization to the parties in conflict, to the witness, or to others who stand outside. The witnesses had best relinquish their claim over bearing witness and let the events play themselves out as they may. The witnesses themselves may willingly accept this redefining of their role and come to participate as spokespersons for the ideology of conflict and division. They may testify to the inevitability of the conflicts, the wisdom of promoting division, and the wisdom of relinquishing their claim to being a witness.

So, the net effect of "ethnic cleansing" is to commit not only the perpetrator to a collective mentality of fear and hatred of difference, and violence, but to also commit survivors and witnesses to support it as well.

When we talk about creative artists bearing witness to "ethnic cleansing" over the past two plus years, we are really speaking about those who have deployed their artistic skills as witnessing professionals to make art as resistance to this contemporaneous genocide and its ideology of conflict and division. Artists who hoped that their art would lead to some better outcome on the ground. That it would save lives and save Bosnia.

When the creative artist, like the human rights worker, journalist, lawyer, or psychiatrist, functions as what Robert Jay Lifton has called a witnessing professional,[6] the work produced operates within a number of positivistic claims—that the experience of genocide is knowable, that the methodology can adequately represent it, that others will be receptive, and that the work will effect some changes that can make a difference in the world.

Despite the artworks they created, the genocide continued. Bosnian Muslims died and the West did nothing. The witnessing professionals' claims, valid as they may be, did not carry the day. The creative artist witnessing professionals, who have allowed social realities to make a claim on both the integrity of their artwork and on their role as creative artists, struggle personally with these matters.

We who are concerned about art addressing social realities must struggle too. When art is being used to wage a battle against a genocide and that battle is lost, then what's left for art? As with Lawrence Langer I reject the mythological view that would have us rejoice in those precious stories or images that spellbind us with the "triumph of the human spirit" or the heroic achievement of the individual artist.[7] This position has in fact appeared, in what is undoubtedly "ethnic cleansing's" most celebrated text to date, *Zlata's Diary*,[8] the journal of a young girl who survives the siege of Sarajevo—a heavily promoted narrative which offers us an affirmative, heroic, and living facsimile of Anne Frank—free of many of the psychological, social, and political complexities that complicate our relationship to "ethnic cleansing" in Bosnia.

Langer's analysis of the daunting problems faced by the artist of the Holocaust[9] are in part challenges shared by the artist of "ethnic cleansing." The Nazis' and the Serbian nationalists' "calculated malice" works against the "dramatic spirit," mass murder eradicates any prospect of a character's understanding of or control over his or her life and human cruelty defies imaginative capacity. What some artists of "ethnic cleansing" discussed in this text have done, however, is to shift their focus away from the scenes of atrocities and to look closely at the witnessing itself. What makes these works compelling lies less in their depiction of the realities of evil and its destructive impact, and depends more upon their capacity to give us a powerful experience of the human struggle to discover what can be done about knowing, remembering, inscribing, preventing, and living with genocide.

Such a witnessing imagination is a mental process that centers on seeing, knowing, and connecting with an other's experience of traumatization so as to facilitate transforming one's relationship with violence and its destructiveness through one's actions of remembering, inscribing, opposing, and/or transcending those traumas. The witnessing imagination sets a frame which serves as a powerful bearer of the knowledge of genocidal evil and its destructive impact on human life but which also permits the contemplation and affirmation of core relationships that have been destroyed, transformed, or heightened by the experiences of traumatization.

Because the witnessing imagination is in essence a force that emerges out of the relationship between the survivor and the witness, its mentality centers around encounters and bonds between those who are situated within a traumatic experience, and those on the outside. The witnessing imagination always keeps alive a certain tension which comes of this relationship between the inside and the outside positions, even if that means sacrificing the clarity that would come of sticking entirely to either view exclusively. In the witnessing imagination, the inside position of the survivor and the outside position of the witness are inter-dependent on one another. Ideally, the witnessing imagination allows a fluidity between these two positions, both interpersonally and intrapsychically. Survivors may become witnesses to other survivors, or even witnesses to themselves—a survivor/witness. The witnessing imagination can create artworks of unusual power, whose inherent qualities compel the viewers to expand their capacity for witnessing. In art of the witnessing imagination, the relationship between the survivor and the witness is both the origin of aesthetic tension and the area targeted for change.

It follows from our awareness of the different positions in the survivor-witness relationship that we might make some imperfect but useful distinctions between art made by the survivor-witness from the inside, in comparison with the witness from the outside. I will discuss the survivor/witness writer Zlatko Dizdarevic and the survivor/witness visual conceptual artist Sanjin Jukic, and the outsider witness playwright Karen Malpede.

Zlatko Dizdarevic is a journalist for Sarajevo's daily newspaper *Oslobodenje* and a writer who bore witness to the genocide from the inside while it was happening in his acclaimed book *Sarajevo: A War Journal* and in other well publicized writings.[10] Dizdarevic's writings on Sarajevo are not journalistic, as that term is usually understood. Though he presents some facts, he is not objectively reporting factual information. He writes about the truths that have emerged out of his experience as a survivor. He speaks to us with the fierceness and desperation of a survivor who fears that he, and his city, will not survive.

Dizdarevic places the truth at the center of his writings. "The truth itself is 'occupied,' " he writes. "Instead of the truth of what is actually being done to our city, people will be told monstrous lies by those who have come to liberate us." His work is to strike out at those lies—"the lie has slithered in amongst us"—and to be the bearer of the truth. He tells the truth that no one wants to hear, "Nothing is the way it used to be, and it never will be again." He is writing to those in the West, to awaken these potential witnesses to genocide that they might save Bosnia and also "to broadcast a warning" that if they continue to ignore Bosnia it is at their own peril.

Dizdarevic is acutely aware of the complications of communicating from within the experience of a genocide to those positioned outside: "Maybe all of this is actually senseless and no use to explain to anybody outside Sarajevo. Nothing here can be explained to anybody who isn't here." He has asked himself: Will 70,000 copies in five different languages make people think a little bit differently than yesterday, or is the real result nothing?[11] He lives with the uncertainties and the exhaustion that any survivor knows, of trying to make others see a truth, and not knowing if you are getting through to them. Still that takes nothing away from the dead-on accuracy of his vision.

He assaults the lies that obscure the harsh realities of genocide by saying, "It's an outbreak of sheer madness, and no one knows what it's all about. . . . It is a war in which everyone fights everyone else, and you can't make sense out of it." He articulates one of the most feared lasting consequence of the genocide, "Deportation is the ultimate humiliation that can be inflicted on a human being. No one can go on living with the memory of it without a desire for revenge."

Sanjin Jukic is a young artist from Sarajevo whose work has been exhibited and published internationally.[12] Jukic defines his aesthetic approach as conceptual and cites as major influences Joseph Beuys, John Cage, and Robert Wilson. By conceptual Jukic means the prominent role given to the idea in shaping his artworks. The function of the concept is to concentrate the experience of the viewer upon the experiential world defined by the concept and to isolate the viewer, the artists, and their interaction through the artwork from many things other. It could be said that the fragmenting and disconnecting effect of genocide begs for setting a strong conceptual frame.

Jukic was interested in the appeal of the Serbian nationalistic epic myth to Serbian people and the West's failure to notice and effectively intervene in response to the genocide.[13] Jukic specifically implicated the Western media for failing to adequately represent the genocide in a manner that would offer a serious challenge to the values, ethics, and norms of Western democratic society. Jukic's conceptual focus is on the position of the viewer as witness, and how one's capacity for witnessing is mitigated by certain forces or factions such as the media, culture, politics, ideology, and trauma.

In his work "I Like America and America Likes Me," Jukic juxtaposes the two nation's flags and two maps above an Oriental-style table upon which rests an American Coca-Cola, a pack of Marlboroughs, and a Bosnian Turkish coffee server. On one level, these everyday objects bear witness to the Bosnian struggle for basic survival and the fight to maintain and strengthen their culture by the execution of creative artworks. On another level, the viewer is asked to bear witness to the more superficial images of the relationship between America and Bosnia—the American utopian vision of multi-ethnic coexistence in Bosnia, to the Bosnian utopian vision of Western consumer capitalism. On a deeper level, the viewer is invited to reflect upon America's interest in Bosnia and Bosnia's interest in America—and to discover what are the common principles and values and ethics that define the relationship or must be reworked at this moment of crisis in the relationship.

Jukic's approach centers around performance. Each work sets forth an experiential space that invites or demands the viewer's interactive participation. (Literally, in my case. Sanjin and I sat together within his artwork for our conversation—he under "Sarajevo likes America" and I under "America likes Sarajevo"—and experienced the tenderness and respect of two brothers while participating in a broader dialogue across the boundaries posed by geo-politics, culture, and traumatization.) The viewer sees the artworks as objects and is also asked to see oneself as a subject within the world defined by the artwork. Simultaneously, you may have the experience of being a witness to the content of the artwork, a witness to the genocide implicated in the artwork, a witness to yourself within the experience of the artwork, a witness to your position as a witness in relationship to this genocide. The focus in the world of Jukic's art is less upon the precise social situation being witnessed and more on the multiple determinants of the witnessing process and the impact it has on what is being witnessed.

Karen Malpede is an American Jewish woman playwright who has published eleven plays.[14] The latest play which she wrote and directed was produced in Italy and New York. She sees all her plays as revolving around one common theme: "I am always interested in juxtaposing sexual and political violence with the possibility of eros and liberating empathy."[15] As a Jew she experienced genocide in Bosnia as all too reminiscent of the Holocaust. As a woman, Malpede made the connection between violence against women in general and the historical innovation of rape as a specific method of genocide demonstrated in the Serbian forces' mass rape of non-Serb women.

Her new play, "The Beekeeper's Daughter,"[16] is an example of artistic witnessing from the outside. It is a drama about the crises of witnessing that occur in the encounters between a woman survivor of genocide and rape, and a group of intellectuals and artists in a freely creative environment. Malpede consciously chose to dramatize the genocide as it entered into a world very much outside the locations of killings, atrocities, and terror in Bosnia. The idea for the play came to her "during an idyllic trip to Greece and Italy this past summer when, nevertheless I was aware the whole time of the war in the former Yugoslavia so near to us in space and time and yet, so very opposite in circumstance. . . . I've been thinking about what it means to be from the outside writing about something about which I have no firsthand experience whatsoever."[17] The playwright knows that she could have chosen to write a text that would try to get inside through depicting unrelenting images of brutality, but chose instead to portray the possibilities for affirmative self-transformation in the wake of severe traumatization. "The Beekeeper's Daughter" is essentially a drama about how Bosnia plays in the world outside—about us and how the historical events in Bosnia enter into our lives—and about our capacity for witnessing.

Malpede creates an aesthetic experience that powerfully challenges the distance, numbness, and misunderstandings that have plagued our knowing of the genocide and its traumas. When the witnessing imagination confronts "ethnic cleansing"—the first televised genocide—in the theater, we come to enter into an unfamiliar, startling, live interpersonal world; seeing and feeling a thousand gestures of the hand, heart, mind, and soul.

Karen Malpede's theater of the witnessing imagination seeks not to take us out of our lives with brutal images of atrocity. Rather, she and her cast present us with a group of characters into whose lives we can enter because they are a part of that great multi-ethnic and multi-cultural soup of the world city. "Beekeeper" presents lives that are passionate, complex, tragic, transcendent, contradictory, even hilarious. Lives that bear unmistakable traces of extremity. Lives that are lived in the presence of history. Not one-dimensional victims, but fully realized lives of survivors of genocide, rape, suicide, and other hardships who, despite it all, bear great compassion for the self and the world.

Malpede's practiced interpersonal approach to the theater provides the perfect fundament for a theater of witnessing. "Beekeeper" gives us relationships between survivors and witnesses that come alive through a sequence of scenes that function as testimony encounters. The vicissitudes of Admira Ismic as a survivor of mass rape, or the visionary poet Robert Blaze, as a witness, are made clear through the tensions and struggles they experience in relationship with each other and others. Witnessing and recovery are not events, but processes, nor are they simply dyadic, but familial, and communal. The presence of Admira and the awareness of experienced atrocities that she embodies ricochets in and out of all the characters and their relationships with one another, and with the group as a whole. It is through our immersion in this intensive aesthetic experience that we are placed at risk of having a more consequential knowing of genocide, survivors, and witnessing.

In keeping with our awareness of the survivor-witness relationship, we must again think about how art witnessing genocide might function for outsiders who are not witnesses, for outsiders who are witnesses, and for survivors. For the outsider who has not borne witness, art of the witnessing imagination seeks to provide you with a new experience that will put you into relationship with genocide and its survivors. It does far more than report on that day's news events or give new information, advance a political position, sentimentalize, or shock with brutal images. It gives you a story that has not yet been told, an image that has not yet been shown, a truth that has not yet been grasped. It offers you narratives and images that depict not only the experience of traumas' destructiveness, but also the life that once was, the current life, recovery, and the future possibilities. A story that will be absorbed into your sense of your own life and pierce the self, and not become split off or marginalized by virtue of its extremity. Zlatko Dizdarevic's writings constitute one such story.

For the outsider who has borne witness, or the witnessing professional, art of the witnessing imagination can make you experience your witnessing differently by directing your attention on the multiple intersubjective phenomenological layering of the witnessing process and the bearing it has upon what is being witnessed, as in Sanjin Jukic's visual conceptual artworks. It can also do so by dramatizing the richness and complexity of interpersonal relationships between survivors and witnesses, such as in Karen Malpede's play.

For the individual survivor, artworks of the witnessing imagination can help you to negotiate your own struggles with obstacles to psychological recovery posed by absorption into either vengefulness or disconnectedness. The piece of psychological work done by the creative artists of the witnessing imagination—as encoded in their artwork—can provide an example in microcosm of how the traumas of genocide can become known and part of a life. Artworks in which identities are indeed strained by atrocities, but still remain genuine, whole, and clear about who they are. Voices that are not consumed by hatreds, nor the denial of them, nor emptiness. They incorporate the images of atrocities, but deploy creative processes such as the Janusian process—where multiple opposites or antitheses are poised together within a creative work—to avoid polarizing solutions and create works which embody a new mode of experience. These works can become touchstones for psychological growth after genocide. And for the larger community of survivors, artworks of the witnessing imagination can also function in the effort towards communalization of the traumas in such a way that may avoid organizing their survivor experience around reactive nationalistic hatreds.

Art of the witnessing imagination, even when conveying direct accounts of experience from within the genocide, is not doing so solely as a conciliation to its harsh realities, but as a specific confrontation with genocidal evil and a refusal of its polarizing mentality—that of the ideology of conflict and division. Art of the witnessing imagination can help us when we find ourselves lacking in sufficient imagination—to deal with traumatic memories, to make meaningful choices, maintain moral commitments, and take effective actions—in the face of genocide.

It is likely that even after the moment we have actually experienced art witnessing genocide as fulfilling its goal of communicating some crucial truth, we will find ourselves struck by serious doubts about its worth to us. Images and words will deteriorate into meaninglessness and purposelessness. We feel that we cannot maintain a grasp onto the stark realties of genocide in a consequential enough way. One obstacle that blocks us has to do with the tremendous difficulties in taking a powerful individual psychological experience and moving it into the social or the political realm of experience. Yet additionally, the drop-off from a moment of connectedness to one of disconnectedness, knowing to not knowing, enthusiasm to despair, is also part of the expected psychological oscillations that are the consequences of the massive psychic trauma of genocide.

Witnessing cannot transcend these psychological realities and it is also not immune to misuse by those seeking to gain the moral high ground from dubious or even evil positions. Art that reports to bear witness may be doing so as a false witness, as was the case in a photography exhibit in Belgrade that depicted the historical genocide against Serbs as a provocation and a rationale for the contemporary Serbian government's genocidal policies.[18] There is something about being a part of the experience of bearing witness which allows one to believe that one is doing "God's work" and to believe that one sees all there is to see—and to be dangerously and selectively blind to unpleasant or conflicting realities.

Art of the witnessing imagination is particularly vulnerable to attack by those who have tried to keep art from addressing social realities. Recently, this became evident in the fierce public debate that has raged around the pejorative term "victim art."[19] Some will assert that the image of the victim is evoked in order to cover up an aesthetic hollowness. Arlene Croce coined the term "victim art" in her assault on Bill T. Jones's "Still/Here," a dance that addresses AIDS. Ironically, Croce had never seen the dance, insisting that she "can't review someone I feel sorry for or hopeless about." In her attempt to make a conceptual statement about art through her criticism, she unwittingly demonstrates some of the major pitfalls in the receiver's experience of art of the witnessing imagination—the dangers of confusing empathy with pity, justice with altruism, and truth with sentimentality.

Art of the witnessing imagination cannot stop a genocide. That requires the moral, political, and military authority of governments—sorely lacking in the tragic case of Bosnia. Art of the witnessing imagination cannot compensate for this absence, but it can stand as a powerful embodiment of our human capacities to affirm life while admitting evil's presence—a necessary but not sufficient ingredient of human resistance to genocide. Art of the witnessing imagination supplies those of us living in the dark shadow of genocidal evil with something we will continue to need and will probably not find elsewhere in our ongoing struggle to deal with the long-term consequences of "ethnic cleansing" in Bosnia.

Notes

1. Stevan M. Weine and Dori Laub, "Constructions of Historical Realities in Testimony with Bosnian Survivors of 'Ethnic Cleansing,'" *Psychiatry*, in press.

2. Robert Jay Lifton, *The Nazi Doctors: Medical Killing and the Psychology of Genocide* (New York: Basic Books, Inc., 1986).

3. Radovan Karadzic, In the Reuters Transcription Service. Interview conducted February 4th, New York, 1993.

4. Jovan Raskovic, *Luda Zemlja* (Begorad: Akvarijus, 1990).

5. Stevan M. Weine, Daniel F. Becker, Thomas H. McGlashan, Dori Laub, Steven Lazrove, Dolores Vojvoda, Leslie Hyman, "Psychiatric Consequences of 'Ethnic Cleansing': Clinical Assessments and Trauma Testimonies of Newly Resettled Bosnian Refugees," *American Journal of Psychiatry* 152 (1995): 536–42.

6. Robert Jay Lifton, lecture delivered at the 9th annual meeting of the International Society for Traumatic Stress Studies, San Antonio, Texas, 1993.

7. Lawrence Langer, *Holocaust Testimonies: The Ruins of Memory* (New Haven and London: Yale University Press, 1991).

8. Zlata Filipovic, *Zlata's Diary* (New York: Viking, 1994).

9. Lawrence Langer, ed., *Art from the Ashes: A Holocaust Anthology* (New York: Oxford University Press, 1995).

10. Zlatko Dizdarevic, *Sarajevo: A War Journal* (New York: Fromm International, 1993); Zlatko Dizdarevic, "Deaths from Natural Causes," *New York Times*, Op-Ed, February 2, section A, 15, 1994a); Zlatko Dizdarevic, "Under the Gun in Sarajevo," *Time Magazine*, February 21, 30–33, 1994b; Zlatko Dizdarevic, "What Kind of Peace is This?" *New York Times Magazine*, April 10, section 6, 36–78, 1994c.

11. Zlatko Dizdarevic, Research interview conducted by Stevan Weine, New Haven, 1994.

12. Sanjin Jukic, exhibition by the artist, included in "Witnesses of Existence," at New York Kunsthalle, 1994a; Sanjin Jukic, Research interviews conducted by Stevan Weine, New York 1994b; Jamey Gambrell, "Sarajevo: Art in Extremis," *Art in America* 82(1994): 100–105.

13. Sanjin Jukic, research interviews with Stevan Weine, New York, 1994.

14. Karen Malpede, "Us," *Women on the Verge: Seven Avant-Garde American Plays* (New York: Applause Theatre Books, Inc., 1993b). Malpede's early plays are in *A Monster has Stolen the Sun and Other Plays* (Marlboro, Vermont: The Marlboro Press, 1987).

15. Karen Malpede, research Interviews conducted by Steve Weine, New York, 1994.

16. Karen Malpede, "The Beekeeper's Daughter." Unpublished manuscript, 1993a.

17. Karen Malpede, research interviews conducted by Steve Weine, New York, 1994.

18. Museum of Applied Arts, Exhibit Catalogue, Belgrade, 1993.

19. Arlene Croce, "Discussing the Undiscussable," *The New Yorker*, December 26, 1994.

21

Religion and Violence

Harvey Cox

And they shall beat their swords into
      plowshares,
and their spears into pruning hooks . . .
                —Micah 4:3

Beat your plowshares into swords,
      and your pruning hooks into spears,
      let the weak say, "I am a warrior."

I have not come to bring peace,
      but a sword.
                —Jesus, Matthew 10:34

All who take the sword will perish
      by the sword.
                —Jesus, Matthew 26:52

When it comes to violence, the record of religion, including that of Christianity and Judaism, the foundational faiths of Western culture, is—to say the least—ambiguous. Sometimes that ambiguity reaches a bizarre level. Last year I attended a memorial service at the Arlington Street Church in Boston to honor two employees of a women's health clinic in Brookline who were shot to death at their job. The man accused of the killing, John Salvi, publicly announced that his lifetime ambition was to become a Catholic priest. The same day the shooting took place,

Philip Berrigan, a former priest, was arrested yet another time for a non-violent protest at an American nuclear weapons facility. One cannot help contemplating the possibility of these two living embodiments of the convoluted relationship between religious faith and violence meeting each other in the same cell block.

Several months later, when poisonous gas was released in the subway system of Tokyo, suspicion soon fastened on a syncretistic religious movement that combines Buddhist elements with both the worship of the Hindu deity Shiva and with millennial/apocalyptic views of the coming of the year 2000. Meanwhile Hindu–Muslim violence on a large scale still breaks out frequently in India, most disastrously in the city of Hyderabad (which was founded by a Muslim king to honor the memory of his dead Hindu mistress.) Tensions between Muslims and the persecuted Christian population of Sudan could explode into war at any point. Television news teems with ugly reports and images of violent incidents that are said to be inspired by religion. Angry Hindus tear down a Muslim mosque. A Jewish settler sprays bullets into Muslims at prayer on an Islamic holy day. At regular intervals pictures of saddened relatives of yet another victim of the bloodshed among Christians in northern Ireland fill the first pages. Muslim militants demand the death of a woman writer in Bangladesh. It seems that everywhere angry people are beating their pruning hooks into swords, often out of a misplaced loyalty to God.

Yet even the most uninformed observer realizes that this blood and gore represent only one face, and perhaps not even the most important face, of religion vis à vis violence today. We know that the great religious traditions have nurtured some of the most courageous and persistent modern advocates of nonviolence and compassion—Gandhi, the Dalai Lama, Martin Luther King, Mother Teresa, and others. We also know that the teachings of these religions are replete with affirmations of the dignity of human life and the responsibilities of human beings to respect and preserve that dignity.

It is also essential of course to make a clear distinction between human conflicts that are principally caused by religiously based hostilities and those that spring from other sources of tension (economic class, national identity, etc.) but within which religious loyalties sometimes worsen rather than mitigate the conflict. It is particularly important to examine what the principal narrative of a religious tradition teaches about such issues as the care of children, the responsibility one has to the poor, the outsider, the sick, the stranger and the prisoner. These are the people who have often lacked the power in any society and have often been a special object of religious terrorism and violence. Too often, however, secondary customs and derivative practices not drawn from the heart of the tradition have been flagrantly misused. In our time of religious resurgence it is especially important to separate out core teachings from secondary add-ons. The work currently being done on the place of women by Muslim and Christian women is a good example. The compassion most religious traditions frequently commend for the homeless and refugees are especially critical in our moment of history. Where then, on balance, do we stand, as we draw close to the twenty-first century, on the vexed and baffling issue of the link between religion and violence?

It is critical to realize that we pose this question in the midst of an unanticipated worldwide resurgence of religion. God, it seems, did not quite die after all. The predictions said that the technological pace and urban bustle of the twentieth century would increasingly shove religion to the margin where, deprived of roots, it would shrivel. It might well survive as a valued heirloom, perhaps in ethnic enclaves or family customs, but religion's day as a shaper of culture and history was over. But, instead, something else has happened. As the twenty-first century begins, a religious renaissance of sorts appears to be going on all over the globe. Ancient faith traditions that some scholars were sure had either been gutted by secularism or suffocated by repression have gained a new lease on life. Buddhism and Hinduism, Christianity and Judaism, Islam and Shinto, and many smaller sects are back in action as vigorous, often controversial, players on the world stage. But the current revival raises at least two inevitable questions: Why is it happening? And, is it good news or bad news?

For most people, the second question is the most urgent one. They want to know what this unanticipated rebirth of the gods means for them personally, and their curiosity often carries apprehensive overtones. Even the people who suspected that the proclamation of the deity's demise was mistaken, and who sensed that neither atheistic communism nor secular modernity would last forever, harbor severe misgivings. And one can see why. Religions are often fused with ethnic and national identities, so religious revival can also revive old grudges and smoldering vendettas. Can a crowded planet survive a dozen simultaneous new great awakenings? Are we moving ahead toward a new age of the Spirit or slipping backward toward another Dark Ages? There is much palaver about the need for "spiritual values," but what if pursuing such values sets one vision against another and transforms the whole world into a Bosnian nightmare of contending zealotries? Will the current renaissance of religions lead toward some peaceful parliament of faiths, such as the one envisioned by the planners of the Great Columbian Exposition in Chicago 100 years ago, or will it ignite a new outburst of jihads, crusades and inquisitions? Where is it all heading?

If the "what-does-it-mean?" question is the more urgent one, the "why-is-it-happening?" question is also impossible to ignore. Why were so many wise and well qualified scholars—not just popular pundits but careful observers who should have known better—so dramatically and demonstrably wrong when they predicted the imminent decline of religion? If God really did die, as Nietzsche and the more recent radical theologians announced, then why have so many billions of people not gotten the message? Was there something fundamentally askew in the reigning philosophical analyses of Western and world culture that caused such respected thinkers to make such a bad call? Why have Yahweh, Allah, Jesus Christ, Khrishna, the Buddha and a host of goddesses, demigods and lesser deities all come back from their premature internment as though to mock the solemn dirges intoned at their funerals?

These questions are posed at one time or another about all the newly resurgent religious movements. But they are pressed most vigorously about two of them in particular: militant Islam and pentecostal Christianity. The reason these two are so often singled out for discussion is easy to see. They are the two fastest growing such movements in the world, and their growth, for various reasons, often evokes in some people a feeling of genuine anxiety. But the two are very different from each other. In recent years a newly invigorated Islam, often misleadingly labeled "Muslim fundamentalism," has claimed the larger share of headlines. The *fatwa* issued against Salman Rushdie and *The Satanic Verses*, the terrorist actions of a group called the "Islamic Jihad"; and other spectacular episodes have kept renascent Islam on the front page. Images of Muslim crowds shaking angry fists and burning books or effigies understandably frighten television viewers everywhere, especially if they know little about Islam or its history and variety.

With pentecostalism, however, the situation is quite a different one. For most people, the pentecostals are people they have noticed, as it were, out of the corner of the eye: a television evangelist prowling the stage, microphone in hand, tie loose and hair askew, glimpsed while a viewer is grazing the channels with a remote panel; a sudden spurt of high-voltage sermonic phrases accidentally erupting from a car radio while the driver is spinning the dial; a jumble of press reports about faith healers, religious con artists, and biblical theme parks. Then it seems to fade from sight again until the next juicy tidbit about the bedroom peccadillos of excitable preachers pops into the news. Besides, if the average outsider knows little about Islam he probably knows just as little about pentecostals and probably thinks of them as just a somewhat noisier and bumptious variety of Christian.

There can be little doubt that the current rebirth of Islamic belief is vastly important. Still, though it only rarely dominates the evening news, the spread of pentecostalism may in the long run be even more significant for the world's future. First, pentecostalism is a more global movement. Unhampered by the need to teach Arabic to its new converts as Muslims must do (so they can read and pray the *Koran*), it can penetrate a kaleidoscope of various cultures and blend in with them easily. Also, as the fastest growing part of what is already the world's largest religion, Christianity, and as a faith that is expanding in precisely those areas where populations are increasing, a study of its uncanny appeal is more likely to yield the most useful answers to the why and what questions we have just registered.

This is the reason why, for the past few years, I have been endeavoring to answer these questions, among others, through the intensive study of Christian pentecostalism. This movement is growing far more quickly than militant Islam, and is spreading in more regions of the world, including, most recently, China, India and the former states of the Soviet Union. I am interested in pentecostalism in part because I believe it is a particularly dramatic example of a much larger and more encompassing resurgence of religion, and can therefore teach us a lot about our common global future.

In my study of the pentecostal movement, I have become convinced that there is indeed something noteworthy going on, and that it is vital that those of us who worry about religion and violence should understand it. Pentecostals do not issue *fatwahs* or any other death decrees. They are not allied to surging nationalist movements. They do not take credit for kidnapping hostages or bombing air liners. Consequently, the spectacular growth of their churches does not often heave into public view. Still, not only are they continuing to grow, I believe their growth holds within it a host of significant clues to the meaning of the more general global religious resurgence we are now witnessing. Paying attention to the appeal of pentecostalism will help us more than anything else to discern whether the present unforeseen global reawakening of religious faith is good or bad news for the human family.

Who are the pentecostals? It should be made clear at the outset that pentecostals are *not* Jehovah's Witnesses, or Seventh Day Adventists or Mormons, all Christian sects that are growing with considerable rapidity though not nearly as fast as pentecostals are. Pentecostals also are *not* fundamentalists. Though the two are often confused, they are not only very different, but often at odds with each other. Pentecostals are vibrant and exuberant. Fundamentalists tend to be rigid and unbending. While fundamentalists stridently insist on the verbal inerrancy of every word in the Bible, Pentecostals love the verse that says "the letter killeth but the Spirit giveth life." The strong pentecostal emphasis on a direct and unmediated experience of the Divine Spirit often puts them at logger-heads with fundamentalists, who insist that all spiritual experience must be channeled through the infallible Word of God in the Bible.

The impression conveyed by the radio and TV preachers—an enter-taining but unrepresentative fringe—can also be quite misleading. Despite the publicity recently lavished on luckless Jimmy and tear-stained Tammy Faye Bakker, the welcome diversion they undoubtedly provided is in no way typical of the worldwide pentecostal movement. Its main growth area is not in America, not on television, and not among white people. Rather it is spreading in face-to-face meetings and mainly out-side North America, among the people of Asia, Latin America, Africa, and in some places in Europe. Like Christianity itself, which came to birth in Palestine but reached its zenith elsewhere, or Buddhism, which was born in India but became the principal faith of the rest of Asia, pentecostalism started in America but has now probably crested in its homeland while it continues to expand and flourish in the rest of the world. (The important exception to this generalization is that in the United States pentecostalism continues to burgeon among Latinos, Asian immigrants and African Americans.)

The Pentecostal credo is a very simple one. They believe that Jesus can not only save their immortal souls but can also heal their mortal bodies. They believe the Spirit can speak not just through preachers but in the dreams, visions and incoherent praise of ordinary people. They believe that this age is a uniquely significant one and that a whole new chapter in God's way of being with the human race and the planet is beginning. They sing joyously, move energetically, and reach out with zeal and compassion to their friends and neighbors, especially those in need. They sometimes experience what to outsiders appear to be mysti-cal trances and they sometimes pray in sounds that some insiders (though not all) claim to be other tongues. They are famous for their sobriety, honesty and good work habits. Most of all, they believe that the Spirit of God is real and powerful, and available here and now to anyone who sincerely opens his or her heart.

Lots of people, of course, have tried in various ways to grasp the mean-ing of pentecostalism. Sociologists, theologians, anthropologists have all taken their turns. But the picture they paint is confused and contradictory. They point out that pentecostalism seems to spread most quickly in the slums and shantytowns of the world city. Is it then a revival among the poor? Well, they concede, not exclusively. Its message also appeals—thought to a lesser extent— to other classes and stations. Its promise of an unmediated experience of God, and of health and well being here and now, not just after death, attracts a wide variety of seekers to congregations where they bask in the warm support of fellow believers and—perhaps most of all—gain a sense of dignity and direction in a world that otherwise offers them little of either.

But just who are these people? Again the picture is not uniform. They vary in color and gender and nationality, though the brown, black and yellow predominate. They may be teenagers or old folks though young adults lead the way. They may be poor or located somewhere in the lower ranges of the middle class: there are not many well-to-do. They are what one writer calls the "discontents of modernity," not fully at home with the reigning values, beliefs, and lifestyles of whatever one might mean by the "modern world." One scholar describes the movement as a "symbolic rebellion" against the modern world. But they often seem just as dissatisfied with the religions of the very traditional world which the modern world is so systematically subverting. For this reason, another writer describes them as providing a *different way of being modern.* Both may be right. Their dislike for both the traditional order and for certain aspects of modern society may help explain why pentecostals welcome the idea that God is not too pleased with "this world"—with its admixture of old and new—either, and that its days are numbered. Paradoxically, though some sociologists believe pentecostals have been uprooted and dazed by the pace of contemporary change, this spiritual movement's demanding moral disciplines and organizational training often equip them to cope with it better. They are refugees from both the tyrannys of tradition and the oppression of modernity, and their faith provides them with what it takes to survive until a new day dawns.

But how much does this tell us? Are sociological or psychological analyses really enough to explain such a truly massive and worldwide phenomenon? One historian has called the pentecostal surge the most significant religious movement since the original rise of Islam or the Protestant reformation. But these historic upheavals have for centuries defied attempts to explain them in merely secular categories, however sophisticated. The present pentecostal wave also seems to slip through such conceptual grids. More and more, even the most skeptical observ-

ers are beginning to concede that—whether for weal or for woe—
something undeniably significant, maybe even epochal, is underway.
Further, the same observers are coming to believe that whatever is happening is not confined to some special religious or spiritual sphere.
They see it as one indication of a much larger and more sweeping
change.

Granted, there are lots of reasons to doubt whether such a Big
Change is actually at hand. It is true that in philosophy and literary
criticism something called "post-modernism" is the rage of the journals.
But intellectuals like to imagine themselves on the cutting edge, and
post-modernism could be one more pedantic self-delusion. Gurus and
crystal gazers talk about a "New Age," but they sound suspiciously like
the aging hippies who twenty years ago were hailing the imminent dawn-
ing of the Age of Aquarius. The "new world order" Desert Storm was
supposed to introduce turned out to be something of a mirage, and
elsewhere in the international political arena we seem to be reeling
backward in time to an era of ethnic and tribal bloodletting, not moving
forward to anything very new at all. There is every reason to share the
skepticism of Ecclesiastes about whether there is ever any "new thing
under the sun." Still, behind the puff pieces and media hype, and despite the overheated atmosphere that will no doubt excite even more
utopian fantasies and millennarian scenarios before 2000 AD arrives,
the question stubbornly persists. Do the pentecostal movement and the
global religious stirring—of which it is undoubtedly a part signal—
something larger and more significant that is underway?

My own answer to this question is at least a qualified "yes." Having
pondered the pentecostal movement for several years and in many different countries, I have a strong hunch that it provides us with an invaluable set of clues, not just about the wider religious upsurge but about
an even more comprehensive set of changes. Further, I do not believe
these changes are exclusively "religious ones." They add up to a basic
cultural shift for which the overtly spiritual dimension is the tip of the
iceberg. I do not see this change as the beginning of the Last Days, as
some pentecostals do. I do see it however as a major reconfiguration of
our most fundamental attitudes and patterns of perception, one that
will ultimately alter not just the way some people pray but the ways we
all think, feel, work and govern.

I think my hunch is well-grounded. As a life long student of religious
movements—Christian and non-Christian, historical and contemporary,
salubrious and demonic—I have come to believe two things about such
movements. The first conviction is widely shared among my colleagues

today—namely, that religious movements can never be usefully studied apart from the cultural and political milieu in which they arise. I do not believe religious phenomena are "caused" by other factors, economic or political ones for example. Still, they always come to life in close connection with a complex cluster of other cultural and social vectors.

I have also come to a second working premise, one that is not as widely shared among my colleagues. It is that although religion neither causes or is caused by the other factors in a complex cultural whole, it is often a very accurate barometer. It can provide the clearest and most graphically etched portrait, in miniature, of what is going on in the larger picture. Freud once said that dreams are the royal road to the unconscious. I am convinced that religion is the royal road to the heart of a civilization, the clearest indicator of its hopes and terrors, the surest indice of how it is changing.

The reason I believe religion is such an invaluable window into the larger whole is that human beings, so long as they are human, live according to patterns of value and meaning without which life would not make sense. These patterns may be coherent or confused, elegant or slap-dash, rooted in ancient traditions or pasted together in an ad hoc way. People may adhere to them tightly or loosely, consciously or unconsciously, studiously or unreflectively. But the patterns exist. They are encoded in gestures, idioms, recipes, rituals, seasonal festivals and family habits, doctrines, texts, liturgies and folk wisdom. They are constantly shifting, mixing with each other, declining into empty usages, bursting into new life. But they are always there. Without them human existence would be unlivable. And they constitute what, in the most inclusive use of the term, we mean by "religion," that which binds life together. Even that most famous of atheists, Karl Marx, after all once said that religion is "the heart of a heartless world."

What then is the source of the immense appeal of pentecostals to the hearts of so many people in so many different parts of our heartless world? When you ask pentecostals why they think their movement is growing at such astonishing speed, they have an answer: because the Spirit is in it. They may be right. But as I have pondered these questions from a more pedestrian perspective, I have become convinced that there is one commanding reason why the movement has had such a widespread appeal. It has been able to speak to the spiritual emptiness of our time by reaching below the levels of creed and ceremony into the core of human religiousness, into what might be called "primal spirituality," that largely unprocessed nucleus of the human psyche in which the unending struggle for a sense of meaning and significance goes one.

The early pentecostals believed they were restoring the original faith of the first apostles. Scholars have sometimes glibly dismissed them as one more "restorationist" movement. My own conviction is that pentecostals have touched so many people because they have indeed restored something. They have helped countless people to recover, on a very personal level, three dimensions of this primal spirituality that I call "primal speech," "primal piety," and "primal hope."

The first, primal speech, refers to the spiritual import of what scholars of religion sometimes call "ecstatic utterance," what the earliest pentecostals called "speaking in tongues," and what many now refer to as "praying in the spirit." In an age of bombast, hype and doublespeak, when ultra-specialized terminologies and contrived rhetoric seem to have emptied and pulverized language, the first pentecostals learned to speak—and their successors still speak—with another voice, a language of the heart.

A second, primal piety, touches on the resurgence in pentecostalism of trance, vision, healing, dreams, dance and other archetypal religious expressions. These primeval modes of praise and supplication comprise what the great French sociologist Emile Durkheim once called the "elementary forms" of religious life, by which he meant the foundational elements of human religiosity. The reemergence of this primal spirituality came—perhaps not surprisingly—at just the point in history when both the rationalistic assumptions of modernity and the strategies religions had used to oppose them (or to accommodate to them) were all coming unraveled.

The third, primal hope, points to pentecostalism's future-oriented outlook—its insistence that a radically new world age is about to dawn. This is the kind of hope which transcends any particular content. It is what the German philosopher Ernst Bloch once called "Prinzip Hoffnung," the kernel of all utopianism, the principled refusal to believe that what we see is all there is or could be. It is what the *Epistle to the Hebrews* calls the "evidence of things not seen," and because it is more an orientation to the future than a detailed scheme, it persists despite the failure of particular hopes to materialize. Thus despite the fact that the pentecostals' vision of the imminence of the visible coming of Christ seemed to be controverted at one level, their tenacity of primal hope has made their message more contemporary with every passing year.

I realize that for many thoughtful people, all three of these qualities of the pentecostal phenomenon—glossolalia, dreams and trances, and millennialism—appear at best merely bizarre and at worst downright scary. But if we think of the three, in the broader perspective of religious history, as the recovery of primal speech (ecstatic utterance), primal piety (mystical experience, trance and embodiment), and primal hope, the unshakable expectation of a better future, then their contemporary recovery becomes a little less baffling. Long before primal scream therapy, dream journals, liturgical dance, psycho-drama, or futurology made their appearances at elite conference centers and expensive weekend workshops, the early pentecostals were spreading their own versions of all of them.

I believe the unanticipated reappearance of primal spirituality in our time reveals much about who we human beings are as we approach the twenty-first century, and that its meaning transcends all merely social or psychological explanations. In an age that has found exclusively secular explanations of life wanting, but is also wary of dogmas and institutions, the unforeseen eruption of this spiritual lava reminds us that somewhere deep within us we all carry a *homo religiosus*. Pentecostalism is not an aberration. It is a part of the larger and longer history of human religiousness, and from my perspective, it constitutes a much more positive and hopeful way of filling the obvious spiritual void of our time than religions that set group against group. In this respect at least it is one hopeful sign amidst so much bleak evidence from other quarters about the links between religion and violence in our increasingly religious and violent times.

There is another reason why—although I harbor some reservations about some aspects of it—on balance I find the emergence of the pentecostal movement a hopeful sign in a dark period. The people who call themselves "pentecostals" trace their modern history to a tiny African-American church on Azusa Street in the black ghetto of Los Angeles. They take their name from a story recounted in chapter two of *The Acts of the Apostles*. The plot describes how the confused followers of the recently crucified rabbi they believed was the messiah gathered in Jerusalem to mark the Jewish holiday that occurs fifty days after Passover (hence the term Pentecost). Suddenly there came a sound from heaven "like the rush of a mighty wind." The Holy Spirit filled them, tongues "as of fire" rested on their heads, and to their amazement each began to understand what the other was saying even though they came from "every nation under heaven" and spoke many different languages. It seemed that the ancient curse of Babel—the confounding of languages —had been reversed and that God was creating a new inclusive human community in which "Parthians and Medes and Elamites and residents of Mesopotamia" could all live together.

This account is what is technically known in theology as a "myth."

Whatever actually happened on that festive Pentecost is lost to the modern historian. But the religious meaning attached to these events still retains an enormous power. What happened was that people from different and often opposing nationalities and cultures *came together*, but they came together *without sacrificing their cultural particularity*. The story might have said that all these different clans suddenly began speaking Aramaic or Hebrew or Greek, and therefore understood each other. But instead it proclaims that they all spoke *their own* languages, and yet were understood. Conservative Christian movements today are often obsessively focused on the Law of God, and fervently believe it should be imposed on modern society. Liberationist theologies tend to emphasize the Exodus, the liberation of a captive people from an oppressor. But the imposition of a divine law wreaks havoc on religious pluralism, and since the Exodus moves on the conquest of Canaan, both these myths can be used and have been used to justify violence.

Pentecost is a different kind of religious metaphor. It speaks of a re-gathering, of the overcoming of hostility and suspicion in a new spiritual community in which the individual qualities of the particular peoples are not erased but maintained. What we require, perhaps more than anything else as we move into the next century are powerful symbolic motifs of unity, narratives of species identity and metaphors of intercultural solidarity. It just might be that the pentecostal movement, which arose on the wrong side of the tracks and started among the least likely people, could provide some of these saving stories. God knows we need them.

22

Back from the Abyss: Symbolic Immortality, Faith, and Human Survival

Roger Williamson

I have recently seen for the first time a remarkable picture by Marc Chagall, "The White Christ," painted in 1938.[1] To paint a picture of Christ crucified is a remarkable thing for a Jewish artist to do. The picture is even more remarkable—a critique of the genocidal murder that was engulfing Europe. In one part of the picture Nazis are desecrating and destroying a synagogue. In another part a horde with red flags are plundering and destroying. A boatload of refugees is being turned away—and in the center, the suffering figure of the murdered Jew Jesus.

How did Chagall intend it to be understood? I do not know. Did the picture serve as the inspiration for Chaim Potok's moving novel *My Name Is Asher Lev*?[2] Again I do not know. But to me, the interpretation is clear. The place of the Christian in today's world of genocide, war and injustice is on the side of those who suffer. The Christian understanding of Jesus is that in this poor, marginal, Jewish peasant God has become human and accepts the limitation and pain of challenging the death-dealing structures of hatred, complacency and injustice. The message of the work of Robert Jay Lifton tells us a great deal about how humans created hell on earth during this century. The transformation for which he calls and which he has sought so intelligently and courageously to inspire is perhaps barely less remarkable than the incarnation. His question is not how God can become human, but whether humanity can become human.

Lifton identifies a number of different modes of symbolic immortality, which give the individual life a greater meaning than that accorded by its short duration.[3] He speaks of a down-to-earth form of transcendence which he calls "symbolic immortality":

269

(1) In the biological mode, we have the sense of living on, psychologically speaking, *in* our sons and daughters and their sons and daughters.[4]

(2) A second mode of symbolic immortality is the one that most comes to mind in many cases—the theological or religious mode. Sometimes that can include the idea of a life after death, as a form of "survival" or even as a release from profane burdens into a higher plane of existence.[5]

(3) A third mode of symbolic immortality is the creative mode, that of individual works, whether great works of art, literature, or science or more humble influences on friends, lovers, families, teachers upon students or vice versa.[6]

(4) The fourth mode of symbolic immortality has to do with nature itself, symbolized as eternal nature in virtually all cultures.[7]

(5) Now there is a fifth mode of symbolized immortality—the direct psychic experience, so intense that, within it, time and death disappear. This, of course, is the classical mode of the mystics. Not only can it be experienced in the contemplation of God or of the universe; but, as Marghanita Laski in particular has written, it can have a number of expressions in such things as song, dance, battle, sexual love, childbirth, athletic effort, mechanical flight, contemplation of the past, or artistic or intellectual creation. These are experiences of "extacy" or "transcendence."[8]

It is common for human beings to want more than just what can be provided in this limited life. This feeling is particularly acute since we live under the threat of a technologically induced, meaningless apocalypse—whether the "bang" of the bomb or the "whimper" of environmental destruction—to paraphrase T.S. Eliot. Lifton has worked this understanding through in a particularly telling way with regard to the threat of nuclear winter. Rather than looking at how to survive and recover from disaster, the possibility of human technology causing a holocaust which would extinguish all human life means that we must grieve,[9] be angry and work to prevent such disaster *before it happens*, rather than hoping we can survive and rebuild.[10] Clearly, as the threat of nuclear destruction has receded, Lifton's work does not lose its relevance, but the suggestive approaches which he has developed need to be applied to the threat of environmental collapse. For faith communities, the importance of symbolic immortality is considerable, particularly as a defence against any suggestion that the termination of human existence would not be such a disaster in the overall scheme of things.

Work against the death-dealing forces of human violence and techno-logically delivered destruction is not an easy task. The Greeks have two myths to which it is important for us to return—they represent two temptations which those who are concerned for the world do well to reflect upon.[11] I propose these two reflections as a correction to some of the dangers of Lifton's over-enthusiastic embrace of Proteus—for rea-sons which will become apparent later.

The first is the myth of *Atlas*—the person condemned to hold up the world. It is important to mention the fate that Atlas suffered for his opposition to Zeus:

> To bear on his back forever
> The cruel strength of the crushing world
> And the vault of the sky.
> Upon his shoulders the great pillar
> That holds apart the earth and heavens,
> A load not easy to be borne.[12]

Thich Nhat Hanh, the Vietnamese Buddhist[13] nominated for the Nobel Peace prize by Martin Luther King, once described a meditation for overworked peace activists. He suggested that as a form of spiritual discipline, one should abstain from reading the newspapers for a three-month period and then reflect honestly about whether the world had become a significantly worse place as a result. This shows us that we do not personally hold up the world. Naturally one would have to say that the Buddhist teacher would have quite another meditation or form of advice for those who are under-involved or simply not interested in the fate of the earth.

The second Greek myth is that of *Sisyphus*,[14] who has to keep rolling a boulder up a hill (presumably the prototypical Rolling Stone), and, as soon as it gets to the top, it rolls down again. This is a symbol for sense-less, unending work, with no prospect of release. Often the work for peace, justice and the protection of the environment feels like this—well-intentioned, against the grain of the universe and fated to eternal frustration. Even if some campaigns are successful, like decades of activ-ity against apartheid, the world's rivers are becoming more polluted, nuclear disarmament has not yet been achieved, the rain forests are being hacked down, Tibet is not free, the debt crisis is not overcome and so on—ad infinitum or, maybe, ad nauseam.

Albert Camus—a favourite author of Lifton's—in his essay *The Myth of Sisyphus* concludes by saying that we must imagine Sisyphus happy.[15] To me, this means that even as we work on the seemingly endless tasks of passing on a habitable, just and peaceful planet to the next generation we need to have some fun and get, and give, some encouragement along the way.

One important step is to be able to see structures of oppression and domination as being largely humanly created and therefore—at least in principle—capable of being dismantled by purposeful, goal-directed human activity. Lifton's creative theoretical work provides an important source for generalizing lessons of universal significance from the testimony of "survivors." Human beings know death, and only we are capable of inventing "grotesquely absurd death."[16]

Lifton sees nuclear annihilation as a "meaningless apocalypse," but does not despair of a human future. *Death in Life*, his great Hiroshima book, stresses that we could learn from the use of nuclear weapons fifty years ago, thereby taking a "last chance" and deriving "knowledge that could contribute to holding back the even more massive extermination it seems to foreshadow."[17]

Over twenty years ago, the Black South African clinical psychologist N.C. Manganyi, in his book *Being-Black-in-the-World* took up and reinterpreted the thinking of Camus by arguing that the absurdity and hopelessness experienced by black people in South Africa was not fate or destiny, but a system of power constructed by white people which made the lives of blacks oppressive and absurd.[18] As a post-apartheid antidote, it is interesting to read a recent book on the lives and beliefs of anti-apartheid activists, *The Spirit of Hope*,[19] in which they were asked where the basic strength and values came from which enabled them to resist apartheid for decades—even at times when objectively there was little chance of success. In many cases, a systematic worldview (Weltanschauung) was a source of order and strength through which the humanist values of resistance to apartheid was expressed—although the actual worldview differed considerably—for some a Christian or Muslim perspective, for others black consciousness, for others Marxism, and for some an eclectic combination of political and religious approaches. It is hard to resist as an individual, and the adherence to an alternative view of reality very often helps to incarnate or give form to the values of an alternative community. To some extent, this is merely a point which illustrates the social construction of reality. As Peter Berger points out, it is as hard to be a witch doctor in a world of logical positivists as it is to be a logical positivist in a world of witch doctors. It is quite simply hard to swim for a long time against the stream, to oppose unjust wars, to work for a just world order and just to ensure nature's survival.

What I have said so far will already make it clear to those familiar with the work of Robert Jay Lifton, why I consider his writings and involvement to be one of the main intellectual resources for confronting the appalling suffering of the "short twentieth century" (from 1914–89) and this current epoch (whatever we eventually call it). The twentieth-century is a period of history which, in the words of anthropologist Marvin Harris, has seen "a war to end all wars followed by a war to make the world safe for democracy, followed by a world full of military dictatorships."[20] We were then promised a New World Order as the reward for agreeing to the Gulf War, as the end of the Cold War gave way to a seemingly endless series of intra-state wars which the international community is unwilling or unable to bring to order.

In the rich countries of the West, there has been a shift away from fixation on nuclear weapons and dread of the "meaningless apocalypse" of nuclear Armageddon. The free-floating anxiety of the Western world has attached itself to the danger of terminal ecological damage. Meanwhile, however, the situation for many in the South remains largely the same—economic poverty, brutal governments, a harsh environment which allows barely subsistence living standards, political repression, "small" but long-lasting wars, the refugee crisis involving over 25 million refugees and at least as many internally displaced persons worldwide, the debt crisis and so on. It does not seem to be overdramatic to present the world in potentially apocalyptic terms, even if one has the fortune to live in one of the enclaves of wealth in the sea of poverty. It seems likely that it will take increasing levels of repression—in both psychological and political terms—to avoid responding positively to what is going on.

These are Lifton's themes: denial, splitting off the awareness of the suffering of others, extreme human situations. It is this deep understanding of what can be learned for the future survival of humanity precisely from the most extreme and dehumanised relations between human beings which makes Lifton's work of such practical value and urgency. I would suggest that it is precisely his work as a practitioner which leads to the depth of his theoretical insights—and precisely this rich theoretical framework which provides inspiration to us to galvanize action.

The issues which have preoccupied me over the last twenty years are illuminated by Lifton's work—opposition to torture, attempts to move churches to respond to violations of human rights, the nuclear threat, military intervention and war—as well as more theoretical theological issues such as how we envisage God's sustaining power in a time when certain humans are quite capable of ending human history, something which hitherto we had considered that only God could do.

The liberative intentions of the counselling professions can be truncated to fit people back into a "normality" which means the death of others. Lifton has written incisively about the use of psychiatry to help to get soldiers fit enough to be reintegrated into active combat again.

> The psychiatrist in Vietnam, whatever his intentions, found himself in collusion with the military in conveying to individual GI's an overall organizational message: "Do your indiscriminate killing with confidence that you will receive expert medical-psychological help if needed." Keeping in mind Camus' warning that men should become neither victims nor executioners, this can be called—at least in Vietnam—the psychiatry of the executioner.[21]

His reflection on the wider implications of this issue contains a far-reaching critique of the therapeutic professions, which is at least as valid for the representatives of religion, theologians, pastors and others:

> Psychiatrists have a great temptation to swim with an American tide that grants them considerable professional status but resists, at times quite fiercely, serious attempts to alter existing social and institutional arrangements. As depth psychologists and psychoanalysts, we make a kind of devil's bargain that we can plunge as deeply as we like into intra-psychic conflicts while not touching too critically upon historical dimensions that question those institutional arrangements.[22]

This issue is put in even more acute form by James Hillman's book *We've Had a Hundred Years of Psychotherapy and the World's Getting Worse.*[23] For the Christian theologian, two thousand years after the Sermon on the Mount, the question is even more acute—particularly if one includes the "fratricidal" relationship with Judaism (Rosemary Radford Ruether) of endemic anti-Semitism, the failure to prevent (or even effectively to repent for) Western colonialism, expansionism and destruction of indigenous cultures, oppression of women and the despoiling of nature.

What is impressive about Lifton is that his development of Freud's understanding is in the service of a wider humanity, not simply aimed at the cure of the individual as the social world goes under. Lifton's in-depth work on such issues as Vietnam, Hiroshima and the Shoah/Holocaust is precisely not to get the individual survivor to come to terms with the fact that the world is a tough place and that ultimately you have to accept that, but rather to learn from these experiences in order to oppose the forces which lead towards genocide and unnecessary destruction.

The same ambivalence which is present in the counselling profession is there in at least as deeply ambivalent a form in any type of religion. To put it in brutal terms: within the tradition in which I live and work, Christian spirituality can be used either as an extra "plus" for those who already have everything, or it can be the motivating force for trying to change unjust structures. Too often it is used as individualistic consolation for those who are already materially comfortable, rather than as a source of strength for struggle for those who have almost nothing.

As the technology of destruction intensifies in deadliness, this contradiction has become more acute. To take a theme of Lifton's, the nuclear threat, Christian responses to nuclear war range all the way from acceptance of its inevitability as pre-ordained to the opposite end of the spectrum, the unconditional requirement to stop the destruction of God's good creation of the Earth.

The Moral Majority and right-wing fundamentalists thus can see Nuclear Armageddon as being in accordance with God's plan for the destruction of the wicked (who, if these new-right fundamentalist theologians are to be believed, in recent times have exhibited a quite remarkable coincidence with the enemies of the USA, whether the Biblical prophesies are applied to the Communist world or Saddam Hussein ("Babylon"). On the other hand, the Christian peace movements worldwide, and significant sectors of the institutional churches, have shown much greater affinity to a theology which requires the prevention of nuclear war. In the USA, the Catholic Bishops can be singled out as the most impressive example.

In his essay on the conscience, Ernst Lange outlines the characteristics of the type of conscience required in a world of permanent crisis and rapid change.

- It must be oriented towards the future
- It must be informed by expertise and knowledge
- It must cross boundaries
- It must be ready to pay the price for life
- It must be a conscience informed by hope[24]

In Lifton's work the threat of nuclear winter is dramatically turned around to teach us the things which make for peace. The realisation that the threats which we face are of such intensity that the grieving work (*Trauerarbeit*) cannot be done afterwards, means that we have to reflect on the threatened catastrophes so as to prevent them happening. Rather than learning from *past* catastrophes which have happened, we must learn from future potential tragedies which have not yet happened in order to avoid them.

And yet there are limits to the effectiveness of Lifton's images of transformation. Too much of the "Protean" self seems to me like a celebration of remarkable people.[25] If the American dream used to be that of the "self-made man," the protean self runs the danger of being the "man-made self" (or, in non-sexist language, the "humanly-created personality") as the highest art-form, or "me-creation as re-creation."[26] Admittedly, Lifton does have a chapter on "The Dark Side"—itself not such a happy choice of title when the focus is quickly concentrated on the black poor.[27]

I would suggest that the next task for Lifton's work is a fuller concentration on the social ethics and social psychology needed. Much of his work has provided brilliant illuminations of the human condition of humanity as a whole, and of individual psychology. The meaning of total threat for the necessary evolution to the "species-being" (avoiding the shortcuts and dangerous traps of pseudospeciation, scapegoating and projection) and the insight into the individual need for symbolic immortality are not yet, from my reading, adequately augmented by social-ethical or social-psychological readings of American society. There is a danger that proteanism is a new variant of the American dream—the inevitable shadow of which is an American and, indeed, a wider-world nightmare. The shifting protean selves surfing on the waves of history are in danger of being unaware of those who drown, never having surfaced to the levels of choice which make proteanism possible or sustainable. For too many of the world's population the question is not how to get to proteanism, but how to get protein in sufficient quantities for survival.

I would like to suggest, using examples from initiatives in which I have been involved over the last decade, areas where Lifton's work has been suggestive and shows the direction for further development of an ecological, social ethics. This would fill the gap between the aspiration for symbolic immortality for the individual and the "species self" as the goal for the whole of humanity.[28]

During my time at the Life and Peace Institute, we ran a project on "Images of the End and Christian Theology." Lifton's work was of central importance to me in the conceptualization of the project—most particularly his insight that human beings, through the development of nuclear weapons have now usurped the ability which only God was previously considered to have, the power to put an end to human history. This has profound implications for how to live faithfully in the Christian tradition post-Hiroshima and post-Auschwitz. For me this is centred in the need to be "true to this earth"—not to treat this world as though it is dispensible in terms of a greater plan, including nuclear annihilation. This work, which produced three reports, also led to my first connections with the Center on Violence and Human Survival through the active participation in the project of Chuck Strozier.[29] Strozier's contribution to the two international seminars went well beyond the intellectual input of his own work on American fundamentalists in the major project on "Nuclear Threat and the American Self," pioneering work in which the interviewing techniques developed through the psychohistorical approach provided detailed insight into the inner landscape of the minds of ordinary fundamentalists and their nuclear fears for the first time.[30] Previous writing on this subject had focussed almost entirely on the leaders, such as Pat Robertson, Jerry Falwell, Hal Lindsey et al., not their many followers. The intellectual cooperation with Chuck Strozier on this issue has developed into a firm friendship—something characteristic of the Center inspired by Lifton—connections emerging between scholars who do not want to be confined within one subject or discipline.

The second area emerges from this, namely religious fundamentalism as a threat to peace. Already by the late 1980s, I had become convinced that the field of ethno-religious conflicts was one which deserved much deeper study.[31] Both religious and racial/ethnic tensions were areas which Western social sciences failed to take sufficiently seriously. Marxists felt that such features of the ideological superstructure could better be explained in economic terms and would wither away. Western liberal theorists felt that religion was a matter of private choice and could be relegated to the individual sphere. Reality refused to respond. The postmodern polarisation of strategy—the choice between ironic, post-modern Proteanism or a dangerous hardening of religious and ethnic identities into fundamentalist political projects—serves as the beginning of a valuable analytical distinction. It is not, however, in itself adequate to describe fully the dynamics of ethno-religious conflict. The work on religion and human rights,[32] which serves as a counterpart to Hans Küng's approach of seeking a "Global Ethos,"[33] and which brought in such fine scholars as Abdulahi An Na'Im from a Sudanese Muslim background, suggests that there are alternatives to a world in which religious and ethnic wars proliferate in an epidemic of intolerance and slaughter. As Küng never tires of stressing, there can be "no peace among the peoples

of this world without peace among the world religions."[34] It is therefore
an encouraging sign when one of the main interfaith organisations, the
World Conference on Religion and Peace, whose 1994 assembly was addressed by the Pope, is devoting serious attention to this issue through
a project on the contribution of religious faiths to resolution of conflicts.

Within Christianity, the main inter-church organizations have also
seen a deepening response to the threats in the contemporary world.
Both the World Council of Churches and the European churches have
begun major attempts to understand and stimulate reflection and action
on the interlocking threats to human survival.

The World Council of Churches, from its 1983 Vancouver assembly
onwards, linked justice, peace and environmental issues in a global process. This led to a worldwide convocation in Seoul, Korea (1991), which
proved how difficult the linkage is, if one wants to move beyond general
affirmations to specific commitments of binding socio-political nature
enjoying worldwide support from the churches. The controversial, but I
would argue necessary, commitment of the World Council of Churches
to liberation in Southern Africa through its Programme to Combat Racism which supported leaders like Mugabe, Nujoma and Mandela when
most white "realist" politicians still regarded them as irrelevant, as ter-
rorists, or both, proved hard to replicate in other fields of injustice. The
Seoul conference did, however, succeed in producing ten affirmations
which now serve as the basis for its "Theology of Life" programme,
which has been given intellectual coherence by Larry Rasmussen, professor of ethics at Union Theological Seminary. Perhaps inevitably, the
statements are formulated in language which requires translation into
nontheological discourse before they can serve as a basis for a wider
dialogue, but that translation is relatively easy and gives the direction
for an ethics of human survival. Power and the accumulation of wealth
are called to account, the dimensions on environmental care and peace
are stressed.

At the European level the process has been similar. By 1989 a major
conference called by the Conference of European Churches and the
Council of European Bishops' Conferences brought together almost
700 delegates from every European country except Albania, representing all the major church traditions, Catholic, Orthodox and Protestant.
One of the central affirmations of that meeting was that there are no
circumstances in the countries of Europe which call for or justify the
use of violence. This statement in May 1989, and the later transition of
communism in which Christians and Churches played no small part, has
failed to produce a durable and peaceful social situation—as the con-

flicts in Central and Eastern Europe, most notably those in former Yugoslavia, indicate. The ineffectiveness of the Christian churches in preventing these conflicts is cause for deep concern. It is perhaps not coincidental that the splits between Orthodoxy and Catholicism of 1054, and between Western Christendom and Islam, are deep cultural faultlines in former Yugoslavia. In terms of Christian response from outside, there is a profound paralysis and inability to achieve effective results from religiously motivated peace initiatives. Indeed, it would not be an exaggeration to say that there is even a deep contradiction between those who analyze the situation primarily in terms of a "need-for-armed-resistance-to-genocide" model and those who approach the issue more from a "negotiation/sanctions/peace/nonintervention" paradigm. The two sponsoring organisations of the 1989 Basel European Ecumenical Assembly are both continuing to engage in contacts with religious communities in former Yugoslavia and to plan for an Assembly on reconciliation in 1997.

These snapshots of the religious challenges in the field of peace, justice and environmental concern make it obvious how vital Lifton's life's work should be to all who wish to address the prospects for human survival from the perspective of faith. There can be no peace without peace between worldviews and religions. The total threat of nuclear, chemical and biological weapons has not yet been overcome. Genocide is not a thing of the past. The brutalization of war and its continuing psychological trauma make Lifton's work with returning soldiers paradigmatic for the many conflict situations worldwide. If we triumph over our environment through too much economic growth, we will destroy ourselves. The search for the "Good Society" (cf. Bellah et al.)[35] must continue to be informed by the type of psychoanalytic and psychological profundity which characterizes Lifton's major works.

Death is part of the human condition. But as the Jewish scriptures tell us, there is a good death, "old and full of years." The work of Robert Jay Lifton is committed to the hope that people everywhere can grow old and reflect on their lives, not have them brutally curtailed. This requires a human society which can tolerate difference. Towards the end of his book *The Protean Self*, there is a deceptively slight sentence: "Inclusiveness is vital."[36] At first, I misread this as: "inconclusiveness is vital." In a time when nuclear and ecological threats are the Damocles' swords hanging over our human existence, acceptance of difference and the binding of terminal technology are the necessary flip-sides of "continuity of life." The human race is "killing, dying, and destroying on a scale so great as to end the human narrative," says Lifton. "We sense that our models should address that threat, but we do not know just how."[37] Let the inconclusiveness continue. Let worldviews which were challenged as "the end of an illusion" (Freud) combine to dismantle the "illusion of the end"—or at least not allow it to come to pass through human folly. Rather than speculating on the nature of the end, let us combine to resist the end of nature. Let the flux of symbolic immortality continue—preventing the closure of nuclear or environmental catastrophe and rejecting the alleged disclosures of the false prophets of apocalypse.

Notes

1. See the reproduction of the picture and commentary in I.F. Walther, I. Metzger, *Chagall* (Cologne: Benedikt Taschen, 1993), 62–65.

2. C. Potok, *My Name is Asher Lev* (Harmondsworth: Penguin, 1974).

3. Robert Jay Lifton, "The Future of Immortality," *The Future of Immortality and Other Essays for a Nuclear Age* (New York: Basic Books, 1987), 10–27.

4. Ibid., p. 14.

5. Ibid.

6. Ibid., p. 15.

7. Ibid.

8. Ibid. It should be noted that religious experience, even in modern Western societies, is much more widespread than is often accepted by social scientists with their bias towards scepticism. See the presentation of the evidence in D. Hay, *Religious Experience Today: Studying the Facts* (London: Mowbray, 1990).

9. An interesting approach from a Buddhist perspective is J. Rogers Macy, *Despair and Personal Power in the Nuclear Age* (Baltimore: New Society, 1983).

10. Robert Jay Lifton, "Imagining the Real: Beyond the Nuclear 'End,' " L. Grinspoon (ed.), *The Long Darkness: Psychological and Moral Perspectives on Nuclear Winter* (New Haven: Yale University Press, 1986).

11. Cp. E. Lange, "Freiheit für Tantalus: Über die Schwierigkeit, glücklich zu sein," in: E. Lange, *op. cit.* pp. 52–70.

12. Cited in E. Hamilton, *Mythology: Timeless Tales of Gods and Heroes* (New York: New American Library, 1969 [1st edn. 1942]).

13. See Thich Nhat Hanh, *Vietnam: The Lotus in the Sea of Fire* (London: SCM, 1967); *The Miracle of Mindfulness* (Boston: Beacon Press, 1987 [revised edn.]); *The Sun My Heart* (Berkeley: Parallax Press, 1988); *Being Peace* (Berkeley: Parallax Press, 1987).

14. "Sisyphus was King of Corinth. One day he chanced to see a mighty eagle, greater and more splendid than any mortal bird, bearing a maiden to an island not far away. When the river-God Asopus came to him to tell him that his daughter Aegina had been carried off, he strongly suspected by Zeus, and to ask his

help in finding her, Sisyphus told him what he had seen. Thereby he drew down on himself the relentless wrath of Zeus. In Hades he was punished by having to roll a rock uphill which forever rolled back upon him. Nor did he help Asopus. The river-god went to the island but Zeus drove him away with his thunderbolt. The name of the island was changed to Aegina in honor of the maiden, and her son Aeacus was the grandfather of Achilles, who was called sometimes Aeacides, descendant of Aeacus." E. Hamilton, *op. cit.*, 298.

15. Albert Camus, "The Myth of Sisyphus," *The Myth of Sisyphus* (London: Penguin, 1975 [1st UK edn. 1955, 1st edn. 1942]), 107–11. See esp. 111.

16. Robert Jay Lifton, *Death in Life: The Survivors of Hiroshima* (Harmondsworth: Pelican, 1971 [1st edn. 1967]), 572.

17. Ibid., p. 573.

18. N. C. Manganyi, *Being-Black-in-the-World* (Johannesburg: Spro-Cas/Ravan, 1973). See esp. "Nausea," 43–8.

19. C. Villa-Vicencio, *The Spirit of Hope: Conversations on Politics, Religion and Values* (Johannesburg: Skotaville, n.d.). The book includes interviews with Frank Chikane, Nadine Gordimer, Albertina Sisulu, Joe Slovo, Desmond Tutu and others.

20. M. Harris, *Our Kind* (New York: Harper Perennial, 1989), 496.

21. Robert Jay Lifton, *The Life of the Self: Toward a New Psychology* (New York: Basic Books, 1983 [1st edn. 1976]), 167.

22. Ibid., p. 169.

23. J. Hillman & M. Ventura, *We've had a Hundred Years of Psychotherapy and the World's Getting Worse* (San Francisco: Harper, 1992).

24. Ernst Lange, *op. cit.*, 77–83. Own translation.

25. Cf. Lifton, *The Protean Self: Human Resilience in an Age of Fragmentation* (Boston: Basic Books, 1993).

26. Here the sustained critique of the "culture of narcissism," which is characterized by a shallow self-love and the individualism prevalent in the societies of mass consumerism, is important. Christopher Lasch, *The Culture of Narcissism* (London: Abacus, 1980); *The Minimal Self: Psychic Survival in Troubled Times* (London: Pan, 1985); and *The True and Only Heaven: Progress and Its Critics* (New York: W.W. Norton, 1991).

27. Robert Jay Lifton, *The Protean Self*, 193 ff.

28. Ibid., 221 ff.

29. Roger Williamson, *Noah's Ark and the Nuclear Inferno* (1990); Roger Williamson (ed.), *Images of the End and Christian Theology* (1990); R. Williamson (ed.), *The End in Sight? Images of the End and Threats to Human Survival* (1993), all published by Life & Peace Institute, Uppsala, Sweden. The two conference reports (second and third of these publications) contain essays by Strozier.

30. Charles B. Strozier, *Apocalypse: On the Psychology of Fundamentalism in America* (Boston: Beacon Press, 1994).

31. Roger Williamson, "Why is Religion Still a Factor in Armed Conflict?" *Bulletin of Peace Proposals* 21(1990): 243–53. This edition contains other articles

on the role of religion in conflict situations presented at a 1989 Life & Peace Institute Seminar in Sigtuna, Sweden.

32. J. Kelsay and S. B. Twiss, *Religion and Human Rights* New York: the Project on Religion and Human Rights, 1994).

33. Hans Küng, *Global Responsibility: In Search of a New World Ethic* (London: SCM, 1991); Hans Küng & K.-J. Kuschel, *Weltfrieden durch Religionsfrieden* (Munich & Zurich: Piper, 1993).

34. Hans Küng, *Christianity and the World Religions* (London: Collins, 1985), 443).

35. R.N. Bellah et al., *Habits of the Heart: Individualism and Commitment in American Life* (New York: Harper & Row, 1985); *The Good Society* (New York: Vintage, 1992).

36. Lifton, *The Protean Self,* 231.

37. Lifton, *The Broken Connection,* 3.

23

Can There Be a Psychoanalysis Without a Political Anaysis?

Bennett Simon

Interviewer: "Herr Professor Freud, from your vantage point in 1995—a hundred years of psychoanalysis—what do you consider to be the goals of analysis, what should the well analyzed person be able to do?"

— Professor Freud:
"To Love, to Work, and to Vote"

Robert Lifton's work has always taken place at the boundary between the political and the psychological.[1] In an ongoing pragmatic way, he has steadily worked in situations that are at the interface of the two, recognizing the shifting and "protean" nature of the boundaries between them. He has opted for active exploration of situations rather than the development of an elaborate theoretical scheme to encompass the private and the public, the intra-psychic and the international. In recent years, as both a psychoanalyst and a politically aware and active man, I have been struggling—with mixed results—to sort out the relationship between what I do as an analyst and what I do as a person working in the political sphere. I have struggled to find for myself a comfortable middle ground between observer and participant, but these terms barely begin to capture the complexity of the problem in the analytic situation and in the world of organized psychoanalysis. At a concrete and feeling level, I have at times been quite comfortable with the two of me—an introspective psychoanalytic self (and the psychoanalytic practitioner that goes with that self) and a thinking and reflective political self (and the person who must make decisions and act in accordance with those reflections). At other times I have been torn and occasionally

283

felt a bit crazed in the struggle to put together my two selves. I have lived with two mottos, "Don't just sit there, do something" and "Don't just do something, sit there," and have not always been sure which of the two to follow in which situation.[2] Overall, I feel I have made some progress in regard to these difficult questions, and that progress includes moving beyond seeing the "personal" and the "political" as sharply dichotomous.

The invitation to contribute to Robert Jay Lifton's *Festschrift* coincided with a renewed interest on my part in these questions, including questions of how one works with particular patients in relation to political issues that arise, or more commonly, that fail to arise. Years ago, I worked with a man with serious problems of connecting with people in social situations, as well as in more intimate love relationships.[3] For a while he seemed to benefit little from therapy, but then began to socialize with greater comfort and greater pleasure. His social activities soon took him into working in a particular political group, a group that had a very different outlook and political stance from my own, (which was characterized by him disdainfully as "standard knee-jerk liberal"). He was enormously successful in working within this group, found a great deal of personal satisfaction, and discovered talents he had not realized he possessed. I was pleased that our work had helped him move forward and out of his shell, abstractly pleased that I had helped him even in the face of the fact that I disagreed with his politics, and uncomfortable that I was somehow giving aid and comfort to political enemies. While I tried to analyze the meanings and significance of his political ideas and values, of how he was using the differences between him and me to enact various childhood scenarios, I realized that I had relatively little to fall back upon in my analytic training for dealing with this situation. All analysts encounter patients with whom they know they cannot work because of some feature or other of the match between analyst and patient, and perhaps we have to include certain political differences as one such factor. With this patient I did not feel that degree of unworkable political tension between him and me, but could easily envision a slightly different situation where that might be the case.

Some years later, a different kind of situation arose in an analytic treatment. I asked a patient to change an appointment on an upcoming Tuesday, election day. I said, without reflection, that I needed to find a convenient time to vote, and if he could conveniently switch, it would be a help. He allowed as how the switch would be fine with him, and I—again, unreflectively—asked him if my request would interfere with his finding a time to vote. There followed a long and loud silence, and an embarrassed (but slightly defiant) confession that "I don't vote" and a reluctance to discuss the whole issue. There was also a long and loud silence on my part, and a "You don't vote!" clearly signaling something between disbelief and disapproval. I began to realize how much my own comments and request, and my response, arose outside of my awareness, and represented a kind of dissociation on my part. I knew that political issues and controversies in his family had been very salient, and yet there was relatively little mention of any contemporary political interests or opinions on his part and little inquiry on my part. I quickly realized how much he did in effect discuss politics, but it was in asides, and slightly sarcastic if not cynical comments—sometimes about positions I held dear, but not necessarily so. But—risky as it was in some ways—it was also extremely important in smoking out a particular set of attitudes and feelings about politics—namely, that there was nothing one could do about it. I honestly felt that I did not have an analytic vested interest in how he voted, but did have a vested interest in whether or not he did vote. Somehow, this situation felt more comfortable than the first one, in part, I suppose, because of more experience, and in part, because, I felt I was doing important analytic work—bringing an issue to the surface that had been suppressed, isolated, and, overall, disconnected. Part of what had to be done was to breathe life into his suppressed and repressed ideals about government and politics, ideals that can easily go underground in our society where it is so easy to be cynical and disillusioned about political participation.

In recent months, this (and other incidents in relation to voting in the course of my work with patients) returned to me with full force when I learned that only 44.6 percent of the electorate participated in the 1994 congressional elections, which produced a Republican landslide, and remembered that in a presidential election the turnout is typically no more than 50 percent.[4] How and when does one discuss voting and not voting with a patient, especially when (the usual case in my experience), the patient spontaneously would hardly bring it up? If there were a serious epidemic of an infectious disease in the community and the patient never talked about it, and, it emerged that he was not doing anything about it, might not the analyst raise an eyebrow? Is not the indifference, ignorance, fear, or cynicism (or a mix of these factors) that goes into someone not voting a rather dangerous act of ignoring problems in the world that can rather dramatically damage us? Is not such an act of "putting one's head in the sand" worthy of analytic examination?

But what constitutes analytic neutrality? What are the ground rules, what in psychoanalytic technique is there to fall back on? Overall, as I reviewed these questions in my mind, I again became aware of how little discussion there was in the course of my psychoanalytic training (New York Psychoanalytic Institute, 1964–1969), especially since a number of the distinguished faculty had themselves come from Europe and trained and or practiced in the politically tumultuous and dangerous years in Europe. A few published autobiographical anecdotes and a few bits of "oral history" were all there were, or at least all I and my classmates knew about. We certainly knew our analysts and our teachers were not "apolitical," for psychoanalytic politics were pretty intense and ferocious. I have come to believe that for many analysts psychoanalytic politics serve as a magnetic pull for all their political energies and instincts.

Accordingly, it was with no small interest that I read of Freud's actual behavior with a patient in some material that I happened upon. Could we get some guidance from him on these difficult matters? Several writers by now have detailed the political setting of Freud's early upbringing and of his later professional life.[5] Austro-Hungarian politics, social and academic anti-Semitism, clearly infiltrated into his dream life, his unconscious life. Freud as Hannibal or as a conquistador are familiar to generations of readers of *The Interpretation of Dreams*. But here we have a rare glimpse of Freud at work in the midst of the turbulent and scary scene of Vienna during the years 1933–1935.[6] It was several years before the *Anschluss*, but still a time of great tension, frequent demonstrations, and often clashes between Nazis and their opponents in the streets. Freud is analyzing a young American poet, Hilda Doolittle (H.D.), who would, years later, write a number of books and poems about her experience with Freud. We have a contemporaneous record of her analysis: letters she wrote almost daily to her woman lover in London, Bryher, about the events of the day, including the analysis. At Freud's request, his patient was providing him with a number of English newspapers and magazines she was receiving from Bryher in England. Freud was apparently keen to keep up with the political events from the perspective of the British press. When she would bring in some publications, he would thank her, put them on his desk and begin the session. One day, "Freud broke his great analytical rule of not noticing mags. and papers, yesterday when I took him the pamphlet. He said, '*what*—in English? Have the English DONE THIS? He almost wept Then he got up, . . . and said most solemnly, 'thank you' . . . (letter of May 16, 1933). In another letter, the poet-patient notes that Freud has been weeping as to what will happen to his seven grandchildren, worrying over what kind of world they will live in (May 12, afternoon). Yet, the impression we get from the letters is that there were these "intrusions" of Freud's spontaneous reactions to the political scene of his day, but his own reactions could not be part of the analytic dialogue—they remained an undiscussed and at least partially undigested part of the analysis. To me this interchange exemplified a recognizable kind of "dissociation" between the citizen-political part of the analyst and the "analytic" part of the analyst. Disappointed in my hopes of learning more about how to manage the tug between the analytic and the political (or the political-personal), I nevertheless was reassured that Freud too was struggling with this problem.[7]

The problematic relationship between therapy and politics came to my attention from another quarter, one where I had not quite anticipated it. In the past six years, in collaboration with my wife, Dr. Roberta Apfel, I have worked in the area of how children are affected by the violence of armed conflict and persecution, both overseas and in our country. In conjunction with this work, which began primarily during a sabbatical year in Israel (1989–1990), we came to know mental health professionals who were actively working both programatically and psychotherapeutically with Israeli and Palestinian children. Consider these situations.

A ten-year-old Israeli boy is being seen in a counseling center near his home in Jerusalem for behavior problems in school (acting too aggressively with his classmates), for some sleep disturbance and nightmares, and for acting much too bossy at home with his mother and his three sisters. It is obvious to all (except to the boy himself) that most of these disturbances began soon after his father was killed in one of the numerous terror incidents that has marked life in Israel for many years. As the counselor works with him, the little boy-struggling-to-become-a-man begins to express both in play and in powerful words tremendous rage at the man who killed his father, and beyond that, rage at Arabs in general, and, on some days, not only rage, but sheer hatred. The counselor, an Israeli in his early thirties with several years of experience working with children, is very much aware of how he is trying to help the child to make sense and meaning of the violent world in which he lives, of the violence and the violent man who killed his father. Simultaneously, he is trying to help him make sense and meaning of the inner world of wishes, fantasies and fears of a ten-year-old boy. He is aware that the child-development texts from which he was taught, whether psychodynamic texts or texts using other developmental schemas, do not depict children whose wishes, fantasies, and fears, from a very early age, are interacting with the threat and actuality of violence, loss, and death. He knows well how so many families in Israel have a history of loss and death in warfare and/or in persecution. He is well aware of the socialization of

Israeli children from a very young age—how they are taught to be wary of and aware of unattended bags, suitcases, packages, *chefetz chashood* (a suspicious object) that may in fact contain terrorist bombs. Yet, he finds himself disturbed after a number of sessions with the boy, and vaguely dreading the meetings. He, the counselor, has his own history of losses in several Israeli-Arab wars, losses of family members and losses of peers and of army comrades. He is a father of young children, with whom he has to discuss things that the children see on television or hear about in the anxious conversations of the adults around them. Politically, he is a man of the moderate left on the Israeli political spectrum, in favor of and working for some long-term peace settlement between Israelis and Palestinians. His own introspection—realizing how himself as a ten-year-old boy enters the dialogue with his patient—conversations with friends, colleagues and a supervisor, helps him see how torn he is between feeling for the child's pain, resonating with the little boy's wishes and fantasies to be a man big and brave and capable enough to get revenge, and a set of ideals that are very much alive and palpable in his own emotional life—both personal and professional ideals. He becomes aware of how much he is also angry at the boy for expressing hatred and desires for revenge so clearly, desires he has struggled so much to deal with.

The Israeli counselor finds that overall he is able to maintain what he feels is a good therapeutic stance with his young patient, but that as outer events impinge (another Palestinian terrorist attack), both he and his patient are thrown off kilter—anxiety, rage, and sadness mount and they do not seem to be in a stable therapeutic zone. The Israeli therapist is aware—and, later in a more advanced stage of the therapy, finds a way to bring it up with his now somewhat older patient—that a Palestinian counselor only a few kilometers away is talking to a young Palestinian boy whose older brother was killed by an Israeli soldier in the course of a stone-throwing demonstration and whose father has been in an Israeli prison for several years. The Palestinian counselor herself has relatives imprisoned for political activities, including some violent activities. Her family has its own history of loss and dislocation.

The two counselors have in fact met from time to time, and, in a limited way, been able to share their concerns and their "psycho-political" dilemmas in working with their respective patients. The chances are small that the two boys will meet, but if they do, will they be able to share and bear their individual and collective pains? Will their therapies/therapists have helped them? Will their (hypothetical) sharing and bearing enhance or interfere with their late adolescent and early adult political activity and stance within their own people and government?

Something like this scenario (fictionalized to the extent that it is conflated from several actual situations) is taking place, *mutatis mutandis*, in other parts of the world and in other settings, where people are fortunate enough to have available some sort of professional counseling and therapy, and unfortunate enough to be living in the midst of ongoing conflict and violence which as individuals they can do little to control.

A second vignette comes from South Africa: a black-township youth comes to a counselor in a program set up specifically to work with youth in this setting, staffed by people politically sympathetic to the struggle for liberation of the South African blacks. He is suffering from headaches and diffuse anxieties, and has only recently felt it safe enough to temporarily emerge from hiding. After a meeting or two, he mentions to the counselor that he is participating in a plan to blow up a police station, in part to even the score for acts of murder, torture, and brutality abetted and/or perpetrated by some of the those in that police station. What is the counselor to do? She knows how much she is tormented both by the plight and suffering of the township youth, and how identified she is with their struggle, and how many lives have been literally or metaphorically destroyed by the system of apartheid. But she also knows how much she is opposed to the taking of human life, how she is haunted by the images of the spouses, parents, and children of the policemen, policewomen, secretaries, and cleaning staff, some, many, or all of whom might be killed in the bombing. Issues of confidentiality, let alone issues of feeling detached enough from the situation to be able to think, analyze, and work with the patient, are also crucial, but are pushed off center stage by the immediacy of the images seizing the counselor. In this particular situation, the therapist quickly sought active consultation with colleagues, with her team, and collectively they came up with some practical working suggestions that helped to "defuse" the situation.[8] Their ad hoc solution represented a confrontation with the painful ethical dilemmas of this (and other similar cases), but did not claim to represent a generic solution.

If it is any consolation for the difficulties that human therapists can encounter in situations of armed conflict, consider the position of God in the following anecdote. A young Catholic girl in Belfast is being interviewed by Robert Coles and she is looking somewhat anxiously at her watch. When he calls this to her attention, she says that she is concerned about getting to the Church on time for a Mass. A nun, her teacher, had told her that the Protestant children are filling their churches praying to God for victory for their side and that the Catholic children must all get in there and pray at least as much and as hard as the Protestants!

Though to therapists in America these may seem like extreme situations, it is well to remember the list of countries in recent decades where there have been both major violence and the presence of counselors, therapists, and in some instances, people as highly trained as psychoanalysts includes: Argentina, Chile, Uruguay; El Salvador, Nicaragua; Israel, Lebanon, Egypt, Kuwait; Algeria; Northern Ireland, South Africa; the countries formerly under Communist rule in Eastern Europe (including East Germany); the former Yugoslavia and parts of the former Soviet Union. To the extent that many others in helping positions and/or professions (without being trained as counselors or therapists) are often in similar positions, the problem is an even more widespread one. Let us not omit the United States from the list, for anyone who has worked with troubled youth in violence-torn parts of our country knows something of the kinds of dilemmas described above. For example, one young woman reveals to the high school counselor that she knows who killed another youth, and/or who may be planning a revenge killing. How does the counselor juggle the need for confidentiality and, perhaps more important, the need to maintain the trust of this young woman, and collude in not apprehending a murderer and/or in not preventing future violence. The answer is: with difficulty.

The counterpart of the dilemmas of the therapist with the patient are the dilemmas of the therapist participating in public, political life. How much can a therapist be publicly visible, taking stands on particular issues, and still be available as a "neutral" person to actual and potential patients who may be of different political persuasions. In my own training when I pointed out to my analyst that his colleague, another training analyst, had signed a petition in the *New York Times* supporting a local candidate, my analyst said this was an unfortunate breach of the analyst's anonymity that could interfere in his neutrality and with his ability to work with patients of every political persuasion. I was skeptical, and though I could not quite articulate it at the time, felt somehow there would be a "return of the repressed," and the apolitical analyst would one day be confronted with his the need for acknowledgment of his or her political persona in the analytic situation. An example of such a "return" is seen in the following clinical anecdote: a white analyst was working with a black patient, and the patient did not appear for analysis the day after Martin Luther King, Jr. was assassinated. The analyst said to himself that black-white issues were simply too charged that day for the patient to be able to deal with them, and, after waiting most of the hour, started to leave his office. To his amazement (and horror!) he realized that he himself had locked the outer door to his office and that the patient had been trying to get in and was still waiting for him! [9]

But how much can an analyst not be someone who takes a political stand, and still be credible to his patients, as someone who cares about the world in which they both live? This problem is illustrated by a debate in the current scene in the nascent Palestinian state between two figures on the mental health scene. The one (more famous) argues that the oppressive political conditions (as well as the attendant economic conditions) must be publicly addressed by mental health professionals as leaders of the society. This includes the task of not only denouncing the Israeli occupation and its consequences (or, since the Oslo Peace agreement other forms of Israeli control), but also denouncing factions and forces within Palestinian society that interfere with the mental health of the population. Thus, he is at odds with the dominant party headed by Yasser Arafat—whom he considers both undemocratic and too collusive with Israel—and expresses the need for Palestinian society to reform itself in terms of attitudes towards violence as ways of resolving conflict, including domestic violence and wife-beating. He publicly declares his positions and feels that whatever problems these positions might create in running his clinic, or in working with individuals or families, there is much more benefit from the example of taking up causes and not suffering silently. Implicitly, he operates on the assumption that his taking of public positions provides a model for his clients in *taking a stand*, not necessarily the same stand he takes—a model of empowerment.

His compatriot argues that for the mental health professional to be identified with a particular party or faction (or criticizing a party or faction) seriously compromises his ability to function in the society as a whole. He argues that the partisan therapist limits himself to taking care of those who are "on his side" and almost automatically shuts out those with different political stances. In the Palestinian case both protagonists in the debate clearly are dedicated to improving the lot of their people, but differ in whether to take an "unneutral" political stance, or a "neutral" political stance—but nonetheless a political stance.

What can we learn from these various situations and can we deduce some more general problems for dealing with the admixture of the political and the private?[10]

(1) From the perspective of psychoanalytic technique and practice, the nub of the problems I have outlined is the question of what constitutes *analytic neutrality*. The term "neutrality" in psychoanalysis is not exactly neutral, and there is a good deal of controversy about what it means theoretically and practically. But the sense of the term I find most useful is that articulated by Anna

Freud: neutrality means that the analyst is situated equidistant from the claims of ego, id, and super-ego. The analyst realizes that different kinds of motives and claims go into shaping any significant piece of psychic life—the moral and judgmental claims of the super-ego, the realistic assessments of external situations by the ego, and the imperatives of aggressive and sexual demands. In any given instance—analyzing a dream, a parapraxis, a piece of behavior in the patient's past or present life, or the patient's attitudes towards the analyst—the analyst is prepared to impartially consider the claims of the three psychic agencies. This principle corresponds to the theoretical position that the products of mental life are themselves compromise formations among the three mental agencies. "Decoding" the meaning, or helping to change what the patient does and feels, entails then the position of analyst as an impartial judge or arbitrator. But in regard to political issues, it means that the analyst must help the patient, especially a patient in our culture, get in touch with ideals and ego-ideals that are as crucial a part of political experience as are motives of power or domination.

In this definition of neutrality, the term clearly does not mean *indifference* to the patient, but rather the most attentive kind of listening and empathizing. In an important sense, the analyst is a *disinterested* party, but hardly an *uninterested* party. Nor is the analyst uninterested in political dimensions of the patient's life and experience, whether or not the patient brings up such issues. But the analyst is *disinterested* from the perspective of understanding how political issues interweave with the patient's other concerns, or how they *fail to interweave.*

If we follow out the analogy of analytic *even-handedness* with judicial even-handedness, we are reminded that in all judicial and governmental situations, neutrality and impartiality, are difficult to achieve, and are themselves subject to many contingencies. Strong institutions and communal ideals of fairness are needed to maintain a government and a judiciary as impartial. But the problem is not only that judges can deceive themselves, or have self-serving motivations, or even be bribed, but that the judicial system is itself highly embedded in a political and historical situation. While on the one hand there is an evolving and autonomous set of legal principles and rules of evidence, there are also pathways by which these principles are not entirely autonomous and uninfluenced by political, social, and historical currents. Analogously, the neutrality of the analyst requires support and continued attention to the cross-currents involving politics in his or her mind. Similarly, the analyst must feel that there is strong support from the society of other analysts for carrying on this process of self-examination and of communal examination of analytic technique in regard to political situations and actions.

(2) Decisions about the analyst's political stance, whether the public stance (or lack thereof), or what is expressed and dealt with in analytic situations, are never *apolitical.* A decision to ask the patient about his voting behavior and a decision not to ask are both decisions with political dimensions. For the analyst not to inquire about voting (or other political activities) can have as much of an impact on the patient's political life as the decision to inquire. The motives of both analyst and patient need to be scrutinized, in the manner appropriate for each of the parties, but they cannot be ignored without it having a political effect and a political dimension.

(3) How the power relationships between analyst and patient are negotiated can become a model for the patient in negotiating power relationships in other spheres, including the political. Analytic technique can provide a powerful example and identification for the patient either in empowering himself and his community and overcoming despair, or it can become a model for passive and resentful acquiescence to bad political situations. (Conversely, for some patients the way the analyst behaves and the kind of atmosphere she or he generates can also allow for adjustment of rather grandiose expectations of what they can change in the world.) The analytic atmosphere also includes some measure of freedom for the analyst to be himself or herself in regard to all the dimensions of his or her personality, and this includes the analyst as a political person. Exactly how each analyst negotiates what constitutes a proper measure of freedom cannot be determined by any rule or rules, nor can it be ignored. But neither patient nor analyst can be "gagged" by the process without great cost.

(4) Questions about the inter-relationship between the political and the personal are never exactly the same for any two patients (nor for any two analysts). In each analysis, there must be an appropriate framing, dissection, and examination of the way the particular patient has experienced and does experience the political dimensions of his or her existence.

(5) A good analysis gradually makes clear how certain pre-existing dichotomies or categories simply are inadequate to encompass the complexities of a particular person's life. Thus, a good analysis can help both patient and analyst move beyond simplistic dichotomies such as "the personal" and the "political." The analytic process itself becomes a model for understanding that in life these spheres are much more interestingly and complicatedly inter-related than most people realize.

(6) No matter how hard you try, you won't get it perfectly right, and you certainly won't get it perfectly right in every instance. There is no perfect neutrality and there is no perfect anonymity. There may well be situations where an individual analyst with particular political views cannot successfully work with a particular patient, and part of psychoanalytic and political maturity is such a recognition. Recall how Freud argued that psychoanalysis is one of the "impossible professions," along with the governing of nations and the rearing of children.

In conclusion, I want to relate a story of one of the great Chasidic masters, Reb Levi Yitzchak of Berdechev (these are not his exact words, but I put them in quotation marks to help us imagine him speaking them). "When I was a young man, I thought I would try and change the world. I did not succeed. I then tried to change my country, and also did not succeed. I tried to change my city, and then to change my family, and also did not succeed in those endeavors. Then I started to change myself, and lo, as I changed myself, my family began to change, then my city, and in turn my country, and finally, even the world." I would add an amendment to his insight. One of the things he learned is a way of changing oneself and of beginning to change others—go out and vote!

I hope that I have demonstrated that an important step in dealing with the problems of the interface of politics and of psychotherapy is to open up a dialogue on the subject. I make no claim for having theoretically or practically solved these issues, but I do make a claim for the empowerment that comes with facing the issues and engaging with colleagues and patients rather than sweeping them under the rug. I thank Robert Lifton for his ongoing commitment for tackling difficult and problematic issues of self and society, and the editors for the opportunity to join with them in dialogue in his honor.

Notes

1. I use "political" here in the sense of Aristotle's statement that man is the political animal, the animal that lives in a polis. I will eschew terms like "cul-

tural" and "social," which have their own long and convoluted histories, and employ the term "political" as a contrast to the psychological, by which I mean both individual psychological and depth psychological. "Social psychological" might be an apt contrast for individual psychological, but it too carries too much surplus baggage.

2. This is a familiar slogan from Alcoholics Anonymous.

3. The case material presented here is in part fictionalized and cases conflated because of considerations of confidentiality.

4. New York *Times*, Sunday June 11, 1995, 16.

5. Carl E. Schorske, *Fin-de-Siecle Vienna: Politics and Culture* (New York: Knopf, 1980).

6. Quotations are from the Winifred Elleman Bryher papers at Beinecke Library, Yale University.

7. Howard B. Levine and Bennett Simon, "Introduction," in *Psychoanalysis and the Nuclear Threat: Clinical and Theoretical Studies*, ed. Howard B. Levine, Daniel Jacobs, and Lowell J. Rubin (Hillsdale, NJ: The Analytic Press, 1988).

8. Gillian Straker, "Ethical Issues," *Minefields in Their Hearts: The Mental Health of Children in War and Communal Violence*, ed. Roberta J. Apfel and Bennett Simon (New Haven: Yale University Press, in press).

9. I cannot locate any printed source for this anecdote and perhaps I heard it reported at a meeting. Published material about inter-racial analyses includes: Eugene L. Goldberg, Wayne A. Myers, and Israel Zeifman, "Some Observations on Three Interracial Analyses," *International Journal of Psycho-analysis* 55(1974): 495–500. Judith Schachter and Hugh F. Butts, "Transference and Countertransference in Interracial Analyses," *Journal of the American Psychoanalytic Association* 16(1968): 792–808.

10. See more detailed discussion of these questions in Philip Cushman, *Constructing the Self, Constructing America* (Reading, MA: Addison-Wesley, 1995) and references there to Irwin Z. Hoffman, "Expressive Participation and Psychoanalytic Discipline," *Contemporary Psychoanalysis* 28(1992): 1–15, and Lane Gerber, "Intimate Politics: Connectedness and the Social-Political Self," *Psychotherapy: Theory/Research/Practice/Training* 29(1992). See also Andrew Samuels, *The Political Psyche* (London and New York: Routledge, 1993), especially 209–66, a questionaire sent to 2,000 analysts and psychotherapists about clinical situations in which political issues appear, or conspicuously are absent, as well as some information on the political background and activities of the respondents.

24

We Must Hear Each Other's Cry: Lessons from Pol Pot Survivors

Lane Gerber

In our contemporary world there are increasing numbers of refugees who are survivors of violence and war. These peoples struggle with frightening and painful memories and images. From those people who struggle "for intimacy with the knowledge of death in the cause of renewed life"[1] there is much to learn, especially given a world that increasingly finds each of us trying to survive violence, environmental degradation, political dislocation, cynicism, meaninglessness, and isolation. Can the rest of us learn from the experiences of these refugee survivors? At this point in human history, we clearly need teachers who can offer models of hope to help prevent ourselves from becoming cynical, numb, and powerless.

N., a Cambodian woman I had been seeing for some time at a local refugee clinic, who suffered much torture and loss (including seeing three of her children killed in front of her) during the Pol Pot time, recently told me about a time when she had been able to leave Cambodia and was staying in one of the refugee camps in Thailand. During this time, the Khmer Rouge periodically attacked the camps and there were artillery shells landing in the camp and automatic rifle fire all around her. On this occasion, the bombardment and the rifle fire were particularly intense. She and all of the others in her section of the camp fled the camp to seek shelter in the forest. The Khmer Rouge forces followed them shooting at everyone. N. described the scene to me as a "flood of people" desperately running and tripping over dead or dying bodies as they tried to escape from what seemed like certain death. As she ran down the road with her two remaining children and her friends from the camp, she noticed a woman sitting on the road holding and nursing her infant and crying. The woman was rocking back and forth and moaning and crying. With gunfire going on all around her, N. stopped. She told her children to go with their friends into the forest and then she covered the woman and infant with her own body. She noticed that the infant was dead, yet the mother still was trying to nurse it. She stayed in that position sheltering the woman with her body until the shooting and fighting finally ended. They were the only ones left alive on the road into the jungle which was now littered with dead bodies.

After hearing this story, which elicited tears from the interpreter and N. as well as myself, I asked her what made her stop when everyone else ran past this woman and child. What made her stop in the midst of all the shooting and fear? I knew her to be a religious person and wondered if that was part of her motivation. She told me that Buddha did not create this war and that Buddha would not end war. "Then why did you stop?," I asked.

She said that she had lost children herself. She knew what it was like to suffer this kind of loss. She said that as she ran down the road she saw the face of the woman and then heard her cry and felt like she knew that face and she knew that sound. She said that she did not know the woman, but she knew the cries and the faces of people who suffered like that. She said that she could not ignore the way that cry and that face called to her.

"But weren't you afraid for yourself when you stopped?" I asked. She said that she and the woman trembled together, but that she had to do what she did. "The woman was in pain. I knew crying and pain, too. That made us related to each other," she said. She continued telling me that during the Khmer Rouge time no one in the Khmer Rouge–controlled work–concentration camps could talk with each other. If people did talk with each other about their hunger or pain, they would be killed. So they worked and often died beside each other, but could say nothing. "We all suffered, but we suffered in ourselves. We could not talk. The suffering was useless. When people hear each other's pain and talk with each other, then the suffering reminds them that they are all the same; they are all people." She continued, "It was so easy to die in Cambodia because we all suffered alone. I could not let that woman on the road suffer that way. The Khmer Rouge wanted us not to act like people. People suffer and it is people who must care for each other when they hear each other's pain. We must say that to all people. We all have pain. We must hear that and see that in each other or we are not people."

This past year a Cambodian woman who works in a community clinic as an interpreter and paraprofessional therapist approached a couple of us about starting a group for Cambodian survivors who wanted to talk about their experience before and during the Pol Pot holocaust. She said that in contrast to many survivors of such horror, she wanted a place just for people who wanted to write about and tell their stories to each other. She needed to do this and thought there were others who felt similarly. She wanted "to live and become healthy and grow," she said. She did not want to just go from day to day making a living but dead inside. She decided that she needed to do this for herself and for her community so that they would know who they were—both the pain and terror of recent years as well as their culture and heritage from the past. She worried about what would happen to a community, her community, that had suffered so and now was placed in a different country. Although she was in a safer country, it was one with different traditions, where violence and separateness and an emphasis on material things and a disregard for spiritual values seemed all too common. She felt that there was something about her story and her country's story that would be of benefit for all peoples to know. She feared not only for her future and for her former country's future, but also, having her children in a Seattle school where shootings are not an infrequent occurrence, for the future of all of us.

So she talked with other Cambodian refugees she knew and arranged for the first of these groups to begin meeting. The other Western psychotherapist and myself who were asked to participate in these groups have been struck on many occasions by the courage demonstrated by so many of the survivors. Having survived unimaginable conditions, some of these people are still desirous of committing themselves to rebuilding a sense of meaning for themselves that might also be useful for others. Certainly not everyone in pain can bear to tell, and in the telling re-live, their stories of horror and death. The remarkable thing is that some can. How is it that these people can still go on trying to live and grow, as opposed to "merely" survive, in the face of all their pain, loss, and deliberate attempts to crush the meanings that their culture, family, and religion provided them?

The other therapist and I talked regularly with each other about these questions and about our experiences with this newly formed survivors group. We invited two other therapists who were working with refugees to join the two of us in exploring these questions. What sustains these people? we wondered. What enables them to keep hope alive?

Our conversations and reflections with each other, done within the context of our own small therapists' group gathered together to better understand what we were witnessing in the refugee groups, seemed and seem to be transformative for us. We have struggled to find words for how we feel and why we are involved in such an often painful task. We have sensed that there is something important to each of us and to all of us whether or not we can find the words for it.

For example, we have wondered with each other why we seem to be drawn to hearing refugee stories that are filled with such pain and loss. Are we simply feeling guilty that pain exists in the world and we are doing less than enough to deal with it? Or, are we doing it because we feel guilty about thus far being safe from the traumas that have happened to these refugees? Perhaps these represent some of our motivations, yet not the largest parts. As we wondered about our own motivations, we also began realizing that while we joined together for one purpose (i.e., trying to understand what enables the refugee survivors to keep hope alive), something more emerged. That is, our conversation about the refugee survivors led us into a deeper exploration and sharing of what our own motivations were and what has enabled us to keep our own hopes alive. And, as we committed ourselves to this deeper sharing, we also created a deeper sense of community with each other. And so, the process continues.

Meanwhile, the survivors' group continued meeting regularly. We, the therapists, continued to be present as witnesses (as opposed to being therapist-leaders) in the groups that the refugees initiated and continued to lead. During one of the sessions, a Cambodian man in his late fifties said, "As long as I can talk to people about what happened to us, then I am alive. They (i.e., the Khmer Rouge) have not silenced me.[2] I live and raise my new family and tell them about what happened and that we have survived to live." Speaking of one's experience in such a manner seemed like an indication of actively declaring one's being and aliveness (in opposition also to the Khmer Rouge prohibition of talking with others who suffered) as well as meaningfully integrating memories from the past into one's present living. Hearing such a statement made the other survivors in their group as well as those of us in our small therapists' "consultation-research-support" group feel a renewed sense of hope. For to "remember the reality of oppression in the lives of people and to value those lives is to be saved from the luxury of hopelessness."[3] Thus, even as we begin to understand how the Cambodian survivors sustain themselves during their pain and grief, so we Western therapists uncover another piece of our own motivations for doing this work during this cynical and disillusioning period of history.

The survivors' groups continue and more of the participant's stories are told and heard. One survivor described some of the torture he saw and heard others endure, how terrifying that was for him and how helpless he felt listening. His own torture, however, was done in an isolated place with "no one to hear me. No one knew what was happening to me. I thought I would die. I wanted to die. I tried to remember people who loved me, but my pain was too harsh. And then I thought of going to the temple when I was a boy. The monks liked me and taught me even though I was very young. They knew that my family was cruel to me and the monks took care of me. As I grew older, they taught me Pali (a language related to Sanskrit that is used in the writings of Buddha). I remembered sitting with the monks while we were all chanting. The monks were talking about suffering, that to live is to suffer. I didn't believe that Buddha would come save me, but I did think about the monks praying with me and that helped me during the torture. I remembered that the monks and Buddha talk about suffering and I thought the monks would care if they heard me. I think that kept me alive. They knew that we suffer and that we must hear each other. They cared for me. I, too, must care for others and not let them be alone with their pain. We must do that for each other or we will all die. It is why I have to work for the Red Cross." (Ed. note: This man volunteers as an interpreter and also as a driver for people who don't have transportation but who need to get to the hospital.)

The next time I and the other three members of our therapist reflection group met, we again tried to put words to the feelings we had when we heard statements such as this one. We wondered anew why we were doing this work. We stumbled over words trying to say how we felt. Finally, one of us began saying, "I felt like something changed in the room. Like everything else disappeared except for him and me. . . . I felt such sadness and heaviness yet I also felt more alive somehow. It's as though those things shouldn't go together, but they do. I felt warm. I felt like there was something more in the room. Words don't do this justice. I know it sounds weird, but it felt like some kind of exchange was happening somewhere between the two of us . . . it was almost like we weren't sitting on chairs. I felt like we were suspended somewhere in the room . . . and like there was something sacred going on. I was thinking afterwards that people think temples or God is sacred. I think that something sacred was happening as he was talking and we were there. I remember thinking, 'this is why we were born. This is what being human is.' "

As we continue talking with each other, we use words such as "gift" and "privilege" when talking about hearing such testimonies. There is something about what we hear from the refugee survivors that makes us feel like we are learning why we live when we hear those people in pain. In responding to their call, we feel like we become human. Although all of us therapists have nightmares, experience headaches, and see frightening images of what we have heard from the refugees, there is also a sense of being privileged to hear another's cry and be able to give recognition to their suffering. And in this process hope seems to emerge between us—and life seems to be chosen over death.

Perhaps we, in our far smaller hurts and pains, felt recognized and heard and consequently less alone ourselves—more closely connected with others, with the world. Clearly we felt thankful that we were able to hear the voice of someone in pain calling out for another. The survivors' perspectives seemed to affirm for them and for us "the inter-human perspective of *my* responsibility for the other person . . . a non-indifference of one to another."[4]

A short time after this discussion, I talked with a physician colleague who works with refugees. I asked her why she continued to choose to work with refugees. She said that she wondered about that herself. She wasn't sure, but found this work "more interesting, more alive." At the same time, a friend of hers had told her that perhaps she did this work because of a need of hers "to be adored." That is, with a population as needy as the refugees with whom we work (refugees from Southeast Asia and Western Africa), there can be a stronger expression of gratitude when one does something to help them than when one works with a "typical" Western patient.

To me explaining this preference based solely on a model of self-interest seemed very limited. Of course, it's nice to feel special and many of us do want this.[5] At the same time, it struck me that this represented a very limited perspective of human motivation.

As we talked more, we began discussing other patients with whom we most enjoyed working. While it was clear that she and I enjoy clinical work generally, there are certain people with whom the work feels most "alive." Interestingly enough we began talking about working with people on the "fringes" or "margins" of society; people who would be described as "other" by virtue of ethnicity or social class or difficult early background, etc. This aspect of "otherness" together with a strong commitment on their part to work to get better made these people ones with whom we most liked working. In reflecting on her (our) preference this physician said, "All these people are considered 'other' by society. Some of them tend to be at the extremes of 'otherness', but all of us have felt 'other' at some point in our lives. I know I have. I think we all know what it's like to some extent and we recognize the 'other's' pain as having been ours, too. So we want to reach out to them. . . . I think we all want a world in which everyone can feel that they belong."

As we talked, our words began to capture more of the meanings that we had struggled with for why we work with these Cambodian refugees. It had been extraordinarily difficult for us to try to put our feelings and motivations into words. Or, when we did, the motive attributed to our words often felt very limiting. For example, we talked about wanting to help the refugees to feel better and to be able to help themselves and their families. While this is true, the reason for this is often solely attributed to our own self interest. That is, helping others feel better makes us feel better about ourselves (more special, more loved, more powerful, etc.). Not negating these possibilities, it was interesting to all of us that there seemed to be fewer words for motivations having to do with helping others because "that's how things should be." Wasn't it possible for us to have motivations that were expressions of our compassion for and interest in the "other" as well as our "self interest?" If this was true, then why did we have such trouble conceptualizing this? And why do we feel silly or naive when we try to say this? And why do the Cambodian survivors speak so easily in terms that convey compassion and inclusiveness?

Perhaps Robert Wuthnow was correct when he said, "In an individualistic society . . . caring is sometimes seen as an abnormality." If this is correct, then it becomes difficult indeed to have an available language that people can use without being looked at askance. "We do not even believe in sharing too deeply in the suffering of others. Our individual autonomy is too important. If caring for others becomes too demanding . . . we call it an obsession."[6] Of course, a larger implication of all this is that if it is hard to find culturally acceptable words for motives related to compassion, or if we sense that when we speak in this way, people close their ears to us, then not only is our understanding of the range of human motives narrowed, but our present and future behaviors also can be limited.

These thoughts were moving in my mind when I talked again with the Cambodian woman who fled the Khmer Rouge raid of the Thai refugee camp and covered the bodies of the mother and the child on the road. During this meeting, she began to tell me of a time that she was badly beaten and then thrown into a killing pit to die. She said that the pit was deep and wide and filled with dead bodies. She awoke, dazed, in this pit, horrified at where she found herself. She was bleeding and weak and felt like she wanted to die, too. She became sickened by the dead bodies and their smells. She slowly tried to climb out of the pit. She described having to climb over bodies while she cried and felt sick and very scared. She did not have enough strength to climb the final distance out of the pit and could only reach out her hand toward the top and moan.

Somehow a man happened to be in this area and heard her and came over to the pit. She said that he heard her and reached down to lift her out. If he had been seen by the Khmer Rouge, he would have been shot. Yet he lifted her from the pit and, because she could not walk, put her on his back and carried her secretly to his family's hut in the jungle. There he and his wife hid her and cared for her for many weeks until she was strong enough to want to flee to Thailand.

N. said that she asked the man why he saved her life. She wanted to know how he heard her and why he stopped especially when it could have been at the cost of his own life. She said that he said, "I heard you cry. I knew that cry from all of us. It was my duty to try to help you."

Perhaps it is the result of living in a culture that emphasized extended family and community, creating more of a we-self than I-self,[7] but it seems easier for the Cambodian survivors to find the proper words when talking of the responsibility of hearing and being compassionate toward the other than it is for us Western therapists.

Emmanuel Levinas, a Jewish philosopher who was in a prisoner of war camp during World War II, teaches that in "suffering, which is intrinsically meaningless and condemned to itself without exit, a beyond takes shape in the inter-human. . . . It is this attention to the Other which, across the cruelties of our century . . . can be affirmed as . . . a supreme ethical principle. . . . Properly speaking, the inter-human lies in a non-indifference of one to another, in a responsibility of one for another."

Levinas and these Cambodian refugees seem to be teaching that human interactions based on the primacy of hearing the other's cry is the acting out of one's humanness—the choosing of life over death. The Cambodian survivors' stories evoke not only pain and horror in the hearer, but also a compassion that links the speaker to the listener in a bond that is powerful and also inclusive—that seems to go beyond the two people involved. For the listener, the experience can be one of hearing the cry of another and in the process of hearing and responding becoming more fully human. If we can allow their voices to really reach into our ears, we are reminded that we too have been vulnerable and cried out for an other. Out of the pain of all the senseless violence, death, and isolation of their life stories the survivors themselves can sometimes feel heard and those of us who are privileged to sit with them can sometimes hear their cry. A cry that on being heard seems to lift the two of us beyond the constraints of our individual selves to humanity in general. In this cry and hearing a more hopeful vision of our self and our species seems to emerge.

Notes

My thanks to Marcia King, Kara Lee Koury, Kim Powers and Roeun Sam for their enlivening presences and their support.

1. Robert Jay Lifton, *The Life of the Self: Toward a New Psychology* (New York: Harper, 1976).

2. See also Elaine Scarry, *The Body in Pain* (New York: Oxford University Press, 1985), 3–59 for a discussion of the use of torture as a process whereby a person is "taught" the futility of having their own voice.

3. Susan Welch, *Communities of Resistance and Solidarity* (Maryknoll, New York: Orbis Books, 1985).

4. Emmanuel Levinas, "Useless Suffering," *The Provocation of Levinas: Rethinking the Other,* ed. Robert Bernasconi and David Wood (London: Routledge, 1991), 100–35.

5. Lane Gerber, *Married to Their Careers* (New York: Tavistock, 1983).

6. Robert Wuthnow, *Acts of Compassion* (Princeton, NJ: Princeton University Press, 1991).

7. Alan Roland, *In Search of Self in India and Japan* (Princeton, NJ: Princeton University Press, 1988).

25

History, Objectivity, Commitment

Howard Zinn

I became aware of Robert Lifton's writings in the early sixties and was encouraged by the existence of a physician-psychiatrist whose powerful conscience led him to explore the most critical moral issues of our time. When I became involved in the movement against the war in Vietnam, Bob Lifton and I began to cross paths, more and more often. Sometimes it was at professional meetings, where our common aim was to challenge scholars to take a stand on the war. At one point, Bob organized a pilgrimage to Washington of artists and academics to protest the war, and we were all arrested for refusing to move from the halls of Congress.

When I began to attend the famous "Wellfleet Seminars" on psychohistory, I was happy to see that the meetings, however impressive were the scholarly credentials of the participants, insisted on connecting with the most urgent questions of peace and justice. I trust that this personal essay on historical objectivity is in the spirit of Bob Lifton's lifetime refusal to remain professionally proper, silent and neutral, in a world desperate for change.

I always started off, in the first class of the semester, whether I was teaching at Spelman College in Atlanta, or at Boston University, by saying something like this to the students: "This is not an 'objective' course. I will not lie to you, or conceal information from you because it is embarrassing to my beliefs. But I am not a 'neutral' teacher. I have a point of view about war, about racial and sexual equality, about economic justice—and this point of view will affect my choice of subject, and the way I discuss it. I ask you to listen to my point of view, but I don't expect you to adopt it. You have a right to argue with me about anything, because, on the truly important issues of human life, there are no 'experts.' I will express myself strongly, as honestly as I can, and I expect you to do the same. I am not your only source of information, of ideas. Points of view different from mine are all around, in the library, in the press. Read as much as you can. All I ask is that you examine my information, my ideas, and make up your own mind."

I think I came to this way of teaching, of writing, because of my own life experience. Before I became a professional historian, I had grown up in the dankness and dirt of New York tenements, had been knocked unconscious by a policeman while holding a banner in a demonstration, worked for three years in a shipyard, and dropped bombs for the U.S. Air Force. Those experiences, and more, made me lose all desire for "objectivity" whether in living my life, or writing history.

This statement is troubling to some people. It needs explanation (after which it may still be troubling, but for clearer reasons).

I mean by it that by the time I began to study history formally (I became a freshman at New York University under the G.I. Bill of Rights, at the age of 27, with a wife, our two-year old daughter, and another child on the way) I knew I was not doing it because it was "interesting" or because it meant a solid, respectable career.

I had been touched in some way by the struggle of working people to survive (my mother and father, among others), by the glamour and ugliness of war, by the reading I had done trying to understand fascism, communism, capitalism, socialism. I could not possibly study history as a neutral. For me, history could only be a way of understanding and helping to change what was wrong in the world.

That did not mean looking only for historical facts to reinforce the beliefs I already held. It did not mean ignoring data that would change or complicate my understanding of society. It meant asking questions that were important for social change, questions relating to equality, liberty, peace, justice but being open to whatever answers were suggested by looking at history.

I decided early that I would be biased in the sense of holding fast to certain fundamental values: the equal right of all human beings—whatever race, nationality, sex, or religion—to life, liberty, and the pursuit of happiness. The study of history was only worth devoting a life to if it aimed at those ideas. I would always be biased (leaning toward) those ends, stubborn in holding to them.

But I would be flexible, I hoped, in arriving at the means to achieve those ends. Scrupulous honesty in reporting on the past would be needed, because any decision on means had to be tentative, had to be open to change based on what one could learn from history. The values, ends, ideals I held, need not be discarded, whatever history disclosed. So there would be no incentive to distort the past, fearing that an honest recounting would hurt the desired ends.

The chief problem in historical honesty is not outright lying. It is omission or de-emphasis of important data. The definition of "important," of course, depends on one's values.

An example: I was still in college, studying history, when I heard a song by the folk-singer Woody Guthrie, called "The Ludlow Massacre," a dark, intense ballad, accompanied by low, haunting chords on his guitar. It told of women and children burned to death in a strike of miners against Rockefeller-owned coal mines in southern Colorado in 1914.

My curiosity was aroused. In none of my classes in American history, in none of the textbooks I had read, was there any mention of the Ludlow Massacre or of the Colorado coal strike.

The labor movement interested me, perhaps because I had spent three years working in a shipyard, and helped to organize the younger shipyard workers, excluded from the tightly-controlled craft unions of the American Federation of Labor, into an independent union of our own. There was little in the college curriculum on labor history, so I undertook an independent course of study for myself.

That led me to a book, *American Labor Struggles*, written not by a historian but by an English teacher named Samuel Yellen. It had fascinating accounts of some ten labor conflicts in American history, most of which were unmentioned in my courses and my textbooks. One of the chapters was on the Colorado coal strike of 1913–1914.

I became intrigued by the sheer drama of that event. It began with the shooting of a young labor organizer on the streets of Trinidad, Colorado, on a crowded Saturday night, by two detectives in the pay of Rockefeller's Colorado Fuel & Iron Corporation. The miners, mostly immigrants speaking a dozen different languages, were living in a kind of serfdom in the mining towns where Rockefeller collected their rent, sold them their necessities, hired the police, and watched them carefully for any sign of unionization.

The killing of organizer Gerry Lippiatt sent a wave of anger through the mining towns. At a mass meeting in Trinidad, miners listened to a rousing speech by an 80-year-old woman named Mary Jones—"Mother Jones"—an organizer for the United Mine Workers. "The question that arises today in the nation is an industrial oligarchy. . . . What would the coal in these mines and in these hills be worth unless you put your strength and muscle in to bring them. . . . You have collected more wealth, created more wealth than they in a thousand years of the Roman Republic, and yet you have not any."[1]

The miners voted to strike. Evicted from their huts by the coal companies, they packed their belongings onto carts, onto their backs, and walked through a mountain blizzard to tent colonies set up by the United Mine Workers. There they lived for the next seven months, enduring hunger and sickness, picketing the mines to prevent strikebreakers from entering, and defending themselves against armed assaults. The Baldwin-Felts Detective Agency, hired by the Rockefellers to break the morale of the strikers, used rifles, shotguns, and a machine gun mounted on an armed car which roved the countryside and fired into the tents where the miners lived.

They would not give up the strike, however, and the Governor called in the National Guard. A letter from the vice-president of Colorado Fuel & Iron to John D. Rockefeller Jr. in New York explained:

> You will be interested to know that we have been able to secure the cooperation of all the bankers of the city, who have had three or four interviews with our little cowboy governor, agreeing to back the State and lend it all funds necessary to maintain the militia and afford ample protection so our miners could return to work. . . . Another mighty power has been rounded up on behalf of the operators by the getting together of fourteen of the editors of the most important newspapers in the state.[2]

The National Guard was innocently welcomed to town by miners and their families, waving American flags, thinking that men in the uniform of the United States would protect them. But the Guard went to work for the operators. They beat miners, jailed them, escorted strikebreakers into the mines.

There was violence by the strikers. One strikebreaker was murdered, another brutally beaten, four mine guards killed while escorting a scab. And Baldwin-Felts detective George Belcher, the killer of Lippiatt, who had been freed by a coroner's jury composed of Trinidad businessmen, was killed with a single rifle shot by an unseen gunman as he left a Trinidad drugstore and stopped to light a cigar.

Still, the miners held out through the hard winter. But when spring came, someone had decided on more drastic action. Two National Guard companies stationed themselves in the hills above the largest tent colony, housing a thousand men, women, and children, near a tiny depot called Ludlow. On the morning of April 20, 1914, they began firing machine guns into the tents. While the men crawled away to draw fire, and shot back, the women and children crouched in pits dug into the tent floors. At dusk, the soldiers came down from the hills with torches, and set fire to the tents. The occupants fled.

The next morning, a telephone linesman, going through the charred ruins of the Ludlow colony, lifted an iron cot which covered a pit dug in the floor, and found the mangled, burned bodies of two women and eleven children. This became known as the "Ludlow Massacre."

I wondered why this extraordinary event, so full of drama, so peopled by remarkable personalities, went unmentioned in the history books. Why was this strike, which cast a dark shadow on the Rockefeller interests, and on corporate America generally, considered less important than the building by John D. Rockefeller of the Standard Oil Company, which was looked upon generally as an important and positive event in the development of American industry?

I knew that there was no secret meeting of industrialists and historians to agree to emphasize the admirable achievements of the great corporations, and ignore the bloody costs of industrialization in America. But I concluded that a certain unspoken understanding lay beneath the writing of textbooks and the teaching of history; that it would be considered bold, radical, perhaps even "Communist" to emphasize class struggle in the United States, a country where the dominant ideology emphasized the one-ness of the nation—"We the people, in order to . . . etc., etc."— and the glories of the American system.

A news commentator on a small radio station in Madison, Wisconsin, brought to my attention a textbook used in high schools all over the nation, published in 1986, entitled *Legacy of Freedom*, written by two high school teachers and one university professor of history, and published by a division of Doubleday and Company, one of the giant U.S. publishers. In a foreword, "To the Students," we find:

> *Legacy of Freedom* will aid you in understanding the economic growth and development of our country. The book presents the developments and benefits of our country's free enterprise economic system. You will read about the various ways that American business, industry, and agriculture have used scientific and technological advances to further the American free market system. This system allows businesses to generate profits while providing consumers with a variety of quality products from which to choose in the marketplace, thus enabling our people to enjoy a high standard of living.[3]

In this overview, one gets the impression of a peaceful development, due to "our country's free enterprise economic system." Where is the long, complex history of labor conflict? Where is the human cost of this industrial development, in the thousands of deaths each year in industrial accidents, the hundreds of thousands of injuries, the short lives of workers (textile mill girls in New England dying in their twenties, after starting work at twelve and thirteen)?

The Colorado coal strike does not fit neatly into the pleasant picture created by most high school textbooks of the development of the American economy. Wouldn't a detailed account of that event raise questions in the minds of young people as it raised them in mine—questions that would be threatening to the dominant powers in this country, that would clash with the dominant ideology, that might get the questioners—whether teachers or principals, or school boards—into trouble, make them conspicuous, as pointed questions almost always point out the questioner to the rest of society?

Wouldn't the event undermine faith in the neutrality of government, the cherished belief (which I possessed through my childhood) that whatever conflicts there were in American society, it was the role of government to mediate them as a neutral referee, trying its best to dispense, in the words of the Pledge of Allegiance, "liberty and justice for all"?

Wouldn't the Colorado strike suggest that governors, that perhaps all political leaders, were subject to the power of wealth, and would do the bidding of corporations rather than protect the lives of poor, powerless workers?

A close look at the Colorado coal strike would discover that not only the state government of Colorado, but the national government in Washington—under the presidency of a presumed liberal, Woodrow Wilson—was on the side of the corporations. While miners were being beaten, jailed, killed, by Rockefeller's detectives, or by his National Guard, the federal government did not act to protect the constitutional rights of its people. But when, after the Massacre, the miners armed themselves and went on a rampage of violence against the mine properties and mine guards, Wilson called out the federal troops to end the turmoil in southern Colorado.

And then there was an odd coincidence. On the same day that bodies were discovered in the pit at Ludlow, Wilson, responding to the jailing of a few American sailors in Mexico, ordered the bombardment of the Mexican port of Vera Cruz, landing ten boatloads of marines, occupying the city, killing over a hundred Mexicans.

That same textbook, *Legacy of Freedom*, in its foreword "To the Student," says: "*Legacy of Freedom* will aid you in understanding our country's involvement in foreign affairs, including our role in international conflicts and in peaceful and cooperative efforts of many kinds in many places."[4]

Is that not a benign, misleading, papering-over of the history of American foreign policy?

A close study of the Ludlow Massacre would tell students something about our great press, the comfort we feel when picking up, not a scandal sheet or a national tabloid, but the sober, dependable *New York Times.* When the U.S. navy bombarded Vera Cruz, the *Times* wrote in an editorial: "we may trust the just mind, the sound judgment, and the peaceful temper of President Wilson. There is not the slightest occasion for popular excitement over the Mexican affair; there is no reason why anybody should get nervous either about the stock market or about his business."[5]

There is no *objective* way to deal with the Ludlow Massacre. There is the subjective (biased, opinionated) decision to omit it from history, based on a value system which doesn't consider it important enough. That value system may include a fundamental belief in the beneficence of the American industrial system (as represented by the passage quoted above from the textbook *Legacy of Freedom*). Or it may just involve a complacency about class struggle and the intrusion of government on the side of corporations. In any case, it is a certain set of values which dictates the ignoring of that event.

It is also a subjective (biased, opinionated) decision to tell the story of the Ludlow Massacre in some detail (as I do, in a chapter in my book, *The Politics of History,* or in several pages in *A People's History of the United States*). My decision was based on my belief that it is important for people to know the extent of class conflict in our history, to know something about how hard-working people had to struggle to change their conditions, and to understand the role of the government and the mainstream press in the class struggles of our past.

The claim of historians to "objectivity" has been examined very closely by Peter Novick, in his remarkable book, *That Noble Dream: The "Objectivity Question" and the American Historical Profession.*[6] Historians, for instance, have not been "objective" with regard to war. In April 1917, just after the U.S. entered the European war, a group of eminent historians met in Washington to discuss "what History men can do for their country now." They set up the National Board for Historical Service in order to "aid in supplying the public with trustworthy information of historical or similar character."[7]

One result was a huge outpouring of pamphlets written by historians with the purpose of instilling patriotism in the public. Thirty-three million copies of pamphlets written by historians were distributed. Most of them, according to a recent study of the role of historians in World War I by George T. Blakey, "reduced war issues to black and white, infused idealism and righteousness into America's role, and established German guilt with finality."[8]

During World War II, the historian Samuel Eliot Morison criticized those historians who had expressed disillusionment with the First World War, saying they "rendered the generation of youth which came to maturity around 1940 spiritually unprepared for the war they had to fight. . . . Historians . . . are the ones who should have pointed out that war does accomplish something, that war is better than servitude." Yet, in the same essay ("Faith of a Historian") Morison declared his commitment to not instructing the present but to "simply explain the event exactly as it happened."[9]

A number of historians, in the cold-war atmosphere of the 1950s, selected their facts to conform to the government's position. Two of them wrote a two-volume history of U.S. entry into World War II, in order, as they put it, to show "the tortured emergence of the United States of America as leader of the forces of light in a world struggle which even today has scarcely abated."[10]

An honest declaration of their bias would have been refreshing. But, although they had access to official documents unavailable to others, they said in their preface: "No one, in the State Department or elsewhere, has made the slightest effort to influence our views." Perhaps not. But one of them, William Langer, was director of research for the C.I.A. at one time, and the other, S. E. Gleason, was deputy executive secretary of the National Security Council.

Langer was also at one time a president of the American Historical Association. Another president of the A.H.A., Samuel Flagg Bemis, in his presidential address to that group in 1961, was very clear about what he wanted historians to do:

> Too much . . . self-criticism is weakening to a people. . . . A great people's culture begins to decay when it commences to examine itself . . . we have been losing sight of our national purpose . . . our military preparedness held back by insidious strikes for less work and more pay. . . . Massive self-indulgence and massive responsibility do not go together. . . . How can our lazy dalliance and crooning softness compare with the stern discipline and tyrannical compulsion of subject peoples that strengthen the aggressive sinews of our malignant antagonist?[11]

Daniel Boorstin, trying to please the House Committee on Un-American Activities, testified before it in 1953. He agreed with it that Communists should not be permitted to teach in American universities—presumably because they would be biased. As for Boorstin, he told the committee that he expressed his own opposition to communism by religious activities at the University of Chicago. And: "The second form of my opposition has been an attempt to discover and explain to students, in my teaching and in my writing, the unique virtues of American democracy."[12]

After studying the "objectivity" of American historians, and noting how many slanted their work towards support for the United States, Peter Novick wondered if that kind of "hubris," the arrogance of national power, played a part in the ugly American intervention in Vietnam, and the cold war itself. He put it this way:

> If ill-considered American global interventionism had landed us in this bloodiest manifestation of the cold war, was it not at least worth considering whether the same hubris had been responsible for the larger conflict of which it was a part? Manifestly by the 1960's, the United States was overseeing an empire. Could scholars comfortably argue that it had been acquired, as had been said of the British Empire, 'in a fit of absence of mind'?[13]

In the 1960s, there was a series of tumultuous social movements, against racial segregation, against the Vietnam war, for equality among the sexes. This caused a reappraisal of the kind of history that supported war and the status quo, either directly, or by avoiding criticism in the name of "objectivity."

More and more books began to appear (or old books were brought to light) on the struggles of black people, on the attempts of women throughout history to declare their equality with men, on movements against war, on the strikes and protests of working people against their conditions—books which, while sticking closely to confirmed information, openly took sides, for equality, against war, for the working classes.

A group of radical historians, sometimes called "revisionists" became prominent in the profession. One of them, Jesse Lemisch, delivered a kind of manifesto for himself and others, challenging the orthodox historians.

> We exist, and people like us have existed throughout history, and we will simply not allow you the luxury of continuing to call yourself politically neutral while you exclude all of this from your history. You cannot lecture us on civility while you legitimize barbarity. You cannot call apologetics 'excellence' without expecting the most rigorous and aggressive of scholarly replies. We were at the Democratic Convention, and at the steps of the Pentagon. . . . And we are in the libraries, writing history, trying to cure it of your partisan and self-congratulatory fictions, trying to come a little closer to finding out how things actually were.[14]

Andrew Carnegie Library
Livingstone College
701 W. Monroe St.
Salisbury, N.C. 28144

This unapologetic activism of the 1960s (making history in the street, as well as writing it in the study) was startling to many professional historians. And in the 1970s and 1980s, it was accused by some scholars, and some organs of public opinion, of hurting the proper historical education of young people by its insistence on "relevance." As part of the attack, a demand grew for more emphasis on facts, on dates, on the sheer accumulation of historical information.

In May 1976, the *New York Times* published a series of articles lamenting the ignorance of American students about their own history. The *Times* was pained. Four leading historians whom it consulted were also pained. It seemed students did not know that James Polk was president during the Mexican War, that James Madison was president during the War of 1812, that the Homestead Act was passed earlier than Civil Service reform, or that the Constitution authorizes Congress to regulate interstate commerce but says nothing about the cabinet.

We might wonder if the *Times*, or its historian-consultants, learned anything from the history of this century. It has been a century of atrocities: the death camps of Hitler, the slave camps of Stalin, the bombings of Hiroshima and Nagasaki, the devastation of Southeast Asia by the United States. All of these were done by powerful leaders and obedient populations in countries that had achieved high levels of literacy and education. It seem that high scoring on tests was not the most crucial fact about these leaders, these citizens.

In the case of the United States, the killing of a million Vietnamese and the sacrifice of 55,000 American were carried out by highly educated men around the White House who undoubtedly would have made impressive grades in the *New York Times* exam. It was a Phi Beta Kappa, McGeorge Bundy, who was one of the chief planners of the bombing of civilians in Southeast Asia. It was a Harvard professor, Henry Kissinger, who was a strategist of the secret bombing of peasant villages in Cambodia.

Going back a bit in history, it was our most educated president, Woodrow Wilson, a historian himself, a Ph.D. and former president of Princeton, who bombarded the Mexican coast, killing more than one hundred innocent people, because the Mexican government refused to salute the American flag. It was Harvard-educated John Kennedy, author of two books on history, who presided over the American invasion of Cuba and the lies that accompanied it.

What did Kennedy or Wilson learn from all that history they absorbed in the best universities in America? What did the American people learn, in their high school history texts, to put up with these leaders?

Andrew Carnegie Library
Livingstone College
701 W. Monroe St.
Salisbury, N.C. 28144

Surely, how "smart" a person is on history tests like the one devised by the *Times*, how "educated" someone is, tells you nothing about whether that person is decent or indecent, violent or peaceful, whether that person will resist evil or become a consultant to warmakers, will become a Pastor Niemoller (a German who resisted the Nazis) or an Albert Speer (who worked for them), a Lieutenant Calley (who killed children at My Lai) or a Flight Officer Thompson (who tried to save them).

One of the two top scorers on the *Times* test was described as follows: "Just short of 20 years old, he lists outdoor activities and the Augustana War Games Club as constituting his favorite leisure-time pursuits, explaining the latter as a group that meets on Fridays to simulate historical battles on a playing board."[15]

Everyone does need to learn history, the kind that does not put its main emphasis on knowing presidents and statutes and Supreme Court decisions, but inspires a new generation to resist the madness of governments trying to carve the world and our minds into their spheres of influence.

Notes

1. U.S. House Mines and Mining Committee, *Conditions in the Coal Mines of Colorado* (Washington: Government Printing Office, 1914), 2631–34.

2. Commission on Industrial Relations, U.S. Senate, *Report and Testimony* (Washington: Government Printing Office, 1915), 8607.

3. Glenn M. Linden, Dean C. Brink, and Richard H. Huntington, *Legacy of Freedom*, Vol. II (New York: Laidlaw Brothers, 1986), 15.

4. Ibid.

5. *New York Times*, April 21, 1914.

6. Peter Novick, *That Noble Dream: The Objectivity Question and the American Historical Profession* (New York: Cambridge University Press, 1988).

7. Ibid., 121.

8. Richard Polenberg, review of George T. Blakey, *Historians on the Homefront: American Propagandists for the Great War* (Louisville: University Press of Kentucky, 1970), *American Political Science Review* (September, 1973).

9. Novick, *That Noble Dream.*

10. Ibid.

11. Ibid.

12. Ibid.

13. Ibid.

14. Ibid.

15. *New York Times*, May 3, 1976.

26

Exposing the Killing System: Robert Jay Lifton as Witness

John E. Mack

Here were those petrified soldiers of all ages
kneeling down, who, here in the middle of the
desert within reach of the enemy's guns, just kept
on murmuring prayers. It was as though the
world stood still and peace had arrived, as though
a gigantic open mosque did arch over us, cover-
ing us in all directions.[1]

Robert Jay Lifton is perhaps our most powerful witness to the dark side
of the human species. In many books, articles, lectures and at the yearly
meetings he has convened over three decades at his summer home in
Wellfleet, Massachusetts, Lifton has been reminding us in powerful language of the relentless destructiveness of which many of us seem capable
under the right political circumstances. He has recorded and analyzed
more fully than any other scholar of our time the conditions under
which human beings contribute actively or passively to acts of mass violence, genocide and, in the case of the threat to use nuclear weapons as
instruments of war, the destruction of much, if not most, of this planet's
life. At the same time Lifton is no dreary prophet, preaching jeremiads
to a deaf or frightened citizenry. For he offers a path of transformation,
a course by which we might avert the likely plight of extinction that we
have so blindly prepared for ourselves.

Lifton starts where, I suppose, all students of human violence must
begin—with the polarities that seem to be built into the human psyche,
our tendency to disown the killing forces in our natures and find other
people to blame for our pain and ill fortune upon whom we may then
vent the hatred and rage that are the outgrowth of our historic wounds.

319

It is this capacity to split our psyches, "doubling," Lifton has called it, that permits Christian Serbs who may at home be kind family members, to murder Moslems from Bosnia, or previously scrupulous physicians in Germany to turn from healing to killing in the service of the state.

In his studies of brainwashing in China, the pressures on veterans in Vietnam, and, above all, of the Nazi Holocaust, the nuclear arms race and the disturbing parallels between them that he has drawn, Lifton has shown all of us who will pay attention the conditions for the final extinction of the human species that we seem, as if deliberately, to be preparing. Other scholars have identified some of the psychological mechanisms and political forces that contribute to mass killing. What is unique, I believe, in Lifton's work is his systematic building of an edifice of understanding that brings together all of the major elements— spiritual, psychological and social—that constitute the killing system. His discoveries are, in many ways, unwelcome. For they reveal to us the shadow side of our natures. But survival of our own species and the many millions of others that human behavior on the planet now threatens must depend on facing up to and coming to terms with this darkness.

Relatively few human beings are so driven by demonic intention that they would deliberately commit or contribute to acts of mass killing. But the conditions of life in the twentieth century, and the institutions that implement our contemporary societal projects, provide the framework that makes mass killing possible, and even inevitable, should we remain blind to the multidimensional killing system that we have created. This system allows all of us to continue to be more or less in a state of denial, oblivious and anxiously helpless, actively or passively nonresponsible, as the progress toward our final solution continues. But Lifton will not let us remain unconscious, unaware of the elements of the killing system. Through penetrating analysis, scrupulous documentation and passionate advocacy he virtually forces us to become conscious of these elements and to emerge from the stupor of our avoidance.

What are the elements or dimensions of the killing system that Lifton has brought to our attention? It is difficult to outline or summarize them as they are set forth or implicit in his various works. Each element operates at more than one level. There is no simple progression, for example, from individual psychological mechanisms to global institutional forces. For (as we are learning from Lifton and other students of genocide like Raul Hilberg and Ervin Staub) individual psychology—most obviously in the case of leaders—is at work in the collective, while the history and present energies of the collective are at work in each individual. But keeping this in mind it seems convenient to begin with individual psychology, working "outwards," not forgetting that all the structures and institutions that human beings have created are once and always products and ongoing expressions of our consciousness, however unaware of that linkage we may have become.

Demonization, the self-ridding of aggression and the projection onto others of our own negativity and self-hatred, is a mechanism that provides a familiar starting point for our understanding of collective violence. Dehumanization—the extreme denial of positive human qualities in the other—is a close companion of demonization. Sociologist James Skelly at a Wellfleet meeting in September 1986 provided moving illustrations of our success in dehumanizing the Soviet Union during the height of the cold war and the nuclear weapons confrontation. One day at school his seven-year-old son was given an assignment to write a sentence on what he would do if he were invisible. "If I were invisible I would go to the Soviet Union and kill them, because they are our enemies," he wrote. The family subscribed to a magazine which showed illustrations of Russian people, including children playing. Seeing these, Skelly's daughter, then six, remarked with surprise, "I didn't know there were children in the Soviet Union."

When accompanied by extreme rationality, the elimination of empathic connection—indeed of any feeling at all (Lifton has called this psychic numbing)—between human beings in one group and those in another, demonization and dehumanization become powerful building blocks for potential mass killing. Dissociation or splitting, which further enables the psyche to declare that another is radically "not me," complete the basic mechanisms of nonresponsibility upon which a society's leadership structure can build in the pursuit of its violent projects.

Ideology, Lifton has so clearly shown us, provides for the collectivity, the justification and intellectual underpinning of the killing projects. Ideology creates a distorting structure of thought, a relatively well ordered but greatly simplified idea or set of ideas, through which a society may seek to organize its economy and deny human complexities. Ideology contains within it hatred or blame of another person or group, sometimes subtle (as in the case of U.S. racism during the Vietnam war), often gross (like Hitler's use of anti-Semitism), that can mobilize a society's killing energies and relieve citizen responsibility for what befalls human beings in the other or "enemy" country or group.

In the twentieth century, as Lifton's work reveals, virtually all political ideologies occur in the context of nationalism, which, in its more intense or extreme forms, becomes itself an extreme ideology. Nationalism is the individual and collective complex of emotion attached to the idea of the state. In the late decades of the twentieth century the national state has seemed to be the only group structure or vehicle through which individuals seem able to fulfill their personal needs and destinies. Nationalism, as Lifton has shown so clearly, has become the overarching ideology of the late twentieth century, as individual citizens feel increasingly powerless and unsafe, ostensibly incapable of living securely and happily except within the protection of an armed nation with rigidly fixed borders. It is in the name of the high purposes of the national state (or of aspiring national states as in the ethnic struggles within the former Yugoslavia), fueled often by religious zeal (holy war), that mass killing becomes possible. Nationalistic leaders become greatly skilled in the use of the psychological mechanisms described above to mobilize their followers in the projects of collective violence ("ethnic cleansing," for example). Lifton's is, however, a voice that invites us to transcend nationalism, as he proposes frameworks of collective security and fulfillment that reach beyond the military state.

Science and technology obviously augment the destructive power of war itself. But in addition, the sterility of the scientific and technological apparatus that is intrinsic to the killing system can also, as Lifton has documented, provide a further psychological distancing of individuals from their feelings, allowing mass killing to become a cold, impersonal, even rational process. One has only to watch children fascinated and benumbed before commercial hi-tech videos in which robotic creatures are mindlessly and emotionlessly blown away to experience the truth of this.

The rational, nonfeeling dimensions of our psyches are further reinforced by the vast institutional bureaucracies that have come to dominate so much of human life. Some of these institutions have been specifically created to implement the killing system. But virtually all of our institutional structures are succumbing to the dehumanizing pressures of technology in this age of computerization and easy mass communication. Vast institutional bureaucracies provide multi-layered shields within which men and women may carry out, sometimes unwittingly, violent projects for which they experience no personal responsibility. Paradoxically people can be connected now with other people everywhere in the world through the vast global informational networks that are growing so rapidly on the planet. It remains to be seen, however, if the net effect of this technology will be to unite us as a species or further accentuate the trivialization of human life and our fragmenting individualism.

Finally, as Lifton has written of explicitly, and as is implicit throughout his work, the extreme secularization of our age, the virtually total loss of a sense of the sacred, has provided the larger context in which anything and everything becomes permissible. Stated differently, the loss of a sense of reverent connection among human beings and between us and nature has eliminated the sense of generational continuity that would enable us to be shepherds over time of human and nonhuman life. This pervasive spiritual impoverishment allows us to contemplate, if not commit, acts of destruction against other human groups and nature itself that would interrupt this continuity and lead, ultimately, to the end of life as we know it.

Alexander Yakovlev, the architect of Mikhail Gorbachev's program of reform, said that in the task of establishing "civilized relations in society" it was necessary "to teach people to think. We have to make them think on their own. Man has to have the freedom of choice, and make his choices by himself."[2] This is necessary not only in totalitarian societies but in democracies as well where commercial messages lull our minds into frozen complacency. Robert Lifton does not proclaim this necessity, but that is precisely what he does. He teaches us to think and to feel, to face head on the truths about ourselves and the program of death in which we are engaged. He asks us to look honestly at ourselves, to recognize the dark side of human nature, to experience and own the polarities in our souls. Then and only then, according to Lifton, can we overcome the complicity of silence that allows so much violence to be committed in our names.

In Lifton's vision the temporary surcease from war in a moment of prayer that Reza Behrouzi saw in a Middle Eastern desert would become a permanent state. Believing perhaps that he must remain faithful to his own secular intellectual heritage, Lifton seems to use religious language sparsely. Yet he has invited us to join him on a spiritual journey, a path of commitment that would transcend human egoistic fixations. He knows that we live now in a world where the interconnectedness and interdependence of the human species within the web of life on this planet is a fact of survival not a utopian hope. Our fate, as Lifton has so often written, is a shared fate. We live or die according to the harmony and balance that we can create in our relationships with other human beings and living species.

Erik Erikson, Lifton's most important mentor, asked rhetorically at the Wellfleet summer meeting in 1983—one of the last he was able to attend—whether humanity lacked an identity. Could we discover our authentic selves and overcome the fragmentation of identity, what Erikson called pseudospeciation? Could we rediscover the souls whose very existence we have denied in the fanatical, fear-driven pursuit of material satisfaction? Can we, like addicts recovering from an attachment to violence, admit our powerlessness before a higher power, and, paradoxically, gain the power to reverse our destructive course? These are, to use again one of Erikson's terms, the kinds of "ultimate" questions that are contained in Lifton's work.

Anglo-Indian philosopher Andrew Harvey said recently, "There is one way and one way only, I believe, that the planet can be saved in time—and that is through a massive worldwide transformation which is simultaneously spiritual and practical, mystical and political. Turning to the light is not, in itself, enough. We have also to act as humble tireless agents of the light, with the light in us, behind us, inspiring and guiding us, to act on all possible spiritual and practical fronts, wisely, calmly and very, very fast."[3] Robert Lifton is one of our "tireless agents," inspiring and guiding us all in a planet-saving mission.

It has turned out that I am writing this on the fiftieth anniversary of the atomic bombing of Hiroshima. For Lifton, Hiroshima has been the essential symbol of human destructiveness. Lost in the debate about whether dropping nuclear bombs on two Japanese cities at the end of World War II was justified because it shortened the war and saved lives is the symbolism of these cosmic acts. For the incineration of Hiroshima, and the nuclear arms race that followed upon it, ultimately confronted humankind with itself. It has shown us that an organized group of people—for that is all that nations are—is capable and willing to annihilate humanity and most of the earth's life in pursuit of what that group considers to be its legitimate purpose or "interests." To have us know fully, without denial, this truth about ourselves as a species is, I believe, Lifton's ultimate prescription. For in such knowledge could lie the power to choose a different course. In his latest book, *Hiroshima in America: Fifty Years of Denial*,[4] Lifton has written, "Confronting Hiroshima can be a powerful source of renewal. It can enable us to emerge from nuclear entrapment and rediscover our imaginative capacities on behalf of human good. We can overcome our moral inversion and cease to justify weapons or actions of mass killing. We can condemn and then step back from acts of desecration and recognize what Camus called a 'philosophy of limits.' In that way we can also take steps to cease betraying ourselves, cease harming and deceiving our own people. We can also free our society from its apocalyptic concealment, and in the process enlarge our vision. We can break out of our long-standing numbing in the vitalizing endeavor of learning, or relearning, to feel. And we can divest ourselves of a debilitating sense of futurelessness and once more feel bonded to past and future generations."

Notes

1. I Have No More Tears." Told by Reza Behrouzi, twelve-year old Iranian child soldier. Recorded by Freidoune Sahebjam, Iranian journalist in exile. Translated from the German original in *Die Zeit* by Koert Gerzon, 1988.

2. Dusko Doder and Louise Branson: *Gorbachev: Heretic in the Kremlin* (New York, Viking Penguin, 1990), 78.

3. Andrew Harvey and Mark Matousek: *Dialogues with a Modern Mystic* (Wheaton, Ill: Quest Books, 1994), 273.

4. Robert Jay Lifton, *Hiroshima in America: Fifty Years of Denial* (New York: G. P. Putnam's Sons, 1995), 356.

Index

327

suffering: masculinity and, 169; recognition and sharing of, 298, 301–4
Sugihara, Chiune, 100–109
Sugihara, Yukiko, 108
survivors: effects of atrocities on, 244, 245; lessons from, 272, 297–305; narratives of, 232; numbers of, 297; psychological recovery, 252; relationship to witnesses, 247, 251, 252; as war experts, 42, 46; as witnesses, 247, 248. *See also* victims
Sussan, Herbert, 45
Suzuki, Kantaro, 9
symbolic immortality, xii, 269–70, 276

technology, 322; in cultural imagery, 180, 182; destructive power of, 66–67, 275, 276–77; high, 177, 181 (*see also* Persian Gulf War); threat of, 270
"technowar," 177
Teller, Edward, 26, 38
Teresa, Mother, 258
terrorism, 113–14, 244, 258
That Noble Dream: The "Objectivity Question" and the American Historical Profession (Novick), 313
theater, 231–33, 250–51
There Are No Children Here (Kotlewitz), 117
Thought Reform and the Psychology of Totalism (Lifton), xiii
Tibbets, Paul, 46
Togo [Japanese Prime Minister], 8
Tokyo War Crimes Trials, 4
tolerance, 134
Tracy, David, 37
transcendence, 269, 270. *See also* symbolic immortality
The Truly Disadvantaged (Wilson), 115
Truman, Harry S., 5, 6, 14, 21; advice re Japanese surrender, 3–4, 8; decision to use atomic bomb, 3–4, 5, 8, 22, 35; invasion of Japan and, 11, 22; policy re atomic bomb, 7; on development, 214
Tsuji, Masami, 106
twentieth century, violence in, 75, 273, 316

underclass, 122n8
The Underclass (Auletta), 117
U.N. Genocide Police Force, 137–48
U.N. Rapid Deployment Brigade, 68
United Nations, 26, 63, 66; enforcement powers of, 64, 150n11; jurisdiction of, 141–42; membership of, 68–69, 70; national interests and, 66; proposed genocide force, 137–48; resolution on genocide, 82–83; volunteer military force of, 67–68
United Peoples Organization, 70
United States: Bosnia and, 249; class conflict in, 117, 313; economic history of, 311–12, 313; foreign policy, 67, 312, 315; invasion of Japan (*see* Japan); moral authority of, 3, 4, 15; national security policy, 3, 14, 29, 112; Soviet Union and, 6, 7, 24, 45; values of, 15
Universal Negro Improvement Association, 112
urban rebellion, 118
U.S. Strategic Bombing Survey, 23, 45
utopianism, 210

values, 265; of alternative communities, 272; history and, 308, 313; international, 67, 72n14, 134; person as unit of, 72n13; of rescuers, 88, 90, 91, 95; of society, 115; spiritual, 259; systems of, 38; tolerance as, 95; of warfare, 186
van Mierlo, Hans, 68
vegetarianism, 221
vertical polarization, 178
veterans groups, 12
victim art, 253
victimization, xiii, 57, 121, 185
victims: of atomic bombings, 45–46; blaming, 117, 120, 187; of development, 216n5; groups as, 79; innocence of, 79–81; psychological effects on, 119. *See also hibakusha*; survivors
Vietnam War, 16, 127–28
Vilna (Lithuania), 101–2

violence: causes of, 226; conflict resolution by, 291; development and, 210, 211; effect on children, 287–88; fear of, 119; high technology and, 177, 181; in Indian religions and society, 220–26; indirect, 209–10; inner-city, 119; mass (*see* mass violence); psychotherapy and, 290; relationship to self, 232, 247; religion and, 257, 258, 268; responses to, 120; against women, 250. *See also* genocide; mass killing
Virchow, Rudolf, 195
Virilio, Paul, 181
Von Kaltenborn, Hans, 25
voting, 123n21, 284–85

Waitzkin, Howard, 196
Walker, Stephen, 161
Wallenberg, Raoul, 102
war, 77; alternatives to, 277; as brutalizing influence, 84; civilian deaths in, 80, 183–84; excitement and, 170–71; facilitating factors, 83; historians' treatment of, 313, 314; holy, 322; just, 64, 81, 157; masculinity and, 166–73, 184–85; against mass murderers, 62; power balance in, 81, 179–80; as precursor to genocide, 78; prevention of, 202; psychological trauma of, 279; relationship to genocide, 76–81, 83; spatiality of, 177; technology's role in, 177, 180–82; as therapeutic, 169–70
war crimes, 82, 83, 133; defenses to, 141; rape as, 157
War Without Mercy: Race and Power in the Pacific War (Dower), 22
Warren, Robert Penn, 33
weapons of mass destruction, 186, 202. *See also* biological weapons; chemical weapons; nuclear weapons

Weil, Simone, 163
Weindling, Paul, 169
Weiss, Peter, 157
We've Had a Hundred Years of Psychotherapy and the World's Getting Worse (Hillman), 274
Williamson, Roger, xvi
Wilson, Robert, 248
Wilson, William J., 114–15
Wilson, Woodrow, 312, 316
Winckelmann, J. J., 165, 172
witnesses: as apologists, 245, 253; ethnic cleansing and, 244–45; mental health professionals as, 300; redefinition of role of, 245; relationship to survivors, 247, 251, 252
witnessing: art as, 243; forms of, xiii, xv; genocidal ideology and, 245; imagination, 247, 250; misuse of, 253; poetry as, 32; process, 250, 251, 252; professionals, 246, 251; shared suffering, 298
Wolk, Herman, 11
World Conference on Religion and Peace, 278
World Council of Churches, 278
World Health Assembly, 197
World Order Models Project, 154
World War I, xv, 172
World War II, xvi: commemoration of end, 9–14; Japanese view of, 12; political alternative to ending, 8, 42; role of nuclear weapons in ending, 3, 5, 8–9, 14, 23
Wuthnow, Robert, 303

Yakovlev, Alexander, 323
Yellen, Samuel, 309
Yitzchak, Levvi, 294
Yugoslavia. *See* Bosnia

Zimmermann, Frances, 221
Zlata's Diary (Zlata Filipovic), 246
Zöberlein, Heinz, 170

About the Contributors

John Broughton is an associate professor of psychology and education at Teacher's College/Columbia University. He is the editor of *The Cognitive Developmental Psychology of James Mark Baldwin,* author of *The Depth Psychology of High Technology,* and founding co-editor of *Psychoculture: Review of Psychology and Culture Studies.*

Paul Boyer is Merle Curti Professor of History and director of the Institute for Research in the Humanities at the University of Wisconsin-Madison. His works include *By the Bomb's Early Light: American Thought and Culture at the Dawn of the Atomic Age.*

Harvey Cox is Thomas Professor of Divinity at Harvard Divinity School and author of *The Secular City* and, most recently, *Fire From Heaven: The Rise of Pentecostal Spirituality and the Re-Shaping of Religion in the Twenty-First Century.*

Wendy Doniger is Mircea Eliade Professor of the History of Religions at the University of Chicago and author of *Other Peoples' Myths* and *The Origins of Evil in Hindu Mythology.*

Ronnie Dugger, a writer and journalist, was founding editor of *The Texas Observer,* but now lives in New York City. He writes for various magazines and his books include *Dark Star: Hiroshima Reconsidered in the Life of Claude Eatherly, Our Invaded Universities, The Politician: The Life and Times of Lyndon Johnson,* and *On Reagan: The Man and His Presidency.* He is working now on books about computerized vote counting and new social-policy ideas. He will be affiliated during 1995–96 with the Shorenstein Center on the Press, Politics, and Public Policy at Harvard.

Kai Erikson is the William R. Kenan, Jr. Professor of Sociology and American Studies at Yale University and author of *A New Species of Trouble: Explorations in Disaster, Trauma and Community* and *Everthing in Its Path: Destruction of Community in the Buffalo Creek Flood.*

Richard Falk is the Milbank Professor of International Law and Practice at Princeton University and co-author (with Lifton) of *Indefensible Weap-*

ons: The Political and Psychological Case Against Nuclearism and *Revolutionaries and Functionaries: The Dual Face of Terrorism.*

Eva Fogelman is a social psychologist, psychotherapist and filmmaker. She is a Senior Research Fellow at the Center for Social Research, Graduate Center of CUNY; founding director of Jewish Foundation for Christian Rescuers, ADL; co-director, Psychotherapy with Generations of the Holocaust and Related Traumas, Training Institute for Mental Health. She is the author of *Conscience and Courage: Rescuers of Jews During the Holocaust,* and is co-editor of *Children During the Nazi Reign: Psychological Perspective of the Interview Process.*

John Fousek is senior program associate of the World Order Models Project. He is completing a book on American nationalism and the ideological origins of the cold war in U.S. public culture.

Elinor Fuchs is on the faculty of the School of the Arts of Columbia University, and has taught at Emory University, Yale School of Drama, and Harvard. Her books include *The Death of Character: Perspectives on Theatre after Modernism, Plays of the Holocaust: An International Anthology,* and the award-winning documentary play, *Year One of the Empire.* She was an organizer of the Citizens' Commitee on Bosnia-Herzegovina.

Lane Gerber is professor of psychology and the Pigott-McCone Professor of Humanities at Seattle University and the author of *Married to Their Careers.*

Charles Green is associate professor of sociology at Hunter College of the City University of New York and former Fulbright Scholar in Sociology at The University of Dar es Salaam, Tanzania. His central area of research concerns the urban condition of Blacks in the diaspora. He recently co-authored (with Basil Wilson) *The Struggle for Black Empowerment in New York City.*

Hillel Levine is professor of sociology and religion at Boston University and director of its Center for Judaic Studies. He is the author of the forthcoming book *In Pursuit of Sugihara.* His previous books include (with Lawrence Harmon) *The Death of an American Jewish Community: A Tragedy of Good Intentions,* and *Economic Origins of Antisemitism: Poland and Its Jews in the Early Modern Period.*

John E. Mack is professor of psychiatry at the Cambridge Hospital, Harvard Medical School, and author of the Pulitzer Prize-winning *The Prince of Disorder* and *Abduction: Human Encounters with Aliens.*

Karen Malpede is author of eleven plays produced in this country and abroad that have been collected in *A Monster Has Stolen the Sun and Other Plays, Women on the Verge: Seven Avant-Garde Plays, Angels of Power and Other Reproductive Creations,* and *A Century of Plays by American Women.* She is the 1994–95 National McKnight Playwrights Fellow and an assistant professor of drama at the Tisch School of the Arts, New York University.

Eric Markusen is professor of sociology and social work at Southwest State University in Minnesota and co-author, with Lifton, of *The Genocidal Mentality: Nazi Holocaust and Nuclear Threat,* and, with David Kopf, *The Holocaust and Strategic Bombing: Genocide and Total War in the Twentieth Century.*

Saul Mendlovitz is Dag Hammarskjold Professor of Peace and World Order Studies at Rutgers University and co-director of the World Orders Model Project and author of *Towards a Just World Peace: Perspectives from Social Movements.*

Greg Mitchell has written extensively on nuclear weapons issues and is the co-author (with Lifton) of *Hiroshima and America,* and author of *The Campaign of the Century: Upton Sinclair's Race for Governor of California and the Birth of Media Politics.*

George L. Mosse is emeritus professor of history at the University of Wisconsin, Madison, and the Hebrew University, Jerusalem. He is the author of *Fallen Soldiers: Reshaping the Memory of the World Wars.*

Ashis Nandy is director of the Centre for the Study of Developing Societies in Delhi, India, and author of *Science, Hegemony and Violence: A Requiem for Modernity* and *At the Edge of Psychology: Essays in Politics and Culture.*

Martin J. Sherwin is the Walter S. Dickson Professor of History at Tufts University. He is the author of *A World Destroyed: Hiroshima and the Origins of the Arms Race.*

Victor W. Sidel is Distinguished University Professor of Social Medicine at the Albert Einstein College of Medicine and Montefiore Medical Center. He is co-president of the International Physicians for the Prevention of Nuclear War, recipient of the 1985 Nobel Prize for Peace, and past president of Physicians for Social Responsibility. He is co-editor of *The Fallen Sky: Medical Consequences of Thermonuclear War* and of *Public Health and War.*

Bennett Simon is professor of psychiatry at Cambridge Hospital, Harvard Medical School, and the author of *Tragic Drama and the Family: Psychoanalytic Studies from Aeschylus to Beckett.*

Stevan Weine is co-director of the Project on Genocide, Psychiatry, and Witnessing and assistant professor of psychiatry at the University of Illinois at Chicago. His writings on Bosnia have been published in leading professional journals. He is writing a book on survivors and witnesses of genocide in Bosnia.

Roger Williamson works for the Board for Social Responsibility (International Affairs) of the Church of England. He has previously been director of the Council for Arms Control, based at King's College, London; director of the Life & Peace Institute, Uppsala, Sweden; and executive secretary (Peace and Human Rights) of the British Council of Churches. His publications include fourteen books (written and edited) and many articles in the fields of peace research, ecumenical theology and social ethics. Among his books are: *Noah's Ark and the Nuclear Inferno* and *Profit without Honour?* on ethics and the arms trade. He writes here in a personal capacity.

Howard Zinn is professor of history emeritus at Boston University and author of *You Can't Be Neutral on a Moving Train: A Personal History of Our Times* and *A People's History of the United States.*

About the Editors

Charles B. Strozier is professor of history at John Jay College and the Graduate Center, City Unversity of New York, where he is also co-director of the Center on Violence and Human Survival. He is a practicing psychoanalyst and senior faculty member of the Training and Research Institute in Self Psychology in New York City. He is the author of *Lincoln's Quest for Union: Public and Private Meanings*, collaborator with Heinz Kohut, *Self Psychology and The Humanities: Reflections on a New Psychoanalytic Approach*, and editor (with Daniel Offer) of *The Leader: Psychohistorical Studies*. Two books are in preparation: *Heinz Kohut and the Self: Psychoanalysis at the Millennium*, and an edited volume (with Michael Flynn) *Two Thousand: Essays on the End*.

Michael Flynn is lecturer of psychology at York College, The City University of New York, and associate director of the Center on Violence and Human Survival, John Jay College, City University of New York. He is a psychotherapist in private practice specializing in the treatment of victims and perpetrators of physical and sexual violence. He is editing (with Charles Strozier) *Two Thousand: Essays on the End*.